KNOWLEDGE AND CLASS

KNOWLEDGE AND CLASS

A Marxian Critique of Political Economy

Stephen A. Resnick and
Richard D. Wolff

The University of Chicago Press
Chicago and London

The University of Chicago Press, Chicago 60637
The University of Chicago Press, Ltd., London
© 1987 by The University of Chicago
All rights reserved. Published 1987
Paperback edition 1989
Printed in the United States of America
98 97 96 95 94 93 92 91 90 89   6 5 4 3 2

Library of Congress Cataloging-in-Publication Data

Resnick, Stephen A.
  Knowledge and class.

  Bibliography.
  Includes index.
  1. Marxian economics. 2. Capitalism. 3. Communist
state. I. Wolff, Richard D. II. Title.
HB97.5.R48 1987   335.4   86–32631
ISBN 0–226–71021–1
ISBN 0–226–71023–8 (pbk.)

Contents

Acknowledgments   vii

1 A Marxian Theory   1
Theoretical Self-Consciousness   1
Concepts of Epistemology   13
Conceptualizations of Society   19
Conceptual Points of Entry   25
Epistemological Differences   30
Marxian Theory and Relativism   33
Postscript   37

2 Marxian Epistemology:
   The Critique of Economic Determinism   38
Marxian Theory and Economic Determinism   39
An Initial Thesis   49
Marx and Engels on Epistemology   52
Lenin on Epistemology   62
Lukács on Epistemology   67
Gramsci and Mao on Epistemology   74
Althusser   81
An Initial Resolution   95
Readings of Althusser   99
Postscript: Parable of Hindess and Hirst   107

3 A Marxian Theory of Classes   109
Different Theories of Class   111
Class Process and Social Relationships   115
Classes: Fundamental and Subsumed   117
Marx's Subsumed Classes   124
Productive and Unproductive Labor: What Is the Working Class?   132
Productive and Unproductive Capital: What Is a Capitalist?   141
Wages and Profits: Analyzing Their Class and Nonclass Processes   149
Class and Person: The Complexity of Class Struggles   158

4 Class Analysis: A Marxian Theory of the Enterprise 164
The Capitalist Industrial Enterprise 166
Class Structure of the Enterprise 170
Managers 174
Owners and Financiers 176
Other Subsumed Classes 177
Class and Nonclass Processes: The Case of Accumulation 184
Contradictions in and Competition among Enterprises 192
The Enterprise and Multiple Class Positions 200
Once Again: What Is a Capitalist? 204
Overdetermination of Productive Capital Accumulation 207
A Concrete Example 213
Industrial versus Financial Enterprises 219
Capitalist versus Noncapitalist Enterprises 226

5 Class Analysis: A Marxian Theory of the State 231
Introduction: The Capitalist State 231
Class Structure of the State 237
Revenues and Expenditures of the State 245
The State and Industrial Capital 253
Contradictions in the State 258
A Concrete Example of Contradictions 263
The State and Revolution 267

Epilogue: Purposes of This Book 275

Notes 283

Name Index 343

Subject Index 347

Acknowledgments

The diverse influences that combined to determine this book are far too numerous to list. Friendships, students, colleagues, and texts interacted with culture, politics, and economics to bring it into existence and shape its qualities. We wish, however, to express our special gratitude for all the members, conferences, and discussion papers of the Association for Economic and Social Analysis (AESA) over recent years. Our good fortune to teach and interact with students in the economics department of the University of Massachusetts, Amherst, where AESA is based, aided the development of this book enormously. Discussion in New Haven and Cambridge-Boston under the auspices of AESA and the American Independent Movement did likewise. This book has benefited from many students' comments on preliminary drafts of its chapters. We also appreciate readers' reactions to our earlier articles in the *Review of Radical Political Economics* (13, no. 4: 1–18) and *Social Text* (no. 6 [Fall 1982]: 31–72). Portions of chapters 2 and 3 are partially based upon those articles. The following readers posed especially important theoretical issues: Claude Menard of the University of Paris, Robert J. Ackermann of the University of Massachusetts, and Fredric Jameson of Duke University. Readers for the University of Chicago Press made very useful suggestions on a number of specific points in the text. Stephen Cullenberg and Thomas DelGuidice read and corrected the manuscript and also prepared the index. Ann Hopkins typed the final manuscript with care. We thank them all.

1

A Marxian Theory

Our purpose is to construct the basic contours of a Marxian theory. This theory differs significantly from other theories. Our specification of Marxian theory involves differentiating it from alternative theories outside the Marxian tradition and from certain alternatives within that tradition. Our formulation of Marxian theory is shaped, in part, by a desire to communicate with both Marxian and non-Marxian readers. When not otherwise modified, the phrase *Marxian theory* will refer to what this work seeks to construct; it is the particular conceptual apparatus we use.

The Marxian theory that this book will expound is already at work in the method of exposition. We use the theory to design its formulation in these pages and to specify its differences from alternative theories. Marxian theory's acute self-consciousness imposes on its practitioners the awareness that their propositions about other theories are statements from within Marxian theory. How we understand alternative theories and their differences from our own is itself an understanding within our theory. In short, this book exemplifies what it seeks to expound.

Theoretical Self-Consciousness

We have indicated briefly how Marxian theory is self-conscious of what it means by the adjective *Marxian,* that is, its position within the Marxian tradition. We will have more to say concerning this position later, but it is already possible to differentiate this Marxian theory from certain alternatives within the tradition. Those do not conceptualize the tradition as a set of distinct theories. They hold their own formulations to be not *a* but rather *the* Marxian theory. Outside the Marxian tradition as well there are many formulations holding that Marxism is a tradition affirming one theoretical position.

Marxian theory is also self-conscious of what it means by the concept of theory per se. The point here is that how any theory operates—how it develops and toward what conclusions it proceeds—depends in part on what its practitioners understand theory to be. The definitions and deployments of the concept of theory are as different as the different theories within which they occur. For that reason their differing concepts of theory are themselves indexes of the differences among distinct theories.

Marxian theory has a distinctive concept of what theory is, that is, a distinct epistemological position. Theory is a process in society. It comprises the production, deployment, and organization of concepts. This is meant broadly to include the interpretation of concepts received from others as well as the rejection of those concepts found unacceptable in relation to other concepts of the theory. At any moment, a theory is a set of concepts. However, since theory is a process, the set of concepts undergoes continuous change.

Marxian theory offers a distinctive thesis to explain the process of theory—the continuous changes undergone by any theory, including itself. These changes are explained in Marxian theory through the use of the term *overdetermination*. The term is borrowed from Freud, Lukács, and Althusser and considerably modified by us.[1] Overdetermination is our conceptual entry point into the specification of what theory is; it is our partisan epistemological position. Since the concept of overdetermination is a basic concept in Marxian theory, its initial definition here will be extensively elaborated in subsequent parts of this book. One form of its elaboration will be seen in our usage of the verb *to effect*. Since we understand *affect* to mean "to influence" and *effect* to convey the stronger meaning of "to constitute," and since overdetermination implies constitutivity, we stress the verb *effect* later on in this book.

To say that theory is an overdetermined process in society is to say that its existence, including all its properties or qualities, is determined by each and every other process constituting that society. Theory is the complex effect produced by the interaction of all those other processes. As such an effect, the process of theory embodies the different influences of its many determinants. In other words, the process of theory exists as the site of a particular interaction of all the influences stemming from all the other processes comprising any society. In this sense these other processes are all the conditions of existence of the process of theory.

Much is at stake in this concept of overdetermination as the choice of language suggests, that is, overdetermination as against determination or determinism. The concept of overdetermination stands opposed to any form of reductionism or essentialism. Indeed, one way to describe the particular kind of Marxian theory developed in this book is to call it strictly antiessentialist or strictly nonreductionist.

By *essentialism* we mean a specific presumption that characterizes many theories both within and outside the Marxian tradition. This presumption holds that any apparent complexity—a person, a relationship, a historical occurrence, and so forth—can be analyzed to reveal a simplicity lying at its core. In relation to conceptualizing causality, essentialism is the presumption that among the influences apparently producing any outcome, some can be shown to be *inessential* to its occurrence while others will be shown to be *essential* causes. Amid the multifaceted complexity of influences apparently surrounding, say, some historical event of interest to an essentialist, one or a subset of these influences is presumed to be the essential cause of the event. The goal of analysis for such an essentialist theory is then to find and express this essential cause and its mechanism of producing what is theorized as its effect.

Among Marxists, for example, one kind of essentialism holds that within the complex of political, cultural, economic, and natural processes comprising a society, the economic are the essential cause of historical change. The noneconomic processes are relegated to the rank of inessential causes and/or consigned to the status of mere effects of economic processes. Among non-Marxists, for example, neoclassical economists often argue that commodity prices are caused essentially by individual preferences and production technology. Other possible causes are ranked as secondary, inessential (derivative from—effects of—the essential), or irrelevant.

Essentialist theories organize their fields of inquiry into contrasting poles of cause and effect, phenomenon and essence, and determinant versus determined. Infinitely diverse and complex webs of causality among aspects of any topic are approached with the intent and goal of locating the presumed underlying polarities of determining causes vis-à-vis determined effects. A topic has been successfully analyzed, from the essentialist perspective, if and when its aspects have been connected to one another in a nexus of causes and effects, determining essences and their phenomena.

Antiessentialism is the rejection of any presumption that complexities are reducible to simplicities of the cause-and-effect type. Instead the presumption is that every element in the context of any event plays its distinctive role in determining that event. Every cause is itself also an effect and vice versa. An antiessentialist or nonreductionist theory refuses to look for the essential cause of any event because it does not presume that it exists. An antiessentialist theory understands every theory (including itself) to be inherently partial, a particularly focused intervention in social discourse. What distinguishes theories, then, is precisely their differing particular interventions by means of their different particular foci. From the antiessentialist standpoint, no theory has found or could have found the essence of anything; that is not the point of theorizing. The point is the particular social intervention every theory makes (see this volume's epilogue).

An antiessentialist Marxian theory must then reject any kind of determinist argument such as the economic determinism that has figured so prominently in the Marxian tradition (see chap. 2). Similarly, any antiessentialist theory must affirm that those particular aspects of any complex topic it treats are not the essences or essential causes of that topic. Whatever the complex reasons why a theory or a theorist focuses upon those particular aspects, it is not because of any presumption that those aspects (or any others) are essential. Indeed, as we shall show, the Marxian theory at work in this book is consistently antiessentialist.

Overdetermination is the positive side of any theory's rejection of essentialism. It is a way of connecting aspects of any topic chosen for attention that avoids all reductionism and essentialism. This means that Marxian theory understands the process of theory to be irreducible to the effect of one or another process in society. There is no essence of which the process of thinking is a phenomenal form. Thinking is not the expression of any other process or processes. There is no question of holding the process of theory to be "more" or "less" determined by this or that other process in society. Rather, each and every other process exercises its distinctive, different effectivity in constituting the process of theory and its products: knowledges.

The concept of overdetermination involves a distinctive notion of causality characteristic of Marxian theory. If all possible entities are overdetermined, none is independent of any of the others. Moreover, each entity will have a different, particular relation to every other entity. Each entity only exists as —or, is caused or constituted by— the totality of these different relations with all other entities. Our concept of overdetermination differs from notions of mutual causality among entities (as in systems of simultaneous equations). It proposes instead a notion of mutual constitutivity among entities.

There can be no question of reducing this notion of causality—this play of differential relations—to any common standard or measure. Among the different relations between any one entity and all those others that overdetermine it, none can be ranked as "more important" or "more determinant" than another. To propose such a ranking is to reduce those differences to a quantitative measure of something presumed common to them all. Such a presumption is precisely what the concept of overdetermination contradicts. To explain the causes of any entity is to construct its differential relations with all the other entities that overdetermine it.

To argue, as we have, that the process of theory is overdetermined by all the other processes in a society requires some initial specification of these "other processes." However we choose to designate them, for example, eating, working, singing, voting, and so forth, in aggregate they comprise what we mean by society. Society is the totality of all designatable processes, of which theory is one. For Marxian theory, each of the "other processes" is conceptualized comparably. Each process in society is understood as overdetermined by all the others, as the site constituted by their interaction.

It follows that the process of theory is overdetermined by all the other processes in society as well as a participant in the overdetermination of each of them. For Marxian theory, the process of theory is therefore constitutive of each and every other process existing in society. This notion of the process of theory as a component of the overdetermined totality of processes known as society carries several implications for Marxian theory.

First, the process of theory loses the privileged and even exalted status it enjoys within alternative theories. It is no longer the essence or "truth" of all other processes in society. It no more expresses their essence than they express its. The process of theory is rather one among the many that comprise society. Its difference from the others lies in its particular characteristics as a changing set of concepts. Its relation to the others lies in the complex web of overdetermination linking all the processes in society. Thus, Marxian theory, as we have specified it, must reject idealism understood as any notion that thoughts determine society or nature. It must likewise reject materialism understood as any notion that natural or economic processes determine society and thinking. Marxian theory rejects idealism and materialism as contesting essentialisms, both of which clash with its commitment to the concept of overdetermination.[2]

Second, the process of theory, when understood as overdetermined, is consequently also understood as contradictory in a particular sense.[3] Given our definition of overdetermination, the process of theory embodies the totality of influences emanating from all the other social processes, its conditions of existence. The process of theory literally contains or comprises nothing but these influences. These are many and varied and push and pull or propel theory in different or conflicting directions. By contradictions we mean the tensions and conflicts produced by these different directions that inevitably characterize any overdetermined process, that is, any process understood as the site of the interaction of all other social processes. For Marxian theory, overdetermination implies contradiction in this sense, and vice versa. Like all other processes in society, the process of theory is overdetermined and contradictory.

The contradictoriness of the process of theory appears on two levels. At one level there are differing and often conflicting theories, that is, sets of concepts. Practitioners within each of these spend part of their time in *criticism,* which we understand as chiefly the specification of differences (contradictions) between their own and other theories. At another level each distinct theory or set of concepts is itself contradictory in the sense that tensions and conflicts exist among the concepts comprising the set. Practitioners within any particular theory typically spend part of their time identifying and seeking to resolve those contradictions within their theory that they can recognize as such. This book seeks to specify contradictions between one Marxian theory and others within the tradition and also to resolve certain contradictions identified within that Marxian theory.

For Marxian theory there is special significance attached to those contradictions of the process of theory that appear as different sets of concepts, different theories. Theories differ in how and what they conceptualize as the objects of their theorizing. They differ in the rules, methods, and taxonomies they observe in linking their respective concepts to enunciate the statements they make. They differ in their definition and deployment of the basic concepts with which they construct their respective sets of concepts.[4] They differ in their definitions of their respective truths and hence their criteria or rules for ascertaining the truths of statements.

It follows that each theory contains its own indexes of truth and falsity; truths are plural and conceptualized differently by and within each distinct theory. Moreover, the epistemological standards used within a theory to validate its truths are as differently conceived—from one theory to another—as are its truths. Thus, to rank different theories by their approximation to some particular epistemological standard(s) presumed to exist above and beyond their differences, for example, "coherence" or "simplicity" or "practical efficacy" or "comprehension of predecessor theories" or "empirical reach," and so forth, is to take a position different from Marxian theory. For the latter, concepts of epistemological standards for theory, for example, concepts of "coherency," "simplicity," and "comprehensiveness," vary from theory to theory. Indeed, the concept of theory varies from theory to theory.

It also follows that each theory's truth—including that produced in Marxian theory—is in no sense the expression of the essence of some "reality." Assertions of that sort, as we shall point out, occur outside the Marxian theory we seek to elaborate here and in contradiction to its epistemological position. Each theory's concept of "reality" as well as of the "truth" about that reality is different. Their differing concepts of reality are indexes of difference among theories, as are their differing concepts of truth.

Marxian theory, then, recognizes no single reality or absolute truth or epistemological standard that can serve to validate one theory as against another. For Marxian theory, validations occur within theories as they subject various statements to their differing criteria of truth. Marxian theory sees itself as one among many different theories, each of which conceptualizes its reality differently and tests its conceptualizations differently. Reality for Marxian theory is a totality comprising contradictions in theory interacting with contradictions within all the other processes that constitute that totality. Marxian theory specifies that interaction as overdetermination. Marxian theory also recognizes, of course, that other theories conceptualize all these matters differently; they take different epistemological positions.

The concepts of overdetermination and contradiction are deployed in Marxian theory to define its particular concept of change.[5] All entities in society change as the direct consequence of the complex contradictions that constitute their existence. To exist at all, for Marxian theory, is to be overdetermined, contradictory, changing, and hence in a state of process. Entities, for Marxian theory, become processes. Marxian theory's concept of theory has therefore to be specified as the concept of the *process of* theory.

For Marxian theory, the contradictions among and within different theories produce changes in these theories and in their interaction. Changes in theories will produce changes in all other processes in society in so far as those processed are overdetermined in part by the process of theory. Changes in the other processes will, in turn, react back upon the process of theory to produce yet further changes in it, and so forth. For Marxian theory, the concept of overdetermination is central to its notion of the ceaseless dialectical interplay between the process of theory and all other processes in society.

Marxian theory's definition and deployment of the concept of overdetermination to understand the process of theory itself differentiates it from alternative theories both within and without the Marxian tradition. These alternatives understand the process of theory in very different ways. From the standpoint of Marxian theory, we may designate the two most important of these alternative ways as empiricism and rationalism.[6] Our argument, then, is that Marxian theory's understanding of the process of theory, its epistemology, differentiates it sharply from empiricist and rationalist epistemologies and the theories within which they occur. Marxian theory is a break from those epistemological positions that have dominated Western philosophy since their initial formulations in the seventeenth century by Locke, Descartes, and Kant. While there were dissents from this tradition, its influence has been extraordinarily pervasive into the present and into the Marxian tradition. Marx, as we read his work, was one such dissenter. His work propounds a distinctive epistemological position different both from the dominant tradition (empiricism and rationalism) and from others who dissented from it.

By the empiricist epistemological position we mean the understanding of theory as a more or less adequate representation of an independent "reality." This reality—or "facts" or "history" or "objective conditions"—is presumed to be more or less capable of revealing its causal relations or structure through the medium of sensory observation or "experience." Via observations, theory is tested against reality. Empiricism posits a distance between thought and reality, thinking and being. It also sets itself the task of overcoming this distance, striving to make theory accurately represent, or correspond to, or adequately reflect, a reality existing independently. Truth is defined as such representation, or such correspondence, or such adequation, and is designated the goal of theory.

For the empiricist epistemological position, all theories confront one unitary reality. This singular reality, accessible through sensory observation, serves as the identical object for all theories and as the absolute criterion or standard of truth for all. A theory that includes an empiricist epistemological position understands its concept of reality as necessarily the concept as well for all other theories. Such a theory determines the truth value of statements within other theories according to *their* adequacy in reflecting *its* concept of reality.

Skeptical empiricists doubt that observations can ever be sufficient finally to establish the nature of reality, but they nonetheless endorse the empiricist epistemological position as the closest possible approximation of "the" truth. Empiricists with perhaps less methodological self-consciousness have fewer or no doubts; they can declare their concepts to be absolutely verified by observation. Despite variations among them, empiricists believe in a unitary reality, in the possibility of its more or less immediate observation, and in the notion that knowledge derives from such observation of that reality.

Empiricism is an essentialist epistemological position. It conceives theory as the expression or phenomenon of an underlying essence that produces it. Reality is the essence that produces, via observation, theory. Empiricist theoretical effort strives to make the phenomenon, theory, the purest (truest) possible expression of its essence: to make theory the mirror of reality. Much of modern analytical philosophy joins in this effort by criticizing linguistic, logical, and other impediments to *the* adequate mirroring of reality.[7]

The essentialism of the empiricist epistemological position contradicts the overdeterminism of the epistemological position of Marxian theory. For the latter, there is not *a* reality that serves as *the* essence of all theory. The different realities conceived within the different theories are overdetermined. This means that these different conceptualizations of realities exist as products of the interaction of all the processes of the social totality. At the same time, these conceptualizations participate in the overdetermination of all those processes. As conceived in Marxian theory, reality includes a variety of theories, all of which are understood to be overdetermined and constituent elements, not the phenomenal expressions of any essence.

For Marxian theory, different theories no more capture the essence of the social totality than do different cuisines or different modes of production or different systems of laws. Each of these is a constituent process of the social totality; each is overdetermined by all other processes and participates in the overdetermination of all. The relation of any one constituent process, for example, the process of theory, to the social totality, that is, Marxian theory's "reality," is a relation of overdetermined part to overdetermined whole.

For Marxian theory, no process in society is passive in the sense of not participating in the overdetermination of all other processes. Thus, the empiricist concept of observation, that is, all sense experience, as a neutral process contradicts Marxian theory. For the former, observation tends to be viewed as passive or neutral, in the sense that it is not a process determining in part what is observed. It is the empiricist's independent standard of truth. For Marxian theory, the process of observation is overdetermined and contradictory. The process of theory plays a part in shaping what is observed and how it is observed; observation is not theory-neutral. Furthermore, observation is no singular, common process among human beings; its overdetermined contradictions appear as conflicting observations among observers. Finally, observation participates, via overdetermination, in determining both the thing that is observed and the process of theory itself. Thus there can be no argument in Marxian theory that observation provides a basically passive medium through which an essence, reality, produces its phenomenon, theory, or that observation provides an independent, intertheoretic standard of truth. Observation and theory are not independent processes; both are overdetermined. Marxian theory's epistemological position stands in contradiction to the empiricist position.

The rationalist is an alternative to the empiricist epistemological position as well as to that of Marxian theory. By the rationalist epistemological position we mean the understanding of the process of theory which holds it to be the means capable of expressing the conceptual essence of reality. The rationalist's reality is singular, much like the empiricist's; it is *the* reality out there whose presumed singular essence is *the* object of all theory. However, unlike the empiricist, the rationalist denies that observation can serve as the needed means to overcome the distance between theory and the essence of reality. Essence is not observed because it is not observable. What is observed in phenomenal reality, and how it is observed, depends upon one's theoretical grasp of the essence of that reality. For the rationalist epistemological position, observation is determined by theory; true observation of phenomenal reality depends upon a true theory of the essence of that reality.

For the rationalist, the task for the process of theory is to capture, to express, the underlying essence of which reality is the phenomenon. The presumption of the rationalist is that this singular essence is more or less accessible to theory and capable of being expressed conceptually. This essence is presumed to be strictly *reasonable,* that is, rational. Theoretical expression of this essence is truth.

Rationalism is an essentialist epistemological position. It conceives the process of theory as the approximation to the theoretical (i.e., theorylike) essence of reality. Because it sees a singular reality as the phenomenon of an essence whose presumed nature makes it accessible to theory, we may characterize the rationalist epistemological position as essentialist.

Rationalism and empiricism may then be characterized as inversely related essentialist epistemologies. Where rationalism makes theory the essence of reality, empiricism holds the inverse position. Where the rationalist holds that theory determines and validates observation, the empiricist holds the inverse position. Where the rationalist claims to make sense of observed facts by means of their essence as specified in the rationalist's theory, the empiricist warrants the sense of any theory by means of its essence in observed facts.

By contrast, Marxian theory is antiessentialist in its epistemological position. The process of theory neither has an essence, as in empiricism, nor is it the essence or any approximation to the essence of anything else, as in rationalism. Rather, the epistemological position of Marxian theory replaces essentialisms by its commitment to overdetermination. That is, the epistemological presumptions of Marxian theory are different from those of rationalism and empiricism. Marxian theory presumes overdetermination; they presume essentialisms, albeit different ones.

For Marxian theory, different theories conceive of different realities and conceive of the process of theory itself differently. For Marxian theory, no one of these theories, including Marxian theory itself, is uniquely warranted by observed facts, as in empiricism. None of these theories, including Marxian theories itself, can proclaim itself the essence of or an approximation to the essence of *the* reality, as in rationalism. Marxian theory conceives of a social reality that is distinct from, external to, and encompasses the different realities conceived in and by different theories. However, precisely because of the externality, its distance beyond conceived realities (the only realities that we *know*), it cannot possibly serve as a universal or absolute measure for them. To do that it would have to be knowable by all, *the* reality for all theory. This is what Marxian theory rejects and essentialist epistemologies affirm via observation (empiricism) and reason (rationalism).

Nor does occasional agreement about something among different theorists warrant, for Marxian theory, any claim that such agreements prove the absolute truth, THE REALITY for all theories, of what has been agreed. For example, Marxists and non-Marxists might agree on, say, "the structure of planets in our solar system." While the existence of such an agreement is interesting and has particular consequences for modern society, it does not warrant the inference/conclusion that the structure agreed upon is therefore the absolute truth about the universe. Agreement is just that; it is not some privileged key to absolute truth. The leap from agreement among some theories to absolute truth valid across all possible theories reveals only the essentialist epistemological standpoint of the leapers.

Indeed, the historical variability of such agreements suggests the pitfalls of inferring absolute truth from agreements. Five hundred years ago, many Europeans agreed that God created and governed social life. However, they disagreed profoundly on the structure of planets, as the conflicts between Ptolemaic and Copernican theories attest. Five hundred years later, dissent over the existence and role of God is rampant, while agreement over astronomy is widespread. From a Marxian perspective there is no sense in attributing an absolute, intertheoretic truth to whatever happens to be agreed upon among different theories/theorists at any moment.

Furthermore, agreement among different theories is itself no straightforward matter. Nations sign agreements only to disagree later about what was agreed, what *agreement* meant or means. Likewise, because two persons utilizing different theories both say they agree on some proposition does not warrant the conclusion for all theorists that they agree in the sense of believing identically. Thus, many of us today might agree that, say, elephants are distinct from toothbrushes. Yet, for us, specifications by each party to such an agreement of what each means by the elephant-toothbrush distinction would differ in all manner of ways. This follows necessarily from our conceiving each party to be uniquely overdetermined and hence differently interpreting and, indeed, seeing the distinction. In short, any agreement would itself be theorized differently within the different theories that are party to the agreement.

Finally, the notion of agreement itself is not, from the Marxian standpoint of this book, some supratheoretical object existing identically for all theories. Does an agreement mean that its parties believe identically? Is that even possible? We think not. Or is an agreement a historically conditioned social device whose meaning varies not only among parties to the agreement but among onlookers as well? What is the meaning of the declaration by different theorists that they "agree" on something? We think that how people understand agreement is rather like how they understand everything else; understandings vary with the differing theories people hold.

From our standpoint, agreement is neither some absolute that is identical to and for all theories, nor does it warrant the presumption that some supratheoretical, absolutely real object causes that agreement. Hence we do not infer absolute reality from the existence of agreement.

For Marxian theory, its reality is conceived as an overdetermined totality. Within that totality it conceives of the process of theory as overdetermined and hence contradictory and ceaselessly changing. Consequently, the different theories are understood to be both internally contradictory and to stand in contradiction toward one another. One index of the contradictions between different theories is their different epistemological positions. To elaborate this index is one way to define Marxian theory in terms of its distinguishing differentiation from alternative theories within and without the Marxian tradition.

There is a second major purpose underlying our attention to epistemology besides the precise specification of Marxian theory. Explaining this second purpose requires a brief statement of what Marxian theory understands as the internal structure of the process of theory itself. That process of theory comprises the definition, production, and deployment of distinct concepts. The relationship among the concepts within any theory is understood as overdetermined. This means that no concept functions as an essence for others within the theory; rather, each concept is overdetermined by all the other concepts within the theory as well as by all the other processes within the social totality. It follows, then, that the distinctive epistemological concepts of Marxian theory participate in the overdetermination of all the other concepts in that theory. Marxian theory's antiessentialist epistemological position is a condition of existence for its antiessentialist conceptualization of society.

In our view theories within the Marxian tradition will be different if they espouse different epistemological positions. Different epistemological positions have significant determining effects on the other concepts of and positions endorsed by those theories. Thus, as we shall discuss futher, epistemological essentialism may well influence a theory's other conceptualizations in an essentialist direction. For example, an empiricist epistemological position within a theory may be conducive to essentialist concepts of social structure and social change, and vice versa. Economic determinism is one such essentialist social theory.

We understand Marxian theory as opposed in principle to essentialism in both epistemology and social theory. We understand that essentialist relations among some subsets of concepts within a theory typically reflect in part and reinforce such relations in other subsets. Therefore, our attention to Marxian theory's pointedly antiessentialist epistemological position is motivated partly by our concern to disentangle Marxian theory from all essentialisms. To separate Marxian theory from essentialist epistemologies should conduce further to separate it from essentialist social theories as well.

We are aware that theories other than our own, both within and without the Marxian tradition, hold very different views of what Marxian epistemology is. Some of these other theories find it to be fully essentialist, a characteristic they may applaud or deplore. Some see Marxian theory as essentialist, and quite properly so, in epistemology but not in its conceptualizations of social structure and change. We shall discuss our reading of these theories in chapter 2. Here we wish simply to affirm that some major contributors to the Marxian theoretical tradition have provided the foundations of what we define as Marxian theory's epistemological position. That is, our understanding of Marxian theory has antecedents, albeit in variously developed forms, within the Marxian tradition.

Concepts of Epistemology

Marx wrote rarely on epistemology. His occasional remarks on the process of theory and its methodology have been subject to diverse and contradictory readings.[8] However, some subsequent writers have sought to make explicit the epistemological position left implicit in Marx's work. Lenin, for example, reasons that Marx left these matters implicit because he thought them largely settled in Hegel's work on epistemology and logic.[9] Lenin insists that what he terms Hegel's dialectical conception of the process of theory is also Marx's. Lenin attacks other Marxists for the dire consequences in their theoretical and political work which flow from their lack of adherence to this concept of the process of theory, that is, this Marxian epistemology. Lenin's reading of Hegel's *Logic* (and of Marx) provides strong support to the formulation of Marxian theory and its epistemological position developed in this book.

Lukács, as well as Lenin, returns to Hegel to work out the specifics of Marx's epistemological standpoint.[10] Lukács also traces the undesirable consequences for Marxian theory of the neglect and misspecification of what he understands as Marx's distinctive epistemological position. In this effort, which continued right to the end of his life, Lukács produces concepts of contradiction and overdetermination upon which we build the Marxian theory in this book. We find comparable formulations and supports in the work of Antonio Gramsci, particularly in his extended discussions of the "philosophy of praxis."[11] Chapter 2 will explore the critical contributions of these and some other major Marxian writers in terms of their significance in the construction of the particular Marxian theory we seek to present.

One theoretician deserves special mention. Louis Althusser has been the key figure in post–World War II Marxism to emphasize the unique epistemological position of Marxian theory and to draw some of its consequences for Marxian theory generally. His work has influenced our readings of Hegel, Marx, Lenin, and others. While we modify and depart in significant ways from his formulations, we owe much to Althusser's formulations (Marx's epistemological break, overdetermination and contradiction, the materialist dialectic, etc.).

The Marxian theory presented in this book builds upon contributions such as these that have circulated, although never predominated, within the Marxian tradition since its inception. Of course, other Marxists as well as non-Marxists read these contributions differently. Nor are we arguing that any one author or any one text consistently formulates one theory; most authors and most texts are informed by several, often contradictory, theories. Our point is only that we can identify certain formulations in certain texts which together move toward a kind of Marxian theory whose development and explicit specification are the goals of this book.

Our theoretical position within the Marxian tradition is also complexly influenced by theoretical formulations outside that tradition. Given our commitment to the concept of overdetermination, we see such influences bearing upon each theory within that tradition, albeit quite differently. Some major contributions on questions of epistemology within non-Marxian theoretical traditions have directly participated in overdetermining the Marxian theory of this book. We have read these contributions as critical commentaries on the established epistemological tradition that we have here divided into empiricism and rationalism.

For example, Wittgenstein's self-critical *Philosophical Investigations* involves a critique of the epistemological positions he had earlier espoused:

> He [Wittgenstein] was trying to demonstrate not that logic and mathematics do not rest on a realistic basis, but only that that basis cannot provide any independent support for them. . . . The sources of the necessities of logic and mathematics lie within those areas of discourse, in actual linguistic practices, and, when these necessities seem to point to some independent backing outside the practices, the pointing is deceptive and the idea that the backing is independent is an illusion.[12]

In the same vein, Thomas Kuhn's investigations into the epistemological bases of modern natural science led him to reject any notion that "changes of paradigm carry scientists and those who learn from them closer and closer to the truth."[13] Rather, Kuhn insists that

> there is another step . . . which many philosophers of science wish to take and which I refuse. They wish, that is, to compare theories as

representations of nature, as statements about "what is really out there." . . . I believe nothing of that sort can be found. If I am right, the "truth" may, like "proof," be a term with only intra-theoretic application.[14]

Paul Feyerabend summarizes his extensive critique of what he terms the philosophy of science:

Theories may be removed because of conflicting observations, observations may be removed for theoretical reasons. . . . Learning does not go from observations to theory but always involves both elements. Experience arises *together* with theoretical assumptions *not* before them, and an experience without theory is just as incomprehensible as is (allegedly) a theory without experience.[15]

We have found the work of Willard Van Orman Quine stimulating because of his critiques of the empiricism that has been and continues to be the dominant epistemological atmosphere in the United States, among Marxists as well as non-Marxists. We read his attack upon the "two dogmas of empiricism"—the claims that "synthetic" and "analytical" statements are meaningfully different and that all meaningful statements can be reduced to (and hence "verified" by) immediate experience—as precisely an invitation to the kind of epistemological standpoint we have here formulated as Marxian. When Quine writes that "total science, mathematical and natural and human, is . . . extremely underdetermined by experience," we respond to the invitation by offering our formulation of the concept of overdetermination.[16] That Quine intends no such invitation, and indeed falls back to a remarkably weak—for him—empiricist position based on a "more thorough pragmatism," does not hinder us from responding critically to the invitation we read in his remarkable and valuable work.[17]

Another contemporary philosopher, a Harvard colleague and student of Quine, has also taken up his invitation by paying particular attention to the matter of Quine's second "dogma." Hilary Putnam goes so far in his critique of empiricism (which he calls "metaphysical realism") to affirm that all truths about "The World" are theory-relative.[18] But, like Quine, Putnam shrinks from developing the implications of such an affirmation along the lines of Althusser's or our formulations. Instead, again like Quine, Putnam falls back to an empiricist position, believing that the different theories must somehow "converge," and echoing Quine's "pragmatism" with the view that the truth of theories is somehow measured by their "success" in the world (as if "success," unlike "truth," were not theory-relative).[19] Perhaps Quine and Putnam were influenced by similar formulations by Rudolf Carnap.

Rudolf Carnap, in "Empiricism, Semantics and Ontology" (1940), sounds quite like Quine.[20] Carnap there distinguishes between two kinds of questions confronting any general theoretical position, or what he terms "linguistic framework." There are the "internal" questions formulated by means of the rules and standards of that framework and treated by them. There are, however, also "external" questions as to the validity of the particular framework per se. Such external questions Carnap declares unanswerable, meaningless, and not even capable of formulation in any theoretical language. Carnap explicitly designates the issue of the acceptance of one or another theoretical or linguistic framework as itself a matter of "practicality," or the "efficiency, fruitfulness and simplicity of the use" of the particular framework. Such acceptance is not, he insists, a matter of or for philosophy or theory generally—as though "practicality" is a standard independent of the philosophical standpoint in which it is specified. To accept such a standard once again introduces the dichotomy between reality and theory central to the rationalist and empiricist frameworks.

Carnap apparently believes that the efforts of traditional epistemology to find and prove some final, absolute "validity" for one or another theoretical—linguistic—framework are not acceptable. We agree. Carnap goes beyond this belief to denigrate the whole epistemological enterprise per se, to declare it meaningless. We do not agree. For Carnap, all epistemology is so much effort at demonstrating final validity. Carnap cannot imagine an epistemological position that is not concerned with such validity, one concerned rather with the causes and effectivities of the different frameworks (including their claims about validity or, for that matter, "practicality").[21]

We have been impressed with what J. M. Bochenski conceives as the relativization of mathematical logic since the days of the supremacy of Bertrand Russell's *Principia Mathematica:*

> The assessment of the relative merits of systems of mathematical logic has become a problem for methodology. If demonstrations are to be carried out a logical system must be assumed: but there are now many such systems. Which one should be chosen?[22]

Again, the invitation we read here is to specify the differences among systems and the overdetermined effectivity each of them has in the social formation. Any specification would itself operate within and by means of one such system. Such a specification, in any case, is how we respond to the invitation, although Bochenski proceeds very differently to argue for a choice among logical systems based on "simplicity."[23] This is, for us, unacceptable. Simplicity is itself variously understood from one particular logical system to another. Hence it is of no value as a neutral criterion among them. It can function as a criterion only from the standpoint of any one particular logical system and *its* concept of simplicity.

The tradition of what may be termed structural linguistics tracing back to Ferdinand de Saussure has exercised considerable influence upon us as well, both directly and through its role particularly in shaping the work of Althusser, as we shall show later. Saussure insists that

> language is a system of differences in which all elements are defined solely by their relations with one another.
>
> . . . .
>
>   The most precise characteristic of every sign is that it differs from other signs. . . . Every sign in some sense bears the traces of all the other signs; they are co-present with it as the entities which define it.[24]
>
> What distinguishes a sign is what constitutes it. Difference creates the characteristic (or the feature) in the same way that it creates value and the unit itself.[25]

In our conceptualization of theory we develop certain of Saussure's notions, particularly those concerned with language's synchronic structure and the "arbitrariness" of its constituent signs, although in ways very different from his own development of them. Instead of vague gestures such as "bears the traces" and "copresent"—and instead of emphasis on the synchronic as against the diachronic—we develop our central concepts of overdetermination, contradiction, and consequently ceaseless change. Further, the Marxian theory we formulate works upon selected notions of Saussure in ways quite different from those exemplified by writers such as Claude Lévi-Strauss, Roland Barthes, Jacques Lacan, Michel Foucault, and Jacques Derrida.[26] These so-called structuralists and poststructuralists (Derrida) either select different parts of Saussure's work to focus upon or develop them differently or both. Thus, while these writers have produced a rich and provocative literature whose influence upon us we acknowledge, it would be inappropriate to attribute any "structuralism" to the Marxian theory we elaborate.[27]

   Finally, we should mention a recent study of epistemological discussions and debates within Western philosophy which highlights several of the non-Marxists to whom we are indebted. Richard Rorty's *Philosophy and the Mirror of Nature* aims to assemble, integrate, and extend the works of those key figures who have, in his view, made the seminal contributions in dissenting from that epistemological position that has retained predominance since Locke, Descartes, and Kant. Rorty, as well as the figures he discusses, are all outside the Marxian tradition. He and they share an opposition to the predominant epistemological notion of the "mind as a mirror," of "knowledge as accuracy of representation" of a singular external reality. Rorty writes defensively; he, too, is evidently a dissenter within philosophy and subject to attacks for being "relativist," "irrational," and "idealist." He counters such attacks not by proposing an alternative epis-

temology but rather by showing that the predominant epistemological position is "misguided" and "self-deceptive," its goal of mirroring reality a
mirage. It ought, in his view, to be "set aside" as an inappropriate problematic much as the previous "scholastic" problematic was set aside several centuries ago.[28]

For us, Rorty's greatest contribution lies in his exhaustive demonstrations that the drive of traditional epistemology to provide absolute foundations for all knowledge as representation of an external reality is equally
vulnerable in all its forms. Analytical philosophy, philosophy of language,
theories of reference, and realism are examined in turn and shown to be so
many efforts to rescue the traditional epistemological position from its successive detractors.[29] Rorty finds them all subject to the same critical pro-
test. All amount to efforts to guarantee that some theory has actually
"touched" the real world out there, has referred to an objective, hard existence, and can, finally, claim an absolute sort of truth across all existing
theories. Rorty concludes that all these efforts fail; "nothing can do what
epistemology hoped to do."[30] Rorty finds that we are left with theories and
their truths, forever plural. They are not commensurate; they do not
dissolve ultimately into an absolute standard of truth, for there can be no
such thing.

The Marxian theory advanced in this book shares something basic with
Rorty and his predecessors in the long debate over epistemology. The general notion of knowledge as accuracy of representation ("mirroring nature") is rejected; so, also, is the concept of philosophy as the somehow
privileged source providing the "foundations" of what can be known. We
even share the "antifoundationalist" view of Rorty and others that philosophy can be understood as a "conversation" among different theories, each
producing its respective knowledges and truths with none having any claim
that it "accurately represents" the "external objective world" vis-à-vis the
others. "The application of such honorifics as "objective" and "cognitive"
is never anything more than an expression of the presence of, or hope for,
agreement among inquirers."[31]

However, we part company with Rorty and his predecessors on a crucial
point, namely, the social context and consequences of the struggle over
epistemology. Rorty and many of his followers see traditional epistemology
as merely a misguided effort to protect the values inherited from the Enlightenment, chiefly the autonomy of science.[32] The latter, in his view, no
longer needs the "ideology" of traditional epistemology to survive; hence
it follows for Rorty that "we" or "philosophers" or "modern philosophy"
can and should reject that tradition. Occasionally, Rorty asserts further that
retaining traditional epistemology threatens the development of new theories by imposing a closure upon thought that imperils the free change in
ways of thinking that Rorty endorses.[33]

For us, more is at stake than what Rorty seems to mean by "Enlightenment values" and "free discursive development."[34] From the standpoint of Marxian theory, epistemological discourse, as a social process, is both overdetermined and a participant in the overdetermination of all other social processes. The changing contradictions of epistemological discourse—the conflicting positions formulated and the social predominance of some over others—influence all economic, political, and cultural processes in society. The contradictions of epistemological discourse have social consequences. By its particular specification of these consequences, which depend on and vary with historical circumstances, Marxian theory arrives at an attitude toward the alternative epistemological positions. Marxian theory thus formulates a partisan epistemological standpoint self-conscious of its own social consequences.

The epistemological position of Marxian theory has been overdetermined in part by both Marxian and non-Marxian theories. Its position is different from the long-predominant alternatives here labeled as empiricism and rationalism. The Marxian theory advanced in this book differs from alternative theories within the Marxian tradition by virtue of its different epistemological position. The latter serves as a significant index of theoretical differences within that tradition.

A second such index is the conception of society characterizing a theory. Marxian theory's distinctive concept of the social totality, as we understand it, marks it off from other theories within the Marxian tradition. Concepts of epistemology and of the social totality together provide sufficient indexes of difference to allow us to establish an initial case for the uniqueness of the Marxian theory in this book. After establishing the uniqueness of its distinctive definitions and deployment of its basic concepts, we will explore its unique substantive contributions to the Marxian tradition.

Conceptualizations of Society

Marxian theory, as we understand it, conceptualizes society as a complex totality of relationships. We will use *relationship* as roughly synonymous with the terms *practice* and *activity.* We understand these terms to refer to multifaceted interactions among and between people and nature. However, such relationships are not the basic analytical unit with which Marxian theory approaches the conceptualization of society as a totality.

The basic unit of analysis in Marxian theory is "process." Every relationship in society is composed of its distinguishing set of processes. The qualities or aspects of any relationship in society are nothing other than its set of component processes. For simplicity of exposition, we shall group all the possible processes comprising any social relationship into four categories: natural, economic, political, and cultural. Variously combined sets of these processes comprise the relationships whose aggregate is society.

By natural processes we mean the movements of matter and energy commonly understood as chemical, biological, physical, and so forth. By economic processes we mean the production and distribution of the means of production and consumption for communities of human beings. By political processes we mean the design and regulation of power and authority in such communities. By cultural processes we mean the diverse ways in which human beings produce meanings for their existences.

These processes, for Marxian theory, never occur in society alone; they appear rather in sets as the distinctive and constitutive aspects of relationships. Thus the theory approaches relationships in society as complex. To understand them requires the specification of their distinguishing aspects, that is, their component processes.

For example, working—human labor to produce some use value—is a relationship. It comprises a set of processes that are its distinguishing qualities. The set includes natural processes, involving, for example, the physical changes in the raw materials being worked up. It includes certain economic processes, involving, say, the performance and appropriation of surplus labor in the work, and certain political processes involving, say, the structure of command among various participants in the work. Finally, the set of processes defining the relationship called working includes cultural processes involving, say, the manner in which the workers conceptualize the social significance of their work. There will usually be not one but many natural, economic, political, and cultural processes comprising any particular relationship to be specified by Marxian theory.

Each of the processes in this relationship is overdetermined by the effects of other processes within it as well as by the effects of processes within still other relationships in society. For a concrete example, consider the Marxian notion of class, an economic process. It is defined as the process of producing and appropriating surplus labor. Laborers are understood to do a certain amount of labor sufficient to produce the goods and services their current standard of living requires. Marx calls this "necessary labor." However, laborers in all societies perform more than necessary labor. They do what Marx calls "surplus labor." This surplus may be retained by the laborers, individually or collectively. Alternatively it may be appropriated directly and immediately by nonlaborers. The latter case is Marx's precise definition of exploitation: when the class process involves nonlaborers appropriating the surplus labor of laborers.

The class process, whether exploitative or not, is different from other economic processes (e.g., commodity exchange, borrowing/lending, saving money, etc.) as well as from cultural, political, and natural processes. Marxian theory often underscores its focus upon class by dividing social processes into class and nonclass categories for its analytical purposes. Chapter 3 elaborates the Marxian concept of class in detail.

The existence of the class process in the work relationship, and thus in society, is partly the effect of particular cultural processes involved with the production and dissemination of specific meanings pertaining to the nature of the labor performed. Such cultural processes might include the widespread distribution and social acceptance of a produced economic knowledge that does not recognize the existence of the economic process of extracting surplus labor. One result could be the nonrecognition by laborers of their own exploitation: they do not "see" it, partly because they conceive it as nonexistent; others in society also hold this view.

Such thinking may occur both within and without this relationship. It may occur, as noted, among workers who continually make sense in this particular way of the nature of their own and others' work and also among managers who produce this understanding of their own and others' contributions to the production of goods and services. The receivers of surplus labor, the exploiters themselves, can share such thinking and thus be unconscious of their own or others' participation in this class process. Outside the work relationships, such thinking in one way or another may be produced, argued, and disseminated by individuals connected to the media, educational institutions, households, state bodies, and churches. The effects of these diverse cultural processes are powerful: they combine together to help secure the extraction of surplus labor. Their effectivity is thus to deny what Marxism, a differently produced knowledge, affirms to exist in society.

As crucial as these effects are to the existence of exploitation, its existence is also partly the effect of particular political processes involved generally with the ordering of social behavior and the ownership of property. These political processes are not more or less powerful in effecting surplus labor extraction than are the cultural ones. They merely add their own different and unique influences to the existence of the surplus labor process. For example, the relationship called working may involve shop stewards, floor managers, and workers themselves participating in the specific political processes of order giving, rule making, and rule enforcing, whose combined effects push the worker to participate in the class process. Consider, for instance, workers selling their capacity to labor, to produce use values. In this instance, political processes may be necessary to insure their working for the prescribed time, a time that includes their participation in the class process of producing surplus labor. If, for whatever reasons, they do not follow the established rules and orders, they may be disciplined or perhaps even fired. Force, then, becomes one of the societal instruments established and used to secure the existence of this class process.

Still other political processes exist in society, outside the working relationship, which produce their own particular effects on the extraction of surplus labor. Laws may be established that vest certain powers in the hands of unions and mangers, permitting them to establish and enforce rules necessary for the extraction of surplus labor. Such laws thus empower some individuals, both within and without the working relationship, to insure that the worker participates in this particular economic process. It follows that the latter's existence is thus secured partly by the effects of these political processes.

Still other laws may establish and enforce private ownership of commodities and property. If, for whatever reasons, workers within this relationship do not own means of production, they may be unable to reproduce their own social existence independent of it. They are, therefore, pushed, in part, to become involved in this relationship (and its processes) in order to receive a needed wage income for selling what they privately own—their labor power. Their exploitation is produced partly by their non-ownership of the means of production.

Besides these cultural and political processes, certain economic processes also help secure the existence of the class process. For example, economic processes of exchange, involving both the purchase of necessary raw materials and labor power and the sale of the produced commodities, may have to exist in order for surplus labor production to take place. Without those exchange processes, the worker might not be able to participate in any production whatsoever. The very performance of labor itself is in part predicated on the availability and purchase of tools, raw materials, and labor power. Similarly, produced commodities have to be sold. If what the worker has produced cannot be sold within a specific price range, then the performance of surplus labor will be undermined. Therefore, taken together, the effects emanating from both the purchase and sale of commodities give as much life to the extraction of surplus labor as do the aforementioned cultural and political processes.

Economic processes external to the relationship of working also produce their own unique effects in overdetermining the existence of the class process. The existence of markets, money, and the accumulation of capital may all help provide certain of those conditions that may be necessary for the class process to occur.

No less obvious than these diverse social effects are those emanating from natural processes. The extraction of surplus labor is in part the effect of numerous chemical, physical, and biological changes occurring both within and without this relationship. Processes of physical change in raw materials help make possible the use values to be sold. Added to this change are the complex natural changes occurring within the body of the worker. The productive activity of this individual is partly the complex product of the human body's innumerable biological and chemical processes. In sum, natural processes add their own unique contributions to whatever social behavior the worker exhibits—in this case, the participation in the class process. Still other effects produced by the processes of nature occur outside this relationship. For example, sunlight, air, and weather are only a few of the endless processes of nature that participate in overdetermining the extraction of surplus labor.

No listing of processes can ever be complete. Indeed, the very conceptual process of specifying them will beget still others in a ceaseless attempt to explain concretely the existence of any one—here the class process. This example illustrates the nature of the class process as a site constituted by the effects of very different social and natural processes. Still additional ones need specification and elaboration. Nonetheless, the logic should be evident: each process adds its own unique contribution to creating or causing the existence of the class process. Its nature is thus caused by their combined effectivity and is itself different from each of theirs. The process of surplus labor extraction embodies, therefore, the totality of effects emanating from this incomplete listing of cultural, political, economic, and natural processes. It would embody as well effects from still others we have yet to specify or even invent. That is why we consider it, and by logical extension all other processes in society, to be overdetermined. Indeed, the use of the prefix *over* becomes a way to signal this different and distinctive way to think about causation.

The alternative is essentialism: the presumption that one or more basic processes of life exist whose effectivity on the class process is more powerful, more important, than the effectivity of the others. Once discovered, the search is over; the list is complete. The ultimate explanation of the existence, the cause, of the extraction of surplus labor has been found: the class process has its essence.

Indeed, several of the social processes listed above have functioned as essences in some of the more famous essentialistic approaches adopted within the Marxian tradition over the last one hundred years. Cultural determinists specify the consciousness or lack thereof of workers as the ultimate cause of the existence of class. Political determinists discover in power, rather than culture, the ultimate origin of workers' exploitation and their class position. Whether it be the workers' lack of control over the means of production or their subjection to the wishes and desires of managers and capitalists, the unequal distribution of power in society becomes the ultimate explanation for the existence of surplus labor extraction. And, of course, the economic determinists have their special place in the Marxian tradition. They are not shy in claiming that after all is said and done, economic factors, typically conditions of production, govern class in the last instance.

In contrast to these essentialistic approaches, we conceptualize each distinguishing aspect of a social relationship as a process and thereby underscore Marxian theory's focus upon the ceaseless change characterizing society and each of its parts. Such change is understood as the consequence of the interaction among processes within any social totality. Marxian theory conceptualizes that interaction by means of its concept of overdetermination. Every class and nonclass process in society is theorized as overdetermined by all the others existing within society and therefore changing it.

To generalize Marxian theory, each process in society is understood as the site of the interaction of the influences exerted by all the others. In other words, the existence and particular features of any one social process are constituted by all the other processes comprising a society. Each social process is the effect produced by the interaction of (i.e., is overdetermined by) all the others. Each process is overdetermined as well as a participant in the overdetermination of every other process in the society. The examples of overdetermining the processes of theory (discussed earlier) and class exemplify the general notion of the overdetermination of social processes specified here.

The generalized concept of overdetermination is accompanied by the parallel generalization of the concepts of contradiction and change discussed earlier. Thus, each social process, understood as overdetermined, is conceived as contradictory. It is the site of influences from all other social processes that push and pull it in all sorts of ways. Its overdetermination constitutes the process's existence and its internal tensions. These produce its movement, its change. Such movement or change in any one process within a society means a change in the influences it exerts upon all other social processes. The latter change and their changes react back upon the first process to change it further. This is true for each and every overdetermined process in the society: hence the notion of ceaseless, complex changes which characterizes the Marxian theory of society.

It follows that each social process is overdetermined uniquely. In other words, each is the unique effect of the totality of all processes other than itself. The qualities of each are therefore different. The pace, direction, and so forth of its changes differ from those of all other processes. Each social process therefore exerts its unique influences in the overdetermination of all other processes.[35]

It also follows that each relationship in society, conceived as a distinct set of social processes, changes as each of the processes of that set change. Moreover, since each social process changes differently, the development over time of any social relationship is conceived as unique and uneven in the sense that each process comprising that relationship changes in its own particular way. Marxian theory's concept of uneven development is constructed by means of its concepts of overdetermination, contradiction, process, and relationship. These latter concepts function, in Marxian theory, as the conditions of existence for the formulation of the concepts of uneven development.

The Marxian conception of society as a totality of overdetermined processes implies a distinctly antiessentialist view of causality in society. No process in society can be understood as the effect of merely one or a subset of other social processes. No one process in society, nor any subset, can be understood as *the* cause of one or more other social processes. In other words, no process can be the essence of another; no subset of social processes can determine another subset.

Theories affirming that some social processes, say, an economic subset, determine or function as the essence of another subset, say, political and cultural processes, are different from and opposed to Marxian theory as we understand it. So, too, are theories affirming that some subset of social processes, say, those comprising certain intersubjective human relationships, determine or function as the essence of others. As we understand it, Marxian theory is different from and incompatible with either economic determinism or theoretical humanism, the latter understood here as a determinism where human subjectivity functions as the essence of other aspects of society. The critique of these two determinisms will be developed in detail in chapters 3 and 4. In any case, the Marxian theoretical conception of society as an overdetermined totality places that theory in opposition to any essentialist or determinist theories of social structure and change, inside or outside the Marxian tradition.

Conceptual Points of Entry

To theorize society as a totality of overdetermined processes and hence devoid of any determining essence(s) implies the question How can one make sense of this totality? If every process in (aspect of) society is complexly overdetermined by *all* the others, any explanation of such an aspect would require an exhaustive examination of all those others and their interaction. Such an examination would be interminable and thorough to the point of incomprehensibility. In other words, if everything about society depends upon and helps shape everything else, how can anything be reasonably explained?

Marxian theory has a particular answer to this question. Marxian social theory has a starting point, but the theory never ends in the sense of a "complete" social analysis. Indeed, one way to distinguish social theories is by referring to their different starting or entry points. By entry point we mean that particular concept a theory uses to enter into its formulation, its particular construction of the entities and relations that comprise the social totality. In any case, Marxian social theory is open; it never completes its formulation of the social totality.

Marxian social theory's entry point is its concept of class. As noted ear-

lier, Marxian theory approaches epistemology with the entry-point concept
of overdetermination; it approaches the theorization of society with the
entry-point concept of class. Class is understood as a distinct social process. As noted, it is the economic process of performing and appropriating
surplus labor. The different forms and analytical implications of this concept of class are developed in chapters 3–5. Marxian theory begins its
analysis of any society by initially specifying the forms of the class process
existing within that society. It proceeds to elaborate how such forms are
overdetermined by all the nonclass processes existing within the social totality and how they participate in overdetermining all those processes.

Given Marxian theory's adherence to the concept of overdetermination,
it necessarily follows that the class process cannot be conceived as the essential cause or determinant of any other process(es) in the society. Marxian theory thus distinguishes between theoretical entry points and theoretical essences; all theories have entry points, while only for some do they
function as essences. Marxian theory has its entry point, but it does not let
that entry point function as an essence. This distinguishes it from theories
whose entry points function as the essences of other concepts or subsets of
concepts within those theories.

To link the initial concept of the class process to other concepts within
Marxian theory is not only the task of the theory; it is at the same time the
enrichment of the theory's conceptualization of class. Each linkage of the
concept of class to other concepts in the theory adds another relationship,
another determination to the concepts that are so linked. As the Marxian
theory is elaborated, then, the entry-point concept of class is increasingly
determined, or, in Marx's terminology, increasingly concretized.[36]

Marxian theory is characterized and differentiated from other theories
by its definition and deployment of the class process as its conceptual entry
point. It is further distinguished by the antiessentialist deployment of its
entry point: locating the class process within the web of overdetermina-
tions comprising society. Finally, and as the consequence of these distinguishing characteristics, it is a unique theory in terms of the increasingly
concretized conceptualization of the class process that marks each step of
its elaboration as a theory.

One possible objection to our argument to this point might take the following form: does this notion of a conceptual entry point reintroduce an
essence after all? Are we not making class an essential determinant of society by designating it our entry point? Our answer is an emphatic no. We
make no claim that our entry point, the class process, has any greater social determinacy than any other process in the social totality. Our theoretical commitment to overdetermination precludes precisely such claims.
From the standpoint of Marxian theory, social analysis must begin some-

where, with one or another constituent social process, to weave its conception of the social totality. What Marxian theory makes explicit is its distinguishing starting point, having already specified its antiessentialist structure by means of its endorsement of the concept of overdetermination. Thus, the Marxian theoretical entry point is no essence. By contrast, as we show in the later chapters of this book, alternative theories within and without the Marxian tradition have different entry points. These may or may not function as determinant essences, depending on whether or not those theories subscribe to the concept of overdetermination.

A second possible objection to our argument so far might be that we have not justified making the class process, as opposed to some other social process(es), our particular entry point. Now, of course, we could articulate an explanation of how our entry point came to be the class process. We would then point to the variety of political, cultural, and economic processes whose interaction overdetermined our deployment of the class process as our conceptual entry point. Among them would be certain educational and political processes in which we have participated, as well as certain imaginative processes in which we conjured up visions of a future society that we might like to see, as well as certain economic processes in which we were constrained to participate, and so on. All these combined to overdetermine in us a certain focus on class in our theoretical work, as well as a feeling that the class components of desired social change had been analytically neglected and badly needed reemphasis (see epilogue).

Marx remarks in the *Grundrisse* that

> if I were to begin with the population, this would be a chaotic conception of the whole, and I would then, by means of further determination, move analytically towards ever more simple concepts . . . until I had arrived at the simplest determination.[37]

The move from "the whole" to "simplest determination" varies according to the theoretical framework in which the move is made. Different thinkers arrive at different entry points and then theoretically concretize them differently. The different "simplest determinations" at work in different theories, or what we term their respective entry points, are overdetermined. From the standpoint of Marxian theory, we would explain its distinguishing conceptual entry point as overdetermined.

This explanation would contain a justification. We would justify the class process as entry point in terms of the current social situation and the available levers for making specific changes in it. We would argue that the kinds of social analysis produced by Marxian theory via its particular conceptual entry point could and would make a significant contribution toward such social changes. But in all this explanation and justification,

Marxian theory is sufficiently self-conscious to acknowledge that its explanation and justification are produced solely by means of Marxian theory.
That is, like all theorists, we use our theory to fashion all our explanations
and justifications, including the explanation and justification of our own
distinguishing entry point. Our understanding of the social situation and of
the possibilities for changes in it are both causes and effects of our theoretical work. Such a justification of Marxian theory on the grounds of its social context and consequences amounts to warranting a theory by means of
the self-same theory.

We are in no way distressed by this. All theories, as we argued above
in distinguishing Marxian epistemology from empiricism and rationalism, erect their own truth criteria, their own standards for testing newly
produced statements, and so forth. We may now add that all theories justify
or could justify their own distinguishing conceptualizations by means of
those conceptualizations; theories erect their self-justifications alongside
their truth criteria.

To be distressed, for example, by the related comment of Saussure that
"in language there are only differences" is to be distressed at the inability
to specify a referent for any element of the language that is independent of
that language.[38] He insisted that "language is a system of interdependent
terms in which the value of each term results solely from the simultaneous
presence of the others."[39] The "infinite regress" of meaning-production is
apparent: no term or concept can take on any meaning except in relationship to all other terms. Thus, we are left with an endless production
of interdependent terms in which there cannot be any absolute standard
or closure. Saussure summarized this nicely as "everywhere and always
there is the same complex equilibrium of terms that mutually condition
each other."[40]

We are not bothered by the nature of this infinite regress of meaning-
production, by this complete rejection of a referent that is independent of
these "interdependent terms" and that may serve as an ultimate ground of
truth for these meanings. To borrow an image from Hegel, the specification of any idea is without meaning; it is completely empty until we begin
to construct its complex determinations, its linkages to other ideas, its conceptual conditions of existence. Only these give it life and character. Thus
each discursive idea of a theory can only take on its meaning in relationship to all the other ideas of the discourse. Each term is thus understood to
exist as the locus of effects emanating from the other terms of the theory.
Its meaning is literally constructed by them.

There must be, as we have said, a starting point to make sense of this
ceaseless mutual effectivity of terms. The Marxian conceptual point of entry of class gives its unique and visible thread to this idea of an endless web

of meaning-productions. Nonetheless, to be consistent with the logic of overdetermination, we understand the meaning of this entry-point concept itself to unfold and change as its conceptual conditions of existence are specified. It thus cannot serve as an essence, a referent whose nature is somehow independent of the other discursive terms that, in fact, give it life. Yet its presence, and by the same token its absence from other discourses, gives a distinctiveness and a particularity to the construction of Marxian theory and its unique language. The entry-point concepts of class and overdetermination endow that Marxian language with its unique effectivity on our lives. It in no way, however, provides an escape from the relativity of theories and their meanings (truths), both of which are implicit in the linguistic contribution of Saussure and very explicit in the notion of overdetermination.

To be distressed by this is to be distressed by Marxian theory's rejection of traditional epistemology. The latter involves a commitment to a more or less accessible external reality that can act as final arbiter among, or final source of justification for, different theories and their different truth criteria. In other words, Marxian theory admits no final, absolute standards for truth, justification, and so forth. Such absolute concepts belong to epistemological standpoints different from and opposed to that of Marxian theory. Hence we understand our task to be the elaboration of the specific differences of Marxian theory as properly prior to an effort at self-justification, one that must, in any case, operate within that theory. We delay our formulation of a self-justification of this theory (and its distinguishing entry point) in the ordering of the sections of this text for another reason as well. To place such justification too early would risk its being traditionally understood as somehow independent of the theory itself. We can make no such claim and want to minimize any chance of its being read into our text.

The relation of our formulation of Marxian theory to the Marxian tradition may be summarized by our definition and deployment of two terms basic to that tradition. *Dialectical materialism* is understood here in terms of the distinctive epistemological standpoint of Marxian theory. *Historical materialism* refers to the distinctive conception of society and the distinctive entry point discussed earlier. Marxian theory includes both dialectical and historical materialism—both concepts of an overdetermined and class-based knowledge of the social totality. More precisely, Marxian theory is a structure of concepts including the two subsets of dialectical and historical materialism. Each subset participates in the overdetermination of the other; that is their relationship within the theory.[41] Neither subset functions as the essence, cause, or final determinant of the other. Neither is deduced or derived from the other. Each conceptual subset is overdetermined by the

other, by yet other concepts in Marxian theory, by concepts formed within
other theories, and, finally, by all the other nontheoretical processes of the
social totality within which the subset exists. That, after all, is how we
define the overdetermination of any social process and hence the overdetermination of the particular processes or theorizing dialectical and historical
materialism.

Epistemological Differences

The Marxian theory expounded in this text includes formulations of how it
differs from other theories. Of course, the practitioners of each theory will
see, or not see, its difference from others in their own distinctive ways.
From our standpoint, essentialist epistemologies formulated within any
theory will differentiate it from Marxian theory. Empiricist and/or rationalist epistemologies are essentialist, as we have shown, in their respective ways of making theory and reality into essences of one another. The
concept of overdetermination within the epistemology of Marxian theory
renders it strictly antiessentialist; hence its difference from empiricism and
rationalism.

Rationalist and empiricist epistemologies abound both within and without the Marxian tradition. We may point to a few of the seemingly limitless
examples. Several theories within the Marxian tradition include formulations to the effect that they, as against alternative theories, are warranted or
proven by "the facts" or "history" or "practice." [42] This is empiricism. In
various forms empiricism has existed as an epistemological position within
non-Marxian theories for centuries as well as being very much alive in current Marxian and non-Marxian theories.

The recent work of a Marxian theorist, E. P. Thompson, is an interesting
example of the subtle persistence of empiricism because it is a self-defense
against the charge of empiricism, a brusque rejection of empiricism as
"obviously" inadequate, and nonetheless also a thoroughly empiricist discourse. [43] This work and its reception by many of its readers exemplify the
continuing strength of the empiricist epistemological standpoint within the
Marxian tradition.

Thompson repeatedly states that it is "obvious" that concepts are never
identical with "the real." Nonetheless, he writes paragraph after paragraph
negating just this "obvious" point. In these paragraphs he discourses at
length about the relation between "historical knowledge" and "its object." [44] This relation is understood as that between concept and reality.
Thus, Thompson writes a discourse about "reality," apparently unaware
that he must of course be dealing with a, or rather *his*, concept of that reality. What Thompson is doing is discoursing upon a relation between two

concepts: "historical knowledge" and "the real object of that knowledge." To impute "reality" to the latter concept, which Thompson repeatedly does, is precisely to collapse a concept into "the real," the self-same "obvious impossibility" he elsewhere rejects. To admit that different theories or knowledges are distinguished, among other ways, by how they differently conceive of their objects is apparently too much for Thompson, in the sense of cutting theory and knowledge from its foundational connection to "the real." His reaction, so widely reproduced in others, is to save the connection by collapsing at least one of his concepts into identity with the real. For Thompson this real-concept is "history," *the* object of Marxian theory. This is the empiricist epistemological standpoint which views "history" as the measure of the validity of alternative theoretical formulations.

Rationalist epistemologies appear as well in both Marxian and non-Marxian theories. Within the Marxian tradition, rationalism takes the form predominantly of assertions that Marxian theory, understood as a singular entity, uniquely captures and expresses the truth of reality. This truth of a reality external to thought is conceived as singular and accessible to a properly specified Marxian theory and to no other theory. Thus, within Marxian theories that contain rationalist epistemologies, propositions are validated in two complementary ways: by reference to authoritative conceptualizations by Marx and selected other Marxists and by referene to observations of "reality" ("facts") whose significance is warranted by those conceptualizations.

An example found throughout Marxian literature past and present is the assertion of Marxian theory's adequacy as the truth of the real against the inadequacy of alternative theories. Thus, Marxian theory is "social and historical" whereas others are not. Marxian theory can handle certain phenomena that are simply beyond the reach of other theories. From the rationalist epistemological standpoint it is evidently necessary to go beyond understanding differences between Marxian and other theories to an absolute position. The goal is to establish the identity of Marxian theory with the essence of social reality, its truth against the "falseness" of alternative theories.[45]

A recent example of a rationalist school within the Marxian theoretical tradition comprises those who specify the epistemological standpoint of Marxian theory as "realist." Their collective hostility to empiricism, or, more precisely, to what they term "positivism," on the one hand, and their abhorrence of the "descent into agnosticism and relativism," lead them to "realism."[46] By this they mean a conception of theory as an

> objective enterprise, the purpose of which is to provide us with true explanatory and predictive knowledge of nature. . . . To explain phe-

nomena is not merely to show they are instances of well-established regularities. Instead, we must discover the necessary connections between phenomena, by acquiring knowledge of the underlying structures and mechanisms at work. . . . We get beyond the "mere appearances" of things, to their natures and essences. Thus, for the realist, a scientific theory is a description of structures and mechanisms which causally generate the observable phenomena, a description which enables us to explain them.[47]

This "realism" is precisely what we have here designated as rationalism. The adoption of a rationalist epistemological standpoint, at least for these realists, signals more than their rejection of what we term empiricism. It exemplifies as well their refusal to break from the long philosophical tradition of essentialist epistemological debates between empiricists and rationalists who share the terrain of "providing true descriptions and explanations of an external reality."[48]

Marxian theory constitutes a break from the tradition of epistemology built around the problematic handed down from Descartes, Locke, and Kant. That problematic posed the issue: How can philosophy warrant the adequacy of thought as a representation of an external reality? Philosophy, and more specifically, epistemology, was defined in terms of a task: to establish the criteria by which it could be determined to what degree any statement was adequately grounded or, in other words, true. Truth was understood as a universal and absolute quality which any statement either possessed or did not possess for all thinkers. By contrast, Marxian theory rejects that problematic, posing the issue of epistemology altogether differently. It is not sensible, in and for Marxian theory, to imagine or seek after any absolute criteria of an absolute truth. Truths are intra- rather than intertheoretic; they are, in a very particular sense, relative to the theories in which they are constructed. This view carries important implications for the distinction between science and ideology for Marxian theory; those are developed in chapter 2.

Beyond its break from tradition, Marxian theory approaches epistemology in a particular way, as the problem of explaining how different theories come into being and interact with their environment. For Marxian theory the task is to specify the overdetermination of theories and the ways they in turn participate in the overdetermination of all the other processes of the social totality (Marxian theory's concept of reality) in which they occur. This task implies that Marxian theory subjects itself to the same specification. And since, as we have argued, theories continually change by virtue of their overdetermined contradictions, it follows that Marxian theory must continually reexamine and change its understanding of them. In so doing, Marxian theory itself undergoes the continual changes whose necessity it affirms.

Marxian Theory and Relativism

Marxian theory's epistemological standpoint may be labeled relativist or conventionalist. Engels and Lenin acknowledged the possibility of the former label explicitly.[49] As a rough designation of how Marxian theory breaks from the dominant epistemological tradition in Western philosophy, the label fits. However, to use that label for Marxian theory requires that we distinguish sharply its meaning in that usage from its meaning when deployed to characterize certain other theories. Those others share with Marxian theory the rejection of traditional epistemology; to that degree they and Marxian theory are all "relativist." However, Marxian theory goes on from that rejection to pose and develop its epistemological standpoint in a way that differs sharply and significantly from the other "relativist" theories. To collapse them and Marxian theory under the singular label *relativist* loses a basic difference between them and Marxian theory. To specify this difference is to add another determination to the definition of Marxian theory.

Within theories very different from what we term Marxian theory, there have been rejections of the traditional epistemology which Marxian theory also rejects. Rorty, for example, speaks of "occasional protests" against the traditional epistemology built around the words of Descartes, Locke, and Kant.[50] He laments that such protests "went largely unheard" until the twentieth century, when an effective break in epistemology was produced. This break, emerging in the later works of Wittgenstein, Heidegger, and Dewey, which Rorty himself seeks to extend, is "relativist." It affirms

> truth as, in James's phrase, "what it is better for us to believe," rather than as "the accurate representation of reality." Or, to put the point less provocatively, they show us that the notion of "accurate representation" is simply an automatic and empty compliment which we pay to those beliefs which are successful in helping us do what we want to do.[51]

Rorty understands his own philosophical work as in part a generalization of Kuhn's distinction between "normal science" and, presumably, abnormal science:

> Normal discourse . . . is any discourse (scientific, political, theological, or whatever) which embodies agreed-upon criteria for reaching agreement; abnormal discourse is any which lacks such criteria. I argue that the attempt (which has defined traditional philosophy) to explicate "rationality" and "objectivity" in terms of conditions of accurate representation is a self-deceptive effort to eternalize the normal discourse of the day, and that, since the Greeks, philosophy's self-image has been dominated by this attempt.[52]

Rorty systematizes "relativist" formulations of epistemology. Other notable non-Marxian theorists have made less developed but similar for-formulations. For example, in the context of political science, Raymond Aron haltingly and not altogether consistently embraces "relativism" vis-à-vis alternative explanations of history. So, too, does Hans Meyer-hoff, although with greater trepidation. Peter Winch, in the context of anthropological discussions, is clearly "relativist" in the sense of his break from traditional epistemology. Harold Bloom is, in this sense, a "relativist" literary critic. Kuhn and Feyerabend are relativists in the philosophy of science; Bachelard and Canguilhem in the history of natural sciences; Foucault in the history of discursive structures generally; and so on.[53]

What distinguishes all these "relativist statements" from the different "relativism" of Marxian theory lies in the manner of conceptualizing the relationship among the different theories with their different truths. For Marxian theory, the relativity of theories and their truths is always particular. The particular set of, and relationships among, such theories existing at any moment are understood as overdetermined and contradictory. Each theory in the set has its particular conditions of existence while it provides a condition of the existence for every other process in the social totality. Each theory is a condition of existence for all the others.

It follows that the social predominance of one theory over others depends upon a precise set of social conditions of existence, that is, a precise set of the divers processes comprising the social totality. These overdetermine the social predominance of the theory, its status as "normal" in Kuhn's sense. Thus, for Marxian theory, the conditions of existence for any theory's social predominance over others include, for example, the class processes within that society, technical processes of transforming nature, legal processes of conflict adjudication, and so on. The predominance of one theory over others also provides certain conditions of existence for those class and other processes.

It follows that the Descartes-Locke-Kant tradition in epistemology has been the predominant theory of knowledge because the conditions of existence of such predominance were produced in European society over the last four centuries. So too were the conditions of existence of the predominance of the capitalist over noncapitalist class processes. Marxian theory is concerned with how the predominant epistemology and the predominant class process provide conditions for each other's existence. It is concerned with how both of these provided conditions of existence for the predominance of certain social theories and vice versa.

The point is that Marxian theory distinctively understands the relation between alternative theories, that is, their "relativity," in terms of their historically specific mutual overdetermination with the rest of the processes in the social totality. Thus Marxian theory neither applauds nor bemoans the plurality of theories and their truths. Rather, it presumes these within its continuous drive to specify their changing positions within the social totality generally and in relation to its class processes in particular.

By contrast, the proponents of "relativist" epistemological positions outside what we understand as Marxian theory have different conceptions of the relationship among theories. Kuhn, for example, sometimes conceptualizes this relationship as a matter of "choice" among alternative theories by an agreeing group—in his case a community of scientists. They agree to choose, among several plausible theories, the one that becomes "normal" vis-à-vis the others, which become "abnormal" or disappear altogether. This choice inaugurates a predominant paradigm. Kuhn wavers, however, and occasionally moves away from the voluntarism of the notion of choice to a kind of apriorism. That is, Kuhn suggests that the predominance of one theory or paradigm gives way to another by virtue of "the *nature of the mind*" when it is confronted with observations clashing with the initially predominant paradigm.[54]

Rorty couches his epistemological position in a rather liberal formulation. He is a relativist only in reaction against the absolutist claims of traditional epistemology. He wants to open up the space of theory, to "keep the conversation going rather than to find objective truth."[55] For Rorty, traditional epistemology involves the closure of philosophy, the belief in a singular absolute truth. Rorty rebels by systematically formulating the various rebellions of his scattered predecessors in the history of Western philosophy. All this is done in the name of the virtue of openness to alternatives, to richness of theoretical diversities. Feyerabend goes a bit further, arguing that such openness is necessary to something he terms "the advancement of knowledge."[56]

What commonly distinguishes these non-Marxian relativists from Marxian theory is their limited interest in the causes and consequences of any set of alternative theories. They limit their arguments to the attack upon traditional epistemology and its notions of absolute truth. Combining Kuhn and Rorty, one might say that the latter promotes openness to the plurality of theories and their different truths, while the former explains normal science as the scientists' choice among those theories. Both these "relativists" eschew an epistemological standpoint that emphasizes how and why this particular set of theories exists, influences life, and changes in this way at this particular historical time.[57] So Kuhn leaves unexplored the question his work raises: why was the choice among alternative paradigms made that way at that time, and why did the field of choice include these but not other paradigms? Rorty is more explicitly aware of the limitations of his own relativism. He takes considerable pains to explain why his epistemological standpoint

> can be *only* reactive, why it falls into self-deception whenever it tries to do more than send the conversation off in new directions. Such new directions may, perhaps, engender new normal discourses, new sciences, new philosophical research programs, and thus new objective truths. But they are not the point. . . . The point is always the same—to perform the social function which Dewey called "breaking the crust of convention," preventing man from deluding himself with the notion that he knows himelf or anything else, except under optional descriptions.[58]

Not only does Marxian theory recognize no such limitations, not only does Marxian theory insist that the point is precisely to engender the predominance of certain theories, but Marxian theory could not reason in terms of "social functions" as if the term could be reduced to some notion of "man" and his freedom from delusions. After all, Rorty's own work would lead one to suppose that "self-delusion" viewed from within one theory might appear very differently, say, as wisdom, from within another. Marxian theory includes an epistemological standpoint whose "relativist" commitment to the plurality of theories and their truths is merely the prelude for the specification of their partisan positions within the overdetermined totality. Intertwined with its epistemology is a social theory of the conditions and consequences of the process of theory. So Marxian theory seeks to send the conversation in very particular directions, just as it explains the social resistance to such directions in terms that cannot be reduced to man's self-delusion or the persistence of outmoded thought.

Marxian theory is not relativist in the limited sense of merely standing in front of a plurality of theories and insisting that no objective truth can ever arbitrate among them. It rather seeks to specify the social constitution of that plurality, of the predominance of certain theories within it (including the theory of absolute truth) and of their social consequences. Moreover, Marxian theory does this with the explicitly acknowledged intent to advance the social position of certain theories as against others, and indeed certain economic, political, and cultural processes against others. Marxian theory conceives of itself in struggle against alternative theories, a struggle that is not advanced but hindered by the predominance of traditional epistemology.

Marxian theory qualifies as an abnormal theory in Kuhn's and Rorty's sense. Hence it should come as no great surprise that it opposes the predominant epistemological position defining such abnormality. Marxian theory has, as one of its conditions of existence, the intentions of its practitioners to accomplish the predominance of Marxian over other theories.

Such predominance is a condition of existence for other social changes sought by Marxists.

However, the predominance of Marxian theory would be a very particular sort of predominance. Its antiessentialist epistemological position and social theory preclude the traditional sort of closure of philosophical discourse that we, like Kuhn and Rorty, oppose and reject. Its predominance cannot involve the claim that it is the mirror of reality or "the truth" of social life. Certain alternative theories within the Marxian tradition make just such claims, which follow from their traditional epistemological positions and essentialist social theories. Such alternative Marxian theories thereby provide theoretical conditions of existence for the closure of discourse and debate. And such closure is itself a condition of existence for all manner of political, economic, and cultural processes that we, as Marxists, oppose, even when they adopt labels such as socialist, communist, or Marxist. To oppose and change such processes requires, we believe, the formulation of a Marxian theory whose predominance, if achieved, will undermine the conditions of their existence.

Postscript

Marx's famous eleventh thesis on Feuerbach states that philosophers have only interpreted the world when the point is to change it. Unlike others, we do not understand this thesis as a statement about what philosophers *ought* to do rather than what they have been doing. Marx recognizes the actual, historical effectivity of the different interpretations of the world. Change is precisely what all existing philosophies and philosophers produce, via what we have termed overdetermination. The point is that *how* different philosophies change the world is part of what Marxian theory seeks forever to specify, precisely in order to accomplish the social changes sought by Marxists. Marxian theory does not involve the determination of the reality or nonreality of alternative theories or philosophies. (Marx ridicules such efforts as "scholastic" in the second thesis on Feuerbach.) The practitioners of Marxian theory seek rather to win the struggle in theory to establish the theoretical conditions of existence for the social changes they favor.

2

Marxian Epistemology: The Critique of Economic Determinism

We seek here to establish two interdependent arguments. First, we identify and discuss those theoretical tendencies within the Marxian tradition that provide basic materials for the particular formulation of Marxian epistemology commenced in chapter 1. Second, we demonstrate how such a Marxian epistemology serves to displace and thereby resolve the long-standing debate over the relation between Marxian theory and economic determinism. The epistemological positions taken implicitly or explicitly by Marxian theorists have been conditioned by and in turn have influenced their positions in the debate over economic determinism.

We intend to show that epistemology matters by indicating some of its effects upon social theory and practical politics. The different epistemological positions that contested within the Marxian tradition were part of its struggles over how to understand and change society. Central to these struggles was economic determinism with its complex theoretical and practical implications. The struggles and debates continue and matter today; epistemological positions, social analyses, and practical politics remain complexly interdependent.

We realize that others holding a different epistemological position would not agree with us that epistemology matters. For them there is a *real* social and historical analysis which is the only way to change the world. Debates over what thinking is, how it works, and how theory should approach concrete analysis are, in their view, merely inconsequential philosophical speculations. Worse still, such debates detract us from our proper business of changing reality by studying it properly, that is, by means of *their* theory. This view of the singular nature of reality and the singularly appropriate way to study it amount to a kind of monotheism. Like other monotheisms, this one can stand no claim that alternatives to it exist; such claims are treated as the attempted destruction of their God, their "History." Thus Adorno attacked traditional epistemologies as a "reflex of personal insecurity" in their search after guarantees of their respective, singular truths.[1]

Marxian Theory and Economic Determinism

An unsettled and unsettling dilemma has beset the theoretical tradition of Marxism since its inception. The problem concerns the relation between Marxism and economic determinism. The historically predominant tendencies within that tradition have affirmed and elaborated variations on the theme that economic aspects of the social totality determine its non-economic aspects. Words and concepts such as *base-superstructure, forces-relations of production, objective-subjective social conditions, proximate-ultimate-last-instance determinism, moral-material incentives,* and many others were borrowed from Marx and Engels or newly invented to specify the identity of Marxian theory and economic determinism. The continuing felt need among Marxists to make this specification is itself a response not only to non-Marxists' criticisms of economic determinism (qua "Marxism") but, more to the point here, a debate with other Marxists' rejection of the identity.

This debate within Marxism continues unabated. It merits the label *dilemma* because no resolution to its antithetical propositions has yet emerged from the rich theoretical and practical history of Marxism. As we propose to show, the greatest Marxian theoreticians typically wrestled with both sides of the dilemma, recognizing its central importance yet ultimately unable to formulate a clear, explicit solution. At the same time, these theoreticians did provide the conceptual materials that permitted some Marxists, shaped by and confronting the particular social conditions of post–World War II capitalism, to overcome the dilemma by displacing it. Their argument focuses on knowing how and why all sides to the debate within Marxism failed to find the answer because they kept asking the wrong question. In other words, the debate over economic determinism within Marxism was consistently posed in terms that clashed fundamentally with the most basic tenets of a Marxian theory of knowledge, a Marxian epistemology. Our thesis is, then, twofold: that the unresolved dilemma over economic determinism within Marxian theory has involved a distinctly non-Marxian epistemology, and that displacing the latter in favor of a Marxian epistemology leads directly to overcoming that persistent and pernicious dilemma.

To say that the debate over economic determinism within the Marxian theoretical tradition involved a non-Marxian epistemological position raises the question What precisely was the epistemological aspect of that debate? Participants on all sides generally shared the traditional epistemological standpoint of the presumed existence of two distinct realms of life: that of "reality" ("being," "materiality," "practice," "the concrete," "actuality," etc.) and that of the thought ("theory," "idea," "abstraction," "concept," etc.), aiming to grasp the truth of that "reality."

The participants divided over what the essential truth was, and they still do. The consistently predominant view has often been labeled "classical" or "official" Marxism in recognition of the general endorsement it has received within and by most Marxian political parties and groups. In this view Marx was and is understood to have discovered the truth, namely, that the economic aspect of social reality determined the noneconomic, specifically the various political and cultural, aspects. Proponents of this view have always undertaken to elaborate how this determination process works in concrete situations and to polemicize against alternative, "false" theories of social reality.

The consistently minority Marxian tendency found the predominant view too strong, too dogmatic, too mechanical, too unidirectional, too narrowly reductionist. In the writings of Lukács, Korsch, Gramsci, Reich, Frankfurt school theorists, Marcuse, and Sartre, to take some major examples, this minority tendency has found basic supports for its rejection of the identity of Marx and Marxism with economic determinism.[2] However, it is more accurate to refer to minority tendencies than to suggest one unified position. Some of the minority offered a humanist position in which the essence of history was "man," or "the human existential predicament," or the "Human project," and so forth.[3] Others held back from any such full-fledged humanism, focusing their work rather on particular demonstrations that specific noneconomic aspects of social reality help shape history, effect economic aspects, and therefore serve to undermine any economic reductionism in Marxian social theory.

The contests among these positions occasioned many variations on their respective themes. However, none resolved matters. One variation, inaugurated by Engels, came to serve as a widely held middle ground occupied by those who both acknowledged that the debate touched something of great importance, yet also accepted it in its unresolved form. Engels offered the interpretation of Marx and his earlier works to the effect that they only meant to say that the economic aspects *ultimately* or *in the last instance* determine the noneconomic:

> It is not that the economic situation is *cause, solely active,* while everything else is only passive effect. Economic relations, however much they may be influenced by the other—the political and ideological relations, are still ultimately the decisive ones.[4]

> Marx and I are ourselves partly to blame for the fact that the younger people sometimes lay more stress on the economic side than is due to it. We had to emphasize the main principle *vis-à-vis* our adversaries,

who denied it, and we had not always the time, the place or the opportunity to give their due to the other elements involved in the interactions.[5]

This formulation indeed grants to both sides of the debate some theoretical space to pursue their respective arguments about the truth of the social reality. It also permits both sides to present a united front toward non-Marxists, since both can jointly proclaim their allegiance to a notion of *ultimate* or *last-instance* determinism exercised upon society as a whole by its economic elements. The remarkable and instructive work of Max Horkheimer of the Frankfurt school offers various illustrations of the complexities attending the occupation of the Engels middle ground.[6]

The history of the unsettled debate presents a picture of recurrent shocks and crises renewing and sharpening the intensity of the debate, followed by relapses into repetitions of but slightly altered positions. Marxian political groups, conditioned in significant ways by the various positions in the debate, forever found and find themselves forced to make basic strategic and tactical decisions involving the assessments of the precise and ever-changing mutual effectivity of the different aspects of their social environment. In such circumstances struggles over the specific strategic or tactical centrality of some noneconomic aspects could and often did develop into theoretical assertions of the primacy, even over economics, of other aspects, for example, the political or class consciousness of the workers, the power of nationalist, sexist, racist, or religious beliefs, the effectivity of parliamentary and military bodies. Against such theoretical developments, loyalists to the economic determinist argument reaffirm their commitment. The debate flares up again; the loyalists drive some out of the ranks of Marxism altogether; the Engels middle ground is once again rediscovered. Marxian political practice, having shaken the theoretical debate, is in turn shaken by the flare-up of and fallout from the debate. The stage is thus set for the next shock.[7]

In many ways the mutual determination of theoretical debates and political practices within the Marxian tradition changes both. The history of the tradition attests to this. However, what remains remarkable, and itself a provocation of this chapter, is the repeated inability of participants in the debate to resolve it. Each flare-up posed and poses anew the problem of how to think through the relation of economic to noneconomic aspects, only to relapse, with much frustration all around, into fruitless, vague disputations about which aspects influence the others more (in the quantitative sense).

The recent history of the New Left in the United States, and the resurgence of interest in Marxian economics which it helped kindle, offers a

case in point. The particular contradictions of postwar United States society concentrated by the exigencies of the Vietnam War interacted with
the political weakness of the domestic radical and Marxian movements to
provoke an intense debate over the theory of social change, particularly
revolutionary social change. Participants in this debate took up, often unknowingly given the extreme weakness of any Marxian theoretical tradition within the United States, what had become fairly standard opposing
positions in the traditional Marxian debate over economic determinism.

Against the theoretical economic determinism and economism in practice identified with the Marxian parties, the New Left affirmed its concerns
for the noneconomic aspects of society that it found intolerably oppressive:
militarism, racism, sexism, alienation, authoritarian hierarchy, undemo-
cratic power, and so on. With exceptions, of course, the New Left counter-
posed various noneconomic determinisms: history was to be reconceptualized as the struggle of white versus nonwhite ("third-worldism"),
women against male oppression, the intrinsic human potential against its
alienating social constraints, democracy against authoritarian hierarchy,
and so forth. Within New Left ranks those especially concerned with economics and economic theory created the Union for Radical Political Economics (URPE). The dominant tendencies within it to date have either rejected Marxism as irrelevant or worked to reconceptualize it in accordance
with the antieconomistic agenda of the New Left. Thus, many in and
around the URPE worked to free Marxian economics from the perceived
economistic flavor of *Capital* generally and of Marx's basic value theory in
particular.

Marxian economics and Marxian value theory in particular were rejected in favor of "political economy." This, in turn, was a term intended
to encompass the widest possible application of economic analysis to the
typical concerns of the New Left. What mattered most to New Left political economy was the social problem addressed; what analytical apparatus
to deploy was a very secondary matter. In general, Marxian theory remains
suspect as too economic, too tied to the rejected economic determinism of
the Marxian parties, although rich with important insights into capitalist
society. Those within the URPE who continue to concern themselves with
Marxian theory seem chiefly interested in correcting, superseding, or reworking it to incorporate the various New Left concerns they champion.

The New Left, and the economic theorists operating within its influences, refused to reduce the noneconomic aspects of the people's struggles
that they confronted to economic bases. Nor did they shrink from the consequences of this refusal. Since they nearly universally identified the
Marxian tradition with economic determinism, they had either to reject
Marxism per se or else endorse a reformulation of Marxism that rejected

the identity of economic determinism and Marxism. Thus, some among them came face to face with the traditional Marxian debate over economic determinism. Not surprisingly, some could line up comfortably behind the positions enunciated by Herbert Marcuse. Parts of the New Left thus took up certain of the anti-economic-determinist standpoints characteristic of the traditional Marxian debate.

These segments of the New Left and its economic theorists also faced up to the problem of how to conceptualize "revolutionary struggles" and "class struggles" when no economic determinist argument was acceptable. Such struggles were shown to involve much more than economics: power struggles, racial struggles, and sexist struggles came to occupy center stage theoretically, "equally" or "more" important for social change than economic struggles, according to the taste of the theorist in question. In the process of working toward such positions, New Left theorists had occasion to rediscover those Marxian theorists whose participation in the economic determinism debates had produced texts with which the New Left could identify: passages in Lukács, Gramsci, Korsch, Wilhelm Reich, and others.[8]

The overwhelming thrust of the New Left and the URPE to date has been along the lines of the traditional anti-economic-determinist position, including the major variants of that position as outlined above. The Engles middle ground has adherents in the New Left generally and in the URPE especially, given its economic focus. There are even some loyalist economic determinists to be found; their numbers may well be increasing in recent years (partly because of changed economic conditions in the United States). There are also the proponents of an "uncommitted" position on the relative mutual influences of economic and noneconomic aspects of society. Such proponents have always boasted of their commitment to concrete social situations, each of which has to be examined in its empirical specificity in order to ascertain the specific mutual effectivity of economic and noneconomic aspects. Political practice and the social contradictions of the United States after World War II interacted to stimulate once again a flare-up of the traditional Marxian debate over economic determinism; as before, despite certain unique features of this flare-up, the debate remains in its unsettled and unsettling state.

What strikes us about all these particular tendencies is their common adherence to the same epistemological terrain, the same epistemological terms of debate. All understood themselves to be approximating in theory the true, essential determination of social reality. Even the few who seriously questioned the common epistemological terms of the debate nonetheless returned to use them when participating in the debate themselves.

All participants in the debate over economic determinism and Marxism appealed to empiricist or rationalist (or both) types of proof for their respective positions. Empiricists appealed to "the facts" as warranting their arguments. They argued that the facts revealed their truth to anyone not so extraneously biased as to be unable to face them. "History teaches" to those not ideologically refusing to learn. "History," from the empiricist standpoint, constitutes not a problem in and for theory but, instead, an independent universal measure of its validity as exemplified in the work of E. P. Thompson discussed in chapter 1.

Within the proceedings and publications of the URPE, empiricism, crude and sophisticated, flourishes as the generally predominant epistemological standpoint.[9] Thus, "political economy" is championed against neoclassical economic orthodoxy on grounds of the former's greater adequacy to historical reality, its validity tested against the independent measure of facts. Within the URPE, positions on the debate over economic determinism frequently also exhibit empiricist epistemological standpoints: "history" shows that economic determinism is or is not true, that racial or sexual determinism is more, less, or equally significant in reality, and so forth. We may readily understand how easily and how often the different tendencies came to see one another as more or less infected by bourgeois bias, blinding them to the truth revealed by the facts.

There was and is also the rationalist proof offered from the rationalist epistemological standpoint of some within the debates. Marxian rationalists, for example, operate from the presumption that Marx discovered the truth of social reality, that his theory captures, and thus is identical to, the essence of that reality. For them disputes over that reality and whether it is economically determined properly reduce to disputes over the precise specification and formulation of Marxian theory. To take an example, important in URPE, an economic "crisis" located in the realm of "reality" is "explained" by properly understanding the relationship in *Capital* between underconsumptionist tendencies and tendencies for the profit rate to fall.[10]

All participants in the economic determinism debate resorted to empiricist and/or rationalist proofs corresponding to their epistemological standpoints in framing their arguments for or against economic determinism and its identity with Marxism. More important, most writers frequently utilized *both* proofs at different points in the texts they produced.[11] The reason for this, we suspect, is that empiricism, when pushed to defend itself, can and often does collapse into a rationalism, and vice versa. To take the rationalist epistemological standpoint first, consider the dilemma of a Marxist with a typical commitment to some sort of materialism. Confronted with the critical demand to justify the rationalistic notion that Marx's theory is the truth of "the real," the final recourse can be and often has been that empirical testing—"practice" in the empiricist sense—has validated the truth of the theory. On the other hand, consider the dilemma of the empiricist Marxist confronting the critical demand to justify his or her epistemological standpoint: How does one verify the independence attributed to "theory," on the one hand, and "facts perceived," on the other? To such questions Marxian empiricists can and often do reply, in what is a rationalist formulation, that their (or Marx's) notion of the two independent realms—that is, their *theory* of the theory-fact relation—is the essence, truth, of the real world. We may here ignore, although it all too frequently occurs, the vulgar, circular proposition that the independence of facts from theory has been empirically proved, since, of course, such an empiricist testing *presumes* what it is supposed to test, thereby violating its own premise.

The tradition of Marxian debate over economic determinism exhibits, thus, rationalist arguments for and against economic determinism by means of increasingly rigorous conceptualizations of the logic of Marxian theory qua *the truth* of the social totality. There are, as well, empiricist arguments for and against economic determinism. This four-part typology of debating positions sheds some new light upon the Marxian theoretical tradition, as may be illustrated by discussions within the URPE. The latter's minority tendency favoring economic determinism included both a rationalist and an empiricist approach. For the rationalists, the essence of capitalist society conforms to the privileged determinant role of economics which they read in Marxian theory. Thus, for them the "mode of production" or the "commodity form" becomes the essence of reality, and their task becomes the careful specification and elaboration of *Capital*'s logic (which they see as identical to capital's logic). By contrast, for Marxian empiricists the economic essence of social life is found in the concrete-real, their "real data." History becomes the data source with which they prove the validity of Marxian theory's discovery of economic determinism in the last instance.

Both of these economic determinist approaches carefully distance themselves from the noneconomic essentialisms predominant within the URPE. Nevertheless, contesting economistic and humanistic positions often build upon the same epistemological standpoint. Thus, we may explain how rationalist-economistic tendencies, as well as their rationalist-humanistic antagonists, would both rediscover Hegel and Marx's complex relation to him in terms of a rationalist reading of Hegel's *Phenomenology of Mind* (for the humanists) and *Science of Logic* (for the economic determinists). By contrast, as shown below, we read Marx as sharing Hegel's rejection of received epistemological standpoints, both empiricist and rationalist, although Marx and Hegel developed this rejection in different ways to different conclusions.

In any case, upon examination of the epistemological standpoints at play in the debates, what is perhaps the most striking is the remarkable

similarity they display to the long prior history of epistemological debate
within traditional philosophy. So we might ask What are empiricist and rationalist formulations doing inside the Marxian tradition generally and in
the economic determinism debates in particular? To put this question in
slightly different terms: Does Marx accomplish a basic break, including an
"epistemological break," from prior philosophy, as he thought he did, or
does he not? If the latter, then perhaps we have no reason to find the epistemological terrain of the economic determinism debate surprising or especially significant.

However, it is precisely our purpose to argue the other way—to sustain
the notion of Marxism's epistemological uniqueness vis-à-vis traditional
epistemologies. We seek to develop a specification of that uniqueness out
of the materials given by some of the greatest Marxian theoreticians, even
while they, too, lapsed repeatedly into empiricist and rationalist formulations that were, and still are, the bulk of the intellectual air everyone
breathes. The traditional debate over economic determinism offers a very
useful context and focus for making the needed specification and demonstrating its importance for Marxism.

We are concerned with the unresolved status of the debate above all because it strikes us as one index, itself both a cause and an effect, of inadequacies and irresolutions within Marxian political practices. On the one
hand, there is a long tradition in Marxism of linking positions in the economic determinism debate to their political contexts. Thus, many Marxists
couched criticisms of the political strategy of the Second International in
terms linked to the economism-evolutionism of writers such as Bernstein,
Hilferding, and others. Lenin's criticisms of what he terms the "errors and
failures" of the economistic tendency within Russian Social Democracy
are similarly linked to its proponents' theoretical commitment to economic
determinism.[12] On the other hand, Lenin linked his critique of certain political "ultra-leftist tendencies" to the "idealist" rejection of economic determinism explicit or implicit in their expressions.[13] Gramsci repeatedly
criticized the spiritualism (and clear anti–economic determinism) that he
identified with Croce in terms of its relation to political practices that
Gramsci opposed.

However, we believe it important to go several steps further in linking
theoretical positions in the economic determinism debate and the Marxian
political practices with which they are complexly and mutually interrelated. Beyond the connection between pro- or anti-economic-determinist
theoretical positions and political practice, there is the connection between
the common epistemological terrain of both theoretical positions and political practice. That is, how do empiricism and rationalism present connections to practical political activities that contribute to provoke us into
the oppositional act of writing this chapter?

Empiricism and rationalism as epistemological standpoints have their own political and theoretical consequences. Empiricism starts from certain givens, the "facts," against which it measures, and thus justifies, the particular theoretical positions of any particular empiricist argument. In proceeding this way there is a built-in tendency to consider these facts as conceptually neutral. Since, in our view, no facts are conceptually neutral, it follows for us that empiricist formulations within the Marxian tradition operate as vehicles for the unacknowledged, unrecognized entry of non-Marxian conceptualizations into Marxian theoretical work.[14] Thus, for example, the empiricist concept of "experience" as an immediate register of facts against which to measure the truth of theory can operate, and we believe often has operated, to introduce non-Marxian conceptions of "daily life" into Marxian theory. We understand Lukács's famous attacks against "bourgeois immediacy" in this sense, as his important recognition that proletarian revolution requires the proletariat to deny, to break the hold of "immediately given everyday life" (Lukács's terms), the equivalent of the empiricists' "facts," upon proletarain consciousness.[15] Marx criticizes Ricardo on just this point:

> When he analyses the *value* of the commodity, he at once allows himself to be influenced by consideration of all kinds of concrete conditions. . . . One must reproach him for regarding the phenomenal form as *immediate and direct* proof or exposition of the general laws, and *for failing to interpret it*.[16]

We would emphasize also that such "givens" of capitalist society, absorbed uncritically into Marxian theoretical practice, contain all manner of idealistic notions alongside various materialist notions with which capitalist society invests the phenomena of its "everyday life." Thus, we would argue, empiricist formulations within Marxism function as an open door welcoming non-Marxian conceptualizations, non-Marxian debates between idealism and materialism, and, most ironically, non-Marxian debates between empiricism and rationalism into the Marxian theoretical tradition, where they are now firmly established. We might offer the following analogy. The uncritical import into the Marxian tradition of non-Marxian concepts ("givens") of freedom, sex, class, race, and so forth is rather like the uncritical import of advanced capitalist technologies into developing socialist societies. Of course to reconceptualize critically is to transform, to change, any "given"; it is certainly not a flat rejection.

Empiricism's open door brings into the Marxian theoretical tradition an often embarrassing, often irrelevant, and generally eclectic collection of disparate confused conceptualizations. Indeed, the traditional Marxian debate over economic determinism is itself the site of contests embodying epistemological standpoints taken over uncritically from non-Marxian traditions. We would make the same argument about the concept of economic determinism itself; it is an import not critically reconceptualized into Marxism from its non-Marxian context. However, we focus on the problem of epistemological standpoints that support the various determinisms afflicting the Marxian tradition and that are also imported without the necessary Marxian critical reconceptualization.

We wish to eject empiricism and rationalism by closing the door through which they arrived. The mistakes and failures of Marxian political practices that have been ascribed, in part, to one or the other side in the debate over economic determinism are, we believe, caused in part by the interminably unsettled status of the debate. Indeed, the middle ground in Marxian political practice, which acknowledges the importance of noneconomic aspects within the context of the primacy of the economic, is the practical counterpart for the theoretical middle ground inaugurated by Engels. Both such practice and theory are characterized by vacillation tending toward opportunist swings between pro- and contra-economic-determinist positions. This is because both operate with a general concept of the basic relation between economic and noneconomic aspects that wobbles between making one the essence of the other, or vice versa, depending on whether such practitioners or theoreticians think themselves to be in first-, middle-, or last-instance determinant circumstances. Our notion is that the unsettled and unsettling status of all positions in the debate follows from replacing the specific epistemological standpoint we read in Marx with uncritically imported non-Marxian epistemological concepts.

In sum, then, the practical political consequences that have followed from *both* sides and from Engels's middle ground, taken in the traditional Marxian debate over economic determinism, make it an urgent task for us to criticize the epistemological terrain of that debate in the hope of displacing it onto a different terrain. This way of resolving the debate may then contribute something to the task of overcoming and correcting the failures of past Marxian political practices and thereby establishing a better basis for the present and the future.

Practically and analytically, a problem remains for Marxism: how to think through the relation between economic and noneconomic social aspects without the essentialist lapse into contentions about more or less determinacy by one or the other. The problem remains that the ceaseless twists and turns of social life have disrupted and repeatedly reversed these contentions without, until recently, bringing into question their common epistemological terrain. One solution to this politically and theoretically important problem lies in specifying the conceptual link between their common epistemological terrain and the essentialism characterizing all participants in the debate.

Such specification focuses on the *ontological* quality of the Marxian debates over economic determinism. Participants argue over the actual, ultimate nature of social being, whose essence their opposing formulations claim to capture or to be. Their essentialisms—in epistemology (how theory is understood) and in ontology (how the world is understood) are the problem. In our solution we shall displace the ontological aroma of empiricist and rationalist formulations and the essentialism they support. We displace these essentialisms because they are key blocs to the necessary resolution of the Marxian debates. We propose a very different, strictly nonessentialist ontological formulation linked to what we read as Marx's original epistemological position: our understanding of dialectical materialism.

We wish not only to sketch the basic contours of our formulation but also to show our indebtedness to and frustration with the Marxian theoretical tradition. We understand that tradition to have both permitted and provoked the shape of our contribution to it. Our intention is that specifying our indebtedness and frustration will itself contribute to the articulation of our position and its context within the Marxian tradition.

An Initial Thesis

The traditional Marxian debates on economic determinism have demonstrated a double essentialism. First, the different positions taken counterpose essentialist ontologies. Economics versus intersubjectivity versus technology, and so forth, contest as proposed essential determinants of the world's social structure and change in the short or long runs. Second, debaters on all sides adopt essentialist epistemological positions: empiricist and/or rationalist. They all warrant their particular positions in the debate by epistemological references to empiricist and/or rationalist criteria of truth as the adequate mirroring by theory of an external reality.

Our thesis is that Marxian theory rejects the double essentialism of the traditional debates; it is overdeterminist in epistemology and ontology (or social theory).[17] In our view, essentialist epistemological positions reinforce as well as reflect essentialist social theory; the two kinds of essentialism provide conditions for each other's continued existence. The uncritical acceptance of essentialist epistemological positions reinforces determinist social theory—economic and otherwise—within the Marxian tradition. By contrast, Marxian theory's commitment to overdetermination in both epistemology and social theory permits it to go beyond the rejection of economic determinism to a resolution of the debate itself.

The centrality of the concept of overdetermination rules out any notion that any one social aspect, such as the economic, can be ultimately determinant or determinant in some last instance of other social aspects. This centrality also carries with it a definition of the particular kind of complexity characteristic of Marxian theory. That theory focuses not on the relative importance of economic versus noneconomic social aspects but rather on the complex "fitting together" of all social aspects, their relational structure, the contradictions overdetermined in each by all.

Marxian theory thus cannot declare an a priori commitment to any notion that some among the constitutive social aspects determine others any more than they are themselves so determined, or, rather, overdetermined. Marxian theory can thus be neither economic determinist, nor determinist in any other way, nor can it differentiate itself from other theories upon that basis.

Here, then, is the resolution we offer to the traditional Marxian debate over economic determinism. None of the economic, humanist, or other debated determinisms is acceptable. All of them are connected to epistemological standpoints different from and unacceptable to Marxian theory as we understand it. The stress of Marxian theory upon economics in general, and upon class in particular, is a matter of its particular conceptual approach to social analysis. That approach should not and cannot be confused with the concrete knowledge it produces. Class has a role of conceptual priority in the former but not in the latter. Marxian theory's overdeterminist epistemological standpoint—dialectical materialism— precludes the sort of ontological arguments for one or another essence of social reality which characterize the debate.

Class as an economic concept is an entry point and focus—not an essence for—Marxian theory and the knowledge it produces. For Marxian theory it is no more determinant of social life than any other aspect. Marxian theory does not need, nor can it sustain, any claim that its particular theories grasp the essence or the truth of *the* social totality, of reality: "The real subject retains its autonomous existence outside the head. . . . Hence, in the theoretical method, too, the subject, society, must always be kept in mind as the presupposition." [18]

Overdetermination, contradiction, and class are specific, basic concepts within Marxian theory that not only mark its epistemological standpoint as sharply divergent from that of nearly all participants in the debate over economic determinism. They also make the task of Marxian theory sharply different from that undertaken by those participants. The latter, reading Marx and especially his emphasis on economics from a traditional non-Marxian epistemological standpoint, come to concern themselves with the question Are economic aspects of social reality more determinant of other aspects than they are determined by them? By contrast, Marxian theory, as we understand it, asks the question How do the nonclass aspects of the social totality function so as to overdetermine its class aspect, and what dynamic is constituted by the mutual overdetermination of both class and nonclass aspects?

The formulation of Marxian theory at work in this book displaces the question underlying the traditional debates over economic determinism. Beyond rejecting economic determinism, it rejects the question of which social aspects are more or less socially influential than others. That question presumes the possibility of an answer; it supposes that some social processes have greater effects than others. One form of economic determinism is the belief that the economy (or mode of production) determines in the last instance the effectivity of other processes in the society. So, for example, the economy or mode of production determines ultimately which of the political, cultural, or economic levels or instances will "dominate" the society. The domination of, say, the cultural level is caused by the economy: the latter is, in the last instance, taken to be the *most* important determinant in society.[19]

This approach assumes that the different levels or instances are independent of each other so that it can identify the influence of the economy as the most determinant in society. The essentialism of the approach requires entities to be given independently so that their "more or less" quantitative effectivity can be discovered. In contrast, we affirm that the nonindependence of entities does not allow us to identify such quantitative determinance.

The conditions of existence of the economy's effectivity are precisely the effects of the noneconomic levels upon it. The relative autonomy of the economy only exists by virtue of the effectivities of all the other entities upon it. Its qualitative and quantitative determination in the society is thus (over)determined by all others. This determination therefore cannot be identified independent of the determinations of all other entities. Since all determination is mutual among all social processes, no one determination can be "more or less" important.

The idea that some social processes are more important than others is inconsistent with our concept of overdetermination. We ask rather why any theorists would seek to reduce the different and mutual effectivities of different social processes to a uniform quantitative ranking. We argue that one explanation lies in their epistemological positions. Consider, for example, empiricists and rationalists who rank alternative theories according to their approximation to a singular truth. Not surprisingly, this ranking of theories is conducive to a ranking of determinants within their particular theories. We have here an example of how epistemology can matter, that is, how particular epistemological positions may lead to posing particular questions and producing correspondingly particular analyses of society and history. By contrast, our epistemological position, involving the concept of overdetermination, precludes ranking theories vis-à-vis any singular, independent standard of truth. In parallel fashion, our social analyses do not suppose or seek to determine the ranking of social processes' effectivities in terms of more and less. We thus produce different concrete social and historical analyses form those holding different epistemological positions.

Marxian theory can resolve the traditional debates over economic determinism by setting aside the presumptions and terms of the debate along with the various debating positions. In their place Marxian theory pursues the task of specifying the mutual overdetermination of the class and nonclass processes constituting society. Marxian theory's rejection of determinism in favor of overdetermination covers the internal workings of Marxian theory as well. The entry-point concept of class is itself complexly overdetermined in its meanings and role within Marxian theory. Thus, class is a concept from which Marxian theory begins; it is likewise the objective toward which the theory aims. As the next chapters show, the very point and process of Marxian theoretical work—the "concentration of many determinations" in its concept of class—are to develop and change that concept.[20] Thus, each Marxian analysis begins with an initial concept of class, explores its relations of mutual overdetermination with nonclass social processes, and thereby transforms it into the initial concept available for subsequent Marxian analyses. The Marxian theory of the dialectic embodies the dialectic of theory.

Moreover, all the nontheoretical aspects/processes of the social totality within which Marxian theoretical work takes place also participate in overdetermining the contradictions, and hence changes, in Marxian theory's concept of class. For Marxian theory, as we understand it, its own concept of class is related to other concepts and to nontheoretical aspects of the social totality by mutual overdetermination. Thus, class is neither the essence of social reality nor the essence of the structured set of Marxian theory's constituent concepts.

The Marxian tradition that contained and contains the interminable determinist debate has always had its own contradictions which include the formulations from which we have constructed our critical resolutions of that debate. Our discussion of such formulations is intended to anchor our initial thesis and, more important, to elaborate its conceptual apparatus.

Marx and Engels on Epistemology

The views of Marx and Engels on epistemology should be treated against the background of Hegel's teachings on that subject. They acknowledged those teachings as influential upon their methodology.

In the *method* of treatment . . . Hegel's *Logic* has been of great service to me. . . . If there should ever be time for such work again, I would like to make accessible to the ordinary human intelligence, in two or three printers sheets, what is rational in the method which Hegel discovered.[21]

There are indeed passages in Marx where he very closely paraphrases the originals in Hegel.[22]

Hegel's *Phenomenology of Mind* of 1807 contains an introduction devoted largely to a critique of the received philosophical tradition of epistemology. He there attacks the traditional philosophical approach that sought an independent criterion establishing true knowledge before proceeding to produce knowledge. Hegel rejects the empiricist tradition explicitly for its attempt to establish verification through sense perception as the truth criterion for any and all theories, any and all knowledges. He also rejects the truth criteria established by both Kantian and Cartesian epistemologies. As a recent acute observer has noted:

Hegel's objection applies quite generally to epistemology as traditionally conceived. *Any* principle which specifies some criterion of what can and what cannot count as authentic knowledge must itself appeal either to that criterion (circularity) or to some other criterion (regress).[23]

Hegel's "phenomenological" solution to the inadequacy of traditional epistemologies, which he summarized as "we shall here undertake the exposition of knowledge as a phenomenon," is not germane here because it clearly carried no weight for Marx; nor did Hegel's notions of Absolute Idea.[24] But Hegel's critique of epistemology was, we suggest, accepted by Marx, providing him with the basis for formulating an alternative theory of knowledge and truth, of the relation between thinking and being.

György Lukács explicitly recognized another insistence of Hegel's to which Marx's epistemology was seen as deeply indebted: "There is no immediate knowledge. Immediate knowledge is where we have no *consciousness* of mediation; but it is mediated for all that."[25] Marx and Engels also operate with a notion of all knowledge as mediated by concepts or what Marx usually refers to as "categories." In other words, what distinguishes knowledges from one another are the mediations, the conceptual frameworks, the logical methods informing their production. Marx and Engels follow Hegel in insisting that

not only the account of scientific method, but even the notion itself of the science as such belongs to its content, and in fact constitutes its final result. . . . It is essentially within the science that the subject matter of logic, namely, thinking or more specifically *comprehensive* thinking is considered.[26]

Marx once ridiculed an admirer who complimented his work in *Capital*, volume 1, for "moving with rare freedom" in empirical detail: "He hasn't the least idea that this 'free movement in matter' is nothing but a paraphrase for the method of dealing with matter—that is, the dialectical method." [27]

From the very few passages where Marx directly discusses his view of the production of any particular knowledge, we infer that he understands it as the deployment of concepts to select, define, and transform features of—stimuli from—the concrete environment. Each knowledge or science is thus a process in which a particular conceptual response to the environment continually extends, elaborates, and revises its conceptual apparatus according to the ever-changing determinations of its environment. This response involves the construction of new concepts, the rejection of others, and the systematic ordering of the growing body of such concepts. In both his earlier and later writings Marx gives strong indications of such a view of knowledge. In 1844 he rejects the empiricist notion that sense perceptions provide independent evaluations of the truth of alternative theories: "The *senses* have therefore become directly in their practice *theoreticians*." [28] In 1857 he argues that

> the concrete is concrete because it is the concentration of many determinations, hence unity of the divers. It appears in the process of thinking, therefore, as a process of concentration, as a result, not as a point of departure. [29]

For Marx, what is (or can be) known is conceptually produced.

At the same time Marx sought to specify that concepts and conceptual frameworks are neither innate, absolute, nor essences of "reality," but are themselves produced: "the thought process itself grows out of conditions," [30] or "the logical categories are coming damn well out of 'our intercourse.'" [31]

> It is not the consciousness of men that determines their existence, but, on the contrary, their social existence determines their consciousness. [32]

> [The concrete] is the point of departure in reality and hence also the point of departure for observation and conception. [33]

For Marx, then, theories themselves are produced by the natural/social environment which can be known only through such theories.

While Marx's writings clearly put him outside of any empiricist or rationalist epistemological standpoint, they only gesture toward his own epistemological position. This must be constructed from his suggestions as a synthesis of the two kinds of propositions cited above, as the particular "negation" of both empiricism and rationalism that also "preserves" something of what is negated.[34]

The influence of Hegel's formulations is present in Marx's notion of the process of producing knowledge or science as a particularly circular process.[35] Theory begins and ends with concretes: one concrete produces theory while the other is produced in and by theory. The point is that these concretes are different. Marx's epistemological standpoint concerns precisely the specification of these concretes, their difference, and their relation. For Marx the concrete that determines theory is conceptualized as the "concrete-real," and the concrete produced by thought is the "thought-concrete."[36] For Marx, *knowledge process, theory,* and *science* are synonyms designating the particular process connecting the concrete-real and the thought-concrete.

Marx presumes that an environment exists. Once again Marx's presumption is illuminated as a reflection upon Hegel's formulation: "That which constitutes the beginning, the beginning itself, is to be taken as something unanalyzable, taken in its simple, unfilled immediacy, and therefore *as being,* as the completely empty being."[37] Marx cannot and does not, as we read him, presume that any statement he may make about that environment could ever be other than a statement within his own particular conceptual framework. Alternative conceptual frameworks can and do make different statements. Marx, then, conceives of a natural and social totality in his particular way; he formulates his particular concept of the concrete-real. He goes further and formulates the manner in which such a concrete-real determines the different conceptual frameworks and the different thought-concretes they each produce. Marx is not naïve; he theorizes his own theory as determined in like manner. Indeed, what Marx argues is that each conceptual framework produces its own particular, different concepts of concrete-real, of thought-concrete(s), of thinking, and so on.

Marx's concrete-real is his conception of the presumed environment as an actual, material, natural, and social totality. It is the source of the divers stimuli to which thinking is one among the different responses humans make. Marx's concrete-real is the locus of the natural and social processes that combine to overdetermine every component of the thinking process, including its contradictions.[38] The products of thinking, the particular responses that differentiate each science's manner of recognizing and conceptually elaborating stimuli, are the thought-concretes. The thought-concretes of the different sciences are the "concentrations of the many determinations" they each bring to bear upon the stimuli they can recognize by means of the conceptual apparatuses they each deploy.

Knowledge, for Marx, is the process connecting the concrete-real to the thought-concretes. The knowledge process that connects both concretes connects also the ceaseless transformation of *both*. In specifying and elaborating this mutual transformation, we can show Marx's break from all previous traditional epistemology and his unique development from Hegel's work.

Engels summarized his and Marx's general approach as follows:

> [From Hegel we took] the great basic thought that the world is not to be comprehended as a complex of ready-made *things*, but as a complex of *processes*, in which the things apparently stable no less than their mind images in our heads, the concepts, go through an uninterrupted change of coming into being and passing away.[39]

The processes, then, that comprise the concrete-real are forever changing. Thinking, which is one of those processes, is forever changing, that is, producing changed thought-concretes. At the same time, any change in the thinking process, in thought-concretes, changes the concrete-real in two ways: on the one hand a change in thinking *is* a change in a component process of the social totality, and, on the other hand, any change in thinking impacts upon all the other social processes, thereby changing them. In turn, a changed social totality reacts back upon the thinking process to change it in the ceaseless dialectic of life.[40]

For Marx, then, thinking is a process of change: change in both the concrete-real and thought-concretes. Thinking cannot, therefore, be conceived as *either* the cause/essence of the concrete-real *or* as its effect. Rather, thinking is both a creative, active constitutive part of the concrete-real *and* a process overdetermined in and by that concrete-real. This was a major theme of Marx's critique of materialism.[41] The contradictions between and within each distinct science are both effects of the overdetermination of thought and causes of the ceaseless movement and change of thought-concretes and hence of the concrete-real. The same holds for the contradictions within each of the other processes comprising the social totality.

For Marx, knowledge cannot be conceived in the traditional epistemological terms of independent subjects seeking knowledge of independent objects. Knowledge is not an activity of a subject over against an object. Such subjects and their thinking are rather understood as overdetermined by objects, including those to which the thinking may be directed. The objects conceived in traditional epistemology are impossible for Marx since he conceives all objects as overdetermined by the totality of social processes, *including* the thinking process of subjects.[42] For Marx, objects *of* thought are understood at the same time as objects *for* thought, since the thought process participates in the overdetermination of such objects. Moreover, such objects include the thought process itself—the different sciences or theories as objects of analysis. The different theories conceptualize one another and themselves in different ways.

In Marx's conceptualization, thinking is a process whose overdetermined contradictions generate different sciences each with its own concepts of subject and object. Therefore, Marxian epistemology clashes with empiricism: the conception of a singular (absolute) truth of a given reality. For Marxian theory, empiricists conceive of the object of their knowledge, their concrete-real, and instantly declare it to be identically the object for—and thus the validity measure of—all other knowledges. The empiricist standpoint rejects the proposition that different theories or sciences conceptualize their respective concrete-reals differently. Theorists embracing an empiricist epistemological standpoint will judge alternative theories as "greater" or "lesser" in truth, understood absolutely as approximation to the one concrete-real permitted by that standpoint. Their critical activity is focused on ranking theories according to degrees of approximation to the truth. It is at best a very secondary matter to investigate the social causes and consequences of the suspect persistence of the false or less true alternative (as in the academic specialty of sociology of knowledge). Empiricists see theory, differences among theory, and theoretical criticism in a manner sharply different from what we read as Marx's view.

Where empiricists accord a privileged place to their concepts of the concrete-real, rationalists accord privilege to their concepts of the governing cause, logic, or origin of their concrete-real. Like their empiricist twins, the rationalists also seek an absolute truth. For Marxian theory, rationalists conceive of a concrete-real that has a unique truth—understood as cause, logic, origin, or telos—that can be captured or expressed in a thought-concrete, that is, rationally. All thinking is presumed to aspire to express such a truth; alternative thought-concretes are critically ranked according to their approximation to such a truth. Rationalists see theory, differences among theory, and theoretical criticism in a manner sharply different from Marx's view.

Marxian theory's epistemological standpoint (dialectical materialism or the specification of the relationship between concrete-real and thought-concrete) is radically different from traditional epistemology. Moreover, Marxian theory makes this difference an important part of its argument against those sciences that include traditional empiricist or rationalist standpoints. Refusing to erect an "independent" criterion of "truth" across the different sciences, Marxian theory seeks rather to specify carefully its concepts of the changing differences among sciences and of the social causes and consequences of those differences. Such specification is what Marx means by criticism. Criticism delineates the different ways in which different sciences conceive of their objects, their subjects, and of the knowledge process. Such criticism, in Marxian theory, seeks to pinpoint the differences between Marxian and non-Marxian theories and to determine their different social consequences. The point is to show the relationship between theoretical differences and the social changes sought by Marxists.

Difference is the key element of Marx's notion of criticism. Marxian theory refuses to accept the claim of any particular conceptualization of the concrete-real—that is, of any particular thought-concrete—that it is identical to the world itself, to "ultimate reality." This is the sense of Engels's formulation:

> The two of them, the concept of a thing and its reality, run side by side like two asymptotes, always approaching each other yet never meeting. This difference between the two is the very difference which prevents the concept from being directly and immediately reality and reality from being immediately its own concept. Because a concept has the essential nature of that concept and cannot therefore prima facie directly coincide with reality, from which it must first be abstracted, it is something more than a fiction, unless you are going to declare all the result of thought fictions.[43]

Marx is more blunt in dismissing any epistemological perspective that claims its concepts, its theoretical truths, can ever be other than particular thought-concretes different from being per se (or "reality"):

> The vulgar mob has therefore concluded that theoretical truths are abstractions which are at variance from reality, instead of seeing, on the contrary, that Ricardo does not carry true abstract thinking far enough and is therefore driven into false abstraction.[44]

Notice here that Marx is not criticizing Ricardo on the—for Marx—unacceptable grounds of some discrepancy between Ricardo's concepts and "reality." Rather, Marx's criticism proceeds on the very different grounds that Ricardo's abstractions, his particular concepts, and also his particular mode of conceptualizing are different from Marx's and in that precise sense "false."[45] Ricardo's notions of value, price, capital accumulation, profits, and so forth are different from Marx's; that is their "falseness" for Marx. Marx's specific definition and mode of criticism are implied by his epistemological position.[46] Falseness is not a matter of their relation to some "concrete reality," which, as we have seen, Ricardo and Marx conceptualize differently as well. Marxian criticism seeks to establish how, why, and with what consequences Ricardian and Marxian sciences *differently* produce their *different* thought-concretes.[47]

Marxian theory refuses to entertain the illusion that the "realism" of one or another theory, its "proofs" for its supposed "correspondence" to the "real," determine its truth also for other theories—in that sense its absolute truth. Marx was contemptuous of such illusions: "All that palaver about the necessity of proving the concept of value comes from complete ignorance both of the subject dealt with and of scientific method." [48] Wittgenstein came later to hold similar contempt for such illusions. [49]

Marxian theory's affirmation of the internality and relativity of each conceptual framework's claims to truth implies that the survival of any particular framework can hardly be explained in terms of a correspondence to "the real." The rise and fall of particular theories cannot be reduced to functions of "the truth" or even of "their truths." For example, Ricardians still work theoretically within and upon the conceptual framework of Ricardian (or "neo-Ricardian") economics; the neoclassical and Austrian school economists work within theirs. And Marxists must still criticize these theories without spurious references to their respective "inadequacies," to what they all see differently as "the real." As Marx put it in the second of his *Theses on Feuerbach:* "The dispute over the reality or nonreality of thinking which is isolated from practice is a purely *scholastic* question." The "practice" referred to by Marx and Engels is their concept of the different interaction between each theory and the concrete-real of which it is an overdetermined constituent. In our reading, the Marxian conception holds that the social formation, its concrete-real, will overdetermine the birth, development, and death of each theory, its evaluations of its truths, and its social consequences. To play on a related remark of Marx's, we might say that a theory ends only when all the conditions— economic, political, and cultural—of its existence end. [50] The social conditions for the existence of Ricardian, neoclassical, Austrian, and Marxian economic theories—although changed over the last one hundred years— are in place. Thus, Marxists today continue to face conditions requiring criticism of alternative theories, a criticism informed by the specific epistemological standpoint of Marxian theory.

The Marxian epistemological standpoint received a particular elaboration by Engels. While his elaboration served to clarify further the specifics of that standpoint, it has also served to trouble and provoke later Marxists. For both reasons it deserves attention. Gratefully citing Hegel, Engels argues for the position that "one leaves alone 'absolute truth,' which is unattainable . . . instead, one pursues attainable relative truths along the paths of the positive sciences." [51] The key word here is "relative." Engels explicitly recognizes the relativity of the truths established by the different sciences.

Engels's recognition is most emphatically not equivalent to an indifference to these different truths and the sciences that constitute them. The passionate commitment of Marx and Engels to their science and its truths, their linkage of their science to a class revolutionary project, the thoroughness and intensity of their criticism of alternative sciences—all attest to their active discrimination among relative truths. It simply never occurred to them, apparently, that partisanship in theory, in what they call the class struggle in theory, requires any denial of the scientificity of the theories of some of their opponents (the nonvulgar ones). It did not occur to them, we suggest, largely because their epistemological position would not permit any such formulation. As we argued earlier, Marxian theory does not permit such formulations today: to hold that there are some "absolute" as against "relative" truths in the terms previously specified strikes us as a position that does not belong within the Marxian theoretical tradition.

Engels's argument about the relativity of truths was not a move toward any notion that the "best theoretical posture" lies in a judicious or "best" selection and collection of insights from the relative truths. Marx made this point sharply and unmistakably:

> The *academic form,* which proceeds "historically" and, with wise moderation, collects the "best" from all sources, and in doing this contradictions do not matter; on the contrary, what matters is comprehensiveness. All systems are thus made insipid, their edge is taken off and they are peacefully gathered together in a miscellany. The heat of apologetics is moderated here by erudition, which looks down benignly on the exaggerations of economic thinkers, and merely allows them to float as oddities in its mediocre pap.[52]

Marx here aptly dissects what remains academic high fashion today: formulations that flatter their own eclectic mingling of fragments from Marxian and other scientific systems as "correcting," "improving," or "going beyond" Marxian theory.

Marx and Engels's notion of the relativity of truths thus differs from the modern positivist notion of relativity as the greater or lesser approximation of theories to the "absolute truth" or "reality" as they usually term it. For Marx and Engels, unlike the positivist tradition, "trial and error" refer to each theory's internal process of problem posing and problem solving. Each science has its distinct ways of conceiving the trials it undergoes, of perceiving and interpreting its errors, and of drawing its particular conclusions therefrom. The relativity of truths refers to the distinctively different ways in which each science defines, deploys, increasingly determines, and changes its conceptual components.

To conclude this brief investigation of Marx and Engels on epistemology—and to underscore its importance for resolving the Marxian debate over economic determinism—we may reconsider some famous quotations often cited to illustrate their basic approach to social analysis.

According to the materialist conception of history the ultimately determining element in history is the production and reproduction of real life.[53]

Economic relations, however much they may be influenced by the other—the political and ideological relations, are still ultimately the decisive ones, forming the keynote which runs through them and alone leads to understanding.[54]

In the first quotation the important words are those that open the sentence; in the second, the important words close the sentence. Given the epistemological position we read in Marx and Engels, these quotations define precisely how the particular science of Marx and Engels constructs its particular knowledge of its object, social history. "Real" or "material" life is a summary term to designate their particular conception of the concrete-real. "Economic relations" is a summary term to designate the distinguishing emphasis, the "keynote," within their particular thought-concrete, their "understanding" as against that of other thought-concretes. "Economic relations" define what we have called "the entry point" of Marxian theory.

Consider Marx's famous summary statement:

The conclusion we reach is not that production, distribution, exchange and consumption are identical, but that they all form members of a totality, distinctions within a unity. Production predominates not only over itself, in the antithetical definition of production, but over the other moments as well.[55]

His point was to specify what distinguished his science from others. Again, the first sentence indicates Marx's concept of the concrete-real as a totality of mutually overdetermining and overdetermined "members" or "distinctions" or sites. The second sentence indicates which concepts Marx defines and deploys distinctively within his science—which concepts "predominate" in the specific sense of serving as the beginning and the end, the entry point and the goal point of his strictly nonessentialist theoretical process.

We may now offer an initial summary of our reading of the epistemological standpoint in Marx's and Engels's writings. They conceive of a natural/social totality, their concrete-real, which has overdetermined a particular set of theories or sciences over the last 150 years. One of these, Marxian theory, defines a particular concept of class which operates as its entry point into social analysis. Marxian theory's positive goal is to elaborate its thought-concrete as a social totality of mutually overdetermined, contradictory class and nonclass processes. Marxian theory's critical goal is to specify the nature and social position of theories different from itself.

Marxian theory understands itself (and, for that matter, any other theory) to be both cause and effect of the concrete-real, an overdetermined and also constituent process within the social totality.

Insofar as our representation of Marx and Engels's epistemological standpoint is accepted, it follows that the debates over economic determination as the essence of social reality are not germane to Marxian theory. As we have presented matters, Marxian theory cannot and need not offer any assertions about the ultimate nature of social being. Economics is determinant in the last instance only in the very restricted sense that an economic concept, class, is the entry point into the scientific workings of Marxian social theory. That theory neither looks for nor finds any one process or aspect of the social totality exercising any "more" determinant influence on the others than any of those others do on it. The very pertinence of the terms of the debate have been displaced on the grounds of their incompatibility with the epistemological position of Marx and Engels as here presented.

Of course we recognize that readings of the texts of Marx and Engels other than ours are possible and connected to other knowledges of their epistemological standpoint. Here we ask only that the reader consider the plausibility of our reading and reflect with us upon its implications in permitting an original resolution to the economic determinism debate within the Marxian theoretical tradition.

In the next sections we consider some of the greatest Marxian theoreticians who were prompted by various urgent practical and theoretical tasks, including those directly linked to the economic determinism debate, to try to specify the particular epistemological standpoint of Marxian theory. The importance and, indeed, centrality they assigned to such a specification in their work will be apparent. While we do not think they succeeded, we share their basic concern with epistemology. Moreover, they provided certain concepts and suggestions we found indispensable in constructing our specification of Marxian theory's epistemological standpoint and applying it to the economic determinism debates.

Lenin on Epistemology

Repeatedly disturbed by certain readings of Marx and Engels that were widespread among those considering themselves Marxists in Russia, Lenin came eventually to locate one chief support for such readings in their epistemological standpoints.[56] So important did he deem the political implications of such readings that in 1907–8 he devoted enormous time and energy to publishing his criticism of these standpoints. His critique consisted of differentiating them from his own reading of Marx and Engels's epistemological position. Again, a few years later, during World War I, Lenin returned to the task of thinking through the specificity of a Marxian epistemology, of making explicit what Marx had left largely implicit. Despite urgent political preoccupations and a remarkable output of other writings in 1914–16, he filled notebooks with detailed paragraph-by-paragraph commentaries on Hegel's *Logic* and other writings.[57] Although not well known, Lenin's work, we believe, provides indispensable materials for a specification of the distinctively Marxian epistemological position and of its important connections to Hegel's work.

Following Lenin's own emphases, we focus on two basic questions for which Lenin offered answers: What is the relation between thinking and being for Marxian theory? And what is the particular Marxian definition of the relativity of all sciences and their truths? The answers as well as the questions are interdependent.

> Aphorism: It is impossible completely to understand Marx's *Capital,* and especially its first chapter, without having thoroughly studied and understood the *whole* of Hegel's *Logic.* Consequently, half a century later none of the Marxists understood Marx!![58]

This remark summarizes Lenin's many notebook entries recognizing Hegel's crucial contributions to Marxian theory. In Lenin's view the epistemological position of Marx, Engels, and Marxian theory depends upon and incorporates a great deal of Hegel's work. Lenin's appreciative return to Hegel constitutes no disagreement with Marx and Engels, although they left no documents comparable to Lenin's notebooks. It reflects rather the different social conditions within which they theorized and publicized. Marx and Engels initially presumed Hegel's wide influence, the widespread acceptance of his philosophic achievements. They sought to distance themselves critically, to build upon, but also—and more emphatically—to build away from what Marx termed "that mighty thinker." Moreover, as Hegel's influence rapidly withered across the middle of the nineteenth century, Marx and Engels noted the process with great regret lest their criticisms contribute in any way to the spreading disregard for Hegel.[59] By Lenin's time, in his view, neglect of Hegel's accomplishments had become a contributing factor to the return of Marxists to pre-Hegelian epistemological positions embodying empiricism, rationalism, and the essentialism typically associated with them.[60] For Lenin, the theoretical return to Hegel and to his critiques of Hume and Kant was a matter of immediate political importance, of specifying and strengthening Marxism in Russia. He sought to reawaken Russian Marxists to Marx's closeness to Hegel: "Dialectics is the theory of knowledge of [Hegel and] Marxism. This is the "aspect" of the matter [it is not an "aspect" but the essence of the matter] to which Plekhanov, not to speak of other Marxists, paid no attention."[61]

Lenin is especially impressed with one particular short section of Hegel's *Logic* entitled "The Idea." [62] Not only does Lenin value the critiques of Kant formulated there; he also reads in those pages "*perhaps the best exposition of dialectics.* Here, too, the coincidence, so to speak, of logic and epistemology is shown in a remarkably brilliant way." [63] In this section and the passages immediately following, Lenin formulates his concept of the distinctively Marxian epistemological standpoint.

Lenin declares his full agreement with Hegel, that the relation between thinking and being can be neither of the following two traditional epistemological alternatives: the object of thinking is what it is by virtue of what thinking puts into it, or thinking is what it is by virtue of what its objects give to it. Either alternative is rejected for its one-sidedness. Instead, the relation between thinking and being must be understood as the unity of these one-sided alternatives. Lenin specifically argues that concepts are "subjective" and "abstract," but "at the same time they express also the Things-in-themselves"; he insists that "nature is *both* concrete and abstract." [64]

Lenin here refuses to ascribe to any knowledge either the label "subjective" or "objective." Each conceptual framework or theory is subjective—held and developed by persons—as well as objective, a process within and constituent of the objective natural/social totality. By its partiality, that is, by the particular conceptual framework it deploys to build up its particular knowledge, each theory participates in shaping, in determining that totality. In Lenin's usage of terms drawn from Hegelian and pre-Hegelian philosophy, each theory is shaped by the "things-in-themselves," while the theory simultaneously participates in shaping the "things-in-themselves"; it makes them "things-for-us," objects of this theory's knowledge. [65] Each theory is thus objective—it reflects "things-in-themselves"—and also subjective: it helps shape these things in its particular way.

Thus, Lenin shares with Hegel the view that the natural/social reality about which humans theorize is a unity in the following sense:

> What exists in *reality* as soon as there is a *Reality of which one speaks*—and since we in fact speak of reality, there can be for us only Reality of which one speaks—what exists in reality, I say, is the Subject that knows the Object, or, what is the same thing, the Object known by the Subject. This double Reality which is nonetheless one because it is equally real in each aspect, taken in its whole or as Totality is called in Hegel "Spirit" (*Geist*) or (in the *Logik*) "absolute Idea." [66]

> To the extent that the scientist thinks or knows his object, what really and concretely exists is the *entirety* of the Object known by the Subject or of the Subject knowing the Object. [67]

Lenin, like Hegel, distinguishes himself from epistemological standpoints that conceive of subjects and objects isolated from one another and do not proceed from their indissoluble unity as constituent aspects of one another.

For Lenin as for Hegel, the truth is the whole, the totality. It is the entirety of all the objects known in and to the different sciences; it is the entirety of the processes—knowledges—that encompass the knowers and the known.[68] For Lenin and for Hegel this true totality encompasses all the processes of nature and society, including thought. More precisely, this true totality encompasses a mutual interconnection of each process with all the others. Thus, in some basic ways Lenin and Hegel hold similar conceptions of what we have termed the concrete-real. Lenin summarizes the similarity of conception as follows:

> Every notion occurs in a certain *relation,* in a certain connection with all the others. In the alternation, reciprocal dependence of *all* notions, in the *identity of their opposites,* in the *transitions* of one notion into another, in the eternal change, movement of notions, Hegel brilliantly *divined precisely this relation of things, of nature.*[69]

Lenin reads Hegel to the effect that insofar as the process of thinking both "reflects and creates" the concrete-real, it is exactly like all the other processes that comprise the concrete-real.[70] In effect, Lenin holds a concept of the concrete-real in which it shapes each different process of nature and society even while it is shaped by them; it is the totality of such processes. Moreover, Lenin locates contradictions in each such process and hence in the human beings defined in and by those processes. These contradictions generate the movement, that is, the change in people, which is at the same time their changing of the concrete-real. Thinking is, for Lenin, "in the eternal process of movement, the arising of contradictions and their solutions." The concrete-real changes by and through its contradictions among which "the strongest contradiction [is] between thought and object which man eternally creates and eternally overcomes."[71]

In his studies of Hegel, Lenin finds formulations of totality and contradiction of thinking and being, which he shares and which he finds implicit in Marx and Engels. Hegel's explicit formulations assist Lenin's approach to a conceptualization of the concrete-real and of causality very much like the notion of an overdetermined, contradictory concrete-real discussed above.[72]

> Cause and effect, ergo, are merely moments of universal reciprocal dependence, of (universal) connection, of the reciprocal concatenation of events. The all-sidedness of the world, which is only one-sidedly, fragmentarily and incompletely expressed by causality.[73]

At the same time, Lenin follows Marx in rejecting Hegel's arguments that his formulations are some absolute truths above and beyond alternative formulations (Marx termed these arguments Hegel's "mystifying side"); Lenin's rejection concerns his notion of "relative truths."

Lenin understood each scientific process, each particular theory, to contain a "relative truth." This he distinguished, although in an unfinished argument, from "absolute truth." The latter "is composed of the sum-total of relative truths":

> For Bogdanov (as for all the Machians) the recognition of the relativity of our knowledge excludes the least admission of absolute truth. For Engels absolute truth is made up of relative truths. Bogdanov is a relativist; Engels is a dialectician.[74]

> The distinction between subjectivism (skepticism, sophistry, etc.) and dialectics, incidentally, is that in (objective) dialectics the difference between the relative and the absolute is itself relative. For objective dialectics there *is* an absolute *within* the relative. For subjectivism and sophistry, the relative is only relative and excludes the absolute.[75]

Lenin's vigorous assertions about the relativity of truths certainly did not dilute his passionate defense of and contributions to one science, Marxism, against others. The socialist transformation of society had a particular theory as one of its constituent elements: for Lenin that was Marxism. He argued that the status quo too had its constituent theories, including theoretical eclecticism.[76] Lenin's writings sought continually to sharpen Marxists' understanding of Marxian theory's specific difference, including its epistemological standpoint, and to win adherence thereto.[77] The "struggle" for the predominance of a particular theory had to be waged by this author of the aphorism: "There can be no revolution without a revolutionary theory."

Lenin's formulations throughout his many writings are neither consistent nor always precise in terms of their specific epistemological implications. He defends some arguments by reference to the "facts" in a manner warranting the label *empiricist*.[78] He writes occasionally as though he believes that the different relative truths comprise some sort of progression toward higher truths, with Marxism the highest to date (echoing certain similar formulations by Engels).[79] His specifications of his epistemological position are at times inconsistent, incomplete, and uneven.

Nonetheless, his position demonstrates how intensely he wrestled with the specification of a Marxian epistemology, how important a task he took it to be. Moreover, his position is clear on certain points at stake in this book. Marxian theory is one among others; it produces a knowledge containing a relative truth different from the other relative truths of different theories or sciences. The epistemological foundation of Marxian science, dialectical materialism, is different from the traditional epistemologies of the other sciences it contends with. This difference involves an explicit rejection of both sides of the traditional philosophic debate between empiricist and rationalist epistemologies.

Lenin did not, of course, restrict his specification of the difference between Marxian and non-Marxian theories to matters of epistemology and the methodological implications of Marxian epistemology. He went on to focus upon Marxian theory's concern with the whole social "complex of opposing tendencies, by reducing them to precisely definable conditions of life and production of the various *classes* of society." [80] For Lenin, Marxian science offered its particular truth against the alternatives, building this truth around its set of most basic concepts. This set included a particular concept of knowledge, a particular concept of classes, and a particular concept of the social totality.

Our reading of Lenin, then, places his propositions concerning history and knowledge squarely within the context of the elaboration of and ceaseless change in the Marxian theoretical tradition and the truths emerging therefrom. Our reading, encouraged directly by epistemological statements offered by Lenin himself, does not understand the broad sweep of his propositions about the social totality as reductionist assertions about some last-instance determinant essence. Far from endorsing an economic determinist tendency within the traditional Marxian debate, Lenin seems to us to warrant a rejection of the epistemological terms of that debate and its participants on all sides.

Lukács on Epistemology

György Lukács was a close student of Lenin's writings, including those formulating a distinctive position on epistemology. Lukács's emphasis on the importance of Hegel for understanding Marx contributed to epistemological statements, similar to Lenin's, both in Lukács's studies on dialectics and in his aesthetic writings. [81] He shared Lenin's concern that the neglect of the specifically Marxian epistemological standpoint often combined with the influence of "contemporary bourgeois concepts . . . [to] introduce confusion" within the Marxian tradition generally. [82] Lukács also made key contributions of his own.

The history of Lukács's political positions as well as his voluminous writings is a particularly complex story of shifts as well as developments of his standpoint. Current notions of his work and its significance vary even more than he did. To avoid misunderstanding and to clarify the particular and limited purposes of our concern with Lukács, we sketch very briefly two current types of attitudes toward Lukács. One attitude views him as a "Marxist revisionist" possessing "affinities with early Marx" and sharply opposed to the economic determinism of "orthodox Marxism." [83] Those with this attitude typically welcome Lukács's concerns with the subjective side of social revolution, while being deeply distressed by Lukács's suggestion that the proletariat or, worse still, the Communist party may be understood as the revolutionary subject.[84] A second attitude, more directly concerned with epistemological matters than the first, criticizes Lukács for his "realism" which it understands as his theoretical commitment to the idea that one theory is more correct, more truly reflective of "reality," than alternatives: the target here is Lukács's "rationalism."[85]

These and other general attitudes toward Lukács's work typically focus on those formulations in his work that in fact offer considerable basis for their judgments, both hostile and approving. However, a type of approach taken recently by two students of Lukács's work strikes us as more fruitful generally and particularly in terms of Lukács's contributions to the specification of Marxian epistemology. This type of approach focuses on what it finds as basic tensions or contradictions in Lukács's work: it is interested in the particular way Lukács posed and struggled with these contradictions, rather than particular and occasionally one-sided expressions of one or another aspect of such contradictions. Istvan Meszaros understands Lukács as struggling in new and important ways to theorize the relation of subjectivity and objectivity in social history.[86] Fredric Jameson focuses upon Lukács's struggle to make the Marxian notion of reflection something much more and much richer than the passive, simply determinist notion of images (thoughts) imprinted on the mind by "reality."[87]

Like Meszaros and Jameson, we are interested in the particular way Lukács posed a basic question: in our case, the relation of thinking and being. Similarly, we are interested in how Lukács posed and struggled with the closely connected question of the relation between the social totality and any of its constituent parts. It is, in our view, Lukács's ultimately unsuccessful struggle to think these relationships through to some satisfactory resolution that produced, along the way, important contributions toward our particular notion of Marxian epistemology. In discussing Lukács briefly, our very limited goal is to suggest what these contributions are.

Hegel's importance for an understanding of Marx was summarized by Lukács as follows:

> Hegel's tremendous intellectual contribution consisted in the fact that he made theory and history dialectically *relative* to one another, grasped them in a dialectical reciprocal penetration. Ultimately, however, his attempt was a failure. He could never get as far as the genuine unity of theory and practice.[88]

Theory and historical reality, to use Lukács's terminology, are aspects of a "complex of processes." Between them there lies "the unbridgeable abyss between concept and reality," that is, neither aspect may be collapsed into or reduced to the expression or effect of the other:

> For the reflection theory this means that thought and unconsciousness are orientated towards reality but, at the same time, the criterion of truth is provided by relevance to reality. This reality is by no means identical with empirical existence. This reality is not, it becomes . . . and to become the participation of thought is needed.[89]

For Lukács, reality shapes thinking while it is also shaped by thinking. Lukács breaks from traditional epistemology, from the empiricists' and rationalists' strivings to make their thoughts adequate to some essence of a separate, independent reality. Lukács breaks from the post-Hegelian return to variants of traditional epistemology in Europe; he returns to the dialectical positions of Hegel and Marx in order to build from them. Thus Lukács recommences, within Marxism, the development of a distinct epistemological standpoint

> which had been ignored by university philosophy during the entire second half of the nineteenth century. . . . Man is not *opposite* the world which he tries to understand and upon which he acts, but within this world which he is a part of, and there is no radical break between the meaning he is trying to find or introduce into the universe and that which he is trying to find or introduce into his own existence.[90]

In his own brusque summation, Lukács endorses Lenin's view that dialectics is an epistemological standpoint: "*the act of consciousness overthrows the objective form of its object.*"[91]

Lukács often expresses himself in formulations emphasizing how subjectivity, especially the self-conscious subjectivity of a revolutionary proletariat, could and would transform objectivity. He understands his own attack on "immediacy"—the effort of bourgeois theory to equate itself with some "given" reality—as a contribution to the overthrow of bourgeois society. Lukács also often writes about all thought as shaped and limited by its particular social environment.[92] Lukács both champions subjectivity smashing reification and affirms that thinking reflects objectivity. Depending on which expressions touch a reader's concerns, Lukács might appear as some sort of humanist or "revisionist" Marxist, or, alternatively, as a sophisticated version of rather vulgar reflection theory. What matters to us are his efforts to specify a dialectic— a particular Marxian epistemological standpoint that combines or unifies (and thereby changes) both these one-sided alternatives.

Hegel's affirmation that "the truth is the whole" is likewise fundamental for Lukács: "Marx's dictum: 'the relations of production of every society form a whole' is the methodological point of departure and the key to the *historical* understanding of social relations."[93] The social whole comprises, for Lukács, not things but continually changing "*aspects of processes.*"[94] Thoughts are such aspects of the process of history: they are both shaped by and participate in shaping that process. Lukács's concept of the social whole serves him to unify the one-sided standpoints of traditional epistemology, whether empiricist or rationalist, idealist or materialist.

Lukács's concept of the social whole serves also as the touchstone of his struggle to unify the subjectivity and objectivity of the human being in history. Lukács expresses this unity as an imperative directed to the proletariat: "Man must become conscious of himself as a social being, as simultaneously the subject and object of the socio-historical process."[95]

Lukács's concept of the social totality specifies that all its processes are in an uninterrupted flow of mutual interaction. Moreover, Lukács is at pains to carry this specification in a particular direction. He is concerned to argue that the mutual interaction is also mutual constitution: each aspect of the social whole does not exist other than in and by these interactions. Thinking exists as a social process by virtue of its determination by the social whole, that is, all the other nonthinking processes. The thinking process, in turn, participates in the determination of every aspect of the social whole. Perhaps Lukács's clearest formulation of what we would call an "overdeterminist" conceptualization of the social whole is the following:

> But even the category of interaction requires inspection. If by interaction we mean just the reciprocal causal impact of two otherwise unchangeable objects on each other, we shall not have come an inch nearer to an understanding of society. This is the case with the vulgar materialists with their one-way causal sequences (or the Machists with their functional relations). . . .
>
> The interaction we have in mind must be more than the interaction of *otherwise unchanging objects.* . . . Every substantial change that is of concern to knowledge manifests itself as a change in relation to the whole and through this as a change in the form of objectivity itself.[96]

Lukács carries further the return to Hegel undertaken in Lenin's notebooks and criticisms of nondialectical theory. Lukács builds upon Lenin's reaffirmation of society as an "ensemble of relations," as a universe of reciprocity among all its elements, to produce a notion of the social whole as a moving process of mutually constitutive aspects. Like Lenin and, indeed, like Marx, Lukács strives to produce a materialist, historical reading of Hegel's dialectics. Lukács's achievement is to go somewhat further than they did and, above all, to make remarkably explicit a detailed statement of the particularly Marxian notion of dialectics, that is, the particularly Marxian epistemological standpoint and Marxian conception of the social whole.

Lukács's advance is indispensable for subsequent elaboration and development of Marxian dialectics, of a Marxian epistemological standpoint. Certainly our formulations built around our notion of overdetermination, as well as Althusser's arguments, depend upon as well as differ from Lukács's work in many and complex ways. We illustrate this point in pondering the significance of Lukács's choice of terms in a speech to an international congress of Marxian philosophers in 1947:

> The materialist-dialectical conception of totality means *first* of all the concrete unity of interacting contradictions . . . *secondly, the systematic relativity* of all totality both *upwards* and *downwards* (which means that all totality is made of totalities *subordinated* to it, and also that the totality in question is, at the same time, *overdetermined* by totalities of a higher complexity . . .) and *thirdly, the historical relativity* of all totality is changing, disintegrating, confined to a determinate, concrete historical period.[97]

This particular quotation of Lukács's suggests that he, rather than Althusser, was the first to appropriate (and thereby modify) Freud's notion of overdetermination, for the purpose of developing the specification of Marxian theory.

Lukács's concepts of the dialectical interaction of thinking and the social totality lead him to echo Lenin's attitude toward the relativity of "truths." Lukács's notion of the "falseness" of theories or "ideologies" other than his version of Marxian theory should not, we believe, be assimilated to an empiricist or rationalist framework, since Lukács rejected them. In other words, Lukács's notion of "false" theory is not a notion of such a theory's inadequacy to some separate "reality": rather, theories and their truths are limited, relative, and conditioned by their respective "concrete, historical function and meaning . . . within a unique, concretized historical process."[98]

> For if concepts are only the intellectual forms of historical realities then these forms, one-sided, abstract and false as they are, belong to the true unity as genuine aspects of it.
> In so far as the "false" is an aspect of the "true" it is both "false" and "non-false."[99]

In our language, Lukács's formulations were moving toward a concept of the concrete-real as constituted in part by the different thought-concretes whose existences were overdetermined within and by that concrete-real. In the language of one of Lukács's most careful and perceptive interpreters,

> The relation between the world, the significant universe in which men live, and the men who create it is inseparable, a relation in a double sense: the subject is part of the world and in fact introduces meaning there practically, but this world is part of the subject and

constitutes it. This circle, a vicious circle for a static philosophy, is no problem for a dialectical study of history.[100]

For Lukács the Marxian positions on the dialectical interaction of being and thought and on the relation of economic to noneconomic aspects of the social totality (his "social being") are very closely interwoven and interdependent. For Lukács the basic Marxian conception of social being affirms it as a complexly overdetermined totality in which economic aspects are not "more" important than noneconomic aspects.

> This specific, seldom understood and paradoxically dialectical method is related to the already mentioned insight of Marx's to the effect that economic and extra-economic phenomena in social life continuously transform themselves into one another, and stand in an insuperable relationship of interaction; . . . This reciprocal mutual penetration of the economic and non-economic in social existence reaches deep into the doctrine of categories itself.[101]

Yet Lukács also refers to what he terms the "ontological priority" accorded within Marxian theory to economic concepts of production relations.[102] We read this notion of priority as signifying that these concepts are selected, in Marxian theory, as entry points for the discursive construction of social being. Lukács's comments on the practice of an artist may serve to clarify what we think he means by "ontological priority":

> The intention of a work of art, an artist or a type of art cannot be oriented to the extensive totality of all social relations, but that a choice has had to be made, from objective necessity, in so far as specific moments of the totality are of predominant importance for a specific artistic project.[103]

For Lukács, Marxian theory has as its defining intention or project an analysis of overdetermined social being in which economic aspects are of "predominant importance." Such predominant importance is not understood as an inherent quality of the economic aspects of social being (such an approach leads to "a one-sided and hence mechanical causal sequence which falsifies and simplifies the phenomena").[104] It is rather a matter of which of the mutually overdetermined and overdetermining social aspects are selected as predominantly important *for* the particular project of Marxian theory.

Lukács draws heavily on *Capital* to illustrate Marx's dialectical method in constructing social being from the standpoint of economic concepts as entry points.

> The very construction of *Capital* shows that Marx is dealing with an abstraction, for all the evidence adduced from the real world. The

composition of *Capital* proceeds by way of successive integration of new ontological elements and tendencies into the world originally depicted on the basis of this abstraction.[105]

Lukács examines in detail the theoretical process involving this "abstraction," that is, the dialectical process of progressively transforming abstract concepts into ever new thought-concretes. However, Lukács also returns repeatedly to the key theoretical place of production relations within this developing, changing, discourse:

> The transformation of surplus-value into profit, and of the rate of surplus-value into the profit rate, is of course a methodological consequence of the cancellation in the third volume, of the abstractions of the first. Even here, as we have seen in the case of all these abstractions of Marx and the concretizations that supersede them, surplus-value remains the foundation; it simply leads to a further relationship that is equally real, and remains dependent on the original one.[106]

Lukács is here seeking to articulate how Marxian entry-point concepts become both raw materials and means of production for the production of new concepts. Such new concepts, being worked-up transformations of the initial abstract concepts, retain a link, a dependence, upon them; this is what confers upon the latter the designation of "ontological priority."

Our reading of Lukács, like our understanding of Marxian theory, is different from alternative readings and theories within (and without) the Marxian tradition. We find in Lukács's concepts of social totality, of the dialectic between thought and social being, and of the "ontological priority" characteristic of Marxian theory some of his most important contributions to Marxism generally and to the explicit formulation of a Marxian epistemological standpoint in particular. We find these contributions notwithstanding his frequent formulations that conflict with or flatly contradict them, because we understand such formulations as extremities within his oscillating struggles to work through the concepts most basic to his theoretical and political labors.[107] Despite his occasional remarks supporting economic determinist positions within the traditional Marxian debate over economic determinism, and despite the widespread reading of Lukács that renders him a theoretical humanist (man is the essential determinant of social life), in our view his basic formulations of dialectics and of a Marxian notion of the overdetermined social totality take him outside that debate. Those formulations rejected de facto the terms of that debate, rejecting its appropriateness given his reading of the foundations of Marxian theory.

It is no disrespect for Lukács's contributions to Marxian theory to insist that they raised as many problems as they resolved. His key concepts of totality, mutual interaction of aspects, unity of subject and object in the process of knowing (thinking), and unity of history generally are begging for elaboration and specification. Moreover, they provoke basic questions for which Lukács provides little in the way of answers. Is there some particular way that Marxian theory approaches totality differently from other theories that recognize the centrality of such a concept? How is social change exactly specified within a totality from a Marxian standpoint (a question all the more important in view of what functionalisms and structuralisms have done in this area)? What exactly is class as a concept within the social totality (given Lukács's heavy usage of the concept, the near absence of definition is troublesome indeed)? What exactly is the relationship in Lukács's thinking between his concepts of totality and overdetermination?

The centrality of such questions for Marxian theoreticians was underscored by the particular and often original way Lukács struggled with the task of specifying the relationship among Marxian theory, the Marxian epistemological standpoint, and Marxian revolutionary objectives. That underscoring is Lukács's achievement and contribution. He simultaneously builds upon the Hegel-Marx-Lenin connection he recognizes and opposes the theories within Marxism that conflict with that connection. Gramsci, as we shall show, enriched and expanded on Lukács's questions in ways that set the stage for and indeed began constructing answers to them.

Gramsci and Mao on Epistemology

Our attention to Antonio Gramsci and Mao Tse-tung will be more condensed than our discussions of Lenin and Lukács. No ranking of their different merits and importance should be inferred from this treatment. Rather, it is their different standpoints within the broadly defined Marxian theoretical tradition, combined with certain similar comments on epistemology and economic determinism among them, that invite this limited attention.

The section titled "The Philosophy of Praxis" in Gramsci's *Prison Notebooks* contains several key passages seeking to specify how Marxian theory differs from bourgeois theory and how Gramsci's reading of Marxian theory distances him from other Marxian tendencies.[108] Gramsci grapples directly with the concerns motivating this book when he speculates about the reasons for traditional Marxism's disregard for the specificity of the Marxian theory of knowledge, that is, its distinctive epistemological position as Gramsci understands it:

> If the philosophy of praxis affirms theoretically that every "truth"
> believed to be eternal and absolute has had practical origins and has
> represented a "provisional" value (historicity of every conception of

the world and of life), it is still very difficult to make people grasp "practically" that such an interpretation is valid also for the philosophy of praxis, *without in so doing shaking the convictions that are necessary for action.*[109]

Later in the same passage Gramsci attacks what he evidently takes to be one major factor causing traditional Marxism "to become an ideology in the worst sense of the word, that is to say a dogmatic system of eternal and absolute truths." The point raised here by Gramsci is hardly a minor one; Marxism's epistemological standpoint is unique, difficult to grasp, and yet indispensable if Marxism is not to become dogmatic. For Gramsci, Marxism's rejection of absolute truth is not equivalent to its acceptance of any form of indifference toward the different truths specified in different conceptions of social life. Marxism's rejection of notions such as Absolute Truth, Science, Scientific Method, and History, as well as the non-Marxian epistemologies within which they are theoretically located, is itself a key ingredient of its struggles against alternative theories.

Gramsci is no doubt right that stressing Marxism's *relative* truths will challenge widely and deeply held beliefs in various sorts of absolute truths among Marxists as well as others. Yet Gramsci insists upon such a challenge as part of the class struggle in theory for the hegemony of what Gramsci understands as Marxian theory. For Gramsci, concepts of absolute truth, being complexly interwoven with all the other social conditions of the capitalist social formation, are properly and necessarily the targets of Marxian criticism. Thus, stressing Marxian theory's epistemological standpoint is not only a defense against dogmatism; it is also a necessary component of the Marxian project. It contributes to accomplishing the interdependent (i.e., overdetermined) theoretical, cultural, economic, and political conditions for a transition to communism. Thus, Gramsci devoted much of his writing to the specification of the distinctive epistemological standpoint of Marxian theory. For him this task of specification clearly constituted a key part of his battles against bourgeois hegemony both inside as well as outside the Marxian tradition.[110]

Gramsci insists that Marxian theory is

an integral and original philosophy which opens up a new phase of history and a new phase in the development of world thought . . . [and] goes beyond both traditional idealism and traditional materialism . . . while retaining their vital elements . . . [and] its originality lies not only in its transcending of previous philosophies but also and above all in that it opens up a completely new road, renewing from head to toe the whole way of conceiving philosophy itself.[111]

A term central to Gramsci's formulation of the distinctive Marxian philosophy is *dialectics* or the distinctively *dialectical* materialism of Marxian epistemology.[112] In various contexts he opposes dialectics to the dominant conceptions of knowledge, of the relation between thought and being that predominate within traditional Marxian theory. For example, Gramsci ridicules what he terms the "common sense" notion of the objective reality of the external world.[113] To believe that the human mind can and does grasp directly and immediately the concrete reality is, he argues, not Marxian theory but rather "mysticism . . . of religious origin." For Gramsci this commonsense notion, so basic to the traditional Marxian theory, was opposed to a dialectical epistemological standpoint: "We know reality only in relation to man, and since man is historical becoming, knowledge and reality are also becoming and so is objectivity, etc." [114]

In the language of this book Gramsci here understands reality, that is, *his* concrete-real, as including the totality of concrete-reals constructed in and by all existing thought-concretes. Gramsci repeatedly emphasizes the dialectical interaction, the mutual determination, the ceaseless process of development within and between reality (i.e., Gramsci's concept of the concrete-real) and all the different knowledges Gramsci recognizes (including the knowledge produced in and by Marxian theory).

To take another example: Gramsci's critique of Nikolai Bukharin's *The Theory of Historical Materialism: A Popular Manual of Marxist Sociology* in the *Prison Notebooks* includes an attack on his epistemology as well as his economism. Gramsci suggests that Bukharin's unacceptable economism is closely linked to his epistemological standpoint. That standpoint, which Gramsci calls "vulgar materialism," is further characterized as "idealism upside down, in the sense that the speculative categories are replaced by *empirical concepts and classifications which are no less abstract* and antihistorical." [115] Gramsci castigates Bukharin for the eclectic mixture of empiricism and rationalism characterizing his epistemological standpoint. Bukharin is seen as taking "givens" from empirical "reality" and making them the rationalist essences of the process of that reality. Gramsci is especially outraged by the particular manner in which Bukharin eliminates any dialectical epistemological standpoint from his specification of historical materialism. Bukharin treats dialectics as merely a minor matter of formal logical inquiry:

> But if the question is framed in this way, one can no longer understand the importance and significance of the dialectic, which is relegated from its position as a doctrine of knowledge and the very narrow of historiography and the science of politics, to the level of a sub-species of formal logic and elementary scholastics.[116]

We share something of Gramsci's outrage but direct it now at those theoretical children of Bukharin (including the rebellious ones) who produce their Marxian knowledges still without much grasp of Marxian dialectics, that is, Marxian epistemology, and its integral role within Marxian theory and politics.

Gramsci linked his campaign to restore dialectics to center stage in Marxian epistemology to his campaign against economism in Marxian theory as well as in political practice. That Gramsci was a determined opponent of economic determinism within the traditional Marxian debates on that question is generally recognized. However, what notion of social determination he did support continues to be a matter of considerable dispute.[117] In any case, Gramsci repeatedly attacks economic determinism, as in his celebrated critique of Achille Loria's concept of "historical economism."[118] Indeed, it is widely agreed that Gramsci's elaboration of his famous concept of hegemony is in large part a sustained critique of and alternative formulation to economic determinism.

As we read Gramsci, his critique of economic determinism is particularly important precisely because it is *not* a notion of determination that replaces economics (relations or forces of production, or classes, etc.) with some other final, ultimate, or "last instance" cause. Rather, Gramsci's insistence on the specificity of a Marxian epistemological standpoint helps him reject the common epistemological standpoints implicit in either economism, humanism, or any other last-instance notions of determinism. Gramsci rejects the terms of the traditional Marxian debate over economic determinism as well as the economic determinist position per se.

Gramsci rejects vigorously any reductionist explanations of historical change referring explicitly to Engels's letters to Bloch and Starkenburg cited earlier.[119] He argues that the search for ultimate, last-instance causes stands in direct contradiction to Marxian theory. It is, he writes, "one manifestation of the 'search for God,'" which characterizes Bukharin's book as well as the predominant tendency within the Marxian tradition exemplified by that book.[120] In passages reminiscent of and in all likelihood directly inspired by Hegel's and Lenin's parallel writings cited earlier, Gramsci challenges the mechanical concepts of cause and effect for purposes of Marxian social analysis. This is the context for his attack on Bukharin's book for its philosophical standpoint as reflected in its economic determinism:

> The historical dialectic is replaced by the law of causality and the search for regularity, normality and uniformity. . . . In mechanical terms, the effect can never transcend the cause or the system of causes, and therefore can have no development other than the flat vulgar development of evolutionism.[121]

As against determinisms, economic or otherwise, and against their philosophic foundations in concepts of cause/effect, Gramsci counterposes his notion of Marxian theory's approach to social formations. That approach investigates social formations as the "ensemble of relations which each of us enters to take part in." [122] For Gramsci, Marxian theory's concept of the concrete-real is that of an "ensemble of relations" understood to be constituted as a "necessary reciprocity between structure and superstructure, a reciprocity which is nothing other than the real dialectical process." [123] Gramsci could accordingly define Leninism as "a unitary system of thought and practical action in which everything is held and demonstrated within reciprocal relations, from the general world view to the smallest problems of organization." [124]

Gramsci's anti-economic-determinist position and his complex elaboration of his concept of hegemony testify to his belief in the prime importance of the careful specification and development of what he sees as the unique and revolutionary philosophical position of Marxism. He emphasizes the full significance of the struggle among theories for hegemony. He argues insistently against tendencies within Marxism that would collapse its specific difference, including its distinctive epistemology, and assimilate it to bourgeois theory.

Gramsci, we believe, clearly belongs among the minority tendencies within the Marxian theoretical tradition discussed in this chapter. We warrant this view by reference to his concerns with the specific differences of Marxian theory, his justification of that concern in and by his concept of hegemony, and his approach to what we call an overdeterminist, rather than determinist, standpoint in Marxian social analysis. That he does but merely begin to specify Marxian epistemology and Marxian theory's dialectical concept of social development is something he knows and admits: "It is not enough to know the *ensemble* of relations as they exist at any given time as a given system. They must be known genetically, in the movement of their formation." [125] His work necessarily was largely negative, aimed to distance Marxian theory from that assimilation to bourgeois theory accomplished in and by the predominant tendency within the Marxian tradition. Gramsci's contribution was to widen and deepen the space within which Marxists could carry forward the task of specifying Marxian theory as he saw it, a task he justified as intrinsic to the Marxian goal of hegemony.

Mao Tse-tung too was a close student of Hegel, Marx, and Lenin's notebooks on Hegel. His 1937 essays "On Practice" and "On Contradiction" demonstrate the basic importance he attaches to their formulations of the epistemological foundations of what Mao understands to be Marxian theory.

> In philosophy, neither "rationalism" nor "empiricism" understands the historical or the dialectical nature of knowledge, and although each of these schools contains one aspect of the truth . . . both are wrong on the theory of knowledge as a whole. [126]

Both essays are remarkable for their insistence on the centrality of the concepts of dialectics and contradiction within Marxian theory, including what Mao understands as its epistemological standpoint.

After the Chinese revolution Mao found it again necessary to explain the practical political importance of grasping what he understood as the distinctive Marxian epistemological standpoint. His essays "On the Correct Handling of Contradictions among the People" of 1957 and "Where Do Correct Ideas Come From?" of 1963 attest to his conviction that socialist development urgently requires and depends upon this particular epistemological standpoint among the people generally and Communist party cadres in particular.[127]

> The ceaseless emergence and ceaseless resolution of contradictions is the dialectical law of the development of things . . . whether in the natural world, in human society, or in man's thinking.[128]

> Matter can be transformed into consciousness and consciousness into matter.[129]

Mao reaffirms the centrality of his interdependent concepts of dialectics, contradiction, and epistemology. He also directly reproaches Chinese Marxists for ignoring, neglecting, giving mere lip service to, or directly opposing these concepts.

> It is therefore necessary to educate our comrades in the dialectical materialist theory of knowledge, so that they can orientate their thinking correctly, become good at investigation and study and at summing up experience, overcoming difficulties, commit fewer mistakes, do their work better, and struggle hard so as to build China into a great and powerful socialist country and help the broad masses of the oppressed and exploited throughout the world in fulfillment of our great internationalist duty.[130]

Beyond insisting that his epistemological concepts are indispensable for successfully waging class struggles, Mao makes some significant contributions toward their specification and elaboration, building upon the groundwork prepared for him by Hegel, Marx, and Lenin. Arguing against idealism and mechanical materialism, Mao defines Marxian theory as a knowledge process concerned to identify the contradictions, or contradictory aspects, that constitute each and every possible object of such knowledge: his "universality of contradiction." For Mao, Marxian theory specifies the social totality as a complex structure of processes, a contradictory totality of its constituent, particular contradictions.

> The contradictory aspects in every process exclude each other, struggle with each other and are in opposition to each other. Without

exception, they are contained in the process of development of all
things and in all human thought. A simple process contains only a
single pair of opposites, while a complex process contains more.
And, in turn, the pairs of opposites are in contradiction to one another. That is how all things in the objective world and all human
thought are constituted and how they are set in motion.[131]

Each of the contradictory aspects of social processes can, then, only exist
in its relation to all the other contradictory aspects: "Without its opposite
aspect, each loses the condition for its existence." Each aspect is seen, in
Mao's formulation, as the location or "identity" for the contradictory influences of all other aspects: "On the one hand they are opposed to each other,
and on the other they are interconnected, interpenetrating, interpermeating
and interdependent, and this character is described as identity."[132]

The logic of Mao's concept of contradiction clashes with reductionism,
the notion of a social process having a cause, an essence. It clashes with
both the humanist and economic determinist counterpositions in the traditional Marxian debate over economic determinism.

When the superstructure [politics, culture, etc.] obstructs the development of the economic base, political and cultural changes become
principal and decisive. Arguing this way avoids mechanical materialism and firmly upholds dialectical materialism.[133]

Mao's extensive writings repeatedly stress that the task of Marxian theory
is the specification of the contradictions constituting any concrete object of
Marxian analysis. He emphasizes that understanding a contradictory reality requires a focus upon the mutual interaction among contradictions and
their aspects and, even more important, "their transformation into each
other."[134] Unfortunately Mao's terminology refers to "principal and secondary" contradictions, which connotes "more and less" social effectivity;
we reject this connotation for the reasons given earlier.

Mao contributes more than a rejection of economic determinism and the
affirmation of a distinctively dialectical, Marxian epistemological standpoint (notwithstanding occasional economic determinist and empiricist expressions found in his voluminous writings). He also affirms a particular
direction for the future elaboration of Marxian theory. He points toward
theoretical elaboration built around his central concept of contradiction
and his closely related critique of determinism. Mao finds the basis for
pointing in this direction in his particular readings of Marx and Lenin as
well as in the necessity to combat among Marxists what he deemed powerful and dangerous tendencies of a reductionist, determinist nature. Like
Lenin, Mao saw an urgent need for a revolutionary theory, including a distinctively Marxian epistemology, as a condition of existence for social

change toward socialism. What Mao's philosophical writings point to, what they invite, is what he himself only initiated: an explicit formulation of the Marxian epistemological standpoint and its connection to Marxian social analysis. As argued below, Althusser's work is in important ways a direct response to Mao's invitation.

Althusser

Since World War II one Marxian thinker in particular has focused attention upon this struggle to specify the epistemological standpoint of Marxian theory, its uniqueness, and to utilize such a specification in a reformulation of Marxian theory generally. Louis Althusser draws heavily upon all of the thinkers discussed above as well as upon the tradition of Western philosophy generally. Althusser responds directly and intensely to the complex circumstances surrounding his membership in the French Communist party since 1947. He also responds to the distinctive French intellectual tradition of the last fifty years involving the complex structuralist movements (de Saussure in linguistics, Lacan in psychoanalysis, Lévi-Strauss in anthropology) and the singular French school of philosophy/history of science (Gaston Bachelard and Georges Canguilhem).[135] It is this latter school's remarkable emphasis on the epistemological foundations of scientific paradigms that evidently influenced significantly Althusser's particular contributions toward the specification of Marxian theory's epistemological standpoint.

In the early 1960s Althusser published a group of essays (*For Marx* and *Reading Capital*) with two overriding and interdependent purposes.[136] The first purpose is to "draw a line of demarcation between Marxian theory and the forms of philosophical (and political) subjectivism which have compromised it or threaten it: above all, *empiricism* and its variants, classical and modern—pragmatism, voluntarism, historicism, etc." The second is to specify the "epistemological break" accomplished by Marx in separating himself scientifically from the set of social theories (including their epistemological standpoints) existing in his environment as he found and entered it. Althusser locates Marx's break, his founding of a new, distinctive science (including its distinctive epistemological standpoint), in his passage from earlier "humanist" formulations to the very different "dialectical materialist" position embodied in *Capital*. Althusser designates the earlier formulations as "idealist notions on which depend contemporary interpretations of Marxism as a 'philosophy of man' or a 'Humanism.'" The very different "problematic" of *Capital* embodies what is new and original, what precisely separates Marxian theory from the prior tradition of philosophy, of social sciences, and of their epistemological standpoints.

The usually tedious literature on the exact dating of Marx's change of scientific position as well as that concerned to document certain strands of continuity across the whole of his work are mostly irrelevant to Althusser's goal: to establish the break that Marx accomplished. That Marx's break was built upon and responded to alternative scientific positions, that Marx's changed theoretical position therefore had all manner of complex strands of continuity to its precursor sciences (including his own earlier position), is exactly what Althusser argues in his specification of "epistemological break." In this he follows, albeit with modifications, Bachelard's original formulation of the concept of an "epistemological break." Althusser conceives of such a break as the sketchy inauguration of a new problematic, a new and different way of posing questions about newly and differently perceived/conceived objects. Thus the new problematic of *Capital* contains the invitation to set to work its problems and its suggestions for their solutions.

Althusser's notion of *break* is trivialized and even rendered absurd when read as an argument denying continuity within Marx. The issue is not continuity per se, but rather how we are to understand the operation of such continuity. For Althusser, Marx's earlier theoretical position—together with non-Marxian theoretical positions and indeed together with the non-theoretical (i.e., political, cultural, and economic) aspects of the social totality—all combine to overdetermine the break Marx is understood to have accomplished. For Althusser, as for Hegel, a change or negation is always determinate; it is the change or negation of something particular and thereby bears the imprint of that particular. Marx's break is such a change. *Capital*'s continuity with the sciences it separates from lies precisely in its being a break particularly from them.

Althusser's 1960s essays present the most detailed and exhaustive examination of the epistemological foundations of Marx's work yet undertaken. They also represent direct critical encounters with tendencies within Marxism that Althusser opposes. Althusser's intense focus upon the philosophical underpinnings of Marxian theory is closely linked to his view of the "crucial tasks of the Communist movement *in theory*":

> —to recognize and know the revolutionary theoretical scope of Marxist-Leninist science and philosophy:
> —to struggle against the bourgeois and petty-bourgeois world outlook which always threatens Marxist theory, and which deeply impregnates it today. The general form of this world outlook: *Economism* (today 'technocracy') and its 'spiritual complement' *Ethical Idealism* (today 'Humanism'). Economism and Ethical Idealism have constituted the basic opposition in the bourgeois world outlook since the origins of the bourgeoisie. The current philo-

sophical form of this world outlook: *neo-positivism* and its 'spiritual complement,' existentialist-phenomenological subjectivism. The variant peculiar to the Human Sciences: the *ideology* called "structuralist." [137]

These words summarize Althusser's goals in his writings.

Whatever his successes and failures in working to achieve these goals, Althusser has certainly contributed toward reestablishing the centrality of the epistemological aspect of *any* specification of Marxian theory. He offers a particular specification of Marxian theory and makes explicit its epistemological aspect. He does this around the two central concepts of overdetermination and contradiction. Drawing upon the Marxian texts discussed above as well as certain pre-Marxian texts (such as those of Spinoza, Hegel, and Montesquieu), Althusser's specification is unique in its scope, comprehensiveness, and the sharp critical edge with which it confronts the predominant tendencies within Marxism. What Karl Korsch more generaly called for in the 1920s (with some remarks along lines reopened and developed by Althusser) won for him then the kind of sharp disapproval that has occasionally befallen Althusser. [138] The difference is that in Althusser's time it has been possible for many to appreciate and take up the task of specifying the philosophic particularity of Marxian theory in ways that simply did not materialize earlier.

In Althusser's view, Marx did, and Marxian theory must, reject empiricism. Marxian theory affirms both definitions of and a relation between thinking and being that are radically different from the empiricist conceptions of thinking as a realm separated or distanced from the realm of its given objects, the real. The gap separating these realms can be bridged, for empiricism, because the truth (essence) of reality is contained within the givens of experience (observations) contemplated by the mind. But what is given needs also to be adequately received: empiricists understand thinking to aim at abstracting the truth (essence) of reality by means of a method adequate to the task. The empiricists' truth is, in the last analysis, singular. It is presumed to exist "out there, in the real" and to be the identical goal of all theories, of all sciences, which are then properly ranked—at any moment of or over time—according to their approximation to the singular goal they are all presumed to share. Such a reality serves to validate one knowledge against another by some notion of the correspondence or identity of the realm of concepts with objects existing (external to theory) in the other realm.

Empiricists, for Althusser, close or bridge the gap between the two realms by the absolute declaration that all thinking, all sciences, all the various thought-concretes are finally unified in their aim to capture the singular truth of "the given reality." Anyone questioning the unified aim is dismissed typically as perverse and/or as "antiscientific," as someone absurdly proposing to cut thinking loose from its proper, singular goal and anchor. For empiricists, denial of the unified aim of all thought-concretes amounts to advocacy of a chaos of disparate conceptions and to a "relativist" inability to choose or discriminate (i.e., rank) among them by an absolute standard (i.e., the unified aim). For empiricists, anyone espousing alternative epistemological standpoints is engaged in sacrifice of science (singular) and the facts to ideology and dogma. For empiricists, one index of the scientific progress of human history is the grounding of theory in science and facts and the refutation of ideology on that basis.

Marxian theory's epistemological standpoint, in Althusser's view, is radically different from empiricism precisely in its rejection of the unified aim, that is, in its alternative, dialectical conception of thinking and being and their relation. Marxian theory holds that different conceptual frameworks (or thought-concretes or knowledges or sciences) share only one quality, namely, they are all overdetermined by and participate in the overdetermination of all the economic, political, and cultural aspects of the social totality (Marxian theory's concrete-real) within which they occur. Their respective objects of analysis (their respective concrete-reals) differ, as do the respective conceptual apparatuses they elaborate in constructing their different knowledges of their different objects. Among the infinity of facts, each science's facts are always selected for scrutiny, gathered, and quite literally "seen" or "observed" in and through its conceptual framework. The "facts" per se can thus never provide any final criterion of truth *between* such different frameworks.[139] Each science's facts are thus selectively produced in and by the interaction between the conceptual framework defining that science and the social totality within which the framework occurs (which includes the facts stressed in other sciences). Each science differentially conceptualizes the facts it recognizes, its claim to truth, and its history. The moment anyone specifies an object of analysis as independent of its conceptual framework is, for Althusser, the moment of existence of a non-Marxian approach to knowledge and society.

The different conceptual frameworks also produce different understandings of one another, that is, of the existing set of thought-concretes. For Althusser, Marxian theory has its concrete-real, which includes its conceptualization of the determinate differences among alternative sciences (such as its differences from empiricist epistemology under discussion here). Marxian theory knows, however, that its concrete-real, its conception of being, of the social totality, is precisely *its;* it declares no unified aim of all the alternative conceptual frameworks.[140] For Althusser, the relation between thinking and being in Marxian theory is one of a mutual determination between part and whole, both equally "real." The whole is primary

(Althusser's reading of "being determines consciousness"), but the reciprocal lines of determination must also operate (thinking is a constituent process of being). The effort to specify the tension between whole and part—the changes each works in the other, the dialectic of thought and being—this is Marxian theory's alternative to the empiricist striving to close the gap between thinking and reality by absolute declarations of unity in the aim to merge thought with the essence/truth of the given being.

The finding that a theory makes unacceptable epistemological, in this case empiricist, claims about the validity of its propositions does nothing for Marxian theory other than underscore a basic difference between such an empiricist theory and Marxian theory. Since, for Marxian theory, each theory produces its own validity criteria along with its own testing procedures for its own propositions, it is no more possible for Marxian theory to dismiss an empiricist theory as "false" than it is possible to admit it as "true." What Marxian theory can and must do, Althusser suggests, is specify and affirm its difference—in this case, as so far discussed, an epistemological difference—from such an empiricist theory. Althusser argues that Marxian theory must investigate what consequences for the other propositions of such a theory may flow from its empiricist epistemological standpoint, in order for Marxian theory to specify further its difference from (its knowledge of) that theory.

Althusser likewise rejects rationalist epistemology as fundamentally incompatible with Marxian theory. For Althusser, what is real is not identical with what is rational. Concepts are not and cannot be the essences of which reality is an expression, any more than concepts are or can be the phenomena of some essential reality. Like empiricism, rationalism involves the conception of a gap between the two realms of thinking and being needing to be closed or bridged. Rationalism performs this closure by conceiving that ideas can express or capture what it conceives as the singular essence/truth of reality and that all theories are so many attempts to reach those particular ideas whose logic is that which governs reality.

Thus, both rationalists and empiricists search for the singular, independent truth. The former find it in the internal logic of thought external to experience; the latter find it in experience as external and given to thought. Consequently, both share a common commitment to a singular Truth, Science, and History. Also, both must eschew the notion of overdetermination for it entails the refusal to reduce differing claims to truth to a final criterion of logic or experience. Indeed, this very refusal appears to be dogmatic, if not dangerous, to those who are epistemologically blinded by their different standpoint (should we write *dogmatism*?) and its commitment to a singular Science and Truth.

The disputation between empiricist and rationalist epistemological standpoints is rejected by Althusser. Throughout *Reading Capital* it is referred to as a dispute situated "on a terrain" or in a context or within a philosophic space that is itself incompatible with Marxian theory. Hence both sides are rejected.

For Althusser, what distinguishes Marx from the other sciences he contended with is in large part the "epistemological break" he made from them. As Althusser sees it, for Marx, concepts, theories, and the thought-concretes are not connected to the concrete-real as *its* essence or *its* truth. At the same time the concrete-real and the various thought-concretes cannot be conceived independently. In Althusser's formulations, the various thought-concretes exist as both partial causes and effects of the Marxian theoretical notion of the concrete-real. Neither thought-concrete nor concrete-real is conceived as the essence, origin, or determining subject vis-à-vis the other. Rather, each is an effect of the other in a particular way whose specification (via the key concept of overdetermination) is the definition of Marxian epistemology or "dialectical materialism." In one way, Althusser's rejection of empiricism and especially of rationalism contradicts charges that he adheres to what is widely understood as structuralism. That is, he did not and indeed he could not consistently hold that the structures of his theoretical formulation correspond to (are the essence/truth of) social reality.[141]

Many of Althusser's critics fail to appreciate his rejection of both empiricism and rationalism, that is, his change of epistemological terrain—just as Althusser has charged them with failing to appreciate Marx's "epistemological break." Such critics, when proceeding from an empiricist standpoint, can only read his attack upon empiricism as necessarily tantamount or equivalent to a rationalist position to which they then counterpose their empiricism. E. P. Thompson's essay cited in the previous chapter proceeds in this way. Ironically, and significantly, two other critics of Althusser, Barry Hindess and Paul Q. Hirst, while themselves explicitly antiempiricist and antirationalist, nonetheless can read Althusser's antiempiricism as likewise equivalent to a rationalism, such as Thompson does. The subtlety and force of Hindess and Hirst's critique requires the extended discussion offered in the last section of this chapter. In any case, all three of these critics do not address the difference in epistemological terrain that Althusser occupies and believes Marxian theory to occupy.[142]

In constructing a specification of Marxian epistemology, Althusser takes an interesting cue from Montesquieu, who defended his own *Spirit of Laws* by insisting that he was "not treating of causes, nor does he compare causes: but he treats of effects and compares effects."[143] Althusser formulates the epistemological standpoint of Marxian theory as one that views thought-concretes and the concrete-real as mutually effective and mutually constitutive. Concepts and theories are complex effects of the concrete-real (the materialist thesis), *and* the concrete-real is an effect, in part, of the divers theories existing within it. (The idealist thesis would hold an extreme version of only this latter proposition, typically removing the words *in part* and changing *theories* to *theory*.) Marxian epistemology recognizes and builds from an irreducible interplay between the mutual effectivities of concrete-real and thought-concretes. Marxian theory proceeds by elaborating the movement or motion of this interplay, its dialectic, as its unique concept of knowledge, its epistemological standpoint. Althusser cites both Hegel's notion of reason as the critique of intellect and Engels's remark that "the dialectic sets concepts in motion" in his argument that Marx's first *Thesis on Feuerbach* amounts to an invitation to specify a particular epistemological standpoint.[144]

Neither the empiricist nor the rationalist can hold such a dialectical materialist position. Rationalists must reject any claim that, for example, political experience continually shapes and changes every theory because such experience is one determinant of the social process of producing theory. Specifically, the thesis of the social overdetermination of thinking, logic, and science is impossible for the rationalist. In the last analysis, rationalists conceive of logic and science as independent of experience (the concrete-real) so that they may be offered as the ultimate source and standard of the Truth of all experience. The empiricist joins in this holy defense of the Truth, while simultaneously offering a different version of it. Empiricists must reject any claim that conceptual frameworks, say a Marxian standpoint, constitute experience (the concrete-real). Rather, thinking aims to extract from the given experience, reality, its essential truth; thought strives to conform to that inherent truth. In contrast, for Althusser's formulation of Marxism, no object experienced (observed) exists independent of thought: all thought participates in the overdetermination of reality as its object.

Althusser states that knowledge is understood in Marxian theory as a process of production in which concepts function as raw material, means of production, and outputs. This process, thinking, is one among the many processes comprising the social totality. It is an effect of all processes other than itself, the site of their interaction; it is constituted as a process by the particular interaction of all the other processes. Those other processes— observing, eating, working, voting, teaching, singing, and so forth— grouped for expository ease into economic, political, and cultural processes (or "levels" or "instances") are all participants in the constitution of the thinking process. In Althusser's adaptation of Freud's initial usage, the thinking process is overdetermined by all the other social processes, as, indeed, is every other distinct social process.[145]

In turn, then, the thinking process is one constituent of every other distinct social process. Thinking and its conceptual elements always participate in the overdetermination of each and every other social process. In this sense, concepts effect, are constituent processes of, the social totality, that is, Marxian theory's concrete-real. Moreover, it follows that the totality and the particular process of knowledge cannot be collapsed into identities, for that would confuse the whole and its part. Similarly, making either the whole or its part an essence, with the other a mere expression of that essence, would lose the interplay, the mutual effectivity, the overdetermination that embodies, for Althusser, Marxian theory's most basic commitment to the universality of motion, process, change.

We may complete this brief overview of Althusser's specification of dialectical materialism as Marxian theory's epistemological standpoint by focusing upon his concept of contradiction. For him, it is the other side of—the concomitant of—overdetermination and hence equally as basic a component of Marxian theory's conceptual framework. Moreover, Althusser's concept of contradiction emphasizes the necessary complexity of all contradictions, as against notions of contradiction that are simply dualistic opposites.[146] That is, because each distinct social process is the site constituted by the interaction of all the other social processes, each contains "within itself" the very different and conflicting qualities, influences, moments, and directions of all those other social processes that constitute it. In this sense, argues Althusser, each social process is the site of, or "contains," the complex contradictoriness inseparable from its overdetermination. Each social process exists, for Althusser's Marxism, only as a particular, unique concentration of contradictions in its environment. As one of those social processes, thinking too contains its political, economic, and cultural contradictions that appear both as different, contradictory theories and as those inconsistencies within each theory or conceptual framework that forever arise and provoke the knowledge process. In Althusser's formulation, *any* object of analysis for Marxian theory is approached in terms of specifying its existence as the site of overdetermined contradictions and thereby explaining both its dynamic and its relations of complex mutual effectivity (e.g., mutual constitutivity), with all other objects of Marxian theory. Althusser exemplifies his approach in his reading of Marx's *Capital*.[147]

Althusser finds, then, that the thinking process is forever in motion, activated by the contradictions that define it. Thinking is thus forever changing, as is every other social process. As each social process is changed, so its constituent role in all other processes changes. Changing thinking changes the social totality of which the thinking process is one part; a changed social totality in turn changes thinking, and so on. Dialectical materialism is this conception of the relation of thinking and the social total-ity, or being. Through his conception of dialectical materialism, Althusser understands each theory or science as a constituent part of the social total-ity; each is thus very real, a part of the concrete-real. At the same time he understands each theory or science as constructing its own, particular, dif-ferent knowledge of a concrete-real; each thought-concrete is overdeter-mined by the social totality, in contradiction to other theories, and also exhibiting its own internal contradictions. This concept of dialectical ma-terialism, Marxian theory's epistemological standpoint, is different from the terrain upon which empiricism and rationalism contend as epistemo-logical standpoints. Marxian theory thus embodies, for Althusser, an epis-temological break from the previous philosophic tradition in epistemology, and this break serves to provide one key differentiation of Marxian from non-Marxian theory.

Althusser includes Marxian science as one among the several sciences overdetermined in and by the contemporary concrete-real, for example, a capitalist social formation. Marxian science no more captures the essence of the social totality or reduces to some mere reflection of that totality than it accepts any other theory's claims to do so. Rather, Marxian theory em-phasizes its differences from non-Marxian theory and seeks to integrate those differences into its particular knowledge of the contemporary capi-talist social formation.

Marxian theory's particular constructed knowledge of its relation to the non-Marxian theories contending with it in any social formation precludes the problem of "relativism" that concerned Lenin and others, as we have noted. Althusser's formulation of Marxian theory's epistemological stand-point leads him to demonstrate how both non-Marxian theories and the various theoretical tendencies within the Marxian tradition function within the social totality.[148] For Althusser, Marxian theory specifies its differences from other theories in order to articulate how the different theories impact differently upon the social totality and, more particularly, upon the revolu-tionary project of Marxism. On this basis, Althusser's Marxian theory takes a partisan position toward and makes a judgment on each alternative social theory it recognizes.

Marxian theory proceeds, for Althusser, from a "revolutionary class theoretical position," or, alternatively phrased, with a class revolutionary project.[149] That is, Marxian theory has two basic objectives. The first is to produce a class knowledge of society, to construct a kind of knowledge of the overdetermined and hence contradictory and changing social totality that focuses upon class. Thus, the attention of Marxian theory centers upon specifying the particular contradictions of class, how they are over-determined by all the political, cultural, and economic aspects/processes of the social formation under analysis, and how in turn class contradictions impact upon all those other social aspects. The second objective is to help change the class structure of its contemporary social formations (which is only partly accomplished by and through the achievement of the first objective). In Althusser's reading, Marx's contribution lay in his particular specification of the class aspect of society and hence the class aspect of social change. He made this contribution by emphasizing (but without making an essence of) this aspect in his theoretical constructions, his "revolutionary class theoretical position."

Marxian theory's particular truth and its particular objectives are mutually determining and distinguishing characteristics of that theory; moreover, they set it in complex patterns of contention with various other social theories. The latter are variously characterized by and affirm different objectives and truths. They must critically confront Marxian theory as it must critically confront them. Thus, for example, theorists whose epistemological standpoint affirms a unified aim of science (singular) to extract the truth (singular) of reality (given) seek to deny, on the most profound level, Marxian theory's claim to exist as one alternative theory among others. Such theorists may then differ over whether to dismiss Marxian theory altogether, to grant it a few scattered "insights" into *the* reality, or to reconceptualize Marxian theory itself as holding to their epistemological position. By contrast, Marxian theory, as Althusser conceives it, approaches such theories and theorists as more or less serving socially to block, deflect, or alter in various ways its class revolutionary project. Marxian theory's recognition of the variety of truths under theoretical construction in any social formation rejects any relativist indifference or inaction toward them. As Gramsci noted and Althusser reemphasizes, this recognition is Marxism's necessary precondition for an effective criticism of them, that is, the achievement of theoretical hegemony over them.[150] For Althusser, the theoretical hegemony of Marxian theory is a condition for (and a constituent aspect of) a changed class structure and of a changed social formation. Thus, Althusser's important essay "The Object of *Capital*" is an attempt to show exactly how Marxian theory differs from classical economic theories in its basic conceptualization of its *object*, its knowledge construction.[151] Moreover, the essay is replete with arguments on the social implications of this difference in object and in the associated concepts of time, causality, and so forth.

Althusser's specification of dialectical materialism is epitomized in the phrase "process without a subject." Taken directly from Hegel, Althusser means it to designate the mutually effective interplay between thinking and being in which neither is the subject, origin, or independent cause of the other.[152] Althusser also deploys "process without a subject" to define Marxian theory's concept of history. Using the same phrase pointedly underscores how Althusser sees the linkage between Marxian theory's epistemological position and its concept of history. That concept begins from a notion not unlike Gramsci's concept of the "ensemble of relations" discussed earlier. Althusser develops it further to arrive at a definition of the social totality as a complex structure of entities variously referred to as processes, aspects, instances, levels, moments, and so forth. As we shall see, the vagueness that attends the absence of a clear and consistent choice among those terms of reference is unacceptable and remediable. At this point, however, what matters is Althusser's understanding of this structure as one in which all the entities participate in the overdetermination of each, its contradictions and its dynamic.

We read Althusser's very particular choice, definition, and development of the concept of overdetermination as the affirmation that noneconomic instances or levels of society are just as determinant upon economic aspects as the latter participate in determining, or rather, overdetermining the former. Althusser rejects any essentialism within either dialectical or historical materialism. No one aspect or instance is the essence of any other. There is no subject of which the social totality is the predicate: no essence, no origin, and no telos. Rather, history is seen as the ceaseless interplay or mutual effectivity of aspects or instances. It is a process without a subject, theistic or otherwise. Althusser's notion of dialectical materialism rules out any essentialist concept of society and any essentialist concept of knowledge.

Althusser's usage of overdetermination, process without a subject, and so on has provoked a storm of controversy over his approach to human subjectivity and intersubjectivity.[153] He certainly does not and in fact cannot see them as passive, as merely socially determined, without also seeing them as determining in their own right. Precisely because he conceptualizes them as aspects/processes of persons and hence of the social totality, they are *both* overdetermined by and participate in the overdetermination of all the economic, political, and cultural aspects of the social formation in which they occur. The "relative autonomy" of each human subject and of intersubjectivity refers in Althusser to their being understood as particular sites of overdetermined, natural, and social processes and as such sites generating their own particular effects as well. This is just parallel to the relative autonomy he accords to each constituent process (or aspect) of the social totality. We might paraphrase Althusser's antiessentialism as follows: there are effective subjects and intersubjectivity generated *in* history but no subject(s) or intersubjectivity *of* history.

Althusser's formulation of Marxian theory around the key concepts of overdetermination and contradiction is also a criticism directed against theoretical humanism and economic determinism within the Marxian tradition. By humanism Althusser means the view that human subjects are somehow, in some last instance, ultimate determinants or originators of social processes, of history.[154] We might restate Althusser's position by focusing upon the "free will" issue always closely linked to humanist formulations. Humans have "free will." They have the mental capacity to conceive, struggle with, and choose among alternative courses of thought and action. The point of Althusser's argument is that the contradictions, constraints, and consequences of this mental capacity, this struggle, and its reach ("freedom") are fully endogenously overdetermined in and by the social formation in which they occur.

For Althusser economic determinism is simply an alternative essentialism to that of humanism; it is the view that economic instances or structures (variously the "forces" and/or "relations" or "modes" of production) are the subject *of* history. In his earliest essays he makes clear his opposition to economic determinism and to those Marxists who endorsed it: "The superstructure is not the pure phenomenon of the structure, it is also its condition of existence."[155] He rejects either essentialism as incompatible with Marxian theory, just as he rejects the essentialism of empiricist and rationalist epistemologies. In his view, essentialist concepts of society and history reinforce essentialist epistemological standpoints (rationalism and empiricism) and vice versa.

Having read Marxian theory as dialectical materialist and antiessentialist in the manner here summarized, how does Althusser contribute to the traditional Marxian debate over economic determinism? At the level of epistemology he unambiguously rejects the terrain of the debate. His specification of the unique difference of dialectical materialism, of Marxian theory's epistemological standpoint, implies the consequent rejection of any claims to validate the essentialism of the economic determinist tendency by appeals to "the facts" or to "case histories" (empiricism). It implies as well the rejection of rationalist claims that Marx's theory captures the essence of social reality, an essence it "finds" to be economic. Thus, Althusser's work shows a continuing strain of hostility toward economic determinist formulations, a hostility directed particularly toward the epistemological standpoints implicit in such formulations.

However, despite the rejection of all forms of essentialism required by his overdeterminist position, apparent concessions to economic determinism appear often in Althusser's work. His essays return repeatedly to the thorny issue of economic determinism "in the last instance," which he seems to endorse as a feature of specifically Marxian theory. Yet in his 1962 essay "Contradiction and Overdetermination," his strong position on the antiessentialism of Marxian theory leads him to the following remarkable statement: "From the first moment to the last, the lonely hour of the 'last instance' never comes." [156] Here Althusser comes close to accompanying the epistemological basis of his rejection of the economic determinism debate with a direct dismissal of economic determinism. Yet his 1974 essay "Is It Easy to Be a Marxist in Philosophy?," despite his demonstration of the polemical purposes of Marx's statements, comes close to a reading that affirms substantive commitment to "last instance" economic determinism. [157]

We would argue, thus, that Althusser has not resolved the matter of economic determinism and its relation to the Marxian theoretical tradition. His contribution has been to show that the usual epistemological aspects of economic determinist positions, their empiricist or rationalist aspects, render them outside Marxian theory, as do the parallel epistemological bases of the more or less anti-economic-determinist tendencies within the traditional debate. However, freed of these epistemological aspects, a kind of economic determinist argument still survives, although just barely, in Althusser's formulation of Marxian theory. The clearest statement of this argument emerges in his conception of the overdetermined social totality as a structure of instances or aspects "articulated in dominance," namely, the last-instance dominance of the economic aspects over the noneconomic. How such a formulation could possibly be reconciled with an anti-essentialist notion of Marxian theory remains an unanswered problem in Althusser's work. We shall return to and transform this problem in the concluding section of this chapter. On the other hand, a major component of Althusser's work is the consistent hostility that characterizes his attitude toward economic determinist arguments as they are typically presented within the Marxian tradition. After all, overdetermination is a concept aimed squarely against economic determinism and offered precisely as an alternative to it within Marxism. Notwithstanding Althusser's incomplete elaboration of the concept of overdetermination and evident uneasiness about it, it stands as an indispensable step away from economic determinism and other comparable essentialisms within Marxism. His specification of the unique epistemological standpoint of Marxian theory effectively pulls the rug from beneath the claims to validity of the overwhelming bulk of pro- and anti-economic-determinist arguments comprising the economic determinist debate. Apparently, Althusser cannot take that last step in extricating Marxian theory from that debate, cannot see a way finally to let go of the ontological sort of primacy and privilege accorded the economic in and for Marxian theory. So he both affirms that Marxian theory cannot and does not capture any economic or other essence of the concrete-real and yet also affirms that for Marxian theory the social totality is approached as a structure of instances articulated by the ultimate determinance of the economic.

We can point to another symptom of Althusser's hesitancy to develop

sufficiently the critical epistemology he reads in Marx. His continuing
struggle with the terms *science* and *ideology,* like that with last-instance
economic determination, signifies a certain unwillingness to draw the conclusions his work suggests. In *Reading Capital,* Althusser rejects explicitly
empiricist notions of the difference between true and false theories, yet he
develops a distinction between ideology and science that comes close to
reproducing that difference.[158] Althusser writes frequently of sciences
being born out of ideologies where the latter are understood as merely the
*"imaginary relationship of individuals to their real conditions of exis-
tence."* [159] By contrast, science is something more, something presumably
not imaginary, something involving a "mechanism" whereby "the production of an object of knowledge produce[s] the cognitive appropriation of
the real object." [160] To be fair, Althusser also writes as if the term *ideology*
ought to designate those theories that constitute "concrete individuals as
subjects," as distinguished from theories, or rather sciences, that constitute
"subject-less discourse." [161] This position comes close to ours if understood
as simply a classification of differences between theories, without imputa-
tion of any absolute truth/falsity to them.

Althusser himself came to recognize that his original differentiations of
science from ideology tended toward the rationalist view that Marxian theory grasps the truth of the world whereas other theories—ideologies—
miss that truth, are false. He explicitly repudiated the rationalism of that
early view. He even went so far as to assert that from the standpoint of
Marxian theory, epistemology amounted to the study of all the social conditions of the totality of "already existing knowledge," including presumably Marxian theory in that totality.[162]

But Althusser could not quite proceed to our formulation, whose ground
he had prepared, that the social totality includes a variety of theories (alternatively named sciences, knowledges, ideologies, conceptual frameworks,
etc.) that cannot be distinguished by their truthfulness unless one allows a
transtheoretical truth criterion. This is precisely what Althusser's critique
of empiricism and rationalism rules out. Thus, *ideology* is simply a pe-
jorative applied by various theories to one another for polemical purposes,
while science functions as a compliment in much the same fashion. Then,
as we have argued, Marxian theory justifies itself not by empiricist or rationalist claims about the Truth, but by its specification of the relation between all existing theories and the social changes it supports.[163]

Alternative theories, like alternative cultural, economic, and political
forms, undergo continuous changes and continuously changing relations
with one another. These relations include periods of struggle among the
alternatives for social hegemony. There is struggle among theories as there
is among, say, modes of painting or electoral processes or class structures.
In our view, the causes and outcomes of these struggles are overdetermined

in and by the totality of social and natural processes. There is no end to theoretical changes and struggles, that is, no final, absolute, Godlike arbiter warranting one among the alternatives as best or truest. Marxian theory rejects as well the secular forms—essentialisms—of this basically religious absolutism, that is, the claims of empiricists and rationalists to have an absolute warrant for their theories. The empiricists' essential truth or "factual reality" and the rationalists' essential truth of reason are, for Marxian theory, simply the modern, secularized version of religion's old claim to a single truth warranted by God. Against such claims, religious or secular, old or new, Marxian theory counterposes its conceptions of contradiction and overdetermination and hence difference and struggle. Marxian theory, as we understand it, struggles against absolutist claims to truth (singular) such as those embedded in the traditional distinctions between science and ideology. Althusser provided key means for this struggle but did not carry it through to break fully from the religious prehistory of epistemological guarantees of truth (singular).

Perhaps Althusser, like Gramsci, hesitated to stress this conclusion on the science/ideology relation reached in his own self-criticism for fear of shaking the convictions of Marxists who believed their theory was truth as against others' falsity. However, this hesitancy left Althusser open to the charge of remaining an essentialist in epistemology, specifically a rationalist. Similarly, his hesitancy on last-instance economic determinism left him open to the charge of being an essentialist in social theory, specifically a sophisticated economic determinist. Thus Althusser's hesitancy to take the next step and break unequivocally from essentialism *of* theory (rationalism) and essentialism *in* theory (economic determinism) carried the risk that his great innovative formulation of the concepts of overdetermination and contradiction would not be properly and fully appreciated. As we shall show, Hindess and Hirst, among other careful readers of Althusser's work, were to focus on these two hesitancies, to miss the centrality of the concept of overdetermination, and to criticize Althusser precisely on the grounds of being a rationalist and economic determinist.

By contrast, our reading of Althusser propels us to shake off his hesitancy, to take the steps he pointed to, and thereby to use the developed concept of overdetermination to settle accounts with such critics of Althusser. More carefully and securely than the Marxian predecessors he depended upon, Althusser has provided the basis upon which to resolve the debates over economic determinism within Marxism.

An Initial Resolution

We propose that Althusser's specification of the unique epistemological standpoint of Marxian theory be accepted, but also extended further than he undertook. We propose that Althusser's arguments against any essentialism within Marxian theory be strengthened and extended to overcome the inconsistency or at least the ambiguity contained in his recurrent formulations of "economic determination in the last instance." We believe that elaborating Marxian theory in these ways offers a resolution to the economic determinist debate within the Marxian theoretical tradition. Our initial resolution follows.

Marxian theory is sharply distinguished from other theories or sciences by the combination of its dialectical materialist position and its concept of society. Marxian theory's specific difference cannot be reduced to either the matter of epistemological standpoint or the matter of the concept of society or to any subset of concepts. Since each theory, including Marxian theory, is a set of mutually constitutive, mutually overdetermined concepts, the differentiation between theories must finally concern the entirety of their respective knowledges. Thus, our focus upon epistemology and upon society, or rather, upon the concepts of knowledge and social totality, is to be understood as a focus upon two selected indexes of the differences between Marxian and non-Marxian theories. The choice of these as opposed to other possible indexes simply shows our indebtedness to the path-breaking work of Althusser in reestablishing the specific difference of Marxian theory around these two particular concepts.

As we understand it, then, Marxian theory holds that all theories, including itself, are overdetermined discursive formations of concepts. Marxian theory holds further that all theories produce distinct knowledges of the social totality in which they exist and by which they are overdetermined. Some of these theories produce essentialist knowledges, assigning to some social aspect(s) the role of origin, cause, telos, or subject of the other aspects (or assigning such roles to extrasocial, extrahuman entities). Marxian theory is, by contrast, nonessentialist or antiessentialist; it recognizes no aspect as the essence of another—no origin, no telos, and no subject. Finally, for Marxian theory, no theory is or expresses the essence of an external reality and no theory is the phenomenon of such a reality functioning as its essence. Society is an overdetermined totality of mutually effective, mutually constitutive social and natural processes that are so many aspects of the totality. Marxian theory allows no essentialism *of* theory (rationalist or empiricist epistemology) and no essentialism *in* theory (determinist social theory).

Marxian theory, while definitely antiessentialist, does deploy a particular manner of constructing its knowledge of the social totality. It is motivated by, focused upon, and aims at an ever-deeper knowledge of a selected subset among the many aspects of the social totality. These are economic aspects and, in particular, the class processes and their interrelations within the social totality. The particular, unique concepts of class and of overdetermination in Marxian theory operate as the entry points, guiding threads, and objects of the knowledge produced in and by Marxian theory. This knowledge aims to specify both how the class relations it designates as its objects are overdetermined by the nonclass aspects of the social totality and how those class relations participate in the overdetermination of those nonclass aspects. This knowledge aims, by means of exactly this specification, to determine the contradictions in those class relations and the dynamic motion that those contradictions produce.

Thus, Marxian theory embodies a particular way of thinking about society, history, and the process of thinking itself: dialectically materialist, antiessentialist, and with class as its focus. Every aspect of a social totality—political and cultural no less than economic—is a proper object of Marxian theory, but an object conceived and thought through in a unique manner. This uniqueness is exemplified by its fundamental commitment to its concepts of overdetermination, contradiction, and class. Marxian theory asks of every nonclass aspect of a social totality: How does that aspect participate in the overdetermination of the class aspect? To which contradictions within the class aspect does it contribute? What is its relation to the class dynamics of the social totality? This way of thinking about the social totality is part of what sharply differentiates Marxian from non-Marxian theory.

The task of Marxian theory is to construct a knowledge of an ever-changing overdetermined social totality. This includes the knowledge of the ever-changing, overdetermined nature of its own conceptual apparatus.

Our formulation of Marxian theory around some basic indexes of its specific difference from non-Marxian theories leads us to certain conclusions regarding the long economic determinist debate within the Marxian tradition. First, that debate occurred upon a non-Marxian epistemological terrain that was questioned by Marx, struggled over by leading Marxists, and finally critically displaced by Althusser. Second, the latter's specification and reestablishment of the centrality of dialectical materialism not only undermined the epistemological terrain of the debate; it also raised further questions about the essentialism practiced by its participants on both sides. And third, rejecting the essentialism and non-Marxian epistemological standpoints that have characterized the debate serves to reformulate Marxian theory and its distinctive contributions.

Our initial resolution to that debate begins, then, on the basis of the displacement of its epistemological terrain, that is, on the basis of a different concept of Marxian theory itself than that supported by most of the debaters. We have broken with the notion that Marxian theory either needs or can countenance any commitment to "economic determination in the last instance." Marxian theory's emphasis on economics is, in our view, a distinguishing aspect of its particular focus in approaching the social totality, that is, in constructing its particular knowledge of that totality. That focus is the specification of the relationship between the structure and dynamic of the class process and all the other processes that comprise the overdetermined social totality.

In Marxian theory its concept of class becomes a key conceptual tool to make sense of this infinity of social processes. Using the abstract concepts of class and overdetermination, a class knowledge (thought-concrete) is produced—a particular specification of the social totality. Building from those two concepts, Marxian theory produces a class knowledge of social being in which each human subject occupies specific class and nonclass positions. These positions, occupied by human beings, are constituted by all the processes of the social totality. The goal is to specify exactly how and with what consequences the contradictions and dynamic of these positions are overdetermined. The result of this particular theoretical production is then a picture of reality (a thought-concrete) that stresses the mutually overdetermining class and nonclass social processes together constituting society.

The initial resolution offered here distinguishes between that produced picture and the conceptual tools necessary to produce it. Class has a particular theoretical location of primacy in the latter, but not in the former. The traditional Marxian debate over economic determinism has confused the two. But to confuse the two is to embrace a non-Marxian epistemology and open the door once again to essentialism.

However, if class has this unique role to play in the logic of the theory, then does it form some sort of essence? Has a form of essentialism slipped back in by making class a key concept from and with which a knowledge of society is produced? The answer is no, because the commitment to overdetermination makes the attribution of essentiality impossible to any aspect of the social totality. Moreover, the centrality of class in the uniquely Marxian theoretical approach to social analysis is itself understood as overdetermined; Marxian theory's concept of class is itself undergoing the processes of change implied by its status as overdetermined by other concepts and by all the nonconceptual aspects of the social totality. It too is a process without a subject.

Marxian theory as we understand it is a ceaseless process of posing and transforming its particular concepts in its particular way. Each and every Marxian elaboration of its abstract concepts of class and overdetermination toward more concrete, that is, more determinate, specifications of particular social formations is understood to react back upon and change those abstract concepts. Marxian theory recognizes no unchanging components either in society or in itself.

Class then is one process among the many different processes of life chosen by Marxists to be their theoretical entry point so as to make a particular sense of and a particular change in this life. The choice of this entry point is understood to be overdetermined by both class and nonclass aspects of social life. No choice is determined by only theoretical or other cultural, political, or economic aspects of social life. In our view, Marx chose class as his conceptual entry point because he thought that the social reformers and revolutionaries with whose goals he sympathized did not understand the class aspect of the society they sought to change. They missed, in his view, how class changes had to be part of the revolutionary agenda if the agenda were to be accomplished. Thus he set to work to define what he meant by class and to specify the mutual overdetermination of class and nonclass aspects of the society to be changed: capitalism. In our view, Marx only began that project; it remains a key task today. The social changes we want still include the class changes upon which Marx focused in commencing his overdeterminist social analysis. So it remains to carry forward Marx's project and for many of the same basic reasons that prompted his beginning. We intend the subsequent chapters of this book to contribute to carrying this forward.

For us, Marxian theory rejects both the conventional pro- and anti-economic-determinist positions in the traditional debate in favor of an altogether different formulation of both the object of the theory and its method of analyzing this object. Our resolution of the debate consists in showing that it poses a question of essential determination that has no place in what we understand as Marxian theory, although it does within alternative theories. Thus, our initial resolution implies that instead of continuing the unsettled and unsettling economic determinism debate, the task for Marxian theory is to disengage from it critically and to renew Marxian social analyses on a different theoretical basis.

Readings of Althusser

Our initial resolution is proposed with full recognition and acknowledgment of its dependence upon the traditional Marxian tendencies we oppose and upon the theoretical formulations discussed earlier in this chapter. Both produced analyses that, in different ways, complexly provoked and made possible Althusser's breakthrough in reformulating Marxian epistemology and social theory. Our development of Marxian theory is in turn deeply indebted to our particular reading of Althusser's work.

Our reading poses the question of alternative readings of Althusser involving critical attacks upon his view of knowledge and society. One theme is that Althusser's work is informed by a rationalist epistemology. Despite his repeated disclaimers, his work is understood to be part of that French

structuralist school in which mental manipulation of elegant models of social structures captures the essence of a reality conceived as independent of
thought. For the more common humanist critique, the key Althusserian
summary concept of "process without a subject" represents the hated
structuralist thesis understood to leave no theoretical space for intentional
human action or free will: human beings are mere recipients, "bearers," of
specified effects produced by changing structures. As noted, the confusion
here is between (human) subjects *in* and *of* history. Althusser rejects the
latter but not the former. Althusser seeks to theorize human subjects as
overdetermined *in* society and thereby actively producing in turn their
effects. However, he rejects notions of subjects or intersubjectivity as the
cause, origin, telos, or logic *of* history and society: "What is at stake here
is something quite different: the *theoretical* pretensions of the humanist
conception to explain society and history."

> This is to suppose that social relations are relations which only in-
> volve *men*, whereas actually they also involve *things*. . . . Naturally,
> human individuals are parties to this relation, therefore active, but
> first of all in so far as they are held within it.[164]

Of course in Althusser's work one can find evidence of a structuralist
approach, of a rationalist epistemology, of economic determinism, of empiricism, and even of theoretical humanist traces. The rejection of the traditional epistemological terrain by Althusser does not necessarily imply that
his work bears no trace of the positions from which he distances himself.
To employ the concept of overdetermination is to understand that the activity of Althusser is constituted by new theoretical developments as well
as by those developments he rejects, by inconsistencies, by polemical arguments, and by political and economic developments comprising the social totality in which he exists. Such is the case with all thinking, be it
involved with Marxian epistemology, psychoanalytic theory, mathematical
reasoning, or anything else. It is, of course, possible to imagine and expect
that Althusser or Marx or any human being could be free from all such
factors, could and should be capable of expressing one conceptual framework purely and exclusively across voluminous writings. However, that
amounts to thinking within a non-Marxian framework, to be forever searching for the absolute truth.

Yet to read Althusser's work from an alternative position to ours (i.e., a
nonclass, non-overdeterminationist position) is to read each structuralist,
rationalist slip of his as the essence of his work. Even if points of initial
agreement across alternative readings are discovered, when given their
full, elaborated meanings within the alternative positions, they turn out to
be points of disagreement. Indeed, to affirm that either a particular critique
directed against Althusser or a contribution of his could or should be con-

vincing to any "reasonable observer" is equivalent to affirming the existence of textual passages or facts to whose intertheoretic truths all (reasonable observers) may appeal.

Overdetermined positions juxtaposed against each other—this is what we understand to be the nature of theoretical criticism, the synonym of theoretical struggle. No doubt such an understanding is unsettling to those who are epistemologically comfortable with the conviction that a logical, analytically sound, unbiased critique should persuade any reader bright enough to understand it. For them our understanding is equivalent to accepting as logical the bizarre and the outlandish. But these words themselves, the very meaning of them, only exist within and through those overdetermined discourses that deploy them.

Our reading of Althusser's contributions bears some considerable resemblance to one other particular and close reading, which has, however, led its proponents to a development of Marxian theory very different from our own. Hindess and Hirst and their associates "settle their accounts" with Althusser, whose importance they acknowledge, very differently from the way we do.[165]

Therefore, we propose here to "settle accounts" with Hindess and Hirst. This is necessary because their reading, like that of others, misses what we see as Althusser's greatest accomplishments. It is appropriate to consider their critique of Althusser since it finds him to be essentialist in epistemology (rationalist) and in social theory (economic determinist), and since it must then follow that Althusser offers no resolution of the traditional Marxian economic determinism debates of the sort we have constructed from his work. Finally, our critical differentiation from Hindess and Hirst, whose importance to our work we recognize, will hopefully preclude readers from assimilating our work to theirs while demonstrating anew the specific difference of the approach taken in this book.

To a degree, Hindess and Hirst propound lines of argument quite like our formulations: essentialist theories both of knowledge and of society are rejected. However, in contradistinction to our argument, they pronounce Althusser's work to be basically essentialist, to express a rationalist and determinist position. Hindess and Hirst thus offer a position they distinguish from that of Althusser and indeed from that of Marx.[166] To their credit, they pursue the logic of their position on Althusser and so discover the work of Marx (most importantly *Capital*) to be likewise essentialist at its most basic level. Like Althusser's writings, Marx's too are found to suffer from a rationalist epistemology and a determinist view of society. It is then this particular contradiction—significant similarity to our theoretical position, yet just as significant difference—that requires us to examine their critique against Althusser.

The critique of Althusser (and to a large degree of Marx as well) presented by Hindess and Hirst flows directly from a basic thrust of their works: the rejection of epistemology as such. For them, *all* forms of epistemology must involve a conceptual dichotemization—a gap—between thinking and a reality conceived to be independent of thought. In their definition, any epistemological standpoint must then posit a necessary relationship to bridge, via some correspondence, the so-conceived gap. Since in their view all forms of epistemology must affirm this particular distinction and correspondence, so must any Marxian epistemology, for example, dialectical materialism. As we propose to show, such a view impels Hindess and Hirst to read, understand, and criticize in both Althusser and Marx a rationalist epistemological standpoint. Once their initial premise is granted, the logic of their critique is sound.

There is a striking affinity among Hindess and Hirst's views on the nature and consequences of rationalist and empiricist approaches in Marxism, the position we advance, and Althusser's views on non-Marxian epistemology.[167] The several works of Hindess and Hirst provide a superb critical evaluation of rationalist and empiricist forms of epistemology and their relation to different theories of society. Especially noteworthy is their critical study of the theoretical role of economism in Marxism. They also offer an alternative approach to developing a theory of society that we find particularly fruitful for Marxian work. They do not, however, make explicit the theory of knowledge informing their approach, since all theories of knowledge are presumed to imply an "inescapable dogmatism that is entailed in the epistemological project itself."[168]

In Hindess and Hirst there exists no theoretical place for those concepts of overdetermination, contradiction, the Marxian dialectic, and the epistemological break of Marx that receive elaboration by Althusser and in our work. Instead, Hindess and Hirst see in this work a continuation of certain pre-Marxist rationalist traditions. They literally cannot entertain the possibility of a distinct Marxian epistemology that is neither empiricist nor rationalist; they cannot see in dialectical materialism such an epistemological standpoint as Althusser can and we do.

The work of Hindess and Hirst offers a classic example of the significant consequences of one's epistemological position upon any form of theoretical endeavor. Since they produce a knowledge of Marxism with a basic thesis that *all* epistemology posits first a distinction and then a correlation between thinking and being, it must follow that they discover either empiricism or rationalism or complex combinations of both in *any discourse claiming any epistemology,* Marxism included. No Marxian or non-Marxian discourse can offer any "epistemological solution" to their posed epistemological dilemma of the distinction/correlation couple since epistemology as such is defined (and thus in their view forevermore dogmatized) as starting with such a couple. For Hindess and Hirst the only acceptable "solution" is the rejection of epistemology per se. This is perhaps their key discovered truth. It also has significant consequences for their understanding of the Althusserian contribution to Marxism, to its theory and politics.

What they have accomplished, then, is a simple but brilliant conflation between particular epistemological positions that posit distinctions between thinking and being and epistemology as such. The former positions certainly may be rejected from a Marxian epistemological position as we have shown. However, a Marxian position need not and, we think, cannot reject epistemological discourse per se. Dialectical materialism is the particular Marxian formulation of the relationship of thinking to the social totality. It is the Marxian position on epistemological discourse, the Marxian epistemological standpoint. The radically different non-Marxian epistemological standpoints affirming the dichotomy/correlation couple have been and still are the dominant philosophical standpoints inside and outside the Marxian tradition. It is their predominance and their social consequences that require the Marxian theory we elaborate to distance itself from them by developing its particular Marxian epistemology.

The key here is *not* epistemology as such, but rather different approaches to the epistemological enterprise. Rather than emphasizing different epistemological truths existing within and through different discourses, Hindess and Hirst reject the epistemological enterprise as such. They thereby establish their particular truth of the dogmatism of the whole enterprise, that is, of all alternative epistemological standpoints, including Marxism. But *their* truth seems to become *the* truth; differences seem to give way to an absolute. Their notion of epistemology comes to exist independent of its being conceived in their conceptual framework. It thus provides them with a new standard of validation to which all discourses can be compared. When Hindess and Hirst use terms such as *indefensible dogmatism, impossible,* and *no rational debate* to refer to different epistemological positions or to the epistemological enterprise itself, they evidently believe that they have discovered a truth that does indeed transcend all discourses.[169] And that is certainly not Althusser's position nor ours.

For Hindess and Hirst, Althusser's work is a classic example of a rationalist approach within Marxism since it rejects empiricism but not epistemology per se. Hence, for them it offers little in the way of solution to the dilemma of the Marxian determination debates posed in this chapter. In fact, their argument suggests that the theoretical role of the concept of determination in the last instance in Althusser's work only leads us back to economism. Let us explore that argument.

Marxists have long been reading and interpreting rather differently the few specific pages Marx ever wrote concentrating on his method. One object of this book is to present our understanding of this method as well as to demonstrate the different theoretical and political consequences of different readings and interpretations. Hindess and Hirst *read* those pages of Marx and Althusser's elaborations of them as formulating a rationalist enterprise. This particular reading informs all of their subsequent arguments. Of course, this position must be juxtaposed against our argument concerning Marxian dialectics, that is, overdetermination, to appreciate the significant gap between their approach and ours.

Hindess and Hirst especially focus on the phrase "appropriation of the concrete in thought" as signaling the rationalist presumption that the essence of the concrete-real, conceived to be independent of thought, can be captured and expressed in thought.[170] They determine that the particular logic of Althusserian (and Marxian) theory is inextricably intertwined with its, for them, rationalist and hence essentialist epistemological standpoint. They then pose the question: What exactly is the logic or causal order of Marxian theory as elaborated by Althusser that presumes to capture the essential truth of the concrete-real?

They answer that Marxian theory structures its nonepistemological concepts like its epistemological concepts, namely, in an essentialist manner: it privileges certain concepts as the essences of other concepts, which then function as the phenomenal form of these privileged concepts. For them the essence in the Marxian theory of society as elaborated by Althusser is the economy or mode of production, determinant in the last instance. Rather than focusing on the concept of overdetermination, which Hindess and Hirst read as of no importance, they read in Marxism a traditional notion of causation in which certain *distinct* entities determine (albeit complexly) others: economy determines (is essence of) society. For them the essentialism of Althusser and Marx are twofold: in their epistemology and social theory. It lies in their rationalist view that their theory captures (is) the essence of society, of an entity conceived to be independent of thought. Second, it lies in their economic determinism.

Hindess and Hirst themselves connect their rejection of *all* epistemologies as necessarily essentialist (rationalist or empiricist) to their rejection of *all* concepts of the social totality as necessarily essentialist (determinist in one way or another):

> But what I and my co-authors are arguing for is the rejection of the concept of totality itself, and, therefore the rejection of the problems of the relations of the political, economic and other "instances" in terms of hierarchy of causal effectivity, relative autonomy, etc.[171]

This sentence shows that these writers literally cannot imagine a concept of the social totality that is not conventionally determinist, having one or another determining essence. This follows from their lack, because they could not read it in Althusser, of his concept of overdetermination or a development of it such as ours.

A key political accompaniment to their critique of epistemology is their effort to develop a new "socialist" strategy freed of traditional Marxian dogmatism, whether in the form of the Althusserian rationalism or the empiricism so prevalent in British and American radicalism. For Hindess and Hirst, the mode of production functions as traditional Marxism's essence whose necessary effects are the various other aspects of the social totality. Thus, they argue, political conflict within a social formation would be understood within traditional Marxism as a complex expression of the mode of production. Here class struggle is reduced to merely its economic aspect, thereby allowing no theoretical or political space for noneconomic effectivity within that struggle. In reaction against this, Hindess and Hirst, like so many others, offer a nonessentialist, "nondogmatic" approach that does indeed allow politics and culture to have their own specific effectivity not reducible to some economic essence. For them, no existing Marxian theory allows this.

The concept of overdetermination, for Althusser as for us, precisely negates the possibility of forms of essentialism in Marxism. It is the key concept shaping the difference and distance between Althusser and the empiricist, rationalist, and determinist currents in the Marxian tradition. Indeed, theoretical commitment to overdetermination means that no concept in the structure of the discourse is understood as an entity from which other entities can be deduced or derived as necessary effects. Instead, *each* concept is a condition, never an essence, of the others' existence. If so, then the critique that Hindess and Hirst levied at Althusser or Marx cannot be sustained from what we have defined as the dialectical materialist (overdeterminationist) position.[172] The latter affirms that each and every concept is never an essence or a predetermined given in the discursive logic, and is subject to revision the moment the theoretical process is posited. Our position also precludes a rationalist epistemological standpoint since no one among the many constituents of the social totality, such as one theory (e.g., the Marxist), can be the essence, the determinant, the truth of the totality. Rather, the set of contesting theories comprises one contradictory, constituent aspect of the overdetermined social totality.

Why might Hindess and Hirst have difficulty with our formulation of Marxian theory? After all, the concept of overdetermination can be deployed to produce a profoundly antideterminist solution of the long economic determinism debate within Marxism. The answer rests with the rejection by Hindess and Hirst of epistemology, which rules out their understanding of the Althusserian concept of overdetermination. Paradoxically, their very rejection of epistemology blocks them epistemologically from grasping Althusser's key philosophical contribution. Their own departure from Marxism, as we understand it, illustrates the consequences for social theory of positions taken on epistemology.

Hindess and Hirst's criticism of Althusser as summarized here bears an ironic resemblance to that advanced by E. P. Thompson and discussed in the previous chapter. Both critiques understand Althusser to have specified a rationalist approach in which the logic of the theory reveals or captures the essence of a reality conceived to be independent of thought. Both critiques operate with the premise that Althusser has an epistemological position and that such a position *must* be either empiricist or rationalist since, by the definition of epistemology common to both, no other epistemological alternative is conceivable. Althusser's withering attack upon empiricism then leads both to the conclusion that Althusser's must be a more or less classical rationalist epistemological position. Hence they both attack him from the vantage point of such a conclusion. Interestingly, Hindess and Hirst read Marx essentially as a rationalist, where Thompson reads him approvingly as an empiricist. Thereby, each side attributes to Marx one or the other classical position in epistemology. Neither imagines that Marx made an epistemological break of just the sort Althusser sought to specify and recall to Marxists' attention.

Hindess and Hirst have no sympathy with the empiricism informing Thompson's view of society, even though they all share similar conclusions concerning Althusser's rationalism. From the standpoint of Hindess and Hirst's rejection of epistemology, Althusser may be seen as simply turning Thompson on his head, thereby substituting a crude idealism for an even cruder materialism.

For us, what is common to both of these critical views is far more significant than their differences. Simply put, Thompson, as well as Hindess and Hirst, does not accept the epistemological break of Marx as elaborated by Althusser. This is the key point. Althusser begins his approach to Marx with a discussion of this epistemological break. To miss or reject this point is to accept implicitly or explicitly an alternative position. Thus, Thompson, Hindess, and Hirst fall into the same camp despite their particular differences. By not accepting or understanding the concept of overdetermination, they remain mired within the largely sterile arguments concerning idealism versus materialism, rationalism versus empiricism that have plagued Marxism for over one hundred years and traditional philosophy for many hundreds of years more. For Hindess and Hirst, in particular, this is an ironic negation of the very theoretical and political task they initially set for themselves.

Postscript: Parable of Hindess and Hirst

Let us imagine a theoretical odyssey. This is a story of two folks starting out with an understanding of the world that is informed by a rationalist approach. From this position they reject the empiricism so prevalent in the theoretical work with which they are confronted. Now, events change. The particular social turmoil of the 1960s produces those changed political and theoretical conditions that challenge their rationalist position. In particular, the often-heard cry of the 1960s New Left to"be relevant" makes them acutely uncomfortable with their seemingly nonrelevant and thus nonleftist approach. Our two folks question their notion of their rationalistically conceived truth of this rapidly changing world. They ask How do we know that the conceptual framework within which we operate is true? They ask further Is our conceptual framework a complex part of the very oppression with which we are confronted and against which we struggle? If the latter question has an affirmative answer, then that struggle against oppression requires its concomitant theoretical struggle against that very framework. So in relation to events and to a new, politically healthy doubting of existing theoretical approaches, including their own, they begin a quest, a search for a theory that will be relevant to current struggles and secure in its objective of ending oppression. So ends the first part of this odyssey.

The second part beings with the quest. Their first book (*Pre-Capitalist Modes of Production*) is in fact an empirical testing of alternate frameworks. It indeed discovers via Althusser a "coherent" and "pertinent" approach in Marxian theory, as appropriately modified. But the initial modification does not go far enough for them: their break with Althusserian and thus their own rationalism is not complete. On the high road of truth seeking, where concepts of coherence and pertinence point the way, they reexamine their first book and discover there, perhaps to their chagrin if not political horror, both rationalism and empiricism. The Marxian concept of determination in the last instance, which they had used, is recognized as an index of rationalism (which they had rejected). Their use of case studies to prove the validity of last-instance determinism is in effect empiricism (also rejected). Their second book (*Mode of Production and Social Formation*) critically reviews their first. Our two folks confront their own swinging back and forth, to and from rationalism and empiricism, never quite able to escape the inevitable dogmatism of the swing. They finally come to see the dogmatism and swinging as inherent in the epistemological enterprise as such. They conclude, in their second book—which is the turning point in their quest—that their own position on epistemology per se is the problem.

The new and correct answer to the demand of relevance and ending oppression is the rejection of all epistemologies. They must reject their old rationalism as influenced by that of Althusser and Marx. They must also reject the empiricism they had foolishly slipped into in reaction against rationalism. These rejections move them onto the true high road of finding a coherent and relevant approach to social life, to those economic and political and cultural struggles that characterize that life. Indeed, it is the only way to "socialism," now embraced. Their quest continues, but despite having put Marx to rest, he returns as their ghost, never really present in, but continually haunting their new texts (*Marx's Capital and Capitalism Today,* vols. 1 and 2).

There is always a final lesson to be learned from a parable. Our two folks' rejection of epistemology as a dogmatic enterprise puts them in the awkward company of many contemporary analytical philosophers, on the rather basic question of thinking about thinking. As noted in our previous chapter, analytical philosophy ultimately rejects or at best is indifferent to epistemology. This follows from its basic pragmatism grounded in empiricism. Indeed, American social scientists, radical or not, generally think of the epistemological dimension of all theory, if they think of it all, in terms of a methodological itch to be scratched, but not worth more effort than that. This, however, is not true of our two folks. They have thought long and hard, and more often than not rather brilliantly, about epistemology and its consequences. But then what is the moral of the Hindess and Hirst odyssey? Simply put, it is: To seek the Truth is to find it; but beware of the company for they are you.

3

A Marxian Theory of Classes

One distinguishing characteristic of the Marxian theory at work in this book is its entry-point concept of class. The theory organizes the social theory it elaborates by focusing upon the relationships between class and nonclass aspects of society. It presumes that these relationships are not essentialist; rather, all aspects of society are approached as distinct processes such that each is overdetermined by all the others. This presumption and approach are other distinguishing characteristics of our understanding of Marxian theory.

Still another distinguishing characteristic lies in the particular concept of class that is our entry point into social analysis. Our premise is not only that several markedly different concepts of class exist within the Marxian tradition. We share Raymond Williams's view that these different concepts appear in "a whole range of contemporary discussion and controversy . . . usually without clear distinction."[1] We also share the premise of other Marxists that theoretical struggle over the concept of class is central to the development of Marxian theory and political practice.[2] The widespread deployment in Marxian literature of terms such as *class, working class,* and *capitalist class* usually proceeds as if "their significance is universally familiar and that everyone indeed possesses their notion, [and] rather looks like an attempt to dispense with the only important matter, which is just to give this notion."[3] Our particular reading of Marx's theory of class, conditioned by the conceptualization of Marxian epistemology developed in the previous chapters, results in concepts of class, working class, and capitalist class that differ sharply from the predominant conceptualizations within the Marxian tradition.

Across the range of Marx's writings, the term *class* is used in different ways. In his concrete historical writings, such as *The Eighteenth Brumaire of Louis Bonaparte* and *The Civil Wars in France,* and in political documents such as *The Communist Manifesto,* Marx uses *class* to refer to more or less unified groups of people in social conflict. These groups are sometimes understood as objective economic categories defined typically in terms of property criteria. However, these groups are often defined in more subjective terms such that a class exists only if and when persons are conscious of common interests and unify themselves in actual social struggles against others. Beyond the ambiguous intermingling of these different conceptions of class in Marx's writings (and in the Marxian tradition noted by Williams), there is a tension between them. Marxian debates over these concepts have sharp political overtones. If a class is constituted by a position in a property relation, is it then to be also constituted by a self-conscious position within a social conflict? Are these two distinct ways of constituting and hence defining class, or is one reducible to the other? The tension between these concepts has been expressed in the Marxian tradition in the Hegelian terms of a difference between a class-in-itself and a class-for-itself, which implies various political conclusions.[4] In any case, Marx and many Marxists since have worked with concepts of classes as actual, distinct groups of persons defined objectively, subjectively, or by various combinations of references to both criteria.

However, the tensions and certain confusions in Marxian discussions of class are not only a matter of more or less objective versus subjective definitions. More important to us is the problem that Marx also articulated a concept of class that does not refer to a group of persons at all, but rather to one particular social process among the many that comprise social life.[5] In Marx's major theoretical formulations such as *Capital, Theories of Surplus Value,* and *Grundrisse,* he develops a concept of class that refers to a process of producing surplus labor. The analysis of this process and its conditions of existence is Marx's major object in these works. Individuals and groups are then approached by Marx only partially, "only in so far as they are the personifications" of aspects or "moments" of the class process.[6] Individuals and groups are, as Marx fully acknowledges, involved in all sorts of other, non-class processes of social life and hence "personify" them as well.

Marx's theory of class as a process and his self-consciously limited approach to individuals as differing "personifications" of this process suggest that classes not be considered as actual groups of persons. To equate persons with class amounts to reducing the many different natural and social processes constituting persons to only one. Such reduction is unacceptable if we are to adhere to the concept of overdetermination as central to Marxian theory. Moreover, as we shall show in this chapter, individuals typically participate in more than one kind of class process and their interests and alliances with others are determined, or rather overdetermined, by all the processes of social life, not only the various kinds of class processes.

The works of Marx and the Marxian theoretical tradition present, then, a complexity: debates and analyses deploying differing, inadequately distinguished, and by no means consistent concepts of class that play central roles in their respective arguments.[7] We enter this discussion determined not only to distinguish the different concepts of class within the Marxian tradition but also to elaborate one concept into a critique of the others. Class is for us the concept of a particular social process. Marxian class analysis is then the theorization of the overdetermination of that social process, that is, its interaction with all the other processes that comprise its conditions of existence.

As with any serious attention to Marx's theory, our reading must articulate an explanation for our adherence to one concept of class in Marx's work when we acknowledge the existence of others in that work. This is a matter of interpretation, of a critical reading. Our explanation, elaborated in the conclusion to this chapter, lies in our understanding of Marx's references to classes qua groups of persons as a kind of polemical shorthand. They comprise Marx's translations of a complex theory into strategical and tactical sketches of contemporary historical situations. We do not find in these sketches an acceptable theoretically developed conceptualization of class, that is, one consistent with other basic concepts of Marxian theory (overdetermination, contradiction, etc.). However, elsewhere in Marx, especially in the works of his later theoretical maturity, we do find a complex, considerably developed theory of class as a social process. We build upon that theory.

Our approach renders a Marxian theory of class uniquely capable of incorporating and extending the complex multiclass analysis of capitalism Marx began in volumes 2 and 3 of *Capital* and the parallel sections of *Theories of Surplus Value*.[8] The result, as we will show, is a conceptualization of Marxian class analysis different not only from the predominant theories of class within the Marxian tradition, but also from the major dissenting theories in that tradition as well as from the major non-Marxian conceptualizations of class. In chapters 4 and 5 we delineate certain specific consequences of our theory in terms of the resulting analysis of enterprise and state within a capitalist social formation.

Different Theories of Class

Concepts of class are central to Marxian theory and hence to Marxian analyses of concrete social situations. Within the Marxian tradition, the different readings of Marx's own notions of class are closely linked to different interpretations and applications of those notions. While one general orientation has prevailed in that tradition, recently some influential Marxian formulations have advanced a basic criticism of it as well as of Marx's notions of class, and they offer alternatives. We sympathize with the view that traditional Marxian notions of class are generally vague and inadequate. As for Marx's own work, notwithstanding its ambiguities, it does contain a complex, carefully specified concept of classes which stands, we believe, as a critique both of the traditional Marxian theory of class and of the recent efforts to remedy its vagueness and inadequacies.

Most Marxists have traditionally attributed to Marx a dichotomous theory of class, that is, a theory that societies are predominantly characterized by two opposing classes understood as actual social groups. Thus the Marxian tradition works with a prevalent notion of capitalism, feudalism, and slavery, for example, as societies (or "modes of production") predominantly characterized by the class oppositions of capitalists-workers, landlords-serfs, and masters-slaves, respectively. Marx's reference to capitalism in *The Communist Manifesto* is the most frequently cited support for the traditional view: "Society as a whole is more and more splitting up into two great hostile camps, into two great classes directly facing each other— bourgeoisie and proletariat." When distinctions are drawn between social formations and modes of production, the former are typically viewed as comprising sets of modes of production in which one mode dominates the others. Each such mode comprises a distinct two-class opposition. History is then periodized according to which particular dichotomous opposition, that is, which mode, dominated the others. Our concern is to criticize the conceptualization of mode and formation in terms of single or multiple two-class oppositions. Our critique extends as well to the typical non-Marxian attributions to Marx of a similar dichotomous theory of class.[9]

There are some minor variations on the theme that Marx's is a "two-class model." Many Marxian writers have acknowledged that groups designated as "peasants" or as a "petty bourgeoisie" of craftspeople or other self-employed producers of commodities exist as classes outside of the basic two in capitalism, namely, workers and capitalists. But their existence is traditionally dismissed or de-emphasized on the grounds of an intrinsic polarization of society and social change around two primary classes—workers and capitalists.[10] The Marxian tradition and Marx himself are thus widely understood to mean by the term *class analysis* an approach characterized by this basic focus on two-class sets.

Recent Marxian critics of the traditional two-class focus share a concern to define and emphasize the importance of additional classes in capitalism beyond the workers and capitalists. Despite some differences among them, their common goal is to elaborate a Marxian social theory built upon a complex conceptualization of several classes. One influential writer, Nicos Poulantzas, works with a complex concept of class "places" as distinguished from class "positions."[11] His "places" exist at each of three levels of society: economic, political, and ideological. At each level there is a dichotomy between the dominating and the dominated. In the case of capitalism, the capitalists are dominant at each level, and the proletarians are dominated at each. For Poulantzas, these two classes present no analytical problem. However, they strike him as insufficient to carry out an adequate class analysis of capitalism. Other groupings exist that are not similarly "placed" at each level, that is, they are dominant in some while being dominated in others. Poulantzas conceptualizes these as old and new petty bourgeoisie, classes beyond the basic two of that predominant Marxian tradition he criticizes. Poulantzas emphasizes the importance of these extra classes in terms of Marxian theory and practical politics. The thrust of Poulantzas's work is to produce a Marxian analysis of contemporary capitalism by means of his concepts of several class places whose occupants varyingly take the opposed class "positions" in actual social conflicts.

From an appreciative critique of Poulantzas, Erik Olin Wright derives a more complex conceptualization of contemporary classes.[12] Wright has three basic classes: bourgeoisie, proletariat, and petty bourgeoisie; however, he adds three more, which he terms "contradictory class locations," situated structurally among the first three. In addition he also specifies class locations "which are not directly defined by the social relations of production"; these include housewives, students, and others.[13] Reworking an idea of C. Wright Mills, Barbara and John Ehrenreich theorize in terms of four basic classes: workers, capitalists, petty bourgeoisie, and an intermediate group, the "professional-managerial class," whose importance their work underscores.[14]

A second theme common to many recent critics is a focus upon power or dominance relations among persons. Some of these critics redefine class in terms of those relations but not only at the economic level, which they criticize as the unacceptably exclusive concern of the Marxian tradition. For these critics, class relations exist also at the political and ideological levels: wherever interpersonal dominance relations occur.[15] A variant of this theme does not go so far as to collapse class and dominance into identity; rather dominance is treated as the "primary concept" of social relations, and class is demoted to merely the term for the economic locus of dominance that occurs elsewhere in society as well.[16] All these critics see Marx and Marxism as focused too narrowly upon merely economics and two classes. The critics reconceptualize classes to include dominance relations at the other, noneconomic social levels. This permits them to theorize multiple classes, incorporating the contradictions among the several levels, for example, "professional-managerial class," "new middle class," "new working class," and so forth.

The theoretical tendency unifying these critics seeks to displace an economic concept of classes in favor of a political concept of interpersonal relations of dominance as the essential determinant of social change. Here we encounter again the essentialist terrain of Marxian debates: those who make economic classes the essence of social change are criticized by those who counterpose dominance among persons as essence. The critics proudly claim that their approach avoids economic determinism and simplistic two-class models. The loyalists defending economic determinism denounce as un-Marxian both the substitution of political for economic class analysis and the generation of ever more new classes, which blunts the sharp edge of Marxism.

What we earlier termed the Engels middle ground between contesting essentialist positions in the Marxian debate over economic determinism has its analog in the debate over class. Among both critics and loyalists in the latter debate, some have resorted to an approach characterized by heavy reliance upon a notion of "class fractions." [17] In this approach, a more or less conventional affirmation of a two-class model precedes intense analytical interest in all sorts of divisions within both classes. Thus, capitalists, it turns out, exhibit all manner of divisions among themselves; they differ according to their financial connections, capital intensities, size, monopoly power, foreign trade dependence, regional concentration, dependence on state orders or policies, composition of labor forces, personal political allegiances, and so forth. Workers similarly exhibit sexual, racial, ethnic, regional, religious, age, skill-level, and other divisions, such as degrees of community respect. The fractions defined by such economic and/or noneconomic divisions within both classes allow these Marxian writers to explain complex alignments in actual social conflicts when they cannot be explained as struggle between the two classes. This approach permits its devotees to move between simple dichotomous class analysis and class-fraction analysis according to their preference as to which essence is determinate in an actual social conflict. Here economics, there politics, there culture—working either through class or through class fraction—determine the contours and outcomes of social change. Essentialism remains, but its practitioners retain their option to designate different essences in different analytical situations.

Our formulation rejects the common essentialist terrain of the debaters—loyalists, critics, and " class fractionists"—over the proper concept of class and its connection to social change. As we have argued, we do not read Marx as an essentialist. Thus neither economic concepts of class nor concepts of interpersonal dominance or property function in Marxian theory as essences of social change. Rather, a goal of Marxian theory is to explore the relations among the class processes, the processes of interpersonal domination, and the processes of property ownership as conditions of one another's existence. No process is the essence of the others, nor are they collapsible into one another. Nor, finally, do the overdetermined relations of class, interpersonal domination, and property support any claim that the essence of society is some two-class juxtaposition. Marx directly dismissed such claims: "society would be reduced (economically) to the simple contradiction between capital and wage-labour, a simplification." [18]

The method of Marxian theory calls for constructing the "connecting links" between abstract concepts of class as process and the concrete conjunctures of social relationships, social conflicts, and social change. [19] This method does not collapse these links into the simplistic view that such relationships, conflicts, and change are mere phenomena of classes as the ultimate, last instance or final determinant. Yet none of the Marxists debating class has explored the question: is it possible Marx formulated a theory of class that can delineate a relationship (the "connecting link") among power, property relations, surplus labor production, and social conflicts that is not economic determinist, not otherwise essentialist, and not limited to a two-class approach?

Our purpose here is not to examine critiques of traditional Marxian class theory. Rather, we mention them to set the basis for our reading of how very differently Marx conceptualizes social classes. In our view, Marx's concepts provide the basis for a complex class analysis that is different from the dichotomous theory of traditional Marxism and from the kinds of alternative theory exemplified by the authors mentioned above. In any case, Marx's concepts of classes merit far more careful and detailed discussion than any of these critics devoted to them. Not surprisingly, the complex class analysis we find in Marx is far more consistently grounded in his value theory than are the alternative formulations of the critics. In subsequent chapters, we indicate some of its specific analytical capacities as compared to those alternative formulations.

Class Process and Social Relationships

As we read it, Marx's furthest development of the concept of class holds it to be one distinct process among the many that constitute social life. The class process is that "in which unpaid surplus-labor is pumped out of direct producers," or, in other of Marx's usages, "extracted" or "appropriated" from the direct producers. [20] To clarify the definition of class as a particular social process requires that Marx specify what he means by surplus labor. He does this by his often-repeated distinction between necessary and surplus labor. [21] The former is the quantity of labor time necessary to produce the consumables customarily required by the direct producer to keep working. Surplus labor then is the further, the *extra* time of labor the direct producer performs beyond the necessary labor. *Necessary* and *surplus* are historically variable quantities: they are overdetermined. [22]

Thus, where commodity production is involved, Marx speaks of surplus labor as the creation of "unpaid value" since the direct producer has its fruits taken from him or her without receiving anything in return.[23] Also in this sense Marx refers to wages as the "price of *necessary labor*" and to industrial profit "as appropriation of other people's labour" (meaning their surplus labor).[24]

Marx shows his commitment to the class process as the entry point and focus of his social theory in the following sort of summary formulation:

> The essential difference between the various economic forms of society, between, for instance, a society based on slave labour, and one based on wage-labour, lies only in the mode in which this surplus labour is in each case extracted from the actual producer, the labourer.[25]

Through such formulations, Marx distinguishes his from alternative social theories.

This class process is different from all the other distinct processes comprising social life, including both other economic and noneconomic processes. As we argued in earlier chapters, these include both natural processes such as breathing, photosynthesis, and rainfall, and social processes such as thinking, speaking, voting, and manual labor. In our reading, Marxian theory has a particular way of conceiving how these processes actually occur and interact in constituting society: overdetermination. The class process, like any and every particular social process, has no existence other than as the site of the converging influences exerted by all the nonclass processes. All the other processes that combine to overdetermine it are its "conditions of existence."[26] Thus, the conditions of existence of the class process are all the non-class processes in the social totality without whose particular characteristics and interactions the class process could not and would not exist. In turn, the class process is itself one condition of existence of each nonclass process.

In this Marxian conceptualization, distinct social processes never exist alone; they do not occur by themselves. Rather they occur in groups, in subsets of the social totality of processes. This means that while each is influenced, effected by *all* others, it occurs socially in particular groupings of specific *subsets* of social processes. To make this basic point in other terms, the concept of a social process is an analytical device pinpointing the constituent aspects of social relationships, social practices. It is the basic element of Marxian social analysis. *Concrete social relationships or practices are understood, defined as particular subsets of social processes; "aspect" and "process" are conceptualized as synonyms, as the elements comprising social relationships and practices.*

For example, while the class process is overdetermined by all other processes, it typically occurs together with—within social relationships or practices that include—processes of labor transforming nature, processes of exerting and obeying authority among persons, processes of giving and gaining access to property, and processes of language. The social relationship or practice discussed here, which we term the work relationship, has its constituent social processes overdetermined by all other processes, but the relationship itself is a subset of them. By contrast, such social processes as praying or voting or saving money do not typically occur within the same social relationship as the class process, although they participate in the overdetermination of the class process as it does in theirs.

Two people going fishing are involved in a particular social relationship or practice, that is, a subset of processes. This relationship may include or exclude the class process, depending on the social context—that is, the social overdetermination of the relationship. If one of the two receives surplus labor from the other—one is the employer of the other in a capitalist fishing enterprise—then the relationship is a set of processes, including the class process. If instead it is a case of two friends sharing leisure time, the relationship does not include the class process. By contrast, the process of language, speaking, was likely a constituent of both kinds of fishing relationship.

The object of Marxian theory is the specification of the processes and relationships (practices) whose complex aggregate is the social formation, with special focus on the position of the class process in that aggregate.

Classes: Fundamental and Subsumed

Class process is one thing; classes are another. By classes we understand Marx to mean subdivisions among people according to the particular positions they occupy in the class process, to the precise ways in which they "personify" class processes. People participate in class processes; they thereby occupy class positions. Some people perform necessary and surplus labor—Marx's "direct producers"—while others extract or appropriate surplus labor. This conceptualization of class is complex. First, an individual can and typically does occupy more than one class position and so becomes a member of more than one class.[27] Second, Marx specifies more than the two class positions defined as the performers and extractors of surplus labor.

As we have noted, Marx differentiates the two-class groupings of performers and extractors of surplus labor according to the *forms* in which the surplus labor is performed. Different forms coexist in varying combinations across human history. Marx uses *primitive communist, slave, feudal,*

ancient, capitalist, and other differentiations to establish what he terms the
"fundamental classes" of history.[28] Their fundamentality consists in their
place in Marx's theoretical focus and exposition and not, given the antiessentialism of Marxian theory, in any notion that they function as "last
instance," final determinants of social change.

The complexity of Marx's concept of class also emerges in the process
of applying it to social analysis. Society is understood as comprising different fundamental class processes and hence different sets of fundamental
classes at any historical moment. Indeed, Marx prefers the term *social formation* to *society* chiefly to underscore its conceptualization as a formation, an ever-changing structure of different forms of the fundamental class
processes and the individuals who participate in them, the fundamental
classes. The adjective *fundamental* prepares the way to announce another
sort of class process and hence another set of classes. We call these the
subsumed class process and the subsumed classes. They represent our generalization of Marx's analysis in *Capital,* volume 3, of the capitalist form
of the class process, in particular his theorization of classes other than the
industrial capitalist and the productive laborer.

Subsumed classes refers to persons occupying a subsumed class position. Such a position occurs within (is a personification of) a subsumed
class process. It is unlike the fundamental class process because it is neither the production nor appropriation of surplus labor or its products.
Rather, the subsumed class process refers to the distribution of already appropriated surplus labor or its products. The subsumed class process entails two positions: distributor and recipient of already appropriated surplus labor or its products. The existence of the subsumed class process and
all its qualitative and quantitative dimensions is the effect of the interaction
among all the other processes within the social formation. The subsumed
class process and the subsumed classes it defines are overdetermined. It
follows that the subsumed class process participates in the overdetermination of all other social processes, including the fundamental class process.
As Marx sought repeatedly to demonstrate, fundamental and subsumed
class processes are conditions of each other's existences. We intend no implication of a hierarchy of importance in using the terms *fundamental* and
subsumed. Neither class process is more important than the other in shaping
social structure and change. That, of course, follows from this Marxian
theory's commitment to overdetermination.

In the case of the specifically capitalist form of the fundamental class
process, the subsumed class process refers to the distribution of already
appropriated surplus value. As the fundamental class process is the production of surplus value by one class for another, so the subsumed class process is the subsequent distribution of that surplus value to other classes.

The complexity and far-reaching implications of Marx's differentiation between fundamental and subsumed classes have been widely overlooked, notwithstanding his repeated emphasis on that differentiation.

The capitalist directly engaged in production *directly* appropriates the surplus-labour, no matter under what categories he has subsequently to share this surplus-value with the landowner or with the lender of capital.[29]

Surplus-value, therefore, splits up into various parts. Its fragments fall to various categories of persons, and take various forms, independent the one of the other, such as profit, interest, merchants' profit, rent, etc.[30]

[The capitalist] is the person who at first holds the whole surplus-value in his hands no matter how it may be distributed between himself and other people under the names of rent, industrial profit and interest.[31]

Perhaps the clearest formulation of Marx's focus on two different kinds of classes, fundamental and subsumed, appears near the end of *Capital,* volume 2. There Marx aims to prepare the reader for a major goal of the text in volume 3, namely, showing the interaction and interdependence between capitalist fundamental and subsumed classes.

The division of the surplus value—which must always be first in the hands of the industrial capitalist—into various categories, as vehicles of which there appear, aside from the industrial capitalist, the landlord (for ground-rent), the usurer (for interest), etc., furthermore the government and its employees, rentiers, etc.[32]

The subsumed class distributors and recipients of surplus value provide specific conditions of existence of the capitalist fundamental class process. Private owners of land, for example, provide access to the land required for surplus value to be produced and appropriated. To secure such access, a condition of existence of the capitalist fundamental class process, a distribution of surplus value to such landowners must be accomplished: the payment of what Marx, in *Capital,* volume 3, calls capitalist ground rent. Under alternative social conditions, land might not be privately owned. Thus, if land were provided for the performance of the capitalist fundamental class process via a state-run lottery, then access to it would not require a subsumed class process. The process of land ownership participates in overdetermining the existence of a particular subsumed class process.

Similarly, private moneylenders may provide specific conditions of existence of the capitalist fundamental class process, namely, access to quantities of money capital. Under these social conditions, industrial capitalists' access to credit requires that a distribution of surplus value (interest payment) be made to the moneylenders. In Marx's words, "I enable someone else by means of money, etc. to appropriate surplus-value. Thus it is quite in order for me to receive part of this surplus-value." [33] Government, too, provides conditions of existence under certain social conditions, for example, a judicial apparatus for adjudicating and enforcing contractual relations. The existence of the capitalist fundamental class process may then require that a distribution of surplus value to the government be accomplished (in the form of taxes on capitalists). Of course if the government defrayed its judicial costs in other ways, that is, without a tax levy upon surplus value, then it could provide this judicial condition of existence without its requiring a subsumed class distribution.

In general terms, the interaction between the capitalist fundamental class process and all the other processes occurring within any particular social formation will overdetermine which conditions of existence of that fundamental class process require a subsumed class process to exist. Subsumed classes are then the persons occupying the positions of distributors or receivers of the portions of surplus value allocated to secure the provision of those conditions of existence. The overdetermination of both fundamental and subsumed class processes implies that both are contradictory and constantly changing. Marxian theory in general and the rest of this book in particular elaborate a social analysis built upon the overdetermined interaction between fundamental and subsumed classes. Two further examples illustrate the basis of such analysis.

Providing adequate supplies of clean water is a natural condition of existence of all forms of the fundamental class process. Such provision may be accomplished naturally—by rainfall, lakes and rivers, and so forth—and requires no payment to secure it. Here no class process need be involved. If, alternatively, a state apparatus is socially charged to secure the provision of clean water to appropriators of surplus labor, its labor and materials costs may be defrayed by a subsumed class distribution to the state from the appropriators. State officials receiving such a distribution would thereby occupy a subsumed class position.

A third alternative for securing water as a condition of existence of any particular fundamental class process combines a subsumed class payment with a nonclass payment, namely, a commodity purchase. Capitalists buy the water that secures one of their conditions of existence by exchanging money for the commodity water. If and only if water is produced as a commodity will this third alternative be socially available as a means to secure this condition of existence.

This third alternative merits added attention. In *Capital,* volume 1,

Marx repeatedly emphasizes the difference between commodity exchange and the production/appropriation of surplus value. The former is strictly an exchange of values; it is not the site or source of surplus value. Commodity exchange is an economic process, but it is not the fundamental class process or the subsumed class process. When the capitalist *buys* the commodity labor power, this commodity exchange is not the source of surplus value. Rather, "the consumption of labour-power is at one and the same time the production of commodities and of surplus value." [34] Marx sharply distinguishes commodity exchange from the capitalist fundamental class process, his "consumption of labour-power." We propose to further distinguish commodity exchange from the subsumed class process as well. The subsumed class process of distributing appropriated surplus value aims to secure conditions of existence of the capitalist fundamental class process; this subsumed class process need involve no commodity purchase. The latter is a different economic process, a nonclass process. It is, however, possible for both the subsumed class process and the commodity exchange process to be combined, as when appropriated surplus value is distributed by capitalists to purchase commodities as the particular way of securing some condition of existence. Fundamental class, subsumed class, and commodity exchange are three distinct economic processes kept theoretically apart by Marx, notwithstanding his argument that sometimes, under specific historical conditions, they may occur together. In this third alternative, sellers of the water commodity also occupy a subsumed class position: they participate in both the exchange and the subsumed class processes.

Conditions of existence of the capitalist fundamental class process may thus be secured without needing a distribution of surplus value, or they may require a subsumed class process. In the latter case, such a subsumed class distribution of appropriated surplus value may or may not occur together with the separate economic process of commodity exchange.

Another example is the process of educating children for future productive labor. This cultural process is a condition of existence for the reproduction of any form of the fundamental class process, much like the natural process of water provision just discussed. This education process may occur within relationships that include no economic process and hence neither the subsumed class process nor commodity exchange. Thus, children playing together may be involved in relationships that include none of these economic processes but do include processes of education for future productive labor. Alternatively, such education may be provided by a governmental program of free public education. Here the educational process occurs within a social relationship that includes as well the subsumed class process if and when a share (taxes) of appropriated surplus value is distributed to the government for that purpose. Third, the process of educating children for productive labor may be secured by means of commodity exchange, as when education is sold as a service commodity. Here, the educational process occurs within a social relationship that includes as well the commodity exchange process. This relationship could occur when laborers purchase education as a commodity out of their wages or when capitalists buy such commodities for their laborers' families (this last being again a relationship combining a subsumed class process and a commodity exchange process parallel to the purchased water of the previous example). This educational process may occur in all these different kinds of social relationships at the same time, as in the United States today.

Social formations vary from one another and over time in terms of their subsumed as well as their fundamental class processes, according to Marxian theory. Social formations comprise not only various forms of the fundamental class process. They also comprise, for each such form, the subsumed class processes that may be required to secure its conditions of existence. For each social formation, not only its fundamental but also its subsumed class structures are historically variable. Marxian class analysis seeks to specify the complex fundamental and subsumed class positions comprising any social formation chosen for scrutiny. Given the logic of overdetermination, such specification includes the contradictions within and among, and hence the dynamic of, all such classes. Moreover, the Marxian concept of class struggle must correspondingly be disaggregated. Tensions and struggles between occupants of positions within the fundamental class processes must be examined alongside of and in interaction with tensions and struggles between occupants of positions within the subsumed class process. Class struggles are understood to occur over the dimensions and forms of the subsumed class as well as of the fundamental class processes. Ignoring or denigrating the former class struggle in favor of the latter has no a priori justification in Marxian theory. Marx underscores the point in this comment on crisis in capitalism:

> In a general crisis of overproduction the contradiction is not between the different kinds of productive capital, but between industrial and loanable capital—between capital as directly involved in the production process and capital as money existing (relatively) outside of it.[35]

Given that his theoretical entry point is the fundamental class process, Marx organizes his historical analyses through periodization of social history along class lines. The development of a social formation is approached as a sequence of sets of fundamental class processes—for example, feudal, slave, capitalist, communist, and so forth—each with their subsumed class processes. A social formation's history is periodized according to which fundamental class process was prevalent and for how long. Needless to say, Marxian theorists can and do debate and disagree over the issue of prevalence. However, most have agreed that Western Europe may be periodized as a social formation in which the feudal fundamental class process prevailed from the twelfth through the early eighteenth centuries, while the capitalist fundamental class process prevailed thereafter. The capitalist fundamental class process was present in the earlier period, occurring, as Marx writes, "*sporadically,* as something which does not dominate society, at isolated points within earlier social formations." [36] Similarly, the feudal fundamental class process has existed and exists still within the capitalist social formation. The periodization of social formations concerns not the existences of various forms of the fundamental class process but rather their respective prevalences in Western Europe. The prevalent form of the fundamental class process in a social formation gives its name to that formation. Thus the transition from a feudal social formation (feudalism) to a capitalist social formation (capitalism) refers—in Marxian theory—to the emerging prevalence of the capitalist fundamental class process within a social formation in which the feudal fundamental class process had been prevalent. [37] Slave, ancient, primitive communist, and other fundamental class processes have existed across both periods of the Western European social formation. Indeed, Marx divides the earlier history of that social formation into periods characterized by, at various times, the prevalence of each of those fundamental class processes.

The Marxian notion of social change or transition refers to a multileveled development. All the fundamental and subsumed class processes, as well as all nonclass processes within any social formation, are always changing (given their overdetermined contradictions), are always in transition. Marx makes this point about both class processes in communist as well as in other formations. [38] Existing fundamental and subsumed class processes are not only changing, but some are ceasing to exist while new ones are born. The same is true of all the nonclass processes comprising the social formation. However, particular interest attaches to that kind of transition in which the social prevalence of one fundamental class process gives way to another. This is the sort of transition to which Marx devoted his attention in section 8 of *Capital,* volume 1, "The So-called Primitive Accumulation." It is also the sort of transition that the Marxian tradition has usually had in mind when setting its goal as "socialism.' The latter is more or less understood as the transition from the prevalence of the capitalist to that of the communist fundamental class process. In any class, it is always a basic task of Marxian theory to assess all of the transitions in all the class processes of a social formation with an eye toward the possibilities of socialism, that is, the passing of prevalence from capitalist to communist fundamental class processes. For us, then, socialism refers to a particular period and form of transition and not to a particular social formation. Parallel to the historians' debates about transition to capitalism in Western Europe, there can be and are debates over the issue of prevalence in, say, the Soviet Union. A transition to communism there implies the presence of noncommunist fundamental class processes. The capitalist may be prevalent in the social formation while the object of social change is the precise undermining of that prevalence.

Marx repeatedly noted that individuals within a social formation usually occupy multiple, different class positions, both fundamental and subsumed.[39] Thus, Marxian class analysis is doubly complex. First, it must distinguish the various fundamental and subsumed class positions comprising any social formation or part thereof that it proposes to examine. Second, it must specify the pattern of occupation of these different positions by the population of the formation.

Marx's Subsumed Classes

In volumes 2 and 3 of *Capital,* Marx offers a systematic treatment of a sequence of subsumed classes: in this case all subsumed to the capitalist fundamental class process. Three of these are analyzed in great detail: merchants, moneylenders, and landlords. Three receive relatively brief treatments: moneydealers, supervisory managers of joint-stock companies, and owners of industrial enterprises. Marx stresses repeatedly that occupants of subsumed class positions may either be employees of industrial capitalists or alternatively direct their own independent enterprises.[40] One of Marx's favorite examples is the wholesale or retail merchant, the person who performs a commodity exchange process: marketing the commodities produced in the industrial capitalist enterprise to the final consumers. Such marketing is often referred to as the process of realizing the surplus value embodied in capitalist commodities. Realization is a condition of existence of the capitalist fundamental class process. To appropriate surplus value, the capitalist must sell the commodities that contain the surplus value. To secure realization a subsumed class distribution of surplus value is made to such merchants. They occupy this subsumed class position whether the merchant is an employee (sales representative) of the industrial capitalist or the director of an independent merchant enterprise. In both conditions, merchants receive direct distributions of appropriated surplus value from industrial capitalists.

Within the industrial capitalist enterprise, the subsumed class of merchants—the sales department—includes a hierarchically organized structure of order giving and order taking. From the sales director down to the lowliest sales clerk with the least authority, all sales personnel obtain distributed shares of surplus value. Their paychecks all come from the same source: the capitalist's appropriated surplus value. They are all occupants of the subsumed class position of merchant. They are also all sellers of their labor power to the capitalists; they thus combine their subsumed class position with their commodity exchange position.

To the extent that a Marxian class analysis at this level seeks to take into account authority—that is, political, processes occurring among occupants of the same subsumed class position—we note that individuals who occupy the same class position may have different positions of power. So, for example, the corporate vice-president in charge of sales has authority over the sales bookkeeper, the clerks, traveling sales staff, and so forth. This sort of power differentiation within a class illustrates one step in analyzing the interaction of class and nonclass processes in shaping the lives of individuals who occupy varying positions within them.

The class analysis of an independent merchant enterprise is different. The merchant director of such an enterprise occupies a subsumed class position; a distribution of surplus value is received that is *not* combined with any sale of their labor power. Later we shall summarize Marx's detailed explanation (*Capital,* vol. 3, chaps. 16–18) of the mechanism of this distribution to merchants. Here, however, our concern is to show that the clerks, bookkeepers, and other underlings of the independent merchant are *not* subsumed class members. They obtain directly no distribution of surplus value from the industrial capitalist enterprise. Rather they are understood as the sellers of their own labor power as commodities. Their employer, the independent merchant, buys various commodities—ledgers, office equipment, paper, bookkeeping, labor power, and so forth—because such commodity purchases secure the conditions of existence of the merchant as a subsumed class. That is, these commodity purchases are means for the independent merchant to continue to obtain a subsumed class distribution from the surplus value appropriated in the industrial capitalist enterprise.

Payments by an independent merchant to all of his or her employees are not class payments; they are commodity purchases. These laborers do not sell labor power to an industrial capitalist; no surplus value is produced by or appropriated from them. They produce no commodity and no value. They are thus "unproductive laborers," a term Marx uses to distinguish them from laborers who sell labor power to industrial capitalists as well as produce surplus value for them. Indeed, these individual sellers of labor power to the independent merchant share the categorization of unproductive laborer with the subsumed classes within the industrial capitalist enterprise since none of them produce surplus value. The conventional use of one term, *employee,* to identify these different unproductive laborers with productive laborers misses precisely the class distinctions Marx is at pains to draw among all laborers. Of course his purpose, like ours, is to understand class as well as other divisions among laborers in order to facilitate and improve strategies for socialism. This discussion is extended in the next section, "Productive and Unproductive Labor."

To underscore his analysis of merchants as a subsumed class different from either capitalist fundamental class—either producers or appropriators of surplus value—Marx defines them strictly. In the major sections of *Capital* devoted to merchants, he proposes to deal with them only as personifications of two economic processes: buying and selling commodities produced in industrial capitalist enterprises and receiving a share of surplus value from them.[41] He explicitly recognizes that the social groups usually called merchants in Europe personify many other social processes as well. Indeed he discusses elsewhere in *Capital* how European merchants have occupied/personified different class positions in different historical periods and how merchant as individuals sometimes also occupy fundamental class positions as capitalists.[42] However, when Marx discusses merchants as a subsumed class he abstracts from all the other social processes in which they have participated or do participate. He does this not only to pinpoint and develop the concept of what we call the subsumed class process. He does so also because, in his view, the greatest economists of his time had missed the difference he theorized between the buying/selling of commodities and the production/appropriation of surplus value.[43]

Marx wants to emphasize that competition among industrial capitalists necessitated their ability to sell commodities as fast as they were produced. Delays in locating final purchasers interrupted or slowed the production process, reduced the turnover rate of capital, reduced the annualized rate of profit, and thereby worsened the competitive position of any capitalist afflicted by such delays. A historically evolved response is the independent merchant who, as the possessor of a quantum of the money commodity (merchants' capital), serves the capitalists by immediately buying their outputs: the merchant "promotes the productivity of industrial capital, and its accumulation."[44]

Conceived in this way, Marx's merchants direct the circulation of commodities, realizing the surplus value produced by and in the capitalist fundamental class process. Marx's merchants represent one possible form of realization, of the provision of that specific condition of existence. Realization may be accomplished, as noted, by alternative subsumed classes, some of which Marx mentions, such as sales directors and their sales personnel employed directly by capitalist entrepreneurs.

Merchants, strictly defined as subsumed class buyers and sellers of capitalist commodities, deploy a quantum of value in money form (merchants' capital) purely to buy and sell—to circulate commodities: "no value is produced in the process of circulation, and, therefore, no surplus-value."[45] The profit merchants earn is, Marx explains, simply a transfer from industrial capitalists of a portion of the surplus value they extract from productive laborers. Marx locates the transfer in the gap between the price actually paid by the merchant to the capitalist for the latter's commodity and the price at which the merchant resells the commodity.[46] Merchants produce no commodities, no value. Any development rendering merchants unable or unwilling to accomplish the merchanting process will likely block or threaten the existence of the capitalist fundamental class process.

Insofar as merchants are organized as independent, private entrepreneurships, their buying and selling activity must involve a distribution to them of surplus value such that their merchants' capital earns more or less what it would have if invested in capitalist commodity production rather than in merchanting. By contrast, a smaller distribution would suffice if merchanting were accomplished as a "nonprofit" state function. In the latter case, the responsible state administrators could occupy the subsumed class position of merchants. Marx analyses money dealers and money-lenders (bankers) as subsumed classes in terms comparable to those used for merchants. They too provide conditions of existence of the capitalist fundamental class process, for example, foreign exchange transactions and credit, respectively. However, the mechanisms whereby they obtain their cuts of surplus value differ from those of merchants.[47]

Marx's approach to landlords and mine owners as subsumed to the capitalist fundamental class process is somewhat different. The particular condition of existence that they provide, by virtue of their land ownership (right of exclusion), is that of access to the presumedly limited land surface of the globe. Marx argues that exclusive private ownership of land effectively denies to proletarians the access that would enhance their option to cease being proletarians; second, that exclusive ownership also limits capitalists' access to land.[48] In this sense landowners' control of access is the provision of certain conditions of existence of the capitalist fundamental class process: "the landlord plays a role in the capitalist process of production . . . as the personification of one of the most essential conditions of production."[49]

To gain access, that is, to induce this subsumed class to control access in particular ways, capitalists distribute a portion of their extracted surplus value to landlords in the form of capitalist rent payments: as Marx puts it, "Landed property is a means for grabbing a part of the surplus value produced by industrial capital." [50] Such capitalists may be engaged in agricultural or industrial or service commodity production or any combination of these. Competition among these capitalists and between them and the landlords determines the size distribution of rental payments. At the same time competition among capitalists determines the average rate of profit. Together, rental payments and the average rate of profit determine the price distribution of land, as rent flows capitalized at the average rate of profit. [51]

Landlords produce no commodities, no values, and no surplus value. Thus, if they "employ" laborers, for example, purchase the labor power of rent collectors, they do not extract any surplus value from them. Logically, we can broaden Marx's notion of landlords to include similar subsumed classes that function analogously: proprietors of patents, copyrights, trademarks, and so forth.

The broadened notion of landlords as a subsumed class raises the general problem of monopoly and its relation to the capitalist fundamental class process: as Marx writes provocatively, "ground rent . . . constitutes the landlord's revenue, an economic realisation of his monopoly." [52] In this discussion of subsumed classes, we may extend somewhat Marx's remarks about monopoly. In the sense of exclusive ownership, monopoly means control of access to the monopolized item. Monopoly obtains a distributed share of surplus value extracted elsewhere if and to the degree that providing such access is providing a condition of existence of the capitalist fundamental class process. However such a monopoly is achieved, by any individual or group, we understand the latter to occupy a particular subsumed class position for so long as the monopoly lasts. Such a group may, of course, concurrently occupy other fundamental and/or subsumed class positions. For example, industrial capitalists themselves may seek and gain a monopoly of some capital good, raise its price above its value, and thereby add to the surplus value they appropriate directly a transferred portion of other capitalists' appropriations. They obtain such transfers by virtue of their monopoly control of other capitalists' commodity inputs, that is, of the subsumed class position they occupy in relation to those other capitalists.

When Marx discusses briefly the supervisory managers of joint-stock companies, he extends his notions of classes in two important ways. [53] First, he identifies what amounts to another subsumed class, namely, shareholders. When surplus value is extracted in joint-stock companies by means of capital owned by shareholders, then provision of such capital, such means of production, to the directors of such companies, has itself become the provision of a condition of existence of the capitalist fundamental class process. Dividends are a share of surplus value distributed to shareholders for providing the money capital which is a condition of existence of the capitalist fundamental class process: they are conceptually akin to interest payments.[54] By linking as "interest receivers" both shareholders in and moneylenders to industrial capitalist enterprises, Marx can apply to both his extensive discussion of "money-lending capital."[55] Both are subsumed classes obtaining distributed shares of surplus value. Marx terms these shares "a part of the profit given up by capital in the process of functioning to the owner of capital."[56]

The second extension of Marx's class analysis entailed in his discussion of joint-stock companies concerns subsumed classes other than those providing such economic conditions of existence as merchanting, loans, share capital, and so forth. Managerial supervision of productive laborers, as distinguished from their technical coordination, provides a political condition of the capitalist fundamental class process. Managerial supervision provides certain kinds of social behavior among productive workers, without which the production and appropriation of surplus value are jeopardized. For so doing, supervisory personnel obtain subsumed class payments.[57] The same analysis applies to all other managers: in selling their unproductive labor power, they obtain in exchange a subsumed class distribution. Thus, the personnel charged with the accumulation of capital—which capitalist competition renders a condition of existence of the industrial capitalist enterprise—similarly comprise subsumed classes. The famous part 4 of *Capital,* volume 1, devoted to the "Production of Relative Surplus Value," is Marx's detailed demonstration of how and why capital accumulation is a condition of existence of the capitalist fundamental class process.

It follows from our approach here that a modern industrial capitalist corporation will typically display a complex class structure. Besides the two capitalist fundamental classes there will be various subsumed classes such as the directors of merchanting, accumulation, personnel, supervision, advertising, bookkeeping, security, legal services, lobbying, and so forth and their respective subordinates. Certain individuals might occupy either fundamental class position as well as one or more subsumed class positions within the corporation. In any case, whatever tensions and struggles come to characterize relations among these class positions would emerge as "internal" corporate disagreements and conflicts. The capitalist corporation is an institution that—like most others—comprises the site of complex class tensions, alliances, and struggles. Its class analysis is undertaken in chapter 4.

Other providers of political conditions of existence of the capitalist fundamental class process include, for example, the legislators in the state apparatus. The political effects of their various activities—in terms of particularly ordered social behavior—included the securing of private property and contracts. Certainly, innumerable commentators on capitalism have long understood the critical implications for the reproduction of capitalism of any inability to reproduce this security, this political condition of existence of the capitalist fundamental class process.

We may further extend Marx's theorization of what we term subsumed classes to encompass social processes providing ideological or, more broadly, cultural conditions of existence for the capitalist fundamental class process. The subsumed class of directors of the state apparatus often provides, for example, free public education and free public cultural programs.[58] This involves the design and dissemination of concepts of justice, society, work, individuality, and so forth. These concepts function in people's minds as means to construct and construe their life experiences. Belief in and thinking by means of specific conceptual frameworks are cultural conditions of existence of the capitalist fundamental class process. The directors of the state apparatus obtain shares of appropriated surplus value (via taxes falling directly upon that surplus value) to secure such cultural conditions of existence. A detailed class analysis of the state focusing upon its revenues and expenditures is presented in chapter 5.

Cultural processes comprising conditions of existence of the capitalist fundamental class process play their distinct determining roles alongside its economic and political conditions of existence. Only the combined interaction of them all will produce, that is, overdetermine, the capitalist fundamental class process. Any development of these cultural processes in directions inimical to the overdetermination of the capitalist fundamental class process is as potentially dangerous to the reproduction of that class process as similar developments in its economic or political conditions of existence would be.

All subsumed classes are financed directly by the distribution of the surplus value appropriated by capitalists from productive workers. However, the mechanisms and sizes of such distributions vary with the organizational connection between the subsumed and fundamental classes.

Some subsumed classes are organized as privately owned enterprises requiring private capital investment. Merchants and bankers, for example, must in general receive a sufficient portion of the capitalists' surplus value so that what Marx terms the unproductive capital of the former receives the same average rate of profit as the productive capital of the latter.[59] Such unproductive capital outlays—the money used by merchants to buy capitalists' outputs and that used by bankers to lend to capitalists—must earn the average rate of profit. If they do not, the *unproductive* capital outlays will be curtailed or eliminated in favor of the more profitable *productive* uses of such capital. Those eventualities—problems of realization and credit availability—would jeopardize the capitalist fundamental class process. That is, after all, the significance of the designation "a condition of existence."

Our term *subsumed classes* serves both to summarize and build upon Marx's original differentiation between the fundamental classes participating in the production and appropriation of surplus labor and the other classes participating in the distribution of the fruits of that surplus labor. The fundamental capitalist class of performers of surplus labor produces the surplus value which the capitalists appropriate. The capitalists not only appropriate surplus value, they also distribute it. Such distribution is required to secure the conditions of existence of appropriation, just as the appropriation is a condition of existence of the distribution. Thus, persons who occupy the fundamental class position of surplus value appropriator (capitalist) must also occupy the subsumed class position of surplus value distributor.

Thus the term *capitalist* is itself a complexity for Marxian analysis. To be a capitalist means to occupy two distinct class positions within two different class processes. Whatever else they do, capitalists both appropriate (fundamental class position) and distribute (subsumed class position) surplus value. They live, as we shall show, with the contradictions overdetermined in both of the class positions they occupy: shaped by and concerned with the distribution of surplus value as well as its appropriation. The capitalist must decide how to apportion appropriated surplus value among all its possible recipients so as to secure the conditions of existence of appropriation. This decision must be made given the overdetermined, contradictory, and hence ceaselessly changing social processes that comprise the context of appropriation. The decision, the actual subsumed class distributions, will interact with that environment to reproduce, if successful, and to extinguish, if not, the capitalist's class position as an appropriator.

The recipients as well as the distributors of portions of appropriated surplus value are subsumed classes. The recipients obtain these portions for providing certain conditions of existence—economic, natural, political, and cultural—that might not otherwise be available and thereby jeopardize the capitalist fundamental class process. The recipients may function within or without the capitalist enterprise itself; they may be "employees" or nonemployees of the enterprise. If they are employees, then their receipt of distributed portions of surplus value (via the subsumed class process) occurs together with the sale of their labor power (the nonclass commodity exchange process).[60] For nonemployee recipients of subsumed class distributions, no commodity sale of labor power to the capitalists is involved.[61] Merchants, moneylenders, shareholders, and landlords are Marx's examples of such nonemployee subsumed classes; he repeatedly emphasizes that they do not sell any labor power in exchange for their subsumed class receipts.

Of course, all recipients of subsumed class distributions may and usually do in turn make commodity purchases with them.[62] However, these purchases are not fundamental or subsumed class processes, nor do they occur together with them. They are simply commodity exchange processes. Keeping the different processes distinct and determining whether and when they may occur together is a goal of a Marxian theorization of the economic aspects of any social formation. Collapsing these processes together, losing the distinctions, precludes such theorization.[63]

We may summarize the relation between fundamental and subsumed class processes by citing Engels's review of Marx's *Capital,* volume 1. Engels sought to pinpoint how Marx's specific contribution offered a "solution of all those contradictions" of the political economy that preceded him:

> The origin of surplus-value . . . [is] *unpaid* labour, that constitutes the share of the capitalist, or more accurately, of the capitalist class. . . . In general, it is this unpaid labour which maintains all the non-working members of society. The state and municipal taxes, as far as they affect the capitalist class, the rent of the landowners, etc., are paid from it. On it rests the whole social system.[64]

Productive and Unproductive Labor: What Is the Working Class?

Our interpretation of Marx's theory of classes implies a distinct position on and within the continuing debates over different conceptions of productive and unproductive labor. Within the Marxian tradition these debates have usually been linked closely to contesting specifications of "the working class." Our position on classes and on productive and unproductive labor also involves a particular understanding of Marx's concept of working class.

Marx devotes considerable attention to the matter of productive and unproductive labor.[65] He distinguishes between them according to whether they are employed to produce surplus value or are not. His formal definition of productive labor is clear:

> *Productive labor* is therefore—in the system of capitalist production—labor which produces surplus-value for its employer.[66]

> The result of the capitalist production process is neither a mere product (use-value) nor a *commodity,* that is, a use value which has a certain exchange-value. Its result, its product, is the creation of *surplus-value* for capital.[67]

What is less clear and has provoked most of the debate within the Marxian tradition is the positive specification of unproductive labor and its particular place in the social class structure. Yet despite some ambiguous and contrary usages, there is, we believe, a definite notion of unproductive labor developed in *Capital,* volumes 2 and 3. Simply, unproductive labor is that which produces no surplus value. Productive labor is defined in terms of surplus value or, in our terminology, in terms of the capitalist fundamental class process. We understand work as a complex relationship composed of a specific subset of social processes: economic, political, cultural, and natural. Working thus frequently involves persons in thinking, order giving and taking, transforming natural elements, and in performing, appropriating, or distributing surplus labor, among other processes. The work relationship will vary according to which of such processes are involved in it and the different forms such processes can variously take. If and when the work relationship includes the capitalist fundamental class process, that is, when the direct laborer produces surplus value for a capitalist employer, the labor is productive. Otherwise, the labor involved in a work relationship is unproductive.

It follows quite strictly that productive labor, in Marx's sense, does not concern the particular technical or concrete tasks performed by the labor. It does not concern the particular use value resulting from the labor. Nor does it concern the cultural or political or economic relationships among the laborers.[68] It concerns rather a different aspect of the work relationship from all of these, namely, the production of surplus value for the capitalist appropriator thereof.

If and when the work relationship does not contain the aspect of producing surplus value for another, that is, does not include the capitalist fundamental class process, Marx refers to the labor in that work relationship as unproductive. For example, the labor of self-employed persons—what Marx refers to as the ancient fundamental class process—is unproductive labor. The label *unproductive* applies whether or not such self-employed persons sell the output of their labor—goods or services—on the market as commodities. Marx emphasizes that "a singer who sells her song for her own account is an unproductive labourer."[69] We may generalize Marx's argument: when work relationships involve the fundamental class process in any but the capitalist form, the labor performed is unproductive. Hence the labor of feudal, slave, and so forth—performers of surplus labor—is unproductive: no surplus *value* is produced. The products of such feudal, slave, or other kinds of unproductive labor may be sold as commodities, but such commodities do not contain surplus value.

Subsumed classes employed within the industrial capitalist enterprise (e.g., managers, sales personnel, etc.) are also unproductive laborers. The specific work relationships in which they are involved do not include the capitalist fundamental class process. Rather, as noted, they include the subsumed class process and the commodity exchange (their labor power for money) process. Since no production or appropriation of surplus value occurs in their specific work relationships, the labor done by such subsumed classes is unproductive and the labor power they sell is unproductive labor power.

There are work relationships involving neither the fundamental nor subsumed class processes. For example, one neighbor buys and sets to work the labor power of another. When the buyer neither appropriates surplus labor from the seller nor pays for the labor power by an allocation of surplus labor appropriated by this buyer, then it is a case of unproductive labor and unproductive labor power. Here, working involves the labor process and the commodity exchange process (money for labor power) but no class process.

Our class analysis of unproductive laborers shows that they can occupy two different sorts of class positions: either noncapitalist fundamental class positions or capitalist subsumed class positions. They can also occupy nonclass positions when the labor they perform does not occur with either class process. In this way, the first-level differentiation of productive/unproductive labor, which Marx inherited from his predecessors, can be further refined and elaborated through the class analysis Marx works up in *Capital*. He only partly accomplishes the task in his scattered writings on the productive/unproductive distinction. One goal of our work here has been to deploy the fundamental/subsumed class differentiation in order to arrive at a sharper, more developed specification of class differences among laborers (within "the working class").

The terms *productive* and *unproductive labor* serve Marx to distinguish the different social roles of the two kinds of laborers. The terms carry no implication of ranking; productive is no more important—in any sense— than unproductive labor for the reproduction of the social totality in which they both occur. In Marx's own words, "He [the unproductive laborer] performs a necessary function, because the process of reproduction itself includes unproductive functions." [70] Productive labor is what makes possible the appropriation of surplus value by capitalists, while unproductive labor is what makes possible the receipt of distributed shares of that surplus value by subsumed classes. Marx's concepts of productive and unproductive labor are constructed and defined by means of his entry-point concepts of class processes, fundamental and subsumed. The former concepts are elaborations of the latter, incorporating new aspects of the social totality into the theory.

The terms *productive* and *unproductive labor* also serve Marx to comprehend differences within the working or laboring "class," when that term is used loosely to designate an actual group of people in society. More precisely the terms serve to pinpoint class differences within the working class. Notwithstanding the linguistic difficulty here—as *class* is one word used for two different things—the point is that laborers involved in the capitalist fundamental class process and laborers not so involved are *both* involved in work relationships and may both identify as "workers" or a "working class." Whether or not they make such an identification—itself a socially overdetermined matter—both kinds of laborers do work. However, their work is different by virtue of the different class processes present or absent and, in Marx's words, "this difference must be kept in mind and the fact that all other sorts of activity influence material production and vice versa in no way affects the necessity for making this distinction." [71]

Again we reiterate that such class differences within the groups of persons who work—the working "class"—are not ranked higher in importance than all the other differences to which the quotation above alludes. Marx takes pains to make this point in his discussion of the unproductive labor involved in the circulation of commodities:

> In the production of commodities, circulation is as necessary as production itself, so that circulation agents are just as much needed as production agents. . . . But this furnishes no ground for confusing agents of circulation with those of production. [72]

Race, sex, religion, skill, age, education, and many other natural, economic, political, and cultural factors differentiate those who work. All such differences will complexly interact with the class differences that Marx is concerned to specify. That interaction will participate in the overdetermination of whatever consciousness and activities the social group of workers displays. Marx's goal is the class analysis of workers, the class analysis of the "working class." His goal is to add to—and thereby change—the existing knowledge of work and workers. His contribution is precisely the *class* analysis of work and workers. [73] Its purpose is to inform and thereby advance strategies and movements for social change toward socialism by the systematic specification of the class structure of the society to be so changed.

There is an ambiguity in Marx's formulations of productive and unproductive labor which needs to be resolved, especially in view of unacceptable notions of productive/unproductive labor within the Marxian tradition to which that ambiguity has contributed. The ambiguity concerns whether the productive/unproductive labor distinction is to be understood strictly by reference to class processes or also by reference to the use made by the purchaser of the fruits of the labor in question. Consider this statement by Marx:

> For example, the cooks and waiters in a public hotel are productive laborers, in so far as their labor is transformed into capital for the proprietors of the hotel. These same persons are unproductive laborers as menial servants, in as much as I do not make capital out of their services, but spend revenue on them. In fact, however, these same persons are also for me, the consumer, unproductive laborers in the hotel.[74]

In our view, Marx is here mingling two different senses of the word *productive* and thereby inadvertently introducing some understandable confusion. As noted earlier, Marx defines productive labor from the standpoint of its production of surplus value for its employer—regardless of the use made by those who purchase the commodities embodying that surplus value.[75] It is thus a different and not immediately germane question whether particular commodities are purchased as elements of constant or variable capital or neither. If they are purchased for such a purpose, Marx speaks of productive consumption in the sense of their involvement in the production of further surplus value. The alternative—commodities purchased for all other purposes, that is, goods and services exchanged against "revenue"— is deemed unproductive consumption. Now it is clear and fully consistent for Marx to distinguish productive from unproductive *consumptions* in this way. However, he violates his own definition of productive labor if he deduces the unproductiveness of labor from the unproductive consumption of the commodities embodying that labor. Unproductive labor and unproductive consumption are two different activities; each includes a different set of constituent processes. Neither is deducible as the necessary consequence of the existence of the other. The fruits of productive labor may be consumed productively or unproductively and likewise for the fruits of unproductive labor. Marxian theory must reject any deduction of the productiveness or not of labor from that of consumption.

Our understanding and development of Marx's theory of productive and unproductive labor is markedly different from other recent Marxian treatments of this issue. There are some important implications of these differences. These implications serve, we believe, to underscore certain attractive aspects of our formulation.

Recent Marxian discussions of productive and unproductive labor disagree over the connection to be drawn between that distinction and their differing definitions of the working class. Erik Olin Wright affirms, for example, a notion of the intrinsic unity of the working class on the grounds that no "fundamentally different *class interests* at the economic level" exist between productive and unproductive labor.[76] For Wright, both kinds of labor share a structurally determined (derived) interest in "constructing socialism" (a different "mode of production" from capitalism). He downplays the differences of productive and unproductive labor by insisting that their common fundamental interest necessarily and always places them both in the working class.[77] Similarly Harry Braverman arrives at a notion that productive and unproductive laborers "form a continuous mass of employment which, at present and unlike the situation in Marx's day, has everything in common."[78] In contrast to Wright and Braverman, Nicos Poulantzas makes the productive/unproductive labor distinction serve as a "determinant of a class boundary." Poulantzas insists that only productive workers "form part of the working class," and that to include in the working class all wage earners is conceptually inadmissable and politically dangerous.[79] Guglielmo Carchedi has productive and unproductive labor involved in his definitions of the capitalist and "new middle" as well as of the working classes.[80]

Debates over the definition of *working class* have provoked Marxian controversies over productive and unproductive labor for some time. In the 1940s Paul Sweezy argued that unproductive laborers comprised "the so-called 'new middle class'"; he found "an objective bond linking their fortunes with those of the ruling class."[81] In the 1970s a group of British Marxists, variously influenced by theories of a "new working class," took up the debate arguing against the position supported by Sweezy. John Harrison, Ian Gough, Bob Rowthorn, and Alan Hunt argue that finally *all* labor in the capitalist mode of production is productive because in the last analysis it all contributes to surplus value production albeit in different ways, direct and indirect. These different ways are deemed not to "disclose a class boundary between the working class, and some other and opposed class."[82] Gough and Harrison admit that such a notion of productive labor is a departure—necessary, in their view—from the differentiation between productive and unproductive labor given by Marx.[83]

Few of the authors prominent in the Marxian debates devote much substantive attention to the logic and structure of the productive/unproductive distinction per se.[84] Some, such as Sweezy and Poulantzas, adhere more or less to Marx's definition of productive labor and equate it to their rather exclusive notion of the working class. Others, such as Gough and Harrison, tend to depart more or less from Marx's definition in order to derive a relatively inclusive notion of the working class. Still others, such as Wright and Braverman, find the distinction of little theoretical interest or analytical use. None of these writers shows much concern to detail and explore the complex and changing relationships between productive and unproductive labor.

We differ from the authors and the debate discussed above by our focus upon the distinction in detail. We see the need to reassess constantly the changing relationships between productive and unproductive laborers. We differ most importantly from participants in that debate in refusing to define the working class simply as either inclusive or exclusive of unproductive laborers. To make such definitions strikes us as assuming the class analysis of workers as a social group instead of producing it. The virtue of the concepts of fundamental and subsumed classes and of productive and unproductive labor is their usefulness as means for the class analysis of workers.

Workers are people participating in work relationships and therefore in those class processes that may be included in such work relationships. The specific features of different work relationships are determined in part by the various class processes present or absent in those relationships. How human participants in work relationships are affected thereby—naturally, economically, politically, and culturally—is determined in part by the class processes involved in those relationships. Deploying its concepts of overdetermination, class processes, and productive/unproductive labor, Marxian theory aims to specify the different and ever-changing class positions of workers. Further, it seeks to show how those positions—those ways of participating in class processes—participate in overdetermining all the other aspects of workers' lives, including the relations among them and their subjective interpretations of their conditions. One particular goal is to assess both the actuality and potentiality of alliances among workers—among occupants of different class positions—in terms of social struggles. Another goal of Marxian theory is to show the need to add the transformation of class processes to the agenda for social change in capitalist social formations.

We differ also from another major theme in Marxian discussions of productive and unproductive labor; this theme derives the distinction from some criterion of the social usefulness of the goods and services embodying such labor.[85] In so far as certain produced goods and services are judged unproductive or, more generally, socially wasteful, then the labor they embody is defined as unproductive. Such derivations probably stem from Marx's references to "unproductive consumption" cited earlier. Where we read Marx as generally maintaining, despite lapses, a conceptual separation between the productiveness of labor and that of consumption, many Marxists have resolved the matter differently. Either they use, side by side, two different concepts of (or "standpoints toward") productive/unproductive labor, or they go so far as to make a concept of social usefulness into the final determinant of the distinction.

Ernest Mandel is perhaps most explicit in his insistence that Marx's "two standpoints" on the concepts of productive and unproductive labor "must not be confused." He states that one standpoint refers to whether there is "production of new value" and the other refers to whether consumption of the product of such labor serves "the general interests of society." [86] Mandel prefers the latter to distinguish productive from unproductive labor. Similarly, Paul Baran has argued that notions of productive labor must be based on "independent, rational" judgments about what is "socially useful." [87] Other Marxists define such social interests more narrowly as capitalist interests in maximum capital accumulation. Then productive labor becomes that which produces goods and services that are productively consumed. Michael Kidron concludes that "productive labor today must be defined as labor whose final output is or can be an input into further production," and a similar position is taken by Oskar Lange. [88] Ian Gough, John Harrison, and Paul Bullock favor jettisoning Marx's strict definitions; they redefine productive labor as that which produces the elements of constant and variable capital. [89] For these writers, labor engaged in luxury and armaments production, for example, is unproductive because they derive unproductiveness of labor from the final use of the commodities produced by that labor.

The tendency to move away from Marx's basic definition of productive labor as that which produces surplus value is frequently the consequence of an essentialist approach to Marxian theory. Its proponents search for and usually find one aspect of capitalist society that then functions for them as an essence, that is, the final determinant of the other social aspects. For example, those for whom capital accumulation functions in this essentialist manner want to derive the productiveness of labor in terms of its relation to accumulation: the relation to accumulation (essence) determines the productiveness or not (phenomenon) of labor. Similar forms of Marxian essentialism were encountered earlier. For example, Wright seeks to derive the working class (phenomenon) from what he terms "fundamental objective interests" (his chosen essence), while Poulantzas tends to derive the working class (phenomenon) from the productiveness of labor (essence) at the economic level (he has still other essences at his other two levels).

Essentialist modes of reasoning within the Marxian tradition have complex consequences. One of these is worth attention to underscore our difference from such reasoning generally and from its conclusions about the productive/unproductive labor distinction in particular. The overwhelming majority of the Marxian writers who have touched upon the productive/ unproductive labor issue have determined that unproductive laborers in their varying definitions are all a drag upon capitalist society's real interests (or "society's general interests" in some formulations). That is, while "necessary" to capitalism they slow accumulation and represent the costliness of capitalism's irrational necessities. Exposing this irrationality and calculating its "waste" of labor and resources have been mainstays of Marxian critiques of capitalism for some time, as creatively exemplified in the work of Baran and Sweezy.[90]

While we understand the appropriateness of attacking capitalist deployment of labor and resources from a Marxian critical standpoint, we think it is unacceptably one-sided (essentialist) to see unproductive labor as only a negative influence on surplus value extraction and capital accumulation. As emphasized by Marx and by our formulation of fundamental and subsumed classes, unproductive laborers often provide indispensable conditions of existence of (positive supports for) the extraction of surplus value and the accumulation of capital. Thus, for example, the unproductive labor power of an independent merchant's clerk is purchased as a commodity by the merchant. The merchant can make this purchase because of his or her receipt of a subsumed class payment. Such a payment is distributed from the sum of surplus value appropriated by the capitalist making the subsumed class payment. However, Marx repeatedly emphasizes that the unproductive labor of the merchant's clerk makes possible an increased turnover rate for the industrial capitalist's productive capital, that is, an increased capacity for productive capital to appropriate surplus value per unit of time.[91] Unproductive labor is both a cost for and a benefit to the capitalist fundamental class process. Much the same can be shown for all the other sorts of unproductive laborers. Similarly, the state's purchase of the unproductive labor power of public school employees and municipal fire fighters is made possible in part by subsumed class distributions to the state from industrial capitalists. These are certainly withdrawals of surplus value from the latter. Considered in isolation, one-sidedly, they leave less surplus value for capitalist accumulation. However, the teachers' positive contributions to productive laborers' productivity through education and the fire fighters' contribution to reduced losses of productive capital through fire prevention serve as well to enhance the rate of surplus value appropriation.

Finally, we may consider briefly the issue of luxury commodity production. Such production involves productive labor if carried on by capitalists. At the same time, the consumption of such commodities is unproductive; they do not participate as elements of constant or variable capital in the production of surplus value elsewhere in the system. However, the unproductive consumption of the luxury commodity is but one important aspect of its existence alongside another: the productive labor embodied in it. Productive labor and unproductive consumption are different activities within capitalist social formations. They have different consequences and participate in each other's overdetermination. Neither activity is the essence, the final determinant, of the other. The fact that a luxury good is consumed rather than utilized in capitalist commodity production does not determine the productive/unproductive nature of the labor embodied in it.

Our formulation of the productive/unproductive labor distinction in terms of fundamental and subsumed classes avoids essentialism and thereby one-sided analyses. It provides a particular way of understanding the mutually constitutive relationship between both types of labor. Lastly, it provides an approach that captures both the positive and negative aspects of the relationships or, in other words, its contradictory aspects.

Productive and Unproductive Capital: What Is a Capitalist?

In the previous pages of this chapter and in the passages of Marx there cited, the terms *capital* and *capitalist* are given a remarkable variety of definitions and modifying adjectives. Productive is distinguished from unproductive capital; the "functioning capitalist" is differentiated from the merely property-owning capitalist. The industrial capitalist is sometimes separated from the merchant and money-lending capitalists, and there are still other categories of capital and capitalist offered.[92] Given that *Capital* is the title and object of Marx's major mature work, his construction and elaboration of such distinctions hardly seems surprising. Yet it is no exaggeration to state that most works in the Marxian tradition operate with little or no attention to or deployment of Marx's specific differentiations.[93] One likely explanation for this striking state of affairs is the widespread attention given to volume 1 of *Capital* at the expense of volumes 2 and 3 and *Theories of Surplus Value*. In volume 1, whose subtitle and object are narrowed to *A Critical Analysis of Capitalist Production,* Marx uses the term *capital* and *capitalist* per se, generally without differentiations, because he is interested only in one kind of capitalist. While his object there is the capitalist fundamental class process and the capitalist "who extracts unpaid labor directly from the labourers," he explicitly mentions that the others with whom he or she must share this unpaid labor—some of whom he also calls capitalists—will be treated later in volume 3.[94]

As we read Marx, his concept of capital is extraordinarily complex and differentiated, as is his understanding of what a capitalist is. Marx's conceptualizations of capital and capitalist are not reducible to the formulations of *Capital,* volume 1. Our concepts of fundamental and subsumed classes, developed in part from close attention to *Capital,* volumes 2 and 3, may be deployed to pinpoint and clarify Marx's complex definitions of *capital* and *capitalist.* We follow Marx in appreciating that "the conceptual specification of capital encounters difficulties" and that "the exact development of the concept of capital [is] necessary, since it [is] the fundamental concept of modern economics, just as capital itself, whose abstract, re-flected image [is] its concept, [is] the foundation of bourgeois society."[95]

Capital, and hence the capitalist, for Marx, predate by centuries the development of the capitalist fundamental class process. Money, he writes, is "the first concept of capital, and the first form in which it appears; . . . it is found in the earliest conditions of economic development."[96] Elsewhere he speaks of capital "in its two antediluvian forms of interest-bearing capital and merchant capital," emphasizing that "merchant's capital appears as the historical form of capital long before capital establishes its own domination over production," and making the same point regarding interest-bearing capital.[97] Thus, capital and capitalist exist as both historically prior to and different from the notions of capital and capitalist developed in *Capital*, volume 1. In the latter, the capitalist relation is understood to have become—via the so-called primitive accumulation—"the foundation of production," and hence the "productive" capitalist can be analyzed as distinct from the merchant or money-lending capitalists. For Marx there are clearly different types of capitalists.

What then do these different types of capitalists have in common: what makes Marx convey the same name upon them, notwithstanding the differentiating adjectives? The capitalist is, as we have seen, the personification of capital for Marx. Thus we may rephrase our question: what is Marx's concept of capital that makes these very different economic agents—merchants, moneylenders, and surplus value appropriators—personifications of the same process, namely, capital?

Marx's answer begins with the definition of capital. It is "value-in-process," understood as "self-expanding value." Capital "is therefore the constant drive to go beyond its quantitative limit: an endless process."[98] The merchant possessed of value in money form who therewith buys commodities in order to resell them for more money is thereby the personification of capital. Similarly, the moneylender who directly extends to another a quantum of money and receives back a larger quantum is likewise such a personification. And, the "individual" who exchanges a quantum of value for labor power plus means of production and receives back a larger quantum of value in produced commodities is also such a personification. This latter "individual," a recipient of surplus labor performed in a fundamental class process, is not the only agent entitled to the label *capitalist*, not the only personification of capital. Marx is explicit on this:

> Capital as self-expanding value embraces not only class relations, a society of a definite character resting on the existence of labor in the form of wage-labour. It is a movement . . . it can be understood only as motion, not as a thing at rest.[99]

This is the explanation for chapter 4 of *Capital*, volume 1, where Marx elaborates a "general formula for capital" in the famous M-C-M' discussion. There Marx deliberately refers only to the self-expansion process of value and not to its particular personification in production as opposed to merchanting or money lending.

For Marx, then, capitalists exist outside of as well as within production.[100] The latter sort alone are directly involved in the appropriation of surplus labor in the form of surplus value. Marx calls them productive capitalists or, more commonly, industrial capitalists.

These labels serve to distinguish them from unproductive capitalists, those not directly appropriating surplus labor, such as merchants and moneylenders. In our terms, productive capitalists occupy the fundamental capitalist class position of receiver (appropriator) of surplus value. Marx's unproductive capitalists, his merchants and moneylenders, are defined as nonoccupants of a fundamental class position, capitalist or otherwise. This raises the question as to the source of expansion of their self-expanding value.

Marx explains that two alternative mechanisms exist by which merchants and moneylenders personify capital. We have already touched upon the first in our discussion of capitalist subsumed classes. Both merchants who secure realization for industrial capitalists and moneylenders who extend money or credit to them are providing conditions of existence for the capitalist fundamental class process. The shares of surplus value distributed to them as merchants' discounts or interest payments permit the values they dispose of to be expanded. They are thus a subsumed class of capitalists precisely distinguished by Marx from the fundamental class of capitalists. Merchants and moneylenders can personify capital without being subsumed to industrial capitalists. These possibilities are not much discussed by Marx since they fall outside the focus of his work, but he does mention them. Merchants and moneylenders may be subsumed to noncapitalist fundamental classes, for example, feudal lords or slave masters. Alternatively, they may engage in commodity trading and money-lending processes with persons who do not occupy any fundamental class position as receiver of any form of surplus labor, for example, with laborers of all kinds. In the latter case, merchants and moneylenders are capitalists without occupying any fundamental or subsumed class position; they neither appropriate nor provide conditions of existence to any appropriators of surplus labor.[101] "It remains capital for him [the moneylender] even if he does not lend it to the industrial capitalist but to a spendthrift, or to a worker who cannot pay his rent. The whole pawnshop business [is based on this]."[102]

Thus, strictly defined as personifications of self-expanding value, capitalists are differentiated by Marx according to their precise relation to the capitalist fundamental class process, that is, to the appropriation of surplus labor in the form of surplus value. The industrial or productive capitalist is the occupant of the fundamental class position of direct receiver of surplus value: "he is the person who at first holds the whole surplus-value in his hands no matter how it may be distributed between himself and other people under the names of rent, industrial profit and interest." [103] The merchants and moneylenders, the unproductive capitalists, occupy either subsumed class positions or achieve the expansion of their values in relationships that include no class processes.

Our categorization of Marx's definition of and differentiation among capitalists according to their involvement in the fundamental or subsumed or neither class process clashes directly with alternative readings of Marx. In these alternative readings of Marx, a capitalist is defined in terms of property ownership and/or in terms of an active participant contributing significantly to the production of surplus value, for example, supervisor of the production process. We propose to criticize such notions of the capitalist as owner and/or doer along the same lines used by Marx, we believe, to reject such notions.

Implied in Marx's differentiation among industrial, merchant, and money-lending capitalists and in our formulation of capitalist fundamental and subsumed class processes is a particular understanding of private property in the means of production. The social processes that secure private ownership of the means of production for some members of society and exclude others thereby provide one condition of existence of the capitalist fundamental class process. For the latter to exist requires a specific pattern of ownership/separation of the means of production. One part of this pattern focused on by Marx is the separation of the direct producers from such ownership. Marx makes this point many times in his writings: for example, the "separation of labour from the conditions of labour is the precondition of capitalist production." [104] The other side of this pattern is the ownership of means of production by nonlaborers: for Marx, "the *alien quality* [*Fremdheit*] of the objective conditions of labour *vis-à-vis* living labor capacity, which goes so far that these conditions confront the person of the worker in the person of the capitalist—as personification." [105] Marx speaks of reducing the concept of such property "to the relation to the conditions of production" and then defines the capitalist form of this relation as "conditions of reproduction [that] continuously confront labour as *capital*, i.e., as forces—personified in the capitalist—which are alienated from labour and dominate it." [106]

The separation of direct producers from ownership of the means of production is not itself a definition of the capitalist fundamental class process (which is rather the production of surplus labor in value form). It is not ever a pattern of ownership/separation that is peculiar to capitalism, since it is found in slavery, feudalism, and so forth. Nor is it a sufficient condition of existence. It is but one condition for the capitalist form of appropriating surplus labor. But to say this is emphatically *not* to say that the productive capitalist, the occupant of what we have defined as the capitalist fundamental class position of receiver of surplus labor, must himself or herself actually own any means of production. Marx makes it clear that he or she need not. As suggested by the distinction Marx draws between industrial and money-lending capitalists, it is both theoretically possible and currently common for the means of production deployed by the former to be owned entirely by the latter. Bank loans can comprise the capital used by an industrial corporation's board of directors to produce commodities. In other words, the capitalist fundamental class process requires, as a condition of its existence, that direct producers be separated from effective possession of the means of production, *not* that the industrial capitalist need own any.

To elaborate some implications of Marx's particular concept of the relation of property in the means of production to the capitalist fundamental class process, we first address Marx's question of whether the industrial capitalist actually *does* any labor. Our reading of Marx's answer to this question is: basically *no*. The occupant of the capitalist fundamental class position as such does no work; rather he or she obtains the fruits of the labor of others. "The existence of capital *vis-à-vis* labour requires that capital in its being-for-itself, the capitalist, should exist and be able to live as *not-worker*." [107] Marx specifically ridicules the notion of Adam Smith and many others that the industrial capitalist obtains a share of surplus value because of any labor that he performs; he derides "this false view of the labour of superintendence." [108] As far as capitalist production is concerned, he writes, "the cost to the capitalist consists in the capital he advances . . . not in labour, which he does not perform." [109] In short, the person occupying the fundamental class position of capitalist does no work, does not actively contribute to the production of surplus value. Rather the productive capitalist is distinguished by Marx as the passive recipient of surplus value produced by labor; he or she is not a doer except in the very restricted sense of appropriator/receiver of surplus value.

We, like Marx, readily acknowledged that this notion of the industrial capitalist, the personification of "industrial capital as the source of wealth," appears to clash with many popular conceptions of what *capitalist* means. We might add that this notion—in which the capitalist neither does any work nor need own any property—clashes with the predominant formulations within the Marxian tradition as well. Nevertheless, we read in Marx a detailed explanation of how and why his concept of capitalists differs from others and also a justification for his own against those others. This reading concludes our discussion of what the capitalist is.

The central point in Marx's explanation is his argument that individuals usually occupy more than one class position. Indeed, this argument is a corollary of his general approach toward the notion of the individual in society: "Society does not consist of individuals but expresses the sum of interrelations, the relations within which these individuals stand." [110] In our terms, individuals are defined, understood as occupants of various non-class positions (economic, cultural, political) as well as occupants of various fundamental and/or subsumed class positions. Given Marx's focus, the question is to identify which one or more fundamental and/or subsumed class positions are to be designated by the label *capitalist*. To answer this question is to construct a class analysis of the capitalist as the distinctively Marxian definition of that concept.

We have already noted that the industrial capitalist occupies more than just the fundamental capitalist class position of surplus value appropriator. In the latter position the industrial capitalist does nothing. However, in the one subsumed class position necessarily also occupied by such capitalists—distributor of surplus value to subsumed classes—they do something, namely, they distribute. Moreover, the individual who occupies these two class positions associated with the term *industrial capitalist* may also occupy still other class positions. For example, such an individual may also perform productive labor alongside the other productive laborers within the industrial enterprise. He or she might also lend money capital to the enterprise or rent land to it or own shares in it. Marx specifically mentions each of these additional class positions that the industrial capitalist can and often does occupy: "[He] himself is then divided up into different categories." [111] The multiplicity of class positions which these "capitalists" may occupy raises the question: with which of these class positions is labor associated?

Industrial capitalists—as such—do no labor. They get the surplus value produced by productive laborers and neither labor nor give anything in return. Industrial capitalists get something for nothing: industrial capitalists exploit. The Marxian point is to recognize and analytically distinguish the capitalist fundamental class process from all other processes.

By connecting an individual to multiple class positions, Marx introduces an analytical dilemma from which he can and should be extricated. If the occupant of the fundamental class position of productive capitalist may also occupy various subsumed class positions, why does Marx refer to him or her in terms of only *one* of those positions, namely, industrial capitalist? This dilemma deepens when Marx comes to discuss the provision of discipline, control, and supervision of productive laborers within the capitalist enterprise:

> Just as at first the capitalist is relieved from actual labour . . . so now, he hands over the work of direct and constant supervision of the individual workman, and groups of workmen, to a special kind of wage-labourer . . . managers . . . foremen, overlookers.[112]

This means that the person who occupies the fundamental class position of industrial capitalist can and often does cease to occupy the other capitalist fundamental class position of performer of labor (the reference to "actual labour"). Marx extends this point: the industrial capitalist can withdraw as well from occupying the subsumed class position of manager-supervisor. Moreover, he is quite clear that the industrial capitalist does not cease to be an industrial capitalist because he or she no longer occupies the subsumed class position of supervisor:

> It has become quite unnecessary for *capitalists* to perform this labor of superintendence. The capitalist as functionary of production has become just as superfluous to the workers as the landlord appears to the capitalist with regard to bourgeois production.[113]

He denounces the idea that any labor by industrial capitalists as such is necessary, calling any such assertion the view of "vulgarians."[114]

Marx's understanding of what a capitalist is and does amounts to something pointedly different from the functions usually attributed to the capitalist as such in popular discourse and bourgeois economics. The capitalist is not defined by the processes of buying and selling commodities, nor by the processes of controlling, managing, or supervising productive workers, nor by the processes of owning and giving access to means of production. Rather, these are processes providing conditions of existence of the capitalist fundamental class process and hence of the class position whose occupation entitles one to the labels *industrial* or *productive capitalist*. The providers of those conditions obtain distributed shares of appropriated surplus value, hence they occupy subsumed class positions. The person occupying the fundamental class position of appropriator, receiver of surplus value, is thereby a capitalist *whether or not* he or she also occupies those subsumed class positions.

Marx's analytical dilemma emerges when readers contrast this precise and relatively narrow definition of what a capitalist is with the much broader, looser deployment of the term *capitalist* in, for example, volume 1 of *Capital*. There, as elsewhere, Marx has capitalists doing all sorts of things that the narrower, more developed definition assigns instead to various subsumed classes. Disregarding or minimizing Marx's more developed formulations of what the capitalist is, readers can readily come to conceive the capitalist as the active participant in the production process, notwithstanding Marx's many strictures against precisely such views: "It is not because he is a leader of industry that a man is a capitalist; on the contrary, he is a leader of industry because he is a capitalist." [115] In our view, Marx simply did not bring together his various arguments concerning class so as to produce a comprehensive definitional statement on what an industrial capitalist is and does. This is what we propose to do.

We resolve Marx's dilemma by noting that his usage of the category capitalist undergoes an evolution from volume 1 to 3 of *Capital* (as, indeed, do his usages of categories such as commodity, exchange value, profits, etc.). This evolution may be summarized as, first, the positing in volume 1 of the capitalist as a composite figure who occupies several fundamental and subsumed class positions. Second, Marx disaggregates the composite figure into its different components, producing in volume 3 a far more developed and refined definition of various kinds of capitalists. Collecting together the various strands of this disaggregated analysis in Marx, we may complete what we read as Marx's concept of the industrial capitalist. Such a person necessarily occupies at least one fundamental and one subsumed class position. He or she appropriates surplus value in the capitalist fundamental class process and distributes it in the capitalist subsumed class process. As developed in chapter 4, the other fundamental and subsumed class positions he or she may occupy in addition will vary with the distinct histories of particular capitalist social formations and their forms of enterprise.

In statements scattered throughout his work, Marx affirms the importance he attaches to the precise class analysis—that is, the application of his theory of class—of the various agents of economic processes within a capitalist social formation. The differentiation of capitalist fundamental from subsumed classes, most thoroughly elaborated by Marx in his discussions of merchants in *Capital,* volumes 2 and 3, strikes Marx as crucial for his program of social analysis:

> All superficial and false conceptions of the process of reproduction as a whole are derived from examinations of merchants' capital and from the conceptions which its peculiar movements call forth in the minds of circulation agents. [116]

He justifies his differentiation as "all the more necessary, because modern political economy, even in the person of its best exponents, throws trading capital and industrial capital indiscriminately together." [117] In similar fashion Marx justifies his differentiations of money lending from industrial capital and his differentiation of the capitalist as receiver of surplus value from any performance of labor. He argues that the existence of interest on loaned capital "appears" to warrant an unfortunate view of the division between surplus produced outside of production and that produced inside production. To some, says Marx, it "appears" that earning interest is a "sinecure," not connected to "functioning capitalists," that is, those "working" in production and merchanting. The latter are therefore asserted to do labor such that "exploitation itself appears as a simple labour-process in which the functioning capitalist merely performs a different kind of labour than the labourer." [118] Marx denounces this view: "The industrial capitalist is a worker, compared to the money-capitalist, but a worker in the sense of capitalist, i.e., an exploiter of the labour of others." [119] He justifies his own argument as necessary to counter the other view's "apologetic aim of representing profit not as surplus-value derived from unpaid labour; but as the capitalist's wages for work performed by him." [120]

As the last quotation suggests, Marx basically justifies his theory of class in terms of how its use leads to a different understanding of how capitalism works—its laws of motion—from the alternative theories against which he contests. His theory underscores the role of exploitation in modern society. Those alternative theories deny that exploitation exists and affirm instead the "Trinity Formula." The latter ascribes value productivity to land, labor, and capital equivalently by linking them together in ways directly contrary to Marx's conceptualization of the capitalist fundamental and subsumed class processes. "This formula . . . corresponds to the interests of the ruling classes." [121] Marx, by contrast, self-consciously aims by his complex class analysis of workers, capitalists, and exploitation to "shorten and lessen the birth pangs [of] . . . a radical change in the existing relations of capital and labour." [122]

Wages and Profits: Analyzing Their Class and Nonclass Processes

We may now develop and illustrate the explanatory power of our concepts of fundamental and subsumed classes and class and nonclass processes. We may use them to sketch the outlines of a class analysis of wages and profits. We can then begin to fill in these outlines in the final chapters of this book.

In *Capital,* volume 1, Marx concentrated on the production of surplus value in the capitalist fundamental class process. The result, as we have already noted, was the provisional assumption of simple working definitions of *capitalist, laborer, value, price,* and so forth. The complexities of these terms were left to later elaboration when the results of volume 1 could be and were themselves used to produce that elaboration. The concepts of wages and profits need to be elaborated in parallel fashion. We build from the simple provisional formulations needed for Marx's purposes in *Capital,* volume 1, to the richer determinations made possible by *Capital,* volumes 2 and 3, that is, by the conceptualization of fundamental and subsumed classes.

In *Capital,* volume 1, Marx defines wages very simply and generally. They are the payment for necessary labor, which he calls either variable capital or the value of labor power, interchangeably. Thus *wages* is a term designating a particular commodity exchange: typically money exchanged for labor power. Capitalists exchange their value in money (or possibly other commodity) form for equivalent value in the form of the commodity called labor power. Capitalists then consume the labor power they have purchased; consuming labor power means setting it to work and thereby obtaining not merely the labor activity of this hired laborer, but the objectified fruits of such labor. These commodity outputs embody a value that stands in a key particular relation to the value of labor power, that is, wages. The value added by the labor performed by the direct laborer exceeds the wages. The difference is surplus value, the value produced by the unpaid labor, by the surplus labor.

Profits, too, are a relatively simple matter in *Capital,* volume 1. Strictly speaking, profits do not exist as such there; rather the discussion is in terms of the surplus value appropriated by capitalists from direct laborers. The volume is replete with references to capitalists' strivings after surplus value.[123] It is clear, however, that what capitalists strive after is profits, not surplus value. Thus, Marx announces in *Capital,* volume 3, that he had collapsed surplus value and profits in *Capital,* volume 1, into synonymous terms because "profit is nevertheless a converted form of surplus-value, a form in which its origin and the secret of its existence are obscured and extinguished."[124] *Capital,* volume 1, was only concerned to reveal that secret and therefore provisionally ignored the differences between surplus value and profit.

Wages and profits are concepts that remain to be subjected to the complexity of Marxian class analysis. What is the exact specification of profit once we follow Marx in discarding the provisional, *Capital,* volume 1, assumption of its identity with surplus value? Marx never completed such a specification.[125] Nor did he much extend his *Capital,* volume 1, theory of wages other than very brief mentions of the possibilities for them to vary above or below the value of labor power.[126] In part, Marx did not further specify profits for the same reason that he did not specify a more complete notion of wages: "since, like many other things which might be enumerated, it has nothing to do with the general analysis of capital, but belongs in an analysis of competition, which is not presented in this work."[127] However, the further class analytic specifications of wages and profits are possible by means of the concepts that are developed in *Capital,* volume 3, and extended in the earlier sections of this chapter. If, as Marx writes else-where, "profits and wages, although determined by the relation of neces-sary and surplus labour, do not coincide with it, are only secondary forms of the same," then it is appropriate here to offer a precise class analysis of these secondary forms.[128]

The payment of wages within capitalist commodity-producing enter-prises is a complex matter. The wage relationship comprises many differ-ent natural, economic, political, and cultural processes. Our class analysis proceeds by dividing these into two groups: class and nonclass processes. We subdivide class processes into fundamental and subsumed and sub-divide nonclass processes into those that involve money payments and those that do not. Organized in this way, our approach can begin with any of these subdivisions and elaborate an analysis that progressively incorpo-rates the other subdivisions. The method of this incorporation—the logic of Marxian theory as we understand it—is the specification of how particu-lar class and nonclass processes overdetermine each other within the object of analysis—in this case the wage relationship.

In *Capital*, volume 1, as noted, Marx investigates the wage relationship by focusing on two of its constituent processes. One is his prime concern: the capitalist fundamental class process identified as the capitalist's con-sumption of labor power. A secondary concern is the commodity exchange process that is a condition of existence of the capitalist fundamental class process. Marx identifies this as the capitalist's purchase of the commodity labor power from the laborer. Given that *Capital*, volume 1, has a major interest in the fundamental class process, Marx makes the simplifying as-sumption that the prior commodity exchange process is a straightforward exchange of equal values. Wages are set equal to the value of labor power: $W = V$. The wages paid are value in money form exchanged for equal value in the form of the commodity labor power sold by what is clearly for Marx a productive laborer. *Capital*, volume 1, understands wages as the payment received by the productive laborer for this particular commodity that he or she sells: productive labor power. As the seller of labor power, the laborer occupies a nonclass position; as a producer of surplus value, the laborer occupies a fundamental class position.

Given the complex class analysis made possible by *Capital*, volumes 2 and 3, we may develop further what Marx himself recognized as his initial and limited discussion.[129] Our concept of subsumed classes permits us to begin by inquiring whether the productive laborer may also occupy a sub-sumed class position vis-à-vis his or her capitalist employer. If so, this la-borer may also obtain a subsumed class payment from that employer: a sec-ond and additional component of the wage payment.

If a condition of existence of the capitalist fundamental class process is monopolized—in Marx's example, land monopolized by landowners—such monopolists may provide access to the condition of existence only in return for a distributed share of the appropriated surplus value. In parallel fashion, if productive laborers can maintain a monopoly over the supply of labor power, they can obtain a subsumed class distribution from their capitalist employers in return for giving them access to the market in labor power. We may express such a subsumed class payment as W^2 and amend the initial notion of wages as follows: $\hat{W} = W^1 + W^2$, where $\hat{W}$ refers to the total wage payment to such laborers. Such a total wage is now conceived as a complex, composite entity.

The sale of productive labor power accounts now for only part (W^1) of the total wage payment. Another part (W^2) is the receipt of a distributed share of surplus value allocated to secure access to the productive labor power. Such a wage earner occupies two different positions, a nonclass and a subsumed class position, each generating "wage" income: $\hat{W} = W^1 + W^2$. He or she also produces surplus value by participating in the capitalist fundamental class process.

Now it undoubtedly requires labor to erect and maintain any monopoly position in the market for productive labor power or for any other commodity. The wage earner in our example may either perform such labor himself or herself or purchase someone else's labor power for that purpose. Such labor would in either case be unproductive; it results in no commodity, no value, and no surplus value. If the wage earner does such monopoly-maintenance labor, we understand that he or she has purchased unproductive labor power from themselves. Alternatively the wage earners in this example might purchase such unproductive labor power from other persons, as when productive laborers' unions hire staffs.

It is also possible that such monopolists of labor power are not the same persons as those who do productive labor. For example, "gangsters" exercising the monopoly might take into their hands the entire W^2, leaving the wage received by the productive workers no larger than the value of their labor power ($\hat{W} = W^1$). We might anticipate, in such a situation, some conflict over receipt of the subsumed class payment (W^2) between such productive workers and whoever occupies the subsumed class position. Such class conflict might occur complexly intertwined with another class conflict between industrial capitalists and whoever occupies the subsumed class position of labor power monopolist over the size of W^2 or over the very existence of the monopoly itself. The history of labor unions richly illustrates both such class struggles.

To keep from conflating distinct transactions, Marxian theory emphasizes that the subsumed class process (receipt of W^2) is different from the commodity exchange process (productive labor power for money). These two distinct processes are conditions of each other's existence. They are not identical, even if the same person participates in both.[130]

Wages may also include payments that are neither commodity exchanges nor subsumed class distributions. To continue with our example of the productive laborer, we may consider circumstances in which the supply of productive labor power exceeds the demand at a wage equal to the value of such labor power. The sellers of productive labor power will then have to pay for the opportunity to sell their commodity. They must pay for access to the market in labor power. The sum they pay appears as a reduction of their wages below the value of productive labor power. Wages fall below the value of labor power by an amount equal to the nonclass payment made by one party to a commodity exchange to the other. It is not itself a commodity exchange since the productive laborer gets no equivalent value for the payment that he or she makes. It is not a subsumed class payment because it is not a distribution of surplus value. It is a particular nonclass payment, a rebate from the productive laborer to the industrial capitalist taken out of wages paid. If we term this nonclass payment W^3, we may rewrite our total wage equation as $\hat{W} = W^1 + W^2 + W^3$. It follows from our discussion that if $W^2 > 0$, then $W^3 = 0$; if $W^3 < 0$, then $W^2 = 0$.

Nonclass payments included within wages draw Marx's attention in each of *Capital*'s three volumes. Where $W^3 < 0$ and this nonclass payment accrues directly to the productive capitalist, the latter's wage payment (the price of labor power) will be less than the value of labor power purchased.[131] Alternatively, a nonclass payment may flow from laborers to "parasites between the capitalists and the wage-labourer" engaged in the " 'subletting of labour.' "[132] By their control over the access of productive laborers to the market where they sell their labor power, such "parasites" extract a portion of their wages. Then the capitalist will still pay the full value of labor power, but the productive laborers will not receive it since the W^3 portion of it accrues to "parasites." We might anticipate class struggles between, on the one hand, capitalists and "parasites" over who is to receive the W^3 and, on the other hand, between productive laborers and whoever receives W^3 over its size or its very existence.

The term *wages* includes a variable set of payment processes: selling productive or unproductive labor power, receiving subsumed class distributions for access to a monopoly over that labor power, rebating by productive laborers to capitalists, and so forth. Wages refer then to commodity exchanges, subsumed class processes, and still other money transfers. Nor are the class and nonclass processes mentioned above the only ones that may be included within a wage relationship. There are others. For example, a productive laborer may also do a certain amount of supervisory or managerial labor alongside productive labor. In this latter capacity, he or she sells unproductive labor power to the capitalist. It is unproductive because it provides conditions of existence for the capitalist fundamental class process; it does not produce a commodity and hence neither value nor surplus value. We could designate such sales of unproductive labor power as W^4: the wage in question here is a distributed share of surplus value exchanged for the unproductive labor power.

Indeed, unproductive managerial and supervisory personnel directly hired by capitalists are also wage (or salary) earners. If they do exclusively unproductive labor, their total wages ($\hat{W}$) would include only W^4. They sell unproductive labor power (commodity exchange process) in exchange for a subsumed class distribution (subsumed class process). Their wage, $\hat{W}$, is the combination of these two processes as one payment: a share of appropriated surplus value is used to buy their unproductive labor power. Finally, sellers of unproductive labor power may exchange with other than industrial capitalists. In that case, their wage payment is *not* also a subsumed class distribution; it is merely a commodity exchange of unproductive labor power for money, which we may label W^5.

There is thus a general Marxian wage equation as follows: $\hat{W} = W^1 + W^2 + W^3 + W^4 + W^5$, where any wage earner's total wages ($\hat{W}$) can be understood as some combination of one or more of the different subsumed class and nonclass payments discussed earlier. If the wage earner sells some productive labor power, then $W^1 > 0$; if he or she provides access to monopolized labor power, then $W^2 > 0$; if he or she must make transfers to be able to sell labor power, then $W^3 < 0$; if he or she sells unproductive labor power to an industrial capitalist, then $W^4 > 0$; and finally, if he or she sells unproductive labor power to anyone other than an industrial capitalist, then $W^5 > 0$.

The purpose of this reformulation of Marxian wage theory is to call into question the status of the very term *wages* as it is customarily used in both Marxian and non-Marxian analyses. The use of one undifferentiated term, *wages,* conceals what Marxian analysis reveals to be very different class and nonclass processes. *Wages* covers payments for productive and unproductive labor power, commodity purchases, and subsumed class distributions, when their differentiation and interaction is precisely what Marxian class analysis seeks to specify as the basis of its distinctive social analysis.

One purpose of the interdependent conceptualizations of productive and unproductive labor, of fundamental and subsumed class processes, and of class and nonclass processes is to allow the class-analytic disaggregation (and hence, reconceptualization) of the concept of wages. The political implications of this reconceptualization will be briefly suggested. Unity among wage earners cannot be presumed from their status as wage earners, since this is not a singular, common status. Whatever other social differences have to be understood in devising a strategy to unify laborers around certain social-change objectives, the differences in the category of wage earner itself—especially the class differences—need to be understood. This will be facilitated by the sort of reconceptualization of the term *wages* begun here by means of the Marxian class analysis at work in this book.

As appropriators, industrial capitalists are the initial recipients of surplus value in their fundamental class position. They are also the distributors of this surplus value to the various subsumed classes in their subsumed class position. This follows from Marx's definition of *industrial capitalist* as argued earlier. We may represent the two class positions of the industrial capitalist as follows: $S = \Sigma SC$, where S is the surplus value appropriated and ΣSC is the aggregate of subsumed class distributions of this surplus value. Our task then is to specify what profit amounts to when Marx's provisional volume-1 assumption of its equality with surplus value is superseded. We propose here and in chapter 4 to construct a class analysis of, that is, to reconceptualize, profit in a manner comparable to our treatment of wages.

Profit, as that term is generally understood, comprises a subset of all subsumed class payments made by the industrial capitalist, $SC^a + SC^b + \ldots + SC^m$. Subsumed class distributions in addition to this subset, $SC^n + SC^o + \ldots + SC^z$, comprise different, that is, nonprofit, categories of subsumed class payments. For example, rent to the owners of land upon which the capitalist commodities are produced would be a subsumed class payment outside the subset considered to be profits. Similarly, interest on borrowed capital, taxes to the state, and sales discounts given to merchant enterprises marketing outputs would be so considered. So too would be salary payments to supervisory managers: these are subsumed class payments outside the subset typically designated as profits. In contrast, certain other subsumed class payments are considered as elements of the profit subset. Portions of surplus value retained and expended for capital accumulation and the portion paid out as dividends on common stock are usually considered components of industrial capital's profits.

The examples we have chosen do not demarcate definitive boundaries between those subsumed class payments designated profits and those designated otherwise. The reason follows from the concept of subsumed class payments within Marxian theory. There simply is no necessary demarcation among them that would "define" profits. Rather, all subsumed class payments are understood as means necessary to secure certain conditions of existence of the capitalist fundamental class process. The industrial capitalist distributes them toward that end. Taxes secure conditions of existence provided by state apparatuses; distributions for accumulation secure the growth that is a condition of existence; distributions used to purchase unproductive labor power secure supervision; interest and dividend payments secure access to capital funds, which is a condition of existence, and so forth. Salary increments for conspicuous consumption at various levels of the capitalist enterprise's managerial and labor force likewise amount to subsumed class payments designed to secure the external reputation of the enterprise (hence access to credit) and the internal structure of its incentives to its employees.[133] Both these latter are conditions of existence of surplus value appropriation. In terms of Marxian theory's interdependence of fundamental and subsumed class processes, it does not matter which of the latter are labeled profits and which "other."

In other words, once Marx's simplifying assumption in volume 1—that profits equal surplus value—is superseded, it is a matter of convention whether this or that particular subsumed class payment is placed within or without the "profit" subset. For example, in many of Marx's own writings he adopts the convention that what remains of appropriated surplus value after subsumed class payments of rent and interest are made constitutes profit of enterprise. This convention serves Marx's purpose: to locate the central importance of the industrial capitalist (fundamental class process) vis-à-vis other classes not involved in commodity production yet both necessary for the industrial capitalist's existence and sustained by the subsumed class process. This convention enables Marx to criticize the "appearance" of rent and interest as value-determining costs of commodity production rather than as "forms of surplus value."[134] Such criticism lies at the heart of Marx's attack against the dominant tendencies in the political economy of his day: the efforts to theorize industrial capitalists as contributors to production rather than exploiters of labor. Marx's convention also permits him to show how managers' wages are "concealed in the general rate of profit."[135]

Marx's convention is, of course, not the only possible selection of which subsumed class payments are to be designated profits. Alternative conventions might designate only that portion of surplus value allocated to defray the costs of accumulation as profit or accumulation plus dividend payments and so forth. The history of capitalism displays changing definitions of profit, changing conventions governing the selection of subsumed class payments to be grouped in such definitions. Matters are still more complex with respect to definitions of profit *rates* as discussed in chapter 4.[136]

The profits of a capitalist commodity-producing enterprise include the surplus value appropriated from its productive laborers *less* the subsumed class payments conventionally grouped as not-profits, for example, rent, interest, and so forth. However, to complete our class analysis of profits, we must note further possible components of such an enterprise's profits.

As developed in the next chapter, such a firm may obtain subsumed class payments from other capitalist enterprises. It can do this in so far as it provides conditions of their existence as surplus value appropriators. For example, if it exercises a monopoly on any of their commodity inputs, the excess of monopoly price over value of such commodities amounts to a received subsumed class payment. Alternatively, the firm in question might obtain interest payments from another capitalist enterprise to which it lends money or obtain dividend payments from another capitalist enterprise whose common stock it has purchased. Thus, the profits as a capitalist commodity-producing firm include the surplus value it appropriates directly from its productive laborers *minus* those subsumed class payments it makes, which are conventionally designated as not-profits, plus the subsumed class payments it may receive from other capitalist enterprises. However, the class analysis of enterprise profits is still not complete.

We refer to its possible nonclass revenues. For example, a capitalist commodity-producing enterprise may extend interest-bearing loans to its own or other productive and unproductive laborers. These loans are not conditions of existence of surplus labor appropriation since neither productive nor unproductive laborers carry out such appropriation. Thus the interest received on these loans is not a subsumed class payment, but rather a nonclass payment received as a result of the enterprise's occupation of a nonclass economic position of creditor.[137] This discussion is fully elaborated in the next chapter.

Profits, like wages, turn out to be complex entities which include revenues from different constituent processes, both class and nonclass. Further, industrial capitalist enterprises may well supplement the revenues they draw from the capitalist fundamental and subsumed class processes and nonclass processes by means of revenues drawn from noncapitalist class processes.[138] The latter too are typically included in profit statements of such enterprises. Thus, *profits* includes both less-than-appropriated surplus value (since portions thereof are not considered to be profits) and more (since subsumed class receipts from other capitalists and nonclass receipts and noncapitalist class receipts are accounted in profits). This complexity of the term *profits,* revealed by a complex Marxian class analysis, has important theoretical and political consequences.

For example, statistical series of changes in capitalists' profits are usually based upon the profits such enterprises report to various official agencies. Should such profits fall, Marxian class analysis shows that no inference can be drawn about any lesser or greater appropriation of surplus value. This follows because a movement in the aggregate called "profits" can be caused by all manner of alternative movements among each of the constituents of that aggregate. Reported "profits" might well fall while the

Marxian rate of surplus value appropriation rises. In other words, the class significance of changes in profits or profit rates cannot be inferred without the prior class analysis of such profits, although just such inferences prevail throughout the Marxian literature. Missing Marx's careful specification of what he means by profit in his discussion of the tendency for capitalists' profits to fall, most Marxists since have treated reported capitalist enterprises' profits as what Marx had in mind.[139] This leads to conclusions about crises in or the viability of capitalism based simply and directly on such reported profits. This is, we believe, a wholly unacceptable procedure which precisely misses its mark by virtue of *not* carrying out the class analysis of profits that Marx makes possible. It has had and will continue to have correspondingly unacceptable political, strategic, and tactical consequences.

Class and Person: The Complexity of Class Struggles

In Marxian theory, the notion of class struggle is understood as struggle between groups of persons over either the fundamental or the subsumed class processes or both. Capitalist class struggles are defined according to whether the fundamental or subsumed or both class processes are the objects of the struggle. Moreover there are two ways in which class struggles may be focused. They can aim at a quantitative change in the class processes—the division between necessary and surplus labor time and/or the size of the distribution of surplus value to this or that subsumed class:

> Capitalists form a veritable freemason society vis-à-vis the whole working class, while there is little love lost between them in competition among themselves.[140]

> Hence is it that in the history of capitalist production, the determination of what is a working-day, presents itself as the result of a struggle, a struggle between collective capital, i.e., the class of capitalists, and collective labour, i.e., the working-class.[141]

> The struggle between the moneyed and industrial capitalists is simply a struggle over the division of the profit.[142]

Alternatively they can aim at a qualitative change in the form of the fundamental and subsumed class processes. By change of form we mean, for example, a change from a capitalist to a communist fundamental class process, with the corresponding changes from capitalist to communist subsumed class processes.

Fundamental class struggles interact with subsumed class struggles; each is a condition of existence of the other:

Finally since these three (wages, ground rent, profit (interest), constitute the respective sources of income of the three classes of landowners, capitalist and wage labourers, we have, in conclusion, the *class struggle*, into which the movement and the smash-up of the whole business resolves itself.[143]

The traditional Marxian focus on fundamental class struggle has been, we believe, too narrow. It needs to be supplemented by the theoretically informed focus on the specificity of subsumed class struggles and their interdependence with fundamental class struggles. In the concluding section of this chapter, we offer some brief, illustrative examples of a Marxian class analysis of complex circumstances involving intertwined fundamental and subsumed class struggles.

Class is an adjective, not a noun; it serves to demarcate two particular economic processes from all the others—natural, economic, cultural, and political—that comprise the social totality. Human beings are understood and defined according to the myriad social processes they directly participate in. Stated differently, human beings are sites of specific subsets of social processes. It follows that any groupings of human beings, such as social "institutions" like state, enterprise, household, and so forth, are sites of all the social processes that define each member of the grouping.

Since class is an adjective designating merely two of the many social processes that constitute any human beings or any group of human beings, it is problematic to identify persons or groups by reference to merely two of the many different social processes in which they participate. Without extensive qualification, such identification amounts to essentialist discourse: reducing the complexity of person and group to but one of its many dimensions or determinants. Having argued that Marxian epistemology and Marxian social analysis are pointedly antiessentialist forms of discourse, it follows that essentialist usages of the term *class* must be rejected in and by Marxian theory.

Human beings may participate in fundamental or subsumed class processes or both or neither.[144] However, to the degree that they do participate in one or both, they occupy positions within them: performers or appropriators of surplus labor and/or distributors or recipients of shares of appropriated surplus labor. They occupy class positions that are overdetermined and hence contradictory. Each person also occupies a specific subset of other, *nonclass* positions within comparably overdetermined and contradictory nonclass social processes. What is distinctive about each person is his or her occupation of a particular subset of social positions.

How human beings resolve the overdetermined contradictions within which they pass their lives depends upon the interactions between and among the social processes in which they occupy positions and those in which they do not. Human beings are shaped both by the class positions they hold and those they do not hold. All the existing fundamental and subsumed class processes influence each person in a social formation, even though he or she occupies only particular class positions. The same is true of all the nonclass processes within society.

Human beings are born into and remain forever enmeshed within relationships with other human beings, albeit continuously changing relationships. These relationships and the groupings of persons they define are, as we have argued throughout this book, sites of particular subsets of the totality of social processes. Different relationships are distinguished from one another according to the particularity of the subsets of social processes comprising them. Different groups of persons comprise different relationships among their respective members. From the standpoint of Marxian theory as we understand it, the analysis of any social relationship or grouping necessarily involves the specification of all its constituent social processes if it is to be complete. To specify merely the class process within a relationship is then never a complete analysis.

This statement will occasion little difficulty if the relationships in question comprise the group called the family. Few would quarrel with the assertion that the analysis of the class processes included in the family relationships would, by itself, be incomplete as an analysis of the family. But matters seem less clear when the relationship or group under scrutiny is, say, working people or the proletariat or an entity labeled "the working class." Reducing any such grouping to only the class processes and positions constituting it is, however, just as incomplete, notwithstanding the linguistic convention whereby the word *class* is used as a noun, rather than an adjective. Whatever the relationships that define any grouping of persons—whether or not its name is *class*—the two class processes are never more than two among the many social processes that constitute those relationships and hence that group.

Because clarity in these matters is of the utmost importance, both theoretically and politically in the sense of strategically, we propose the following meanings and rules governing the usage of the terms *class* and *class struggle*. We have waited to delineate these meanings and usages until this point in our text in the belief that the prior discussions were necessary as preparations, explanations, and justifications for such a delineation. These may now be combined and focused on a summary statement.

Class, as a term describing two specific economic processes, is further modified by the adjectives *fundamental* and *subsumed*. The two class processes are overdetermined by all the other processes in the social totality just as they likewise participate in overdetermining all of them. Individuals and groups are never constituted merely by class processes. The particular class positions they occupy define them no more or less than all the non-class positions they occupy within the myriad nonclass processes of society. Thus there is no entity, no group of persons, that can be properly designated as a class. For to do so is to reduce a complexity to one of its many components and determinants, an essentialist mode of analysis that is anathema to Marxian theory. Classes, then, do not struggle or do anything else for that matter. The term *class struggle* must refer to the object of groups struggling, not to the subjects doing the struggling.

Groups of persons may struggle over any social process, contesting over its quantitative and/or qualitative dimensions. Only if and when the contest is over the fundamental or subsumed class processes can we properly speak of class struggles. In any case, whatever the objects of groups struggling, Marxian theory seeks to analyze the class processes involved in the relationships that define the group doing the struggling. The goal of the analysis is an assessment of whether and how the relationships and hence the group and hence its struggles may influence the fundamental class process in the society. This is the analytical goal of Marxian theory in large part because and to the degree that the social objectives of the Marxian theorist include a qualitative change in the form of the fundamental class process from capitalist to communist.

Terms like *middle class* or *capitalist class* or *working class* are then simply concepts of groups of persons presented to Marxian theory for its analysis. No great significance is attached to the improper—strictly speaking—usage of *class* as a noun. Marx begins his class analysis by deconstructing the concepts of class inherited from earlier theorists. He produces instead the different fundamental and subsumed class processes and positions discussed in this chapter. He begins as well to deconstruct "the working class" in his explorations of the distinction between productive and unproductive laborers. We have sought to generalize and theoretically unify these beginnings and also to extend the analysis further.

All social groups are defined by relationships among the members of those groups and therefore by, among other social processes, the various fundamental and subsumed class processes that comprise those relationships. It follows that any social group is composed of persons holding a variety of fundamental, subsumed, and/or nonclass positions. Social groups engaged in struggle over any social process can be approached in terms of the class/nonclass composition of those groups. That is the approach characteristic of Marxian theory, given its objectives.

How, then, are we to understand the innumerable sentences written by Marx and repeated countlessly by Marxists ever since in which classes are treated as functioning entities making history? They are, we would argue, a kind of theoretical shorthand inspired by an urgent polemical intent.

Marx was driven by the presumption that desperately needed radical social changes toward justice, equality, and freedom—as he envisioned these—could not be accomplished without certain specific changes in the class processes of his society. He was driven as well by his perception that even those who shared, more or less, his vision of a better society did not understand and appreciate the class components of the changes needed to achieve that society. He thus defined and focused his theoretical and political task as the correction of this defect among the radicals of his day. He sought to bring home to them the specific role and significance of the class processes of social life in social change.

Toward this end, he chose to personify, to anthropomorphize, class positions in his discourse. To his credit, as we noted in the opening pages of this chapter, he states in the preface to the first German edition of *Capital* that he deals with individuals "only in so far as they are the personifications of economic categories, embodiments of particular class-relations and class interest." However, the great majority of his readers and Marxists since have missed the significance of his prefatory caution. They have taken the personifications as actual persons and groups of persons. History has been understood as the clash of entities conceived as classes identified by their connections to property, surplus labor appropriation, power relations, or other criteria as we have seen.

Perhaps the personification of economic categories of social analysis with its inevitably concomitant essentialist overtones—as human groupings were reduced to merely their class dimensions—was chosen by Marx as a discursive device. Perhaps he believed that the device would enhance the readability of his work for readers who occupied productive and unproductive laborers' positions. The device, which followed accepted discursive styles among most of his political economist predecessors and contemporaries, likely did render his formulations more accessible to them and their readers. He probably believed that the profound break with existing social theory accomplished in his work was enough to offer his readers, without at the same time revolutionizing, more than the minimum necessary, the discursive style of argument. Later Marxists, typically without the self-consciousness shown in his preface, continued the discursive style, perhaps for comparable reasons.

Marxian theory has certainly spread remarkably from its beginnings in Marx and Engels. Their strategic choices regarding the best discourse to facilitate its diffusion seem, in retrospect, immune to much criticism. Nor are we concerned to criticize the wisdom of the discursive style chosen *then*. We are determined to criticize the wisdom now in perpetuating that style. Its essentialism, coupled with that substantive essentialism epitomized in the epistemological and determinist social theoretical positions criticized in the first part of this book, render a critique of and departure from the received style of Marxian discourse urgent now. Our focus on class as process and on class struggle as defining social conflict whose object is that process builds upon such a critique and toward such a departure.

We are convinced of the costs to the practical achievement of Marxism's goals of continuing to think by means of anthropomorphized economic categories without recognizing them as such. The elaboration of the class analysis of "classes" begun by Marx is long overdue as the necessary accompaniment to the next phase of class struggles. That elaboration is our goal in defining exactly what the class processes are and are not (e.g., the relation of class to property and to power, versus surplus labor appropriation). It is our goal in defining exactly what class struggles are (and what has been said of class struggles applies equally to class interests). The interests or struggles of persons are determined, or rather overdetermined, by all the processes of social life, not merely by the class processes they immediately participate in. The concepts of class struggles and class interests must refer, in a nonessentialist Marxian theory, to the objects of those struggles and interests.

4

Class Analysis: A Marxian Theory of the Enterprise

This chapter and the next offer two examples of how we use our concepts to produce Marxian class analyses. The particular relationships we focus upon comprise groups called *enterprise* and *state*. We wish to show that the previously specified Marxian notions of class and overdetermination can produce a new and different way of understanding these two groups. Our reconceptualization seeks to ascertain the specific class natures of each—the various fundamental and subsumed class positions occupied by the groups' members. We aim to specify as well the complex contradictions embedded within each: the tensions that characterize each class position and thus the enterprise or state in question. Finally, the reconceptualization seeks to specify the possibilities of class and nonclass struggles among individuals in enterprises and in the state.

The relationships comprising each group are conceived to be themselves comprised in turn of particular subsets of processes. For example, an enterprise is a site of relationships, and each, in turn, is a particular subset of social and natural processes. Conceived in this way, both enterprises and states are sites of relations among individuals; these relationships themselves are understood to exist as sites of processes participated in by these same individuals.

Enterprise and *state* are each quite literally defined to be places, social sites where particular subsets of processes occur. They thus differ from each other in terms of the particular subset of processes comprising each site. The overdetermination of each process engenders the contradictions and thus changes embedded in each. Further, each site is overdetermined by all others in the social formation.

Conceived in this particular way, any site within a social formation may or may not include the fundamental class process. An enterprise, for example, may be the site of processes provided only by occupants of subsumed class positions. A state may be the site of the fundamental class process and therefore include occupants of fundamental class positions. The fundamental class process may occur within a state or enterprise at one time and not at another. Every site exhibits a changing configuration of class and nonclass processes. In Marxian theory there can be nothing fixed in the notion of what an enterprise or state means. Like all entities these too are conceived to exist in change. Indeed, Marx's own notion of an enterprise changes significantly from the first to the third volume of *Capital*. We would forecast a similar result for the state had Marx written his anticipated manuscript on it.

A problem in the Marxian and non-Marxian literature is that the state is often reduced to politics (the state is in the superstructure) and the enterprise to economics (it is in the base). For Marxists, it follows that the appropriation of surplus labor can only take place in the enterprise (the economic base), and nonclass processes occur in the state (the noneconomic superstructure). Problems occur when critics point out that a number of other processes, including financing, lending, teaching, and disciplining, take place in the enterprise while the production and sale of capitalist commodities may occur within the state. If we reject a reductionist logic, no matter its complexity, and consider each site to be overdetermined by its constituent parts, we have no such problems. Indeed, we consider one of our goals to be an analysis of the shifting and different social processes overdetermining these two sites.

We recognize that our formulation of state and enterprise differs from that of alternative frameworks. As argued in previous chapters, any entity is thought, studied, examined as an entity through particular concepts. Social groups such as those discussed in this and the following chapter exist in and through the particular concepts used to understand them, and any statement about them must be from a particular framework. As argued, any other claim would negate our Marxian epistemological approach.

For us, to produce a Marxian knowledge of such groups means to conduct a Marxian class analysis, to carefully distinguish class from nonclass processes in order to highlight the existence and unique effectivities of the former. To not do this means to accept an alternative analysis of such groups, to not engage the Marxian theoretical process. Too often individuals within the Marxian tradition have accepted certain concepts of social groups as neutral, concepts existing separate from and independent of different conceptual frameworks. Such an acceptance of the theory-fact dichotomy has allowed non-Marxian notions of these groups often to dominate Marxian social analysis. What we propose here is something new: a specification of the overdetermined fundamental and subsumed class structure of the enterprise and state. This is what we understand to be a proper Marxian analytical response to, that is, reconceptualization of, these concepts, transforming their meanings in non-Marxian theories into their different meanings for Marxian theory.

The Capitalist Industrial Enterprise

This section seeks to specify the class nature of an enterprise engaged in the production of capitalist commodities. We will hereafter refer to it as a "capitalist industrial enterprise." By *capitalist commodities* we mean those that embody surplus value. Since our main concern here is the industrial enterprise, we do not present any further elaboration of these commodities such as would be necessary if we considered their prices of production. Our approach is as follows. The capitalist industrial enterprise is first designated in terms of its internal class structure. In so doing, we are able to identify a variety of different groups inside the enterprise in fundamental and subsumed class terms. In addition, we will explain how a number of other subsumed classes exist outside the enterprise in relation to its particular internal class structure.

We will conceptualize individuals serving on the board of directors as occupying fundamental and subsumed class positions inside the capitalist industrial enterprise. All individuals hired to manage and/or supervise the enterprise, no matter what their place within the corporate hierarchy, will be shown to occupy internal subsumed class positions. Those hired to perform productive labor occupy internal fundamental class positions. In contrast, we shall identify as external subsumed classes the owners and financiers of the enterprise, merchants selling the enterprise's produced commodities, landlords renting land to the enterprise, monopolists selling commodities to the enterprise, and state functionaries providing a multitude of different social processes to the enterprise.

Once the class nature of such an enterprise is specified, we turn to an examination of its production and distribution of surplus value. Our aim is to show how the fundamental class process, the production of surplus value, both overdetermines and is overdetermined by the subsumed class process and by nonclass processes. To demonstrate this key point our analysis proceeds by dividing the distribution of surplus value into two categories: (1) subsumed class distributions to secure the economic process of accumulating productive capital, and (2) subsumed class distributions to secure economic and noneconomic processes such as supervising productive labor, merchanting commodities, gaining access to means of production, and so forth. We show how each of these distributions to secure nonclass processes overdetermines the other and how all combine to overdetermine the value profit rate.

The next three sections underscore the complex contradictions within the industrial enterprise and its consequently changing class nature. We explore the impact of these changes on both the production and distribution of surplus value. We also elaborate the discussion in chapter 3 on the Marxian notions of *capitalist* and *profits* by showing how the meanings of these concepts are effected and changed by the changing class nature of the enterprise. For us, this provides a class rather than a nonclass analysis of these terms.

The final two sections examine the distinctions between capitalist industrial and nonindustrial enterprises on the one hand and capitalist and noncapitalist industrial enterprises on the other. Such distinctions have significant consequences for both historical and current analysis. For historical analysis, these distinctions are relevant for understanding the changing form of an enterprise both within and between social formations. For current analysis, these distinctions are pertinent for examining differences between capitalist financial and industrial enterprises. The latter suggest a particular way of making sense of the current relationship between relatively large industrial and financial enterprises.

The several parts of this chapter on the enterprise illustrate and underscore the Marxian method of analysis presented in the previous three chapters. Using the concepts of overdetermination and class, we produce our object, the capitalist industrial or nonindustrial enterprise, as a specific overdetermined site in a social formation. Considered as such, the enterprise, industrial or not, is the site of a set of distinct economic and noneconomic processes. As the site of the economic process of surplus value appropriation, the capitalist industrial enterprise exists as a particular location of the performance and appropriation of surplus value. As the site of the economic process of surplus value distribution, it also exists as the location of other economic processes such as purchasing of labor power, raw materials, and equipment and of noneconomic processes such as supervising, commanding, advertising, and public relations. Individuals occupy specific class positions within the enterprise because they participate in either or both the fundamental and subsumed class processes specified to take place there. A variety of other social and natural processes overdetermine the existence of the enterprise, but they do not occur within the purely internal relationships of the enterprise—those occurring exclusively at the site of the enterprise. For that reason, individuals participating in these other social processes are said to occupy class and nonclass positions external to the industrial enterprise.

It follows that a different configuration of internal or external processes changes the nature of the capitalist industrial enterprise and may alter fundamentally its class structure. The absence of the capitalist fundamental class process produces literally a different kind of an enterprise. A radical change in the form in which surplus labor is appropriated produces a noncapitalist enterprise. However, a change in the manner in which, say, the political process of supervision is secured may well change the nature of the enterprise, but may not alter fundamentally its class structure. A radical shift from a highly structured system of authority and command to a much more egalitarian structure in which power to command is democratized and shared within the enterprise can be quite consistent with a changed but still existing capitalist appropriation of surplus value. The class process is a distinct economic process and different from, in this example, the political process of command. By logical extension, this difference holds for all processes that are the conditions of existence of the enterprise's fundamental class process. Thus, a radical change in any subset of the former may contribute to but is not equivalent to a radical change in the enterprise's class structure. To conflate the fundamental class process with its conditions of existence is to obscure the particular insight and contribution of Marx. It is to see, for example, revolutionary class change whenever and wherever there is political change in an enterprise, resulting in its productive and unproductive workers gaining significant control over the management and supervision processes.

The economic processes performed in and by enterprises have often been the focus of both Marxian and non-Marxian theoretical work, which has frequently reduced the enterprise to a purely economic site. In contrast our conception does not make such a reduction. Conceived as an overdetermined site, no one of the enterprise's economic processes (say, the economic process of accumulating productive capital in the example of a capitalist industrial enterprise) is more important, more essential than any other process in governing its development. Thus the nature and complexity of our produced enterprise is far different than that usually specified in the Marxian and non-Marxian literature.[1]

Different *economic* processes occur within the industrial enterprise. Both extraction and distribution of surplus value take place in the capitalist industrial enterprise. Enterprises also participate in the process of purchasing labor power, raw materials, and equipment so as to produce commodities containing value and surplus value. The process of selling finished commodity outputs also takes place in the enterprise. To secure these and still other economic processes, portions of surplus value must be distributed to individuals who perform them. Here the relationship between them and the industrial capitalist includes the economic processes of surplus value distribution (the subsumed class process) and commodity exchange. In this case, these individuals' receipt of a share of surplus value occurs together with the sale of their labor power to the industrial capitalist.[2]

A number of *natural* processes occur in the enterprise. Productive labor transforms physical raw materials and tools into commodities. A variety of different chemical and physical changes also occur within the enterprise among its working population and in its environment. Such natural changes are conditions of existence of the appropriation of surplus value.

Different *political* processes occurring within the enterprise also participate in overdetermining the appropriation of surplus value. Portions of surplus value are distributed to managers to secure the (nonclass) political processes of supervising and commanding productive laborers, of rule and regulation making, and, in general, of establishing, adjusting, and enforcing ordered social behavior within the enterprise. Without such behavior and the political power to enforce it, the appropriation of surplus value would be jeopardized. We must then extend the relationship between industrial capitalist and individuals occupying subsumed class positions to include the managerial performers of this political process of supervision along with the previously listed economic processes.

Advertising is a major *cultural* process performed in large part by enterprises. Such advertising provides conditions of existence of the capitalist fundamental class process by propagating particular conceptions of life, success, work, enterprise, state, household, and so forth. Advertising, for example, helps educate individuals performing productive and unproductive labor to understand that social success in life conforms to and is measured by the accumulation and consumption of commodities. Commodities provide status, pleasure, sex appeal, credit rating, and so forth. Such an understanding influences the level and intensity of demand for commodities. The sale of commodities is a condition of existence of the surplus value embodied within them. If capitalist workers came to believe that social success could be secured in ways other than through the purchase of commodities, the reproduction of the capitalist fundamental class process would be jeopardized. Advertising also acts to shape conceptions of the proper roles of different segments of the population. At one historical moment, for example, women may be portrayed in ads only as homemakers whose success is achieved by satisfying the needs of their families. Advertising educates them to believe that that satisfaction depends, in turn, upon their purchase of particular commodities. Advertising justifies and rationalizes such positions while also creating a demand for capitalist commodities to secure such positions.

Portions of surplus value are distributed to managers to secure this particular cultural process as well as others relating to formulating and establishing explanations of the enterprise's development, different business plans and objectives, sales forecasts, and public relations policy.[3] As analyzed, the relationship between individuals occupying subsumed class positions and the industrial capitalist includes these cultural processes as well as the previously listed economic and political ones. The relationship and thus the enterprise becomes the site of this particular subset of social processes.

All of these class and nonclass processes shape the enterprise in contradictory ways. As the site of the economic process of surplus value appropriation, the enterprise includes individuals who perform capitalist necessary and surplus labor and others who appropriate or receive the surplus. Therefore, the enterprise is one location in society exhibiting contradictions over the appropriation of surplus value and tensions between performers (productive laborers) and appropriators (productive capitalists) of surplus labor. Productive capitalists also hold a subsumed class position by virtue of distributing their received surplus value to other individuals holding various subsumed class positions both internal and external to the enterprise. The enterprise is therefore the site of contradictions between those who occupy the surplus value appropriating and distributing positions and those who occupy different subsumed class positions. It is the site of tensions among those who occupy these different subsumed class positions themselves.

The capitalist industrial enterprise is the site of the political processes of supervision and command. Managers order productive laborers, among others, to work in particular ways. Contradictions and tensions arise between those who perform productive and unproductive labor. Productive laborers produce commodities through some form of social division of labor within the enterprise. Thus the enterprise is the site of overdetermined contradictions in the processes of interaction among the productive laborers and between them and their natural environment. Finally, managers perform cultural processes of producing different forms of explanations of the enterprise's continued existence and its successes and failures: advertising strategies, letters, reports, memos, plans, financial procedures, advice, speeches, phone conversations, and so forth. The enterprise is the site of contradictions among such managers over their differently produced conceptions and explanations of the nature of the enterprise's existence and its development.

We illustrate throughout the chapter how the capitalist industrial enterprise is the overdetermined site of contradictory tensions and conflicts among all the individuals occupying different class and nonclass positions, both internal and external to the enterprise, over both class and nonclass processes. Those contradictions and tensions shape the structure and dynamic of capitalist enterprises.

Class Structure of the Enterprise

An enterprise producing capitalist commodities exhibits a typically complex class structure. Besides the appropriators (productive capitalists) and performers (productive laborers) of surplus value, there will be individuals occupying various subsumed class positions within the enterprise, distributing and/or receiving portions of surplus value for performing social processes of directing, supervising, planning, staffing, purchasing, merchanting, advertising, bookkeeping and auditing, lobbying, investing, and so on. All these economic and noneconomic processes, assumed to take place internal to the enterprise, form a subset of those that must exist for the appropriation of surplus value to take place. This subset is assumed to be provided by individuals occupying different subsumed class positions located within the enterprise. The class structure of such an enterprise involves grouping individuals into three main class features: those who occupy the fundamental class position as performers of surplus value, those who occupy the fundamental and subsumed class positions as receivers and distributors of surplus value, and those who occupy internal subsumed class positions through providing the kinds of social processes listed above and obtaining distributed shares of appropriated surplus value. Individuals who provide various processes outside of this class structure occupy subsumed class positions external to the enterprise if they too receive shares of surplus value, and nonclass positions if they do not.

Because industrial enterprises can be organized in a variety of different forms (owner-operator businesses, partnerships, corporations, etc.), the exact location and identification of the industrial capitalist varies with these forms. For example, in a nonincorporated enterprise, an individual may be simultaneously the sole owner of the enterprise, the appropriator of surplus value, and the performer of various managerial functions. Indeed, in such an enterprise, especially in one whose size is small, the same individual also may perform productive labor alongside the enterprise's other productive employees.

Early capitalist commodity-producing enterprises typified such an organizational form. Here one individual often occupied a number of different capitalist fundamental and subsumed class positions performing (productive and unproductive) labor and appropriating unpaid labor. Perhaps it was Marx's initial confrontation with the predominance of such enterprises in his day that led him to discuss the early "capitalist" as one who did indeed own the means of production, supervise labor, and even perform productive labor in coordinating the production process.[4] In such owner-operated enterprises, the same individual occupies fundamental and subsumed class positions within as well as external to the enterprise. As Marx puts it:

> The employer of capital, even when working with his own capital, splits into two personalities—the owner of capital and the employer of capital; with reference to the categories of profit which it yields, his capital also splits into capital—*property,* capital *outside* the production process, and yielding interest of itself, and capital *in* the production process which yields a profit of enterprise through its function.[5]

The sole proprietorship and the partnership are organizational forms in which individuals are at one moment surplus-value-appropriating capitalists (Marx's "employers of capital") while in their other "personality" they are also owners of capital. Marx's "two personalities" refer, in our terms, to the two different class positions occupied by the same individual. In a sense, because of their participation in these different processes, their fundamental and subsumed class life is the life of the enterprise. The latter does not exist separately from them. This unique personification (e.g., the same individual qua productive and owning capitalist personifies the enterprise) is generally recognized in capitalist society and is usually codified in law. For example, laws passed by individuals occupying subsumed class positions in the state may establish the unlimited liability of the owner-operator, that is, the unincorporated enterprise. Federal tax law in the United States specifies that the unincorporated enterprise does not pay taxes on profits, but rather the owner-operator who occupies different class positions must report received profits of the enterprise as *personal* income. In addition, customers, creditors, and suppliers of the enterprise usually understand legally and traditionally who is responsible for managing the business, owning the business, and receiving and distributing its profits. All these processes locate and identify the industrial capitalist.

Matters are different when considering enterprises incorporated as stock-issuing companies. The main difference arises because of the latter's distinct ability to legally personify different forms of capital. Nonetheless, the logic of identifying the industrial capitalist in the corporation is parallel to that employed in owner-operated enterprises.

In an incorporated stock-issuing enterprise, no matter the complexity of the corporate structure, the industrial capitalists are typically those individuals who sit on its board of directors. They occupy the fundamental capitalist position as the first receivers of surplus value and the subsumed class position as the first distributors of that received surplus value.[6] In their fundamental capitalist class position, board members quite literally do nothing but "sit" and receive the enterprise's surplus value. Their job is not to labor but to receive the labor of others. By contrast, in their subsumed class position, board members do (unproductive) labor by distributing the received surplus value so as to secure its continued receipt. And for this unproductive labor they may or may not obtain a small directors fee (a share of surplus value which they distribute to themselves).[7]

For board members to be designated as the first receivers and distributors of "corporate profits," particular economic, political, and cultural processes are necessary. For example, certain laws have the effect of establishing the concept of a corporation as a distinct legal personality and its board members as personifying or representing that legal entity.[8] Such laws may also permit a corporation to personify different forms of capital. Because members of the board personify the enterprise's productive capital, they receive its surplus value. Because they also personify the enterprise's unproductive capital, they receive interest and dividends if the enterprise lends money-capital to or purchases the stock of other industrial enterprises. In this case, board members occupy subsumed class positions. Finally, if the enterprise lends money to or purchases the stock of financial or merchant capitalists or makes (consumer) loans to productive and unproductive laborers, members of the board occupy nonclass positions receiving interest and dividends on the unproductive capital used for these loans and financial investments. So for board members to be able to occupy these fundamental, subsumed, and nonclass positions within a corporate enterprise, particular political processes involved with producing and enforcing corporate laws external to the enterprise must exist, be enforced, and be reproduced.

In addition, other laws may establish board members as the legal representatives of the corporate owners, elected by them to receive and distribute the "corporate profits." Thus, to appropriate surplus value in a corporate enterprise requires—as a condition of existence—election to the board of directors. Even if these political processes of producing and enforcing corporate laws and of election to the board are secured, still other social processes both internal and external to the enterprise must be present for members of the board to appropriate surplus value. For example, managers must provide them with economic processes of purchasing labor power and means of production (commodity exchanges), political processes of ordering employees' social behavior (designing and enforcing personnel policies), and cultural processes of producing the necessary set of concepts by and through which the enterprise can be maintained (public relations). These are processes that take place inside the enterprise as a site. External to it, landlords, owners, moneylenders, merchants, and so forth must participate in economic processes of, respectively, providing access to their lands and mineral rights, making available their owned means of production, dispensing loans, and providing merchanting. These lands, rights, means of production, and moneys are made available to the enterprise and thus to its board members as their legal users. To be an industrial capitalist in an incorporated business also presupposes then—as conditions of existence of surplus value appropriation—the use of such lands, rights, means of production, and moneys.

In summary, we can say that particular social processes combine to produce the social situation in which individuals as board members receive and distribute surplus value. To quite literally discover such individuals implies the discovery of their conditions of existence. The latter form the criteria by and with which we specify individuals qua industrial capitalists. In the nonincorporated world, different social processes exist and thus the criteria of capitalist identification differ. At any one moment in a capitalist social formation, both forms of industrial enterprise may exist and thus both sets of criteria would be appropriate to use.

Since the corporate industrial enterprise is the main object of our analysis in this chapter, we will have more to say about many of the particular conditions of existence overdetermining board members qua industrial capitalists. However, for the moment we want to emphasize that despite our elaboration of these social processes, board members qua industrial capitalists do not supervise, own, or lend capital. Indeed, if an individual member does participate in the processes of distribution and/or management of capital either as its owner, lender, or supervisor, then in that participation the board member operates not as a surplus-value-appropriating capitalist but as a member of a subsumed class. The logic parallels that used to make sense of the individual who was engaged in a number of different processes in the owner-occupied enterprise. In both cases, the capitalist fundamental class process is defined uniquely as the appropriation, the receiving, of surplus value. And in both cases, subsumed classes, both in and outside the enterprise, in their different relationships to the appropriating capitalist, secure the conditions of surplus value's existence.

Individuals occupying subsumed class positions internal and external to the enterprise can be divided into three distinct groups: those who manage the enterprise and thus comprise what we have designated as its corporate management; those individuals external to this management who distribute means of production and/or money capital to the enterprise and thus can be referred to as its owners and financiers; and finally those who neither manage nor own/finance the enterprise but who provide, external to it, other social processes every bit as important as these.

Managers

The first group receives a share of appropriated surplus value for performing various economic, political, and cultural processes comprising the practice of management. The board of directors distribute a portion of appropriated surplus value to subsumed class managers to perform these nonclass processes. The subsumed class process of distributing a portion of surplus value to them is performed by board members in their capacity (or "personality") as a subsumed class. To sit on a corporate board of directors implies then that an individual occupies at least two different class positions: that of the fundamental capitalist class position (the first receiver of surplus value) and that of a subsumed class position (the first distributor of surplus value). Individuals who are board members may also perform the social processes comprising the management of an enterprise. They would then be recipients of a share of surplus value in the form of managerial salaries. To summarize: individuals who manage the enterprise and who are also board members occupy the fundamental capitalist class position as appropriators of surplus value, and two subsumed class positions as distributors and receivers (as managers) of surplus value.

The importance of this subsumed class group of managers to the existence of surplus value can be summarized simply: their job is to oversee, to manage the enterprise's appropriation of surplus value. In so doing they provide key social conditions for the industrial capitalist to receive surplus value. In any capitalist enterprise, board members qua productive capitalists can only personify productive capital if these (and other) subsumed classes perform processes whose effects are precisely that personification. Marx, for example, refers to the relationship between industrial capitalists and their managers as one in which

> an industrial army of workmen, under the command of a capitalist, requires, like a real army, officers (managers), and sergeants (foremen, overlookers), who, while the work is being done, command in the name of the capitalist. The work of supervision becomes their established and exclusive function.[9]

Among other processes, managers carry out the first phase of productive capital's circuit: they use money capital to purchase means of production (C) and labor power (V). Managers' salaries will be defrayed by distributed shares of surplus value, as will the costs of commodities purchased and used for management purposes. Managers work to induce productive laborers to expend effort in the production process. Part of their job concerns the quantitative and qualitative aspects of this labor effort. Managers may also be responsible for selling the produced commodity. They market the commodities, thereby realizing the embodied surplus value for the industrial capitalists. This is the very surplus value that they have helped induce the productive laborers to produce.

Without the totality of these efforts, industrial capitalists would not realize surplus value. Indeed, to such managers and their theoretical champions, such effort may appear to be the essential cause of the existence of surplus value. Such an approach has generated a literature in which corporate and even economic development have been reduced to effects of managers' decisions and preferences.[10]

Large corporations reveal complex bureaucratic arrays of managers. Directors of corporate departments such as purchasing, manufacturing, sales, research, accounting, and legal occupy managerial subsumed class positions. In turn, each director of a department is responsible for staffing the department with subordinate middle and lower managers. This vertical organization demonstrates how some subsumed class managers are responsible for performing processes of discipline and control over other subsumed class managers. Managing managers, like managing productive laborers directly, is a nonclass process which is a condition of existence of the capitalist fundamental class process. Both managing processes are secured by boards of directors through distributions of shares of appropriated surplus value to the managers.

We may note at this point that the relationship among these different managers includes the political process of command giving. Thus, on one hand, all these individuals occupy the same subsumed class position in that they are participants in the process of management or supervision of the fundamental class process. On the other hand, they enter into relationships with one another in which there is no fundamental or subsumed class process, but there is (among still other processes) a political process of giving/receiving orders.[11]

Indeed, such nonclass political processes of power wielding also exist within the fundamental class itself. For example, as argued, the individual who sits on the board of directors participates in the fundamental class process as receiver of surplus value. In so doing, such an individual also enters into social relationships not only with productive laborers (in which the fundamental class process is a constituent part) and with subsumed classes (in which the subsumed class process is a constituent part), but also with other industrial capitalists. Among the members of the board of directors of an industrial capitalist enterprise there will be political processes of discipline, control, and power wielding. For one industrial capitalist to be elected chair of the board implies that he or she gives orders to, wields power over, the other industrial capitalists on the board. Positions occupied in class processes are distinct from positions occupied in political processes; they are related but distinct.[12]

Owners and Financiers

The second subsumed class group can be divided further into two subgroups: those who hold shares of stock representing legal ownership of the enterprise and its means of production and those who hold credit instruments representing relationships of debt, but not ownership. The first subgroup, the owners of the enterprise, receive dividends for making their means of production available for use in the capitalist fundamental class process. Stockholding is the institutional form of this process of making privately owned means of production available to industrial capitalists. Stockholders also provide conditions for the existence of surplus value appropriation insofar as the holding of such stock supports a higher market price of the shares than would otherwise be the case. Higher prices of shares may permit the board of directors to allocate an increased portion of surplus value to, say, the accumulation of capital and a smaller portion allocated to dividend payments. In this case, individuals who occupy the subsumed class position of stockholders hold their shares chiefly for expected capital gains and tolerate reduced dividend payments. The redistribution from dividend payments to increased capital accumulation makes possible more surplus value appropriation. In addition, higher stock prices may improve the credit rating of an enterprise, thereby allowing lower interest rates to be paid on outstanding indebtedness.

If the enterprise employs a stock option plan as a supplement to subsumed class payments (salaries) to its managers, then higher stock prices may allow the enterprise to pay lower managerial salaries than it otherwise would. Further, such plans could be an incentive for managers to increase their effort (efficiency), thereby reducing the number of potential managers required for any department. In all these cases, higher stock prices secure improved conditions of existence for the enterprise's appropriation of surplus value.

If the enterprise uses such stock option plans or if managers purchase stock on their own account, then such stock-owning managers occupy two different subsumed class positions: one external to the enterprise as its owners (holders of its stock) and another internal to the enterprise as its managers. In any case, shareholders provide, by their ownership process, a variety of economic conditions of existence for surplus value appropriation.

The second subgroup, the subsumed class of debt holders, receives a distributed share of surplus value (interest payments) for the economic process of distributing credit to the fundamental capitalist class process. Such lending enhances surplus value appropriation by, say, facilitating higher accumulation of capital. Here the industrial capitalist is able to use loaned money-capital to expand surplus value. Like stockholders, financial subsumed classes may also facilitate surplus value appropriation insofar as their buying and holding of bonds lowers interest rates, thereby cheapening the cost of industrial capitalists' access to credit. In addition, bond buyers permit managers to borrow to take advantage of special market conditions (e.g., cheap inputs, the holding of inventories, etc.) that can enhance surplus value appropriation.

Other Subsumed Classes

Still other subsumed classes exist in the social formation, besides the two groups of managers and owners/creditors, who provide a variety of economic and noneconomic processes that serve to secure the enterprise's surplus value appropriation process. Produced surplus value is distributed to this third group of subsumed classes in a number of different forms. What we want to underscore here is a key point of the previous chapter: the distributions of surplus value in the form of taxes to state officials, discounts to merchants, rents to landlords, and so forth are as important to the existence of the capitalist fundamental class process as are its distributions in the form of dividends to owners, interest to creditors, and salaries to managers. Hopefully, such underscoring will again help counter any essentialist notion that any one subset of subsumed classes and by extension the nonclass processes in which they participate are *the* essential classes and processes determining the enterprise's existence.

Taxes are paid to the state by industrial capitalists—a subsumed class process—for economic, political, and cultural processes performed in and by the state. Its economic processes often include providing public transport, managing the money supply, and limiting foreign competition. Its political processes include providing laws and regulations, enforcement, protection, and defense. State cultural processes include providing education, art, and research. All of these social processes and still others provided by the state make possible the existence of the industrial enterprise's appropriation of surplus value. For example, a modern condition of existence of commodity circulation is the state's supply of a means of circulation. A condition of existence of the selling of labor power is the state's provision and enforcement of private property laws. Similarly, a condition of existence of surplus value is the state's educational processes. They help produce and disseminate specific conceptual frameworks that reject the notion that industrial capitalists exploit laborers and argue rather that capital and labor cooperate in producing output and divide that output according to their respective contributions to production.

Commercial discounts are given to individuals occupying the subsumed class position of (external) merchants for providing the circulation of commodities produced by the capitalist fundamental class process. This allows the value of produced commodities to be realized speedily in the bodily form of money. A condition of surplus value's existence may thus become the operation of merchants at both ends of the enterprise's M-C-M' circuit. However, since it is assumed that commodities sell at their values, commercial discounts (the institutional form of subsumed class payments to merchants) are given for selling commodities.[13]

The enterprise may also use its surplus value to pay rents to owners of land as well as to pay other owners of minerals, water, and trademarks for access to their lands, minerals, brand names, and so forth. Such access is a condition of existence of the enterprise's appropriation of surplus value. In some instances, the portion of surplus value paid to those holding an exclusive ownership over a trademark or patent can be quantitatively the largest distribution of surplus value. One example is the enterprise in the so-called third world that operates under some form of license agreement with subsumed classes located geographically in the European world. The licensing agreement allows an enterprise to produce and sell particular capitalist commodities; for this privilege, a significant portion of the enterprise's surplus value must be paid to the subsumed class. An enterprise may also distribute a portion of surplus value to monopolists who have exclusive control over commodities (means of production or labor power) required by the enterprise for its production. To gain access to such commodities, payments must be made to individuals exerting such control, that is, occupying such subsumed class positions.[14]

Subsumed class payments are made to still another group of individuals whose relation to the fundamental class process is often missed. Surplus value is distributed to individuals for the more or less conspicuous display of personal consumption. A considerable amount of training, education, and labor time may be devoted to learning the proper way to display clothes, automobiles, jewelry, homes and their furnishings, art objects, books, wines, food, and so forth. Such costly display by industrial capitalists and top managers functions as a lure, an incentive to induce productive laborers to work harder and longer. This amounts to their performing more surplus labor for the appropriating capitalist. Such display also helps justify this performance of labor. Display produces as well as symbolizes significant conceptual and physical differences between performers and appropriators of surplus labor. These differences are personified in styles of dress, eating habits, manners, speech, and so forth. Such differences work to establish a kind of superiority of appropriators over performers of surplus labor. This in turn can serve to rationalize and justify the capitalist fundamental class position. The process of displaying personal consumption can also effect the relationship between industrial capitalists and their lenders of capital. Display can impress the latter group so that they provide credit at a lower cost than they might otherwise have offered. Marx refers to this as "luxury, which is now itself a means of credit."[15] In these and other ways, display can become a condition of existence of the capitalist fundamental class process.

Surplus value is distributed in the form of salaries or other payments to displayers to secure this condition of existence. Industrial capitalists who, for whatever reason, do not themselves occupy this particular subsumed class position must then pay others to display for them. Thus in many modern corporations, some industrial capitalists occupy two separate subsumed class positions as supervisors and displayers. The industrial capitalist distributes surplus value to himself or herself in the form of a managerial salary. One portion of the salary secures the provision of the supervision process. Here the industrial capitalist occupies the subsumed class position of manager. The remaining portion secures the process of display, and here the industrial capitalist occupies the subsumed class position of displayer. Another share of the surplus value may likewise be distributed to different individuals across the managerial hierarchy who also occupy these two different subsumed class positions. All such individuals will then secure two distinct conditions of existence for the industrial capitalist: management and display.

Displayers must strive continually to display conspicuous personal consumption. Any interruption in this process could jeopardize the fundamental class position of the capitalist. Performers of surplus labor might consider appropriators to be insignificantly different from themselves and thus not to warrant their receipt of surplus labor. Creditors might charge significantly higher interest rates. As the development of capitalism in the United States demonstrates, conspicuous display can become a very significant condition of existence of surplus value appropriation.

We can summarize our specification of the class structure of the industrial enterprise in the following equation:

$$SV = SC_I + SC_O + SC_C + SC_R. \tag{4.1}$$

SV is the industrial capitalist's appropriated surplus value. This surplus value is distributed as follows: SC_I represents total subsumed class distributions to its internal management or bureaucracy; SC_O represents payments to its owners; SC_C refers to payments to lenders of money-capital and to financiers; and SC_R stands for distributions to all the remaining occupants of varied subsumed class positions, for example, state officials, merchants, landlords, displayers, and monopolists. This equation highlights our three major subsumed class groupings: SC_I, managers; $SC_O + SC_C$, owners and financiers; and SC_R, state officials, merchants, and so forth.

An important note about this equation (which applies to each and every equation we specify and use) concerns what we mean by the equal sign. For us, the supposition that appropriated surplus value is totally distributed to subsumed classes is only an initial analytical step in our argument. We do, of course, recognize and expect all manner of deviations from equality to occur. Some of these will be specified later. But the analysis of deviation presupposes an understanding of the production and distribution of surplus value that can be most clearly presented using our provisional simplifying assumption of equality.

Toward the end of *Capital,* volume 3, Marx begins to summarize his long discussion of the use of his value theory to make sense of individuals occupying different class positions. He focuses especially on their sources of revenue. Marx contrasts his approach with that of the classical economists which he ironically and critically labels the "Trinity Formula"—the notion of capital, land, and labor comprising three independent sources of income: profits, rents, and wages.[16] The relation of Marx's critique and discussion to equation (4.1) can be shown easily. First, isolate payments to landlords, SC_L, from within SC_R, and call them GR for Marx's ground rent. Next, add $SC_R - SC_L$ to SC_I and call the resulting total the enterprises' profits or Π. Finally, add together dividends to owners and interest to creditors and call that sum payments of interest to providers of different forms of capital (i). Using these definitions, we have the following three value equations:

$$GR = SC_L. \tag{4.2}$$
$$\Pi = SC_I + SC_R - SC_L. \tag{4.3}$$
$$i = SC_O + SC_C. \tag{4.4}$$

Now, add together Π and i in equations (4.3) and (4.4) and call the resulting sum, $\hat{\Pi}$, the gross profit of the enterprise:

$$\hat{\Pi} = (SC_I + SC_R - SC_L) + (SC_O + SC_C). \tag{4.5}$$

Equation (4.1) may now be rewritten in terms of equations (4.2) and (4.5):

$$SV = \hat{\Pi} + GR. \tag{4.6}$$

In Marx's words:

> Profit for capital (profit of enterprise plus interest) and ground rent are thus no more than particular components of surplus value, categories by which surplus-value is differentiated depending on whether it falls to the share of capital or landed property, headings which in no way however alter its nature. Added together, these form the sum of social surplus value.[17]

In our terms, $\hat{\Pi}$ is Marx's "share of capital" and GR his share of "landed property." According to equation (4.6) and this quote of Marx, any income the "capitalist" or landlord receives must be a share of the already produced surplus value. And this "share of capital" can be further distributed, according to equation (4.5), among individuals who are managers, merchants, state officials, owners, creditors, monopolists, and so forth. These are several of the classes discussed by Marx in volume 3 of *Capital* prior to his critical rendition of the Trinity Formula. All of them claim their respective shares of the enterprise's gross profits.

These different shares, together with that of the landlord, represent subsumed class incomes for individuals occupying those subsumed class positions. By virtue of occupying the specific position of appropriating capitalist, individuals receive no such share. Appropriating capitalists receive no income *as such* because they do not provide any of the conditions of existence of surplus value. Indeed, their "job" as industrial capitalist, that is, the process in which they participate, is simply to receive the surplus labor of others while doing no productive or unproductive labor themselves. It follows that insofar as such individuals who occupy the position of surplus-value-appropriating capitalist do receive incomes (whose source is surplus value), they must also hold subsumed class positions as owning capitalists, money-lending capitalists, merchant-capitalists, monopolists, managers, and so forth.[18] In all such positions they must be providing some of the social processes (including the subsumed class process itself) necessary for the existence of surplus value.

We can now show clearly the relationship between our value equations and Marx's critique of the Trinity Formula. First, recall the Marxian equation for the value of capitalist commodities:

$$C + V + SV = W, \tag{4.7}$$

where C is the value of means of production used up during the production period, V is the value of labor power, SV is surplus value, and W is the total value of the commodities. Substituting equation (4.6) into (4.7) yields:

$$C + V + \hat{\Pi} + GR = W. \tag{4.8}$$

Let us rewrite equation (4.8) so that it is net of the value of means of production used up during the production period:

$$
\begin{array}{ccccccc}
V & + & \hat{\Pi} & + & GR & = Y = & W - C \\
\downarrow & & \downarrow & & \downarrow & & \underbrace{}
\end{array}
$$

$$\text{wages} + \text{profit} + \text{rent} = Y = \text{net annual product.} \tag{4.9}$$

In Marx's own words, "capital-profit (profit of enterprise plus interest), land-ground rent, labor-wages, this is the trinity formula which comprises all the secrets of the social production process."[19]

Equation (4.9) summarizes, then, Marx's critical rendition of the Trinity Formula. It shows the three principal sources of revenue (income) received by individuals occupying capitalist fundamental and subsumed class positions. Y refers to the total national capitalist class income; V and $(\hat{\Pi} + GR)$ refer, respectively, to the total wages of productive laborers and the total incomes of subsumed classes. According to Marx:

> The value of the annual product, in which the new labour added by the labourer during the year is incorporated, is equal to the wage, or the value of the variable capital plus the surplus value, which in turn is divided into profit and rent.[20]

Y is equal to the combined sum of wages of productive laborers, profits, and ground rents. Standing by itself, Y abstracts from two different class determinations—the total incomes of productive laborers and subsumed classes.[21]

We thus have a Marxian class analysis of national income. That income is theorized, measured, and "seen" in terms of exploitation and subsumed class distributions. By contrast, it is seen, measured, and theorized in neoclassical economics as the rewards to different contributing factors of production. Neoclassical theory envisions the world in metaphors of harmony. Class disappears and cooperation reigns. The social issue of income distribution is reduced to the mechanical effect of the technical combination of physical inputs used to produce the goods and services people desire. By contrast, in Marxian theory, incomes are not reduced to technology and consumers' desires. Rather they are socially overdetermined by all the class and nonclass processes. Marxian theory then focuses on the class processes and their roles in determining national income and its distribution.

One final point requires mention. In the previous chapter we argued that the meaning of *profit* can be very different depending on which categories are included in its definition. The value equations in the present chapter underscore this important point. So far we have specified two different definitions of profit, the so-called gross profit in equation (4.5) and the profits excluding rents in equation (4.3). Both of these definitions differ from the enterprise's surplus value. This difference poses an interesting question: no matter which definition of profits is used, do changes in an enterprise's surplus value necessarily correspond to changes in its profits? Clearly, the answer must be no. A quick look at our two profit equations shows two different definitions and thus two different deviations of profits from the enterprise's surplus value.

$$\hat{\Pi} = SV - SR. \tag{4.10}$$
$$\Pi = SV - i - GR. \tag{4.11}$$

In either equation, $\hat{\Pi}$ or Π might rise (fall) even if SV falls (rises). So any calculations based upon these and still other definitions of profits that are supposed to indicate the relative degree of success of an industrial enterprise must be interpreted with great care. To put the point differently: a calculated falling rate of profit (using equations such as 4.10 or 4.11) for an enterprise might be quite consistent with a rising value profit rate $(S/C+V)$.[22]

Thus, to conclude that a capitalist enterprise is in a period of crisis because of some calculated decline in profit rate is to make a non-Marxian, nonclass explanation of the enterprise. To base political analyses on such notions of economic crisis is likewise inconsistent with Marxian theory. Such conclusions and analyses are results of not producing a class analysis of the enterprise's profits. It is conceptually equivalent to drawing conclusions about the economic success of a nation's population from a record of its national income, Y. This too abstracts from the fundamental and subsumed class positions that Marxian theory specifies and focuses upon.

Class and Nonclass Processes: The Case of Accumulation

The accumulation of productive capital is one particular economic process that is a condition of existence of the capitalist fundamental class process. Marx refers to the industrial capitalist's securing of this process as "the constant augmentation of his capital becomes a condition of its preservation."[23] Within the enterprise, as we have noted, managers provide this economic process along with a number of other social processes. All of them effect the reproduction of the enterprise. As Marx notes on this point:

> The process of reproduction includes both functions of capital [production and circulation], therefore it includes the necessity of having representatives of these functions, either in the person of the capitalist himself or of wage-laborers, his agents.[24]

We focus initially only on the accumulation process so as to demonstrate and analyze its overdetermined existence. This is a discursive focus: we do not see accumulation as any more essential to the appropriation of surplus value than the other conditions of its existence.

Our particular choice of the accumulation process, however, is influenced by the essentialized approach toward it often found in Marxian texts.[25] There, accumulation of capital functions as the essential force, urge, and goal of capitalist class structures. In contrast, we see accumulation of capital as but *one* among many different processes that provide conditions of existence of the appropriation of surplus value. Accumulation shapes the capitalist fundamental class process in its unique ways, but not more or less than other processes (e.g., management, access to credit, etc.). Indeed, the accumulation of capital is complexly intertwined with many different class and nonclass processes. The relations between accumulation and all other processes are contradictory and changing. We wish to examine some of these relations and their contradictions here.

Productive capital accumulation has as one of its effects the reproduction of the industrial enterprise on an expanded scale. This expansion produces, in turn, still other effects which include impacts upon various commodity markets and other capitalist enterprises' class structures. Let us begin by focusing upon the industrial expansion effect. We will later examine the impact of one enterprise's expansion upon other enterprises.

Rewrite equation (4.1) so as to isolate the revenues distributed to those occupying the subsumed class position of managers:

$$SC_I = SV - SC_O - SC_C - SC_R. \qquad (4.12)$$

Equation (4.12) emphasizes the differences among subsumed class groupings. Increased dividends, interest, taxes, rents, and so forth paid respectively to owners, financiers, state officials, landlords, and others reduce the share of appropriated surplus value available to the enterprise's managers, assuming ceteris paribus. This reduced share for SC_I may produce a smaller productive capital accumulation since less SC_I means less value available to be exchanged for additional constant (C) and variable (V) capital.

Of course, what is held constant here is of some interest. A rise in some or all subsumed class demands on SV may create pressures within the enterprise to alter SV by changing the rate of exploitation. In such a case, increased subsumed class demands by managers, owners, financiers, landlords, state officials, and still others may well be a catalyst for a rising exploitation rate. If so, the distribution of total capitalist class income would shift against productive laborers and in favor of subsumed classes.[26] As we will show, this changed value distribution could allow capital accumulation to expand.

Using the categories specified in equation (4.12), we present three examples showing how relationships among individuals occupying these different fundamental and subsumed class positions overdetermine the enterprise's productive capital accumulation. These examples suggest the difficulty of any predictions concerning the particular direction of capital accumulation when one or more subsumed class distributions change. They also allow us to specify a general formula for the enterprise showing how its rate of surplus value appropriation (the value profit rate) is overdetermined in part by its different subsumed class distributions. The latter are broken down into two broad distributions: one share to secure the accumulation process and another to secure all other social processes. It is the complex mutual effectivity among these three processes—the appropriation and two broad distributions of surplus value—that renders uncertain predictions made about the direction of any one of them.

Consider first the decision of members of a board of directors to expand dividends to owners (SC_O). One effect of such a changed distribution is possible tension and conflict between those who occupy positions as industrial capitalists and those who occupy subsumed class positions as managers. The latter argue that such distributions risk the competitive survival of the enterprise since that depends more on the accumulation of capital than anything else. Such managers sometimes carry their essentialist argument to the subsumed class of owners. They appeal to stockholders to vote for a new board of directors that would redirect surplus value more to them for the purpose of accumulation and less to other subsumed classes (i.e., those, including the owners, who are external to the enterprise). Owners may well be convinced and vote for a new board, expecting lower dividends to be more than offset by higher stock prices due to the increased distribution to the accumulating managers.

In such a case, those individuals voted out of the board of directors now no longer occupy the capitalist fundamental class position within the enterprise. They no longer do so because they failed to secure a particular political condition of their existence as board members, namely, the process of their election by the owners. The latter elected new board members and henceforth distribute to them the use of the means of production. Assuming that these new members also secure all other conditions of existence (e.g., distribution of surplus value to managers, creditors, landlords, etc.), they become the new surplus-value-appropriating capitalists. In this example, the accumulation of productive capital expands because of a conflict between those who occupy the fundamental (the former industrial capitalists) and those who occupy the subsumed (the managers) class positions.

As the second example, suppose an enterprise requires increased money-loans in an era of significantly rising interest rates. Higher finance charges will leave less for the enterprise's retained earnings, which may be defined as $SC_I + SC_O$.[27] Reduced earnings could lead to reduced dividends (SC_O) and/or capital accumulation (a portion of SC_I). Now, assume that industrial capitalists, managers, and owners agree that they will protect the enterprise and their respective class positions by joining together to resist the demands of the subsumed class of creditors, sometimes called finance capital. In this example, industrial capitalists joined by their managers and owners might be said to form an alliance of industrial capital against the claims of finance capital. Suppose a deal is struck between the two different class groupings: industrial capital receives loans at a lower than market rate of interest and, in return, financiers are elected to the enterprise's board of directors. This compromise between industrial and financial capital allows capital accumulation to continue despite generally rising interest rates. It avoids, at least temporarily, likely conflicts among industrial capitalists, managers, and owners over the distribution of the enterprise's lowered retained earnings in the face of higher interest costs. Finally, the compromise provides a new fundamental capitalist class position for the financiers by placing them on the industrial enterprise's board of directors. What this example illustrates is how a complex alliance or compromise between individuals holding different class positions, internal and external to the enterprise, overdetermines the accumulation of productive capital.

Our final example demonstrates that reduced state taxes will sometimes lead to unchanged or even reduced capital accumulation while under other circumstances they lead to its rise. Suppose existing taxes on the enterprise are deemed too high both by individuals who are industrial capitalists and by those who hold different subsumed class positions. Their opposition to high corporate taxes may gain the support of productive laborers. All agree that high taxes on the enterprise do not allow it to perform its "proper" accumulation and employment roles. Consequently, pressures build upon the subsumed class of state officials to lower their claim to surplus value.

Let us assume that such struggle over taxes by individuals occupying those different class positions is successful. A quick look at equation (4.12) suggests that, while it is possible, there is absolutely no guarantee that capital accumulation must rise if taxes fall. Indeed, what may occur is an expansion of all other subsumed class distributions, leaving no additional revenues to distribute to increased accumulation. For example, less taxes provide the extra revenues to distribute to managers for a variety of processes other than purchase of additional labor power and means of production. These could include increased allocations to advertising budgets, expanded purchase of other enterprises' corporate stock and/or bonds, hiring of more managers, and even higher managerial salaries. Extra revenues may also be distributed to owners in the form of increased dividends, to landlords in the form of rents for expanded access to urban land, to financiers for higher finance charges, and so forth.

In this example a redistribution of subsumed class revenues has no necessarily positive impact upon the accumulation of productive capital, despite the clamor to lower taxes for that ostensible purpose. Indeed, decreased taxes will likely produce cuts in various processes provided by the state, and these could have negative effects on the accumulation of capital. For example, decreased taxes may lower state expenditures on education. This, in turn, could reduce the productivity of present and future laborers, resulting in higher commodity exchange values and a lower exploitation rate. If so, then surplus value would be diminished and, ceteris paribus, accumulation would fall. We have an example then of how a reduced subsumed class demand may decrease, on net, the accumulation of productive capital.

We can now summarize the contradictory relationship between the enterprise's accumulation of capital and all of its other social processes. First, consider SC_I alone, the enterprise's retained earnings net of dividends to owners. Let $SC_I = \beta SC_I + (1 - \beta)SC_I$, where βSC_I is the share of net retained earnings distributed to managers for accumulation of productive labor power and means of production ($\Delta C + \Delta V$). Then $(1 - \beta)SC_I$ is the share distributed to managers for securing other social processes internal to the enterprise. Substituting this equation into equation (4.12) and solving for capital accumulation, we have

$$\beta SC_I = SV - [(1 - \beta)SC_I + SC_O + SC_C + SC_R], \qquad (4.13)$$

where $\beta SC_I = \Delta C + \Delta V$. To derive the rate of accumulation of productive capital, divide both sides of equation (4.13) by $C + V$:

$$\frac{\Delta C + \Delta V}{C + V} = \frac{SV - [(1 - \beta)SC_I + SC_O + SC_C + SC_R]}{C + V}. \quad (4.14)$$

Let $\rho = \dfrac{SV}{C + V}$,

$$\lambda = \frac{[(1 - \beta)SC_I + SC_O + SC_C + SC_R]}{C + V},$$

and $K^* = \dfrac{\Delta C + \Delta V}{C + V}$.

For a capitalist industrial enterprise, the accumulation equation may be rewritten as

$$K^* = \frac{\Delta C + \Delta V}{C + V} = \rho - \lambda. \quad (4.15)$$

Equation (4.15) has the following interpretation: ρ is the enterprise's value profit rate or its rate of surplus value appropriation from productive capital; λ is the rate of distribution to subsumed classes for securing social processes (both internal and external to the enterprise); and K^* is the rate of growth of productive capital, the rate of distribution to managers for accumulation. For the rate of accumulation of productive capital, K^*, to be positive, the rate of surplus value appropriation, ρ, must be greater than the rate of other subsumed class demands on it, λ.

For a given ρ, a rise (fall) in λ will decrease (increase) the rate of accumulation of productive capital. For example, increases in the components of λ in terms of higher taxes to the state, discounts to merchants, interest rates to finance capitalists, capitalist ground rent to landlords, and dividends to stock owners will all lower the rate of capital accumulation. It also will be lowered by λ's other component, a rising $(1 - \beta)SC_I$ in the form of higher managerial salaries, advertising, sales and research budgets, administration, and so forth.

This inverse relationship between the rate of accumulation of productive capital and λ holds insofar as we assume that changes in ρ are related to changes in λ in particular ways.[28] We hasten to add that there is no necessity for ρ to change in a particular direction because of a changed λ. For example, increased subsumed class distributions by the enterprise to state functionaries, merchants, managers, owners, financiers, and landlords could increase, decrease, or leave unchanged the rate of capital accumulation. The impact upon the rate of accumulation depends upon the particular impact of these distributions upon ρ. In addition, it is even possible for changes in the components of λ to offset one another so that no net change in λ results, but there is still an impact upon capital accumulation. This possibility depends upon λ's components' differential effectivity upon ρ.

To examine these possibilities in more detail, let us rewrite equation (4.15) in terms of the enterprise's rate of exploitation and organic composition of capital:

$$K^* = \frac{\varepsilon}{k+1} - \lambda, \qquad (4.16)$$

where $\varepsilon = SV/V$, the Marxian rate of exploitation, and $k = C/V$, one version of the organic composition of capital. Now, according to equation (4.16), the two ways for a changed λ to affect ρ is through a change in ε and/or a change in k. We suggest that a good deal of capitalist history could be explained in terms of how the components of λ have overdetermined both ε and k. The questions here concern, for example, how particular nonclass processes such as ordering social behavior, distributing means of production, and making laws overdetermine the value profit rate. The specification of subsumed classes becomes a way to begin to disentangle the contradictory relationships between management, ownership, state, monopoly, finance capital, merchants, and the self-expansion of productive capital, that is, the value profit rate.

A rise in λ to the enterprise's managers effects both numerator (ε) and denominator (k) in equation (4.16), for that is what managers are paid to do: they manage this fraction. Shares of surplus value are distributed to them to enhance the productivity of laborers and their intensity and duration of effort, to engage in research efforts to reduce costs and develop new commodities, to foster the sale of commodities and open new markets, to affect the rate of physical deterioration of machines, and so forth. Increased budgets to the various managerial departments within the enterprise responsible for carrying out these and other tasks are directly and indirectly related to raising ε and lowering k. The resulting higher value profit rate allows an increased rate of capital accumulation to take place if this change in ρ exceeds the change in λ to the enterprise's managers.[29] We then have a positive relationship between K^* and λ. Increased corporate taxes to the state may also produce a higher ρ and thus be a condition for an expanded rate of productive capital accumulation (again assuming that the resulting change in ρ exceeds that in λ). For example, expanded state tax revenues used to improve public education and health programs could enhance the productivity of labor and thereby reduce the exchange values of commodities. This in turn tends to raise the value profit rate by producing a higher ε and, if the value of C commodities falls more than that of V commodities, a lower k. Higher state revenues also may allow a more aggressive foreign policy whose effects might include the enterprise's access to cheaper foreign raw materials and thus to a lower k. In general, state-run processes providing public works, public security, research into new technologies, the supply of money, and insurance all condition the value profit rate of enterprises. In all of these examples, the nonclass processes performed by various state functionaries may well be conditions for an expanded rate of surplus value appropriation (ρ) and thus for the rate of growth of productive capital, K^*, in equation (4.16).[30]

We could expand on these few examples to show in parallel fashion how increased distributions of surplus value to merchants, bankers, landlords, stockholders, and others may produce conditions for a higher rate of productive capital accumulation. They suggest a positive relationship between λ and K^* because of a particular relationship between ρ and λ. We can conclude that under these conditions higher subsumed class payments directed to expanding λ may become a vehicle for raising ρ through both direct and indirect effects upon ε and k and thus for raising K^*.

Equally possible is that a higher λ will have no or even a negative effect upon ρ. Under these conditions, the rate of accumulation of productive capital would fall as surplus value distributions to secure other social processes rose. For example, increased corporate budgets for research and administration to cut costs or develop new products, for exploration to discover new sources of raw materials, and for managers to improve the production process may all come to nought. Increased distributions to provide these and other processes provided by the internal management of the enterprise may not lead to increased surplus value. The state may demand higher taxes to defray increased salaries and material expenses with no consequent positive impact upon ρ. A similar story could be told for increased distributions to secure other nonclass processes provided by subsumed classes. In general, individuals occupying such class positions may demand a higher proportion of an enterprise's surplus value for providing the same or even less in terms of conditions of existence of surplus value appropriation. The rate of accumulation of productive capital would suffer. It would suffer even more if there were a negative impact upon ρ. For example, higher managerial salaries could be coupled with less managerial effort, with waste or inefficiencies that lower the enterprise's value profit rate.

It is also possible for a rising subsumed class distribution to managers to have a negative effect upon ρ and the rate of capital accumulation, even in a situation where managers are working efficiently and waste is minimal. An example of this is useful in explaining recent U.S. corporate history where some enterprises have lost their competitive edge and suffered accordingly. Increasingly, members of boards of directors receive subsumed class payments not in their capacity as providers of conditions of existence of their own surplus value appropriation but rather as providers of other extractors' conditions of existence. These include lending money-capital, purchasing corporate shares, renting land and machines, monopolizing the commodities they produce (gaining monopoly prices), and distributing corporate franchises and licenses. Interest, dividends, rents, monopoly price differentials, and license fees become part of corporate revenues.[31] A complex financial condition has emerged, often requiring the board and managers to devote more of their time, effort, and concern to the administration and direction of these subsumed class positions re other industrial capitalists. It is possible that the board and management become so focused upon the conditions provided to other industrial capitalists that they neglect to secure certain conditions of their own industrial capitalist position. For example, the "traditional" management role of supervising the efficiency of productive capital gives way increasingly to a new role of managing the enterprise's portfolio investments, that is, its loans to and stock holdings of other industrial capitalists. Consequently, the value profit rate falls as the enterprise moves to become a site of conditions provided to these other capitalists.[32] The rate of accumulation of productive capital thus declines, reflecting the enterprise's success in generating these new subsumed class revenues.[33]

These examples point to the richly contradictory nature of the enterprise's value profit rate, its rate of productive capital accumulation, and their connecting linkages. Increased distributions of surplus value to managers, merchants, bankers, and so forth propel ρ and K^* in different, contradictory directions. Individuals holding different subsumed class positions secure social processes that may enhance the enterprise's ρ and K^*; yet the provision of these same processes may also diminish them. Even if in our examples an increased λ to, say, managers raises ε and thus ρ and K^*, it may also set in motion events that counteract that expansion. A raised ε may be a catalyst for producing tension and struggle among occupants of fundamental class positions over the appropriation of surplus value (i.e., a fundamental class struggle). As a result, the enterprise's rate of surplus value appropriation and capital accumulation may suffer. In addition, the raised K^* itself may create conflicts among different industrial capitalists. An expanded K^* in one enterprise can alarm competitors and set in motion struggles over prices, markets, and costs of production. The net result of such competitive struggles could be reduced ρ and K^* for the initially expanding enterprise.

In summary, we can conclude that for any capitalist industrial enterprise, its value profit rate, ρ, rate of productive capital accumulation, K^*, and rate of distribution to secure all other social processes provided by subsumed classes, λ, mutually overdetermine their respective existences. Each is overdetermined in part by the other two; each thus exists in contradiction.

Contradictions in and Competition among Enterprises

As the site of different social and natural processes, each overdetermined uniquely, any one industrial enterprise is pushed and pulled in different directions. It quite literally exists in change. Other sites such as households, the state, and other industrial enterprises impact upon any enterprise in different ways. These contradictory movements or changes produce all sorts of tensions, conflicts, struggles, and compromises among individuals who participate in the different processes that comprise the site of the industrial enterprise. We may illustrate the contradictory nature of that enterprise with some examples.

Different claims on the enterprise's surplus value create a situation of great difficulty for industrial capitalists. One difficulty arises from the uncertainty of differing subsumed class demands for revenue; there is nothing to insure that they will offset each other: for example, higher interest rates coinciding with lower taxes. Individuals occupying different subsumed class positions press their own particular demands, thereby creating conflicts over the relative importance of the particular processes they offer. Some managers demand higher shares of surplus value for capital accumulation, arguing that this process is the essential determinant of an enterprise's financial success. Others demand an increased distribution for expanded purchases of different enterprises' common stocks, arguing that this process governs the enterprise's success.[34]

If we assume that the purchase of other industrial enterprises' stocks, like the accumulation of productive capital, is accomplished for, say, competitive reasons, then board members are faced with increased claims on the existing surplus value by two competing groups within the enterprise: accumulating versus stock-purchasing managers. Both groups secure conditions of existence for a higher rate of surplus value appropriation and thus for an expanded distribution of surplus value to secure still other social processes.

The enterprise can easily become the site of intense conflicts and struggles over the distribution of surplus value (the subsumed class struggle) from individuals occupying variously competing subsumed class positions. The object of such struggles is a change in the distribution of surplus value from those occupying one subsumed class position to those holding a different one. These struggles demonstrate some of the contradictions in the enterprise.

To continue the example, board members who decide to distribute a higher share of surplus value to stock-purchasing managers may alienate accumulating managers. The latter may struggle within the enterprise against such a changed distribution or appeal for support to occupants of subsumed class positions outside the enterprise. In a previous example we argued similarly—that allocation of an increased share of surplus value to dividends risked alienating managers bent on accumulation. Some of them, individually or collectively, resisted such a changed distribution. A possible outcome of such a conflict was the displacement of board members from their surplus-value-appropriating position. Two groups of individuals, certain stockholders and managers, were successful in displacing them. An alternative outcome could have been the loss of their subsumed class position by the managers had they been fired by the board for challenging the latter's decision to raise dividends (or to expand the purchase of other enterprises' stocks). Potential conflicts between those who hold the appropriating position on the board and some stockholders can lead to a particular kind of alliance between them that effectively constrains most other stockholders' political power to replace board members through altered voting rules for stockholders.

Typically, individuals who hold the more important management jobs in an industrial enterprise also sit on the board. They thus occupy multiple class positions. In such situations the board itself displays certain contradictions emanating from its members' participation in different class processes. For example, management, as a group, may be able to garner a significant share of surplus value for itself because some of its members are strategically located on the board to effect such a distribution. Other subsumed classes would then suffer reduced shares distributed to them. In reaction, some of them, such as creditors and owners, may threaten the board with more difficult access to credit and lower stock prices (i.e., struggles over nonclass processes).

Individuals serving on the board are now caught between two different actions. In their subsumed management position they are pushed in the direction of increasing distributions to themselves. In their fundamental class position they are pressed to reduce such distributions to counter the threats of owners and creditors to jeopardize conditions of their existence. In fact, individuals holding subsumed class positions external to the enterprise may even seek board membership to exert their own influence over the distribution of surplus value. If some of them eventually gain the fundamental class position, the board would likely exhibit a new set of contradictions. The key role of the board in the enterprise is often recognizable when individuals holding different class positions compete and struggle over the political process of election to the board (a nonclass struggle). The fundamental class position of appropriating surplus value may be sorely needed when one's subsumed class position is threatened.

Other consequences of struggles over the distribution of surplus value include the board redistributing subsumed class payments concomitant with changes in the form in which its conditions of existence are secured. In the face of rising interest rates and/or demands by finance capitalists to have a voice in running the enterprise, the board may decide to self-finance new productive capital accumulation rather than continue to borrow for that purpose. To maintain accumulation in the face of reduced borrowing, the board of directors must reallocate surplus value so that an increased share is distributed to accumulating managers. The finance capitalists have been displaced. To accomplish this change, occupants of subsumed class positions external to the enterprise may be substituted for those inside. Merchants, external to the enterprise, may take over the sale of commodities (the realization process) formerly performed by sales managers, because these merchants offer the same process for a smaller share of distributed surplus value. In all such examples, the composition of λ changes, reflecting the enterprise's shift from one set of processes to another. Such changes also impact upon the amount of surplus value appropriated, as suggested previously.

It is also possible for industrial capitalists, perhaps in alliance with those occupying certain subsumed class positions, not only to resist increased demands by other subsumed classes, but to go on the offense against them. A state, for example, could have its demands for increased surplus value distributions (higher corporate tax revenues) resisted by an alliance of individuals occupying fundamental and subsumed class positions within and without the enterprise. Through lobbying activity such an alliance may struggle to change certain nonclass processes performed in and by the state, for example, legislation, administration, and judicial procedures. It could also work to defeat hostile legislators and elect friendly ones. As a result, the state could have its tax revenues cut and its hegemony as the sole provider of certain social processes challenged. Nonstate sites would be expected and even encouraged to become the providers of such processes. Newly elected state officials friendly to this alliance would become advocates of such changes. [35]

As a different example, industrial capitalists joined by others holding certain subsumed class positions—including some state officials—could press for new laws that restrict other subsumed classes' ability to claim increased shares of surplus value. Rent controls and interest rate ceilings constrain the revenues received by landlords and bankers from industrial capitalists. Such controls represent the effects of political struggles by occupants of several different class positions.

Difficulties for both the enterprise's internal bureaucracy and occupants of its external subsumed class positions can arise from increased claims to surplus value presented by individuals who produce it. Productive laborers may demand higher wages, thereby threatening the surplus value available for distribution to occupants of various subsumed class positions. This, in turn, threatens the existence of the industrial capitalists.

A successful struggle of laborers to lower ε (a fundamental class struggle) and thus ρ may be followed by a struggle among occupants of subsumed class positions over the diminished surplus value available to be distributed (a subsumed class struggle). Here a shift in the value income distribution favoring productive laborers at the expense of those occupying subsumed class positions can lead some of the latter to maintain or even raise their share of a smaller total at the expense of others. So struggles over the appropriation of surplus value may be conditions of existence of struggles over the distribution of that appropriation.

Conversely, higher subsumed class demands may produce attempts by industrial capitalists to raise ε (possibly setting in motion fundamental class struggles). If successful, the increased exploitation rate may provide sufficient extra surplus value to meet such increased subsumed class demands. In this case, conflicts over the distribution of surplus value become a way to change the production of surplus value.

A shift in the value income distribution against productive laborers also can lead to struggles over the two class processes and struggles over a myriad of nonclass processes. Labor, for example, may press for the nationalization of banks (a political struggle) to reduce the burden upon them caused by industrial capitalists raising ε to defray higher interest costs. If successful, the state would then lend to such capitalists and at a rate below what the banks had charged. The state would receive interest income reflecting the new subsumed class position occupied by it. Assuming as a result that the value income distribution would shift back to its previous level (i.e., a fall in ε to its prior level), we can conclude that a change in the enterprise's rate of exploitation was accomplished by a change in the composition of its λ.

We have specified how contradictions within an industrial enterprise create conditions for tensions and possible struggles over class and nonclass processes both within and without the enterprise. The contradictory nature of each industrial enterprise is also overdetermined by the contradictory movements and struggles within all other enterprises. No enterprise can be passive because its conditions of existence depend on the actions of all other enterprises in its own as well as in other industries. Its contradictory development is overdetermined by interactions within its own as well as within other enterprises' class structures. As different sites, enterprises overdetermine each other's existence. Consequently, the classes constituting each enterprise and their connections to external subsumed classes are propelled in different, contradictory directions by the class and nonclass processes comprising all other enterprises.

To examine this mutual effectivity among different industrial enterprises, we present two examples dealing with a narrow but still important range of effects produced by one enterprise's class structure upon another's. They illustrate that occupants of each enterprise's fundamental capitalist class position, in seeking to reproduce their conditions of existence, overdetermine in contradictory ways the conditions of existence of all other enterprises.

Consider first a board of directors distributing surplus value to its managers for the purchase of additional raw materials and equipment (for the accumulation of circulating and fixed capital), certainly one of its economic conditions of existence. This subsumed class process linking the industrial capitalists to their accumulating managers brings the latter into another relationship with the sellers of raw materials and equipment. Assume, for simplicity, that these sellers are also sales managers, part of the class structure of a different industrial enterprise. We have then a relationship between two different groups of managers, each occupying a subsumed class position as a result of the relationship it has with its own surplus-value-appropriating class. This relationship (between the two groups of managers in the different enterprises) includes neither the fundamental nor subsumed class process. It does include, however, the nonclass economic process of commodity exchange.

Suppose there is a change in the productivity of productive workers in the enterprise producing the raw materials or equipment—which we may call the C-enterprise. Let us attribute this productivity change to a changed distribution of surplus value that improves managerial techniques there. Let us further assume more raw materials are required there as inputs to produce the new use values—C-commodities—resulting from this change in productivity.[36] Because of this, the organic composition of capital, k, rises, and assuming no other changes, the value profit rate falls for the C-enterprise, that is, more value is now required to set in motion the same surplus value. Suppose further that the C-enterprise's decline in value costs per unit output (the consequence of improved productivity) is translated into a fall in the exchange value per unit use value of its C-commodity.[37]

Occupants of fundamental and subsumed class positions in the purchasing enterprise clearly will be affected by the selling enterprise's productivity change. The purchasing enterprise's value profit rate has been enhanced by the cheapening of the C-commodity it buys. We can say, therefore, that a new condition of existence of an increased ρ in the buying enterprise is a decreased ρ in the selling enterprise. This increased rate of surplus value appropriation in the buying enterprise allows an increased rate of distribution of surplus value for a variety of different purposes there.

As follows logically from Marxian value theory, this cheapening of the C-commodity becomes a fall in exchange value per unit in the commodity output of the buying enterprise. This fall, in turn, will affect the class structures of other industrial enterprises. If, for example, our buying enterprise produces a wage-good commodity, called a V-commodity, then a fall in its exchange value consequent upon a fall in its costs of production will make possible an increase in the exploitation rate in all capitalist commodity-producing enterprises (as in Marx's discussion of "Relative Surplus Value" in *Capital,* vol. 1). This includes, of course, the C-enterprise where the productivity change initially took place. A rise in ε in all industrial enterprises, and thus in their ρ, makes possible still further changes in the rate of aggregate capital accumulation and λ, and thus ρ once again.

The particular impact upon the value profit rate of the C-enterprise where the initial productivity change took place depends on a concrete analysis—no general laws can be deduced from these specific changes. Indeed, if the value profit rate of the C-enterprise had a tendency to rise as a result of the V-enterprise's impact upon it outweighing its own rise in k, we could say in this case that a condition of such a rise was the initial fall in its own value profit rate. In other words, the decline in the C-enterprise's ρ acts, via its impact upon other industrial enterprises, eventually to raise its own ρ. This example of mutual interaction among these industrial enterprises located in different industries illustrates once more the contradictions embedded in each of their value categories.

Our second example deals with interactions among enterprises *within* an industry. In this case, the enterprise is the site of nonclass struggles emanating from struggles among the industrial capitalist enterprises themselves. Like the aforementioned class struggles, these nonclass struggles over price, markets, advertising, and so forth overdetermine both the rate of production (ρ) and distribution ($K* + \lambda$) of surplus value in each industrial enterprise in each industry.

The Marxian notion of intraindustry competition and its theory of "surplus profits" involve the redistribution of realized surplus value from less to more efficient industrial enterprises within the same industry.[38] The loss of surplus value by some enterprises (of less than average efficiency) and its gain by others (of greater than average efficiency) result from each selling its commodities at their social, that is, average, value. As Marx makes clear, the sale of commodities is a nonclass process. The class analysis of just this specific redistribution of surplus value approaches it as neither the fundamental nor the subsumed class process. To explain this and extend it toward a Marxian theory of competition, we return to the C-enterprise and now consider it to be only one of many such enterprises all producing a similar C-commodity. An industry is the totality of all enterprises producing a particular commodity.

Suppose there is an increase in the productivity of labor in one enterprise in the C-commodity industry.[39] Industrial capitalists in other enterprises within the industry are affected adversely by this assumed productivity change. Assuming no changes other than those specified, they now realize less surplus value than before because the value of their produced C-commodity, as embodied *private* labor time, exceeds the new, lowered *social average* labor time of the C-commodity.[40] The simultaneous use in this industry of different techniques of production (different forces of production) has created an uneven social environment where one superproductive enterprise gains surplus value at the expense of the others. It gains to the degree that its privately embodied labor time deviates from (is lower than) the new social average. As a reward, the superproductive enterprise earns a surplus profit, a profit above the average, reflecting productivity above the average. This surplus profit earned allows it to increase either or both K^* and λ and thus to further aggravate the situation for the other enterprises within the industry.

The relatively efficient subsumed class of managers of one enterprise has rendered the managers of different enterprises relatively inefficient. Because of this, industrial capitalists in these latter enterprises do not receive the surplus value they had expected. Consequently, members of their board of directors in their fundamental capitalist class position are put in jeopardy. The effects of this are soon felt by occupants of all subsumed and fundamental class positions in these enterprises. A good deal of tension and conflict may result over both class and nonclass processes.[41]

To meet the offensive action of the relatively more efficient enterprise, board members in the jeopardized enterprises must move to change the extraction and/or the distribution of surplus value. In other words, they too must go on the offensive so as to defend their class position(s). They must in effect struggle with one another over each and every aspect of the enterprise's existence, for example, over output price, costs of production, research expenditures, interest payments, taxes to the state, rents, advertising, productive capital accumulation, extension of markets, and so forth. This struggle, in turn, overdetermines the production and distribution of surplus value in each enterprise, setting in motion a ceaseless process of interaction among all enterprises and of change in each.

There is no reason to expect each enterprise to react in the same fashion or for the initially innovating enterprise to passively confront the reactions of others. In addition, there are effects produced by the cheapening of the C-commodity on other industries, as analyzed above, and thus a feedback would occur on the C-enterprises from them. This feedback itself could produce conditions for an entirely new process of productivity change to occur within the C-commodity industry, thereby setting off further tensions and conflicts there.

These tensions and conflicts comprise one aspect of the distinctively Marxian concept of competition. A Marxian theory of industrial competition focuses on the structural and especially class relations within and among enterprises that make them antagonists in their struggles to survive. This theory de-emphasizes the notion of competition as willful acts of enterprises against one another (although, of course, such acts occur). Marxian theory also rejects the claims of neoclassical theory that competition in general assures or tends toward particular economic outcomes such as Pareto optimality. Rather, the Marxian approach defines competition as always a particular nexus of relations among enterprises such that the actions of one board of directors jeopardize the conditions of existence of others. Competition will produce all manner of possible outcomes, depending on the conjunctural configuration of social processes in which it occurs. No essential, necessary, final outcome (telos) governs the effects of competition, given Marxian theory's antiessentialism.

In a complex world of overdetermined interactions, it is not surprising to find—indeed, one expects—that different industrial enterprises develop differently and at uneven rates. As different sites, they are constituted differently and thus embody different contradictions. Consequently, their actions and reactions even to similar events will be dissimilar. Through differential access to finance capital, more efficient management, access to cheaper raw materials, bribes to state officials, reduced periods of turnover of capital and so forth, some enterprises' reproduction may drive others out of business. The successful enterprises grow larger and expand their share of the industry's market and the surplus value realized. Their expanded K^* and λ have become conditions of Marx's "centralization of capital" with its possible lessening of competition. However, such centralization of capital can itself be a condition of increased competition in other industries. Increased size of an enterprise may allow it to diversify its outputs and thus become the site of several different commodity productions. In such a case, entry of new competitors occurs in different industries.

We may summarize this mutual effectivity among different enterprises within different industries: the realized value profit rate of each enterprise, its rate of productive capital accumulation, and its rate of distribution to secure other social processes are overdetermined by class and nonclass processes occurring both within and without that enterprise. Each of these value categories is propelled in contradictory directions by intra- and inter-industry interactions. The contradictory nature of each produces within enterprises all kinds of tensions and conflicts over both class and nonclass processes. It produces among enterprises a complex, changing network of relationships, including competition.

The Enterprise and Multiple Class Positions

Board members within a typical industrial enterprise may individually occupy several different class positions. They occupy the fundamental class position directly appropriating surplus value prior to its distribution. They occupy the subsumed class position as distributors of surplus value in its various forms and sometimes also the subsumed class position of receivers of a small director's fee (a subsumed class distribution from themselves). In addition, they may occupy still other subsumed class positions as recipients of subsumed class payments. Often board members form part of the managerial structure of the enterprise, holding the chief administrative jobs—president of the enterprise or various vice-presidential positions. When board members hold such subsumed class management positions and receive salaries and bonuses, their receipt of a share of surplus value occurs together with the sale of their managerial labor power to themselves as industrial capitalists.[42] Here the subsumed class process occurs together with the process of commodity exchange, and the buyer and seller of unproductive labor power happen to be the same individual. Board members also may own shares of the enterprise's stock, especially if stock option plans play an important role in their compensation as managers. They may then distribute a share of surplus value to themselves in the form of dividends. In sum, we have "corporate individuals" occupying four different class positions: the fundamental one as industrial capitalist, and three subsumed ones as distributors of surplus value, managers, and owners.

Board members may also occupy nonclass positions within the enterprise. They may, for example, receive interest from loans made to anyone other than an industrial capitalist, for example, to productive or unproductive laborers. In this particular relationship between lender and borrower, neither the fundamental nor the subsumed class process is present. In addition, board members may also participate in a variety of relationships external to those within the enterprise which include still additional class and nonclass positions. Besides the capitalist fundamental and subsumed class positions, they may also occupy noncapitalist class positions. And such individuals may occupy a number of different nonclass positions besides those within the enterprise.

Board members occupying these multiple class and nonclass positions embody and experience the contradictions overdetermined in all these positions. These contradictions move them to act. Their behavior in any one position is overdetermined by their different experiences and actions in all such positions. The appropriation and distribution of surplus value within the industrial enterprise, two particular economic processes in which they participate, are overdetermined in part by all the class (capitalist and noncapitalist) and nonclass positions they may occupy. Thus, board members' distribution of surplus value to any particular condition of existence, say to accumulate productive capital, is influenced by the totality of their corporate and noncorporate lives.

The occupation by an individual of several different class positions occurs for a host of reasons. To receive income, individuals must seek (1) subsumed class positions, and/or (2) fundamental ones as performers of surplus labor, and/or (3) nonclass income-producing positions. As suggested, management positions offer significant rewards. Further, board membership allows individuals to be privy to "insiders" information concerning events that affect the prices of various assets and commodities. Such swings in the prices of stocks, bonds, and real estate can earn individuals vast sums in relatively short periods of time. In this case, the capital gains realized result from the occupation of a nonclass position as a buyer/seller of assets. No class process occurs in this relationship between buyer and seller of assets, but the key to any nonclass income so earned may well be the individual's concurrent occupation of the fundamental capitalist class position. In general, board membership facilitates occupation of a variety of different subsumed class and nonclass positions. The latter provide the opportunity to amass great fortunes. Further, occupation of several different class positions allows one to create sizable money funds with which to enter still other class positions, such as a subsumed class moneylender or even the fundamental capitalist and subsumed class owner positions in a new enterprise. This would be a transition of the industrial capitalist from being a board member in one corporation to becoming the new owner-operator of a different business.

Membership on one or more boards can become a condition for membership on several other boards. Individuals would then occupy several fundamental capitalist class positions in these different enterprises. This phenomenon of "interlocking directorates" can easily facilitate individuals' access to a number of subsumed class positions in relation to these enterprises. And occupation of a number of these helps secure the various capitalist fundamental class positions held. Such may be the symbiotic relationship between fundamental and subsumed class positions.

There is an additional reason for multiple class positions that deserves further explanation. An enterprise's competitive position depends to a degree on the class mobility of its board members. The enterprise may gain favorable access to credit if finance capitalists are elected to its board of directors. Such credit can then be used to expand productive capital accumulation, perhaps embodying new techniques of production that lower its relative costs of production and create a competitive advantage, as analyzed previously. In turn, finance capitalists can use their newly occupied fundamental capitalist class position to enhance their other class positions: they gain some control over the distribution of surplus value to occupants of subsumed class positions, including to themselves as moneylenders and perhaps as managers and stockholders if they occupy those positions as well. This control can give them a comparative advantage over other finance capitalists who do not also occupy such a fundamental capitalist class position. Thus finance capitalists may compete with one another over gaining access to membership on different boards of directors.

Besides favorable access to credit, the competitive position of an enterprise depends upon its development of new products and new forms of technology that reduce its costs of production. One way to create a favorable research program to accomplish these two objectives is to build relationships with research scientists, management specialists, and promising students at universities. Such relationships can be improved by appointing particular scientists at these universities to the board. These individuals in their capacity as board members would be industrial capitalists. Similarly, since a condition of existence of surplus value is the sale of the produced commodities, each enterprise attempts to extend its market. One way to facilitate such an extension is to elect a former state official to the board. This may improve greatly the probability of receiving government contracts.

The previously mentioned interlocking directorates also participate in determining the competitive position of an enterprise. For example, suppose that surplus value in an enterprise is distributed to its managers to purchase the stock of other industrial enterprises.[43] This decision may be taken with the expectation that such a subsumed class ownership position will provide the purchasing enterprise with some control over the decisions of the partly owned enterprises. The purpose of such control is the improvement of the competitive position of the purchasing enterprise. Indeed, if nothing else, the enterprise will now be the recipient of dividends and/or capital gains which allow expanded accumulation and nonaccumulation processes.[44] Other considerations likely involve the access to other enterprises' sources of raw materials, to their newly developed commodities, and/or to their markets. However, such a subsumed class ownership position may not be sufficient to achieve the corporate aims. The next move is for some members of the board to attempt a transition to new fundamental class positions by being elected to the other enterprises' boards of directors. These individuals would now occupy several industrial capitalist positions, one in each of the enterprises.

In general, enterprises purchase stock in other enterprises so as to enhance their relative competitive positions. This allows board members in their new ownership positions to directly modify the distribution of surplus value in several enterprises. It can culminate in their becoming board members and thus industrial capitalists in these other enterprises. As a further consequence of such actions, the distribution of surplus value in the different enterprises can become so intertwined that it is as if one combined enterprise now exists. Some enterprises will merge together legally, producing a single enterprise with its one board of directors. The number of industrial capitalist class positions would have declined in this case. The combined capital of this merged enterprise can be an effective weapon against current and potential competitors and can also serve as a financial base with and from which entry into other industries can be achieved.

In any given industrial enterprise, board members may feel forced to distribute surplus value to the purchase of other enterprises' stocks. They do so because industrial capitalists in competitive enterprises are purchasing such stocks for competitive reasons and thus threatening their survival. Some boards may even react to the purchase of their own enterprise's stock by purchasing stock in the acquiring industrial capitalist's own enterprise with the hope of undermining the latter's aggressive action. A competitive scramble for corporate stock results in which individuals serving on different boards in their industrial capitalist class positions are also subsumed to one another in their ownership positions. Of course, still other occupants of subsumed class positions such as finance capitalists may come to play a key role as providers of money-capital necessary to purchase large blocks of shares. Once again, their membership on the board of directors of a purchasing company may become a decisive condition in granting the loan. We have then the resulting phenomenon of "interlocking directorates": in our words, a relatively small group of individuals occupy the fundamental capitalist class positions in several different enterprises.

The composition of an industrial capitalist board of directors reflects the diverse, multiple class and nonclass positions of its members. Besides all being industrial capitalists in the given enterprise, we expect directors to hold several fundamental capitalist positions in different enterprises, to be individually and/or collectively subsumed class owners of stocks and bonds of the given enterprise and/or of others, to be subsumed financiers, and to occupy various subsumed class management positions in the several different enterprises. Directors will also be involved in different nonclass processes internal and external to these enterprises.

The different fundamental and subsumed class positions held by any typical board member suggests the difficulty of any simple class taxonomy of individuals based upon their internal or external relationship to any given capitalist enterprise. At any moment, individuals may well be both "inside and outside" an enterprise—that is, occupying positions as both extracting and finance capitalists, as both owning and managerial capitalists. One objective of Marxian analysis is the exact specification of such multiple class positions and the relative quantitative distribution of internal and external positions held by individuals.

Such an analysis permits us to explain how and why members of the same class positions struggle with one another over class and nonclass processes. We can thus undertake Marxian analyses of class struggles among capitalists. For example, board members holding class positions predominantly internal to the enterprise may want to reduce shares of surplus value distributed to those holding (subsumed) class positions external to it. Some within this latter group may also occupy the fundamental class position on the board of directors. A subsumed class struggle occurs between these two groups despite the fact that both sets of individuals participate in the appropriation of surplus value, the same fundamental class process.

Once Again: What Is a Capitalist?

We noted in the previous chapter how individuals' occupation of different fundamental and subsumed class positions allows us to make class sense of the differentiated Marxian concept of the capitalist. Such an understanding also can help clarify the changing class nature of an industrial enterprise and of capitalism in general. The problem of the capitalist for this chapter is as follows: in *Capital,* volume 3, Marx specifies very clearly the "disappearance" of the capitalist with the development of capitalism and the joint-stock company.[45] In this context, he also refers to the "abolition of capital as private property within the framework of capitalist production itself."[46]

Such notions have generated much controversy over the years. Perhaps they have also contributed to the idea that since by Marx's own admission capitalists have disappeared, other groups of human beings in society such as managers, managers/owners, or financiers have become the key classes wielding economic and political power. Approaches focusing upon these three groups share a common focus upon "control" of the enterprise as the key organizational concept that constructs their understanding of the enterprise. The concept of control or domination comes to define the capitalist, replacing a definition in terms of surplus labor appropriation. Notions such as "who controls whom," "power without property," "corporate capitalist control and power," and "financial power" replace Marxian class concepts in key texts on the "modern corporation."[47]

If by *control, power,* or *domination* is meant the political process of commanding individuals to accomplish some objectives, then, as already pointed out in chapter 3, it is a constituent process of a number of different relationships both within and external to the enterprise. Individuals occupying either fundamental or subsumed class positions can have power or command over others who occupy either position. For example, managers may own no stock but have the power to make major corporate decisions regarding the running of the corporation. They have Berle's "power without property." [48] Their performance of this political process of wielding power is different from the economic one of receiving surplus labor. The former process is a condition of existence of the latter one. Those who wield power as a condition of surplus value's existence and receive payment for so doing occupy a subsumed and not a fundamental class position. The point is not a minor one. Marx did not create a new discursive entry point of domination; his discourse does not produce a "power analytical study of capitalism." Whatever one thinks of the importance and need for such an approach, it is not the Marxian analytical contribution.

Unfortunately, the specificity of the exploitation concept seems to become somewhat confused when Marx personifies it in its human embodiment, the capitalist. As we noted in chapter 3, Marx often refers to the latter as one who not only exploits labor, but also owns capital, commands labor to produce commodities, lends money-capital, and may even sell commodities produced. There seems to be a contradiction here: how can a capitalist personify only productive capital (i.e., productive of surplus value) while also personifying privately owned capital, money-capital, and merchant-capital as well as supervision? Given this seemingly ambiguous specification of one of the key parts of the Marxian approach, perhaps it is not surprising that its readers might seek alternatives, especially those that offer a way to deal effectively with social developments (e.g., managerial or credit revolution) claimed to be beyond the theoretical specification found in *Capital.*

The meaning of Marx's concept of the capitalist, like that of all other concepts, changes throughout the discourse as Marx introduces ever new concepts in his task of constructing a knowledge of capitalism. The meaning of each of these concepts is overdetermined by the effects of all others upon it. Each changes its meaning as these effects change. The notion of a capitalist in volume 3's construction is far different from that in volume 1 because of the more elaborated knowledge of capitalism Marx presents there. The third volume's subsumed classes, absent from the first volume, secure those social processes such as supervision, distribution of credit, land, and means of production, and merchanting that have been introduced and analyzed there in some detail. These processes were not the subject of such an analysis in volume 1. They were assumed to be given to the discussion of capitalism in the first volume of *Capital*, an assumption perfectly consistent with its limited focus on the fundamental class process.

Therefore, the volume-1 capitalist is indeed an individual who appropriates surplus value (the focus of this volume) *and* who participates in several other social processes as listed previously. In contrast, the volume-3 capitalist (Marx's *industrial* capitalist) is more richly and strictly delimited as one who only exploits labor. Other individuals (including Marx's *merchant* and *money-lending* capitalists) within and without the enterprise perform those social processes required for surplus value's existence. Marx goes to great pains to specify the differences among these different "capitalists," and even, to a degree, why they occur.

Marx claims that the change is due to the development and growth of a capitalist social formation. This refers to the increase in the minimum size of an industrial enterprise, resulting from competitive productive capital accumulation and centralization. It refers as well to the associated growth of a credit and banking system. These changed conditions of surplus value's existence are the key foci of the third volume. These changes have, in turn, changed (effected) the nature of the industrial capitalist. All of the above processes now performed by other individuals have been stripped from the industrial capitalist as such, thus revealing exploitation in its pure, naked form.

> With the development of co-operation on the part of the labourers, and of stock enterprises on the part of the bourgeoisie, even the last pretext for the confusion of profit of enterprise and wages of management was removed, and profit appeared . . . in theory, as mere surplus-value, a value for which no equivalent was paid, as realized unpaid labour. It was then seen that the functioning capitalist really exploits labour, and that the fruit of his exploitation, when working with borrowed capital, was divided into interest and profit of enterprise, a surplus of profit over interest.[49]

The "wages of management" are a condition of, not a component of, exploitation.

The volume-1 capitalist has disappeared in volume 3, but *not* the fundamental capitalist class process, not the industrial capitalist. In Marx's own words:

> But since, on the one hand, the mere owner of capital, the money-capitalist, has to face the functioning capitalist, while money-capital itself assumes a social character with the advance of credit, being concentrated in banks and loaned out by them instead of its original

owners, and since, on the other hand, the mere manager who has no title whatever to the capital, whether through borrowing it or otherwise, performs all the real functions pertaining to the functioning capitalist as such, only the functionary remains and the capitalist disappears as superfluous from the production process.[50]

The industrial (or Marx's "functioning") capitalist no longer need also manage the production process or own capital as his or her private property. Whereas in early capitalist enterprises the industrial capitalist was often the only manager as well, now a separate group of managers receives wages for this unproductive labor. Whereas in early capitalist enterprises one individual, the industrial capitalist, was expected to provide his or her own money-capital for the venture, now the industrial capitalist becomes the user of other individuals' money-capital, and the latter become "mere owners," receiving dividends or interest for their investment. To labor or to own and distribute property is to receive respectively wages, dividends, or interest, but not to appropriate surplus value.[51]

The industrial capitalists of volume 3 are then the board members of an enterprise. They appear as pure surplus value appropriators divorced from private ownership of capital and management of production, delegating the latter to managers and converting the former into social capital. They thus receive surplus value for doing absolutely nothing. Engels, in describing the changing nature of the capitalist with the growth of a capitalist society's productive forces and the development of its huge industrial joint-stock companies, writes: "All the social functions of the capitalists are now carried out by salaried employees. The capitalist has no longer any social activity save the pocketing of revenues, the clipping of coupons and gambling on the Stock Exchange."[52]

Overdetermination of Productive Capital Accumulation

The board members' occupation of multiple class and nonclass positions effects every process within the enterprise. To show this, we first derive a new class structural equation for the enterprise. It differs from our previously specified class equation by the inclusion of the revenues from and the expenditures necessary to reproduce the board's occupation of different class and nonclass positions. We then use this equation to show how a particular nonclass process—we will choose the example of foreign portfolio investment by an industrial enterprise—generates a new subsumed class position for its board members with contradictory effects on its productive capital accumulation. Foreign portfolio investment is taken as the illustrative example because of its importance within the Marxian tradition.

The occupation of new class and nonclass positions by the industrial capitalists changes not only the economic process of capital accumulation within the enterprise, but also all other social processes there as well. These changed processes within any one enterprise effect other enterprises within and outside of its own industry. In turn, such effects produce changes in the processes of these other enterprises which feed back upon the initially changed enterprise, thereby creating still additional changes there, and so on.

This continual process of change is a recurrent theme in this and other chapters. Because of its importance, we must make an additional remark about our use of an algebraic model in this section to help explain our argument. Models, like any conceptual entity, are useful discursive devices to communicate particular analytical points. However, they are useless vehicles for understanding the continual process of change central to Marxian theory. The moment they are used to illustrate a point is the moment they are negated (require change) by the need to specify all the different effects produced by this use itself. For that reason, we think of a model, no matter its complexity, as a set of conceptual statements in an argument. And like any other metaphorical statement in a discourse, we use a model to advance ours.

Any industrial capitalist enterprise may be engaged in a number of different class and nonclass processes that can generate three forms of revenues. The enterprise receives surplus value if its board members participate in the fundamental class process and occupy the fundamental class position. If in addition its board members provide conditions of existence to other industrial capitalists, they then occupy capitalist subsumed class positions and receive subsumed class revenues from them. These revenues must be added to directly appropriated surplus value to derive the total revenues of the enterprise. Finally, nonclass revenues must also be added to this revenue total if board members receive revenues by participating in nonclass processes.

The enterprise's distributions to secure these three revenue forms can be divided into the following three portions: a share to those occupants of subsumed class positions who secure the conditions of existence of the enterprise's direct appropriation of surplus value; a share to those individuals who secure the conditions of existence of the enterprise's receipt of subsumed class revenues from other enterprises; and a share to those who secure the conditions of the nonclass revenues received. The following equation summarizes on its left-hand side the class and nonclass revenues received and on its right-hand side its distributions to secure each of these revenues:

$$SV + SCR + NCR = \Sigma SC + \Sigma X + \Sigma Y. \qquad (4.17)$$

Equation (4.17) can be interpreted as follows. SV and ΣSC reflect respectively the board's fundamental class position and subsumed class distributions to reproduce that position; we have already analyzed this. SCR stands for all the subsumed class interest, dividends, ground rents, merchant fees, monopoly receipts, and franchise payments earned by the board in its additional subsumed class positions, subsumed to industrial capitalists external to the enterprise. The total payments to reproduce the conditions of existence of these receipts are denoted by ΣX. NCR stands for all the nonclass revenues earned and ΣY for the total payments to reproduce the conditions for such revenues. NCR includes, for example, interest earned on loans to productive laborers and occupants of subsumed class positions, rents from lands made available to these individuals, dividends received from purchased stock of non-commodity-producing enterprises such as banks and finance companies, and revenues earned from the sale of monopolized commodities (whose prices exceed their values) to productive laborers and occupants of subsumed class positions.[53]

Not all the nonclass revenues received by the enterprise require expenditures. For example, the enterprise may purchase commodities at less than their value, thereby earning the differential abstract labor time for itself (a component of NCR). If the commodity purchased were productive labor power, then as explained in chapter 3, its sellers would make a nonclass payment, W^3, to the buyer (the industrial enterprise) for the opportunity to sell it. This nonclass payment is a component of NCR in equation (4.17). In times when the supply of productive labor power exceeds the demand, productive laborers not only labor for some hours for no pay, but they also pay the industrial capitalist for the opportunity to do so by lowering the price of their commodity. This latter payment or unequal exchange may be the result of changes that have little to do with ΣY.[54]

For a complete specification of an enterprise's revenue and expenditure flows, equation (4.17) would have to be modified to include on its left-hand side a new nonclass revenue category standing for the receipt of revenues from the issuance of new debt and/or stocks and on its right-hand side a category representing the repayment, if any, of such debts and retirements of stock equities. We shall ignore here such additional revenue and repayment categories except to note that a class analysis of them would seek to differentiate corporate borrowings, stock issues, and repayments according to whether or not each was related to a class or nonclass process. Corporate borrowings to generate surplus value would be placed in one nonclass revenue category, borrowings to establish subsumed class positions in another, and debt to establish nonclass processes in still a third. In parallel manner, we would attempt to group on the right-hand side of the equation the debt repayments, interest paid, and dividends distributed, according to which of the three revenue sources such expenditures secured. Interest and dividend payments that secured the conditions of existence of surplus value would be placed in ΣSC, those that secured the conditions for subsumed class positions in ΣX, and the others in ΣY for securing nonclass positions. The repayment and retirement of corporate debt and stock would appear subdivided into three separate categories.[55]

We have noted previously how a board, for competitive reasons, may decide to distribute a portion of surplus value to its managers to purchase the stock of other industrial enterprises. For the same reasons it may also lend money, rent land and means of production, and distribute franchises to other industrial capitalists. It may do these things to defend or expand its competitive position, that is, to secure its conditions of existence. The distributions to accomplish such processes would be contained in ΣSC and not in ΣX. They would be distributions to reproduce the conditions of SV's existence. However, they also generate subsumed class incomes for the board in its different subsumed class positions as collective owners, financiers, landlords, and franchise owners. Therefore, they must be added to SCR, despite there being no ΣX for them. In contrast to this situation, an enterprise's board may distribute surplus value not to secure the conditions of existence of its fundamental class position, but to occupy new subsumed class positions.[56] Such distributions would be in ΣX and not in ΣSC.

In both situations, assuming no other changes, the initial distribution on the right-hand side of equation (4.17) must change to account for the new payments. For example, if the purchase of stock is to secure a condition of surplus value's existence, then, ceteris paribus, there must be a redistribution of payments away from securing one set of processes so as to allow an increased stock purchase.[57] As previously noted, occupants of subsumed class positions charged with providing that set of processes may defend their threatened positions by moving against such stock purchases. A conflict over the distribution of surplus value could develop inside the enterprise. If, instead, the purchase of stock has nothing to do with the competitive position of the enterprise, but is accomplished so that the board can occupy a new subsumed class position, then the reproduction of the enterprise's fundamental class process is placed in jeopardy. Here we have a redistribution away from surplus value's conditions of existence to those processes necessary for the establishment instead of new subsumed class positions taken by the enterprise. Thus, ΣSC falls by the amount that ΣX rises. Once again, a conflict could develop inside the enterprise over the board's "transition" from one class position to another.

This example serves to underscore the point that knowledge of the *presence* of a process itself, here the purchase of stock, is not sufficient to link it to a subsumed class distribution. Only if such a purchase is necessary for the continued existence of the enterprise's surplus value do we place it in ΣSC. That necessity always remains to be demonstrated in terms of the conjunctural social context.

Equation (4.17) has allowed us to modify our previous revenue equation for the enterprise (equation 4.1) and write a new and more general class and nonclass structural revenue and expenditure equation for the industrial enterprise. This equation, in turn, provides the basis to develop a new productive capital accumulation equation for the enterprise that takes into account the fundamental, subsumed, and nonclass positions occupied by its board members. Correspondingly, the enterprise changes its nature by now becoming the site of processes generative of these other class and nonclass revenues. It has developed new sources of revenues, and these, along with the surplus value pumped out of labor, effect its distributions to secure both its accumulation of capital process and many other social processes (including ΣX and ΣY).

To show this, we may solve equation (4.17) for the rate of accumulation of productive capital:

$$\frac{\Delta C + \Delta V}{C + V} = \frac{SV + SCR + NCR}{C + V}$$
$$- \frac{[(1 - \beta)SC_I + SC_O + SC_C + SC_R + \Sigma X + \Sigma Y]}{C + V} \qquad (4.18)$$

Let $\hat{K}^*$ equal the enterprise's new productive capital accumulation rate, $\hat{\rho}$ be its new rate of return from the fundamental, subsumed, and nonclass positions occupied, and $\hat{\lambda}$ equal its rate of distribution to secure the conditions of existence of these different revenues. We have then our new accumulation equation for the enterprise:

$$\hat{K}^* = \hat{\rho} - \hat{\lambda}. \qquad (4.19)$$

Compared to our previous accumulation equation (4.15), $\hat{\rho}$ no longer refers only to the rate of surplus value appropriation from productive capital. It now includes revenues earned from sources other than the consumption of labor power. It follows that the total revenues of an enterprise need no longer equal its surplus value. We can see this more clearly if we write an alternative expression for $\hat{\rho}$ that focuses upon its three revenue contributions. To do this, first define two new rates of return: $r_1 = SCR/X_T$ and $r_2 = NCR/Y_T$. r_1 and r_2 refer to the enterprise's rates of return on its subsumed and nonclass revenue positions respectively. The denominators in these two return rates denote the costs of securing these subsumed and nonclass revenue flows to the enterprise. Included in X_T, for example, would be the value of industrial stocks, bonds, patents, and so forth owned by the enterprise and in Y_T the value of financial or nonindustrial assets owned. Define two "portfolio weights": $\alpha_1 = X_T/(C + V)$ and $\alpha_2 = Y_T/(C + V)$. Each ratio relates the value of bonds, stocks, and so forth held in the enterprise's portfolio to the value of its productive capital. We can now call $\hat{\rho}$ the enterprise's "complex profit rate" comprising the return to its fundamental class position, and the weighted returns to its subsumed and nonclass positions:

$$\hat{\rho} = \rho + r_1\alpha_1 + r_2\alpha_2. \qquad (4.20)$$

Clearly, the more important these subsumed and nonclass weighted revenue returns, the greater the deviation of $\hat{\rho}$ from ρ, or in equation form: $\hat{\rho} - \rho = r_1\alpha_1 + r_2\alpha_2 = (SCR + NCR)/(C + V)$. The new distribution rate $\hat{\lambda}$ also deviates from the old λ to the degree that ΣX and ΣY become quantitatively important, or $\hat{\lambda} - \lambda = (\Sigma X + \Sigma Y)/(C + V)$. Because of the new sources of revenue, $\hat{\rho} > \rho$. However, without further specification, we cannot determine whether $\hat{K}^*/K^* \gtreqless 1$. We will explore this problem in the concrete example of foreign investment presented later.[58]

These deviations or differences between equations (4.19) and (4.15) point to the changing class analytical meaning of an enterprise's "profits" as it participates in subsumed and nonclass processes that generate revenues. The enterprise's "complex profit rate" can rise in equation (4.20) even if the value profit rate stays the same or falls. Conversely, a calculated fall in the "complex profit rate" may signal for some analysts an economic crisis for the enterprise and, if widely experienced, for the economy. This conclusion, however, ignores the class and nonclass composition of such a rate and thus disregards the possibility that the value profit rate is rising and thus creating the conditions for an economic expansion. Indeed, this very rise in one "profit rate" (ρ) may be conditioned by the fall in the other two (r_1 and r_2). And the more important are the two "portfolio weights" in equation (4.20), the more problematic become any conclusions drawn about economic crises from an analysis of changes and movements in only one portion of an enterprise's revenues. Parallel to our discussion in the previous chapter, we can say that the Marxian notions of profits and profit rate embrace completely different meanings depending on what form of revenues are being specified.

In general, we can write a formula for any industrial enterprise's "net profits" that recognizes explicitly the different combinations of class and nonclass revenues received and the different subsumed and nonclass expenditures made to generate such revenues: "net profits" $= (SV + SCR + NCR) - \Sigma Z$, where ΣZ stands for whatever combination of expenditures are deemed necessary by the enterprise to generate such revenues. It denotes the deductions from the enterprise's gross revenues to arrive at some notion of "net profits." Clearly this notion will change as the enterprise not only adds and subtracts revenue positions, but also changes what it considers appropriate to include in the ΣZ category itself. For example, for some enterprises, ΣZ may include all expenditures save those productive and unproductive capital expenditures directed to expand their class and nonclass revenue positions. In this case, "net profits" would equal only that combined capital accumulation.

However, as already suggested in this and the previous chapter, several other alternatives are possible as well. Other enterprises may seek to expand their revenue positions via varying combinations of productive and unproductive capital accumulation along with a variety of other types of subsumed class and nonclass expenditures. The latter could include interest payments to banks, research and development expenditures, and so forth. The meaning of *net profits* would thus vary across these enterprises, depending upon what each included in its particular ΣZ category. Such differences reflect the uniqueness of each enterprise's class and nonclass structure and its particular dynamic in regard to accounting practices, tax laws, fundamental and subsumed class struggles, and competition.

We may conclude that there are many different meanings of the term *net profits*. The same conclusion applies to profit rates. Any calculation of such a rate obviously depends upon what is measured in the numerator and denominator of such a fraction, and, as we just argued, this rate will vary from enterprise to enterprise.

A Concrete Example

Suppose the board of an industrial enterprise distributes a portion of surplus value to its managers for the purpose of investing abroad in the stocks and bonds of foreign industrial capitalist enterprises.[59] The board receives dividends and interest for its foreign portfolio investment and becomes subsumed to foreign industrial capitalists. The investing enterprise does not exploit labor in the foreign land; it provides a condition of existence of such exploitation there. The flow of money-capital into the foreign land is a result of the action of individuals who occupy a subsumed class position, and the return flow of dividends and interest to them indicates a claim on already created and appropriated surplus value. Capital flows, like trade flows, may well be conditions of but are not in and of themselves surplus labor extractions. We point this out because such flows are at times understood to be examples of how one country "exploits" another. Such formulations conflate the fundamental and subsumed class processes: precisely what Marxian theory, as we understand it, seeks to avoid in its class analyses.

We are assuming here that this particular distribution of surplus value to the enterprise's managers for foreign stock and bond purchases is to secure a condition of existence of the enterprise's surplus value. Perhaps the commodities produced in the foreign enterprise are important—say, as productive inputs—to the investing enterprise's competitive position in its own industry. Occupation of the subsumed class positions allows it to have some influence over the foreign industrial capitalists' distribution of their surplus value and thus the exchange value of the commodities they produce. For these reasons the foreign investment is included in the total distributions of surplus value and not in ΣX. Let us now simplify matters by further assuming that there are no other expenditures to establish subsumed class positions ($\Sigma X = 0$), no other subsumed class revenues are received, and nonclass revenues and expenditures do not matter ($NCR = \Sigma Y = 0$).[60] All other distributions other than those for productive capital accumulation and foreign investment can be denoted by $\Sigma \overline{SC}$.[61] The enterprise can choose among productive capital accumulation, $\Delta C + \Delta V$, unproductive capital accumulation in terms of foreign portfolio investment, denoted by ΔA, and distributions to secure other social processes (conditions of its existence), $\Sigma \overline{SC}$. With these assumptions we can write the revenue and expenditure equation for the enterprise:

$$SV + SCR = \Delta C + \Delta V + \Delta A + \Sigma \overline{SC}. \qquad (4.21)$$

The left-hand side of equation (4.21) shows the total revenues of the enterprise greater than its directly appropriated surplus value because of the subsumed class position occupied. The right-hand side shows the different distributions to secure its fundamental class position. Solving equation (4.21) for productive capital accumulation yields

$$\Delta C + \Delta V = SV + SCR - \Delta A - \Sigma \overline{SC}. \qquad (4.22)$$

Let us assume that the enterprise earns a return on its total stock of foreign portfolio investments of r_1. Then r_1 corresponds to the previously defined rate of return to a subsumed class position. Its subsumed class revenues are then $SCR = r_1 A$. Now we will assume that the board decides to maintain a constant ratio between its foreign assets owned and its total wealth ($C + V + A$). It maintains this particular portfolio balance in order to defend its fundamental class position against competitors' intrusions. Such a position is assumed to give the board a nonnegligible influence in affecting the decisions of the foreign board of directors. If its position is threatened, the ratio can always be changed. What this amounts to is the assertion that changes in the ratio are independent of changes in r_1 (or of changes in ρ).[62]

A constant proportion of total wealth held in the form of foreign assets is equivalent to a constant ratio of unproductive foreign to productive capital assets. Let us call this ratio $\alpha_1 = A/(C + V)$; it is the previously defined portfolio weight. Divide equation (4.22) by $C + V$ to derive

$$\frac{\Delta C + \Delta V}{C + V} = \frac{SV}{C + V} + \frac{SCR}{C + V} - \frac{\Delta A}{C + V} - \frac{\Sigma \overline{SC}}{C + V}. \quad (4.23)$$

Using our previous notation and letting $\Sigma \overline{SC}/(C + V) = \bar{\lambda}$ (for the moment a constant), we have

$$\hat{K}^* = \rho + r_1 \alpha_1 - \frac{\Delta A}{C + V} - \bar{\lambda}. \quad (4.24)$$

Since α_1 is assumed constant, we can further simplify equation (4.24) by noting that $A = \alpha_1 (C + V)$ and thus $\Delta A = \alpha_1 (\Delta C + \Delta V)$. Substituting this result in equation (4.24), we have

$$\hat{K}^* = \rho + r_1 \alpha_1 - \alpha_1 \hat{K}^* - \bar{\lambda}. \quad (4.25)$$

Solving equation (4.25) for $\hat{K}^*$ yields the basic-rate-of-accumulation equation for the enterprise:

$$\hat{K}^* = \frac{\rho}{1 + \alpha_1} + \frac{r_1 \alpha_1}{1 + \alpha_1} - \frac{\bar{\lambda}}{1 + \alpha_1}. \quad (4.26)$$

This equation shows the effects of multiple class positions on the enterprise's rate of productive capital accumulation. In our example, the latter depends upon the rate of appropriation of surplus value from productive capital (ρ), the rate of return to a subsumed class position (r_1), its distributions to investment in nonproductive capital as a proportion of its total corporate wealth ($\alpha_1/[1 + \alpha_1]$), and its distributions to all the other processes necessary for its fundamental capitalist class position ($\bar{\lambda}$). If the board decides to increase its foreign investment so as to improve or defend its competitive industrial capitalist existence, the effect will be to raise the domestic rate of productive capital accumulation if the rate of return to the subsumed class position (r_1) is greater than the value profit rate (ρ) less its demand rate ($\bar{\lambda}$). Increased foreign investment will lower the productive capital accumulation rate if the converse holds.[63]

An alternative way of expressing the same result is to define a new profit rate for the enterprise, the internal rate, ρ_1, equal to its rate of productive capital accumulation. This is the rate of return for the industrial enterprise net of all of its expenses and dividends. In the language of accountants, it is the ratio of the net retained earnings of the corporation destined for capital accumulation (βSC_1) to its total productive capital ($C + V$), or $\rho_1 = \hat{K}^*$. Using this result, we can conclude that a decision to invest more abroad will raise, leave unchanged, or lower the productive capital accumulation rate, depending on whether the rate of return to the subsumed class position exceeds, equals, or is lower than the internal profit rate of the enterprise.[64] If the capital accumulation rate is indeed raised, then other domestic enterprises' competitive positions may be threatened, forcing them to react. Under these specified conditions, foreign portfolio investment can serve to raise the domestic rate of productive accumulation and enhance competition.

If we assume all industrial enterprises in a given country are alike, we can derive an aggregate result. The export of surplus value in the form of purchase of foreign stocks and bonds could expand the aggregate productive capital accumulation rate and, assuming no other changes, domestic employment if the foreign return (r_1) is greater than the domestic internal profit rate.[65] Such a capital outflow may also initially relieve pressure on the domestic labor market, perhaps resulting in a price of labor power below its value. This unequal exchange benefits the domestic enterprises. In this eventuality we must relax our prior assumption that $NCR = 0$. The nonclass payment, W^3, paid by sellers of labor power to the enterprise, would become part of the latter's NCR and thus appear in our equation as added revenues to be distributed. Eventually the price of labor power rises as the returned subsumed class revenues enhance domestic capital accumulation and employment. The price may then exceed the value of labor power, setting in motion still other changes. In this new situation of relative labor scarcity, the enterprises' previously positive nonclass revenues have become zero and they must now distribute a share of their surplus value in the form of higher wages (W^2) to their productive workers in the latter's subsumed class positions. This too will affect the expenditures of enterprises.

There is no reason to expect that foreign portfolio investment will leave unchanged the domestic rate of exploitation or organic composition of capital, especially since we have assumed it was undertaken to improve an industrial enterprise's competitive position. Suppose that foreign portfolio investments permit enterprises to gain cheap sources of constant and variable capital. If so, then a rise is α_1 could increase ρ in equation (4.26) through its effects on either or both ε and k (if both, then we assume that C falls in value more than does V). Taking this cheapening of capital into account, we can extend our result as follows. On the assumption that ρ is positively related to α_1, a rise in the propensity to invest abroad in unproductive capital may increase the domestic productive accumulation rate even if the portfolio rate of return is less than the internal profit rate.[66] This is a striking result and one that is consistent with our previous specifications. The decision to distribute surplus value to purchase foreign assets (stocks and bonds) can pay off handsomely for capitalist industrial enterprises, despite a relatively low foreign (subsumed class) return.

This, of course, is what imperialism is partly about: foreign investment creating the social conditions in which cheap C and V will be produced for the benefit of the investing productive capitalists. So occupation of a subsumed class position to foreign industrial capitalists can become a key vehicle for domestic industrial capitalists to raise their rate of exploitation, lower their organic composition of capital, and perhaps garner surplus profits within the industry in which they compete. The domestic productive capital accumulation rate of such enterprises can thus be enhanced through the use of such a subsumed class position.

We hasten to add that there is no necessity for the rate of capital accumulation to rise in these examples. It is possible for the industrial capitalists to expand distributions to the nonaccumulation processes rather than to the accumulation one. They might, for example, distribute extra revenues earned from foreign investments in the form of higher managerial salaries, interest payments, dividends, rents to landlords, merchant fees, and taxes to the state. To see this, relax the assumption of a constant $\bar{\lambda}$. Now assume that the foreign subsumed class return exceeds the internal profit rate. If the board just maintains but does not expand its rate of productive capital accumulation, as we have so far assumed, then the foreign portfolio subsumed class position occupied allows the board to expand its distributions to all of its subsumed classes other than the accumulating managers.[67] Occupants of subsumed class positions other than accumulating managers receive the benefits of foreign investment through higher revenues received. Of course the value-cheapening effect is still at work, and this could act to raise the rate of capital accumulation. In that case, the board would be able to expand distributions both to the accumulation *and* nonaccumulation processes. If, as discussed previously, an increased λ is a condition for a higher ρ, then expanded distribution to λ will permit a still higher accumulation rate to take place.

If enterprises invest abroad when the foreign subsumed class return is relatively low, it is possible to maintain or even increase the domestic productive capital accumulation rate by lowering distributions to occupants of various subsumed class positions. Taking the value-cheapening effect into account makes it possible for the accumulation rate to expand even more. In this case, individuals who occupy domestic subsumed class positions other than accumulating managers would bear the burden of such foreign investment. A shift in the distribution of income against them could lead to reactions by some of them against the industrial capitalists over this form of investment. Bankers, state officials, and so forth could join together in attempts to restrict the capital outflow. Offsetting these changes, decreased distributions to these individuals would adversely effect the value profit rate of enterprises and thus the rate of capital accumulation.

This example of foreign investment generating a subsumed class return could easily be extended to include other types of subsumed class positions and their returns. Such examples further illustrate the overdetermination of the rate of productive capital accumulation. There is one other example that we should comment on, given its place in the previous sections. Enterprises that purchase each others' stocks can produce a situation in which their productive capital accumulation rates will decline. They will decline if their internal profit rate is greater than the expected dividend rate (and capital gain) and if they do not reduce their distributions to their non-accumulation processes. Under these conditions, the aforementioned competitive scramble by boards to occupy such subsumed class positions (as owners) can lead to possible unemployed productive labor as the rate of accumulation declines while stock prices rise. Such stock purchases might serve to cheapen the exchange value of commodities purchased as inputs by those enterprises whose board members occupy the subsumed class position as owners. In addition, some components of λ may decline, offsetting reduced productive capital accumulation. In these cases, depending on the reduced λ and the value-cheapening effect, the rate of capital accumulation could remain the same, fall, or even rise.

Such examples underscore the point of how one process, that of productive capital accumulation, is effected in different ways by the board's occupation of any particular subsumed class position. The rate of productive capital accumulation exists in contradiction because of these different effects. Foreign investment may raise it while in the process contributing to conditions that lower it. There are no general laws that we can produce as to its inevitable movement. What we have theorized here for capital accumulation also could be extended to all processes constituting the enterprise.

To derive concrete results we made very particular assumptions about the enterprise, including the constancy of α_1 and initially of λ. Although we relaxed the fixed λ and could do the same for α_1, deriving increasingly complex algebraic models would not serve our purpose.[68] Our aim was to show how a new class process within the enterprise influenced the process of productive capital accumulation in contradictory ways. Our analysis suggested as well that all other component processes of enterprises were similarly influenced.

Industrial versus Financial Enterprises

When the industrial enterprise becomes the site of processes that generate subsumed class revenues, an interesting question 'occurs: What adjectival label does one give it? Is it still an industrial or has it become, say, a financial enterprise if the lending process becomes an important source of its revenues? The same question could be raised for a financial enterprise that becomes the site of the fundamental class process (a bank that decides to include commodity production in its activities). The focus of these questions differs only in form from those asked of any number of different sites in a social formation, including the formation itself. Our answer is similar for all.

Assuming any enterprise can become the site of the capitalist fundamental class process and also of nonclass processes that generate capitalist subsumed class revenues, then the enterprise is defined as industrial or not, according to which is prevalent. So an enterprise may be labeled industrial despite the existence of processes that generate subsumed class revenues to it. Existence of subsumed class revenues is never the issue; the question of prevalence concerns rather the balance among the processes that generate an enterprise's revenues. Our class analysis of an enterprise always involves then the exact specification of the various class positions of its individuals, the determination of which of the subsets of processes secured by them is prevalent, the changing relationship among all such processes. The answer to the question of prevalence and thus the label chosen for an enterprise is constructed from such a specification.

To distinguish between an industrial and nonindustrial enterprise, let us begin with an enterprise in which the capitalist fundamental class process does not occur. To focus our analysis, we will assume initially that such an enterprise is the site of the economic processes of lending money-capital to industrial capitalists and/or of providing them with access to means of production. Let us call it a financial enterprise. Both financial and industrial enterprises are similar in that both exhibit a class structure, an internal bureaucracy distributing power and authority among individuals, stock ownership, work processes, and so forth. However, the absence of the fundamental class process in the financial enterprise produces different forms of class structure, bureaucracy, ownership, and work process.

The financial enterprise receives dividends and interest from industrial enterprises for securing (via stock purchases, loans, etc.) certain of their conditions of existence. These subsumed class revenues are received by individuals who occupy subsumed class positions on the board of the financial enterprise. They are redistributed by them to bank tellers, clerks, loan officers, accountants, guards, and so forth who perform unproductive labor within the financial enterprise. These performers of unproductive labor do not occupy subsumed class positions for they are not direct receivers of shares of surplus value from any industrial capitalist. Such (unproductive) laborers occupy nonclass positions within the financial enterprise because they sell their labor power to its board members, who occupy subsumed class positions. Managers and clerks of financial enterprises, then, are unproductive laborers who, in contrast to their counterparts in industrial enterprises, do not occupy subsumed class positions. In contrast to occupants of subsumed class positions within industrial enterprises, board members of financial enterprises receive a share of surplus value which is not payment for the sale of their labor power to industrial capitalists. Thus managers and clerks of industrial enterprises and board members of financial enterprises both occupy the *same* class position, but only within the industrial enterprise does the distribution of surplus value occur together with the commodity sale of unproductive labor power. We can conclude that the class position of a board member, of a manager, of a clerk will depend upon whether an industrial or nonindustrial (e.g., financial) enterprise is being specified.[69]

Parallel to an industrial enterprise, a financial enterprise's board and its managers form an internal bureaucracy. Hierarchical power distributions characterize both bureaucracies. However, the class natures of the two bureaucracies differ radically. They differ because the financial enterprise is a site characterized by the absence of productive capital and labor. There are no occupants of subsumed class positions within the financial enterprise other than its board members. The latter are the only occupants of a financial enterprise's *class* structure.

Conflicts and struggles over the fundamental class process differ as well: fundamental class struggle is not possible within a financial enterprise. Unproductive labor there, like productive labor in an industrial enterprise, receives wages for work performed, works intensely and perhaps for long hours, takes orders from managers, works with complex machinery, and joins unions to struggle over all aspects of work life. In all of this, unproductive are like productive laborers save one difference: unproductive laborers do not produce surplus value for a financial enterprise's board members (occupants of subsumed class positions). Struggles over wages, work rules, and mechanization between these unproductive laborers who occupy no class position and the financial board members who do are all possible and may effect in different ways the relationship between productive laborers and industrial capitalists. In other words, although unproductive labor is not productive of surplus value, struggles between such laborers and individuals occupying subsumed class positions in one site in society participate in overdetermining the production of surplus value by productive laborers in a different site.

Portions of the subsumed class revenues received by board members are in turn distributed by them to individuals external to the financial enterprise, including its stockholders, creditors, state officials, landlords, and so forth. Such individuals providing various conditions of the financial enterprise's existence are not subsumed to any one. The relationship between them and the board members of the financial enterprise does not include either the fundamental or subsumed class process. They therefore do not occupy a class position, despite receiving interest, dividends, and so forth for securing conditions of the enterprise's existence. So the class position of stock owners, for example, depends on whether they own shares in industrial or nonindustrial enterprises. In the Marxian tradition this difference is not often recognized. An owner of shares of stock of an industrial enterprise is subsumed to the industrial capitalists; an owner of shares of a financial enterprise does not occupy such a subsumed class position. One consequence of this difference is that successful struggles in some societies to nationalize the ownership of banks eliminate neither a capitalist fundamental nor a subsumed class position since ownership of bank stocks involves neither position. This does not mean, however, that such a change in ownership does not influence capitalist class positions.

A different kind of financial enterprise is not subsumed to industrial capitalists. For example, bankers may provide loans to individuals who occupy the fundamental class position as productive laborers and to occupants of subsumed class positions. These bankers do not occupy a subsumed class position since their relationship to such borrowers does not provide industrial capitalists with a condition for the extraction of surplus value. The interest received by the bankers amounts to nonclass revenues (*NCR* in our previous notation). Of course such lenders and the loans granted influence occupants of both the fundamental and subsumed class positions. For example, savings banks providing mortgages to both productive and unproductive labor help determine the level and movement of interest rates, including the subsumed class interest paid by industrial capitalists to their financial subsumed classes. In addition, mortgage loans impact upon housing prices, a component of the wage bundle of both productive and unproductive labor. Changes in the demand for housing carry over to the demand for productive labor and material inputs. Higher market prices for housing, because of expanded demand fed by bank loans, may allow industrial enterprises to now earn nonclass revenues equal to the deviation of market price from exchange values of the housing commodity. This too produces changes: such industrial enterprises can raise their accumulation of productive capital and/or distribute more to secure other (non-accumulation) processes. A higher "complex profit rate" also may attract flows of capital into the housing industry in various forms, for example, new bank loans, new stock issues, entry of new enterprises. It can also flow in via acquisition of the shares of existing housing enterprises by enterprises in other industries who place new members on the board and proceed to expand commodity production, thereby altering the distribution of surplus value.

A bank may, of course, make loans to both industrial capitalists and others. Its revenues would total the debt payment flows received from the two different positions occupied: one portion from the subsumed class and another from the nonclass position. We assume, as only an initial analytical step in this discussion, that a bank's revenues would be distributed to reproduce each of these positions. A share would be expended to secure the conditions of its subsumed class revenues and another share to secure the nonclass revenues received. Parallel to an industrial enterprise's board of directors, board members of such a lending institution would occupy both subsumed and nonclass positions. Such a bank may alter its revenue distribution so that its loans to one set of borrowers increase at the expense of others. This changed distribution can set in motion a process of struggle over a number of different issues, joined by individuals occupying different combinations of class and nonclass positions.

Parallel to individuals who occupy the industrial capitalist position, individuals who occupy the subsumed class position of financier may seek multiple nonclass and class positions, including the fundamental one. They may, for example, direct their subsumed class revenues to the purchase of each other's stocks or bonds. As board members in one financial enterprise, they would occupy nonclass positions as collective owners or financiers of other financial enterprises, receiving as an entity nonclass revenues of dividends and interest. They may also use their revenues to purchase commodity-producing enterprises' stocks. As owners they would then occupy a second subsumed class position to industrial capitalists receiving additional subsumed class revenues. These ownership positions could become conditions for their election to the boards of either financial or industrial enterprises. In the case of the financial enterprises, they would then occupy additional subsumed class positions; in the case of industrial enterprises, they would occupy fundamental ones.[70]

Again parallel to the competition among different industrial capitalists, financial subsumed classes can interact competitively with one another as each strives to reproduce its conditions of existence. One way boards of directors of financial enterprises improve or defend their subsumed class positions is to accumulate financial capital in the forms of stocks and bonds of other enterprises, both industrial and nonindustrial. The expectation is that accumulating these assets will secure some leverage over those enterprises and their distribution of revenues. This leverage can be used to benefit the financial board's subsumed class position. A next step for them could be election of one or more of their board members to the different boards of the enterprises whose stocks or bonds they acquired. Possibly one of their board members might join the management structure of those enterprises. Individuals who occupy the subsumed class position of financier, like those who occupy the fundamental class position of industrialist, use their occupation of additional class positions to protect any one.

Such an interpenetration of class positions by individuals located in both "banking and industry" is partly what Lenin meant by the term *finance capital:*

> a very close personal union is established between the banks and the biggest industrial and commercial enterprises[,] the merging of one with another through the appointment of bank directors to the Supervisory Boards (or Boards of Directors) of industrial and commercial enterprises, and vice versa.[71]

We say "partly" for Lenin added to this "personal union" of banks and industry other key characterizations of the capitalists studied by him. We may use the class categories of this and the preceding chapter to specify further this "finance capital"—this merger of bank and industrial capital.

Suppose capitalist development has produced a transition from the relatively small owner-operated industrial capitalist enterprise to the relatively large incorporated enterprise. Board members obtain use of capital from different owners and financiers. Occupants of these two latter subsumed class positions have an increasing share of their wealth invested in industrial enterprises. So the volume-1 capitalists, those individuals who once provided their own money-capital for their privately owned businesses, are replaced by board members, that is, volume-3 capitalists, who rely upon owning, lending, and investing individuals external to the industrial enterprise. Marx captured this transition in a remarkable phrase: "transformation of the actually functioning capitalist into a mere manager, administrator of other people's capital, and of the owner of capital into a mere owner, a mere money-capitalist."[72]

We may assume that this transformation of the volume-1 capitalists, the relatively small owner-operated enterprises, into the relatively large incorporated world of the volume-3 capitalists coincides with a process of intense competition within and across different industries, including the financial industry. Indeed, as suggested by Marx, industrial and financial competition provide conditions for such a transformation.[73] Following our previous analysis of competition, relatively inefficient industrial and now financial enterprises will have been eventually forced out of business or into mergers with the remaining more-successful enterprises.[74] Consequently, fewer industrial enterprises are left in each industry to satisfy the commodity demand. Fewer financial enterprises are also left to meet the demands for credit by industrial capitalists. In the case of the industrial enterprises, their minimum size has likely increased dramatically with the growth of their centralized capital.

At any moment in this process, the conditions of monopoly or oligopoly may emerge: the few remaining industrial enterprises establish some form of exclusive control over access to the commodities they produce. They can thus charge a price greater than the value of the monopolized commodity sold. Because of their monopoly power, buyers must pay an amount greater than the commodity's value to gain access to it.[75] The boards of these enterprises enjoy an additional nonclass revenue to the extent that their monopolized commodities are sold to productive and unproductive labor at an unequal exchange and an additional subsumed class revenue to the extent that they are sold to other industrial capitalists.[76]

Monopoly power enjoyed by a few remaining enterprises may also have developed within the financial industry. Relatively large banks, financial holding companies, and so forth charge interest rates higher than the prior, more competitive rate. The subsumed class revenues and nonclass revenues of these remaining financial enterprises also rise. Loans to industrial capitalists increase the former, while loans to productive and unproductive labor increase the latter. So in both industrial and financial enterprises we may expect the emergence of monopoly conditions to produce rising revenues.

The emergence of monopoly conditions in both industrial and financial enterprises, coupled with the phenomenon of a relatively small number of individuals occupying *both* fundamental and subsumed class positions in each other's enterprises, produces what we understand Lenin to have called a "financial oligarchy." This is a group of individuals whose multiple class and nonclass positions in a state of monopolized enterprises yield them both industrial and financial revenues and control over the distribution of such revenues. And according to Lenin, "the 'personal union' between the banks and industry is completed by the 'personal union' between both and the state."[77] In our terms, state officials become members of the boards as well.[78] If we add to this our aforementioned export of capital, we have the last key feature of Lenin's "finance capital."[79]

A financial oligarchy need not conform to one particular kind of grouping of fundamental, subsumed, and nonclass positions. It can take on a variety of different forms. For example, individuals who occupy subsumed class positions as financiers and/or as owners may themselves serve on and even head the industrial enterprise's board of directors and top management positions. Such individuals occupy subsumed class positions in both finance and industry and the fundamental class position in the latter. A different form is where individuals occupying subsumed class positions as owners or financiers of industrial enterprises do not appear on the boards of these enterprises as industrial capitalists and subsumed class managers. However, they can still form alliances with those who do occupy such positions. In this way, individuals may never appear as industrial capitalists, but they use their subsumed class positions to influence industrial decisions over the distribution of total revenues of the enterprise. They may have a degree of control, but do not exploit or manage productive labor. Still another form is where individuals holding subsumed class positions as board members of different financial enterprises and/or individuals occupying different subsumed class ownership positions agree to elect a representative board of directors. Such individuals do not receive surplus value, but through their alliance they control the industrial enterprise.

Situations of mass ownership of industrial enterprises where private property is disbursed over thousands of individual owners can pose a significant contradiction for the industrial capitalist. Election to the board is one condition for them to secure in order to appropriate surplus value, but they may no longer own sufficient shares to secure that political process. The "capitalist" has lost this "absolute control." However, dispersion of ownership also creates the space for them to organize sufficient votes to reelect themselves or their slate of alternatives. Thus, alliances with a few individuals holding particular external subsumed class positions can prove effective in securing this one nonclass process. In addition, emergence of a managerial bureaucracy separate from the industrial capitalists creates another kind of contradiction. Supervision is another condition of their receiving surplus value, but as with their ownership, they no longer are the only managers. Thus the industrial capitalists are dependent upon their subsumed class of managers. In effect, the latter group runs the industrial enterprise—it has Galbraith's management control.[80] Here too alliances— between industrial capitalists and a few key managers—over the distribution of surplus value can be used to secure the former's fundamental class position. As pointed out previously, particular subsumed class managers often appear on the board of directors, one key condition of maintaining their own subsumed class position. It is often in their interests as occupants of both fundamental and subsumed class positions to reproduce the conditions for each of them.

In sum, Lenin's "financial oligarchy" or, in general, various forms of alliances between and among individuals occupying various fundamental and subsumed class positions can become key vehicles allowing such individuals to reproduce their class (and nonclass) positions on an expanded scale and/or to seek new class (and nonclass) positions. Such changing alliances both reflect and help shape the changing class structures of the relationships comprising an enterprise and linking it to other sites in the social formation.

In the case of industrial capitalist enterprises, the different alliances also produce different forms of control over the processes making up the enterprise. Such control can vary from that held predominately by management to that held by financiers or owners. But different forms of this political process do not vitiate either the existence or reproduction of the industrial capitalists. Indeed, they serve as conditions of that reproduction and the exploitation of labor upon which it is based.

Capitalist versus Noncapitalist Enterprises

The meaning of an enterprise and its profits varies according to the class structure specified—different kinds of enterprises and their profits depend upon different forms of exploitation and conditions of existence. This is a Marxian class definition of an enterprise and its profits, in contrast to a market definition. In the latter, the meaning of an enterprise and its profits is not effected by concepts of class. Rather, wherever there is production for a market, there is by definition a capitalist enterprise and capitalist profits. Such a conception is different from and opposed to Marx's definition of capitalism in terms of exploitation and its conditions of existence.

Industrial and nonindustrial enterprises are not unique to capitalism. Such enterprises may exist within feudal, ancient, slave, and even communist social formations. Consider, for example, a Marxian class-analytical approach to a feudal industrial enterprise, one in which feudal commodities are produced and sold. Perhaps such an enterprise operates within the rural manor or urban craft communities of the feudal social formation. Wherever its location, it would be constituted in part by the feudal fundamental class process. Feudal lords would receive surplus labor in the form of, say, corvée performed by feudal laborers. Feudal surplus labor would then be distributed to various individuals occupying internal and external subsumed class positions to secure the conditions of existence of feudal surplus labor appropriation. A portion would go to individuals occupying subsumed class positions as overseers, bookkeepers, purchasers, guards; all of these individuals constitute what we might call the feudal enterprise's internal bureaucracy. Owners of feudal means of production (land, tools, mills, water, etc.) receive a distributed share, perhaps in the form of money rents, for making available the means to feudal lords. These owners, along with moneylenders and merchants who distribute, respectively, credit and merchanting to lords, receiving from them interest and fees, thus occupy feudal subsumed class positions external to the enterprise. Still other occupants of external subsumed class positions include officials connected to whatever court may exist and religious officials. They receive distributed shares for political, cultural, and economic processes provided to lords.

Feudal and capitalist industrial enterprises are alike in that surplus labor is extracted by fundamental and distributed by and to subsumed classes in both. Feudal and capitalist producers of commodities have this commonality—the surplus labor of the serfs and the proletariat is the source of income for much of the population. What distinguishes one industrial enterprise from another, therefore, is not the existence of extraction or distribution of surplus labor, or, in this case, of production of commodities for profitable sale, private ownership of means of production, bureaucracy and hierarchy, size of unit and technology used. Rather, it is the precise qualitative form in which surplus labor is appropriated and distributed. Different forms of the appropriation and distribution processes have as their conditions of existence different economic, political, and cultural processes. It is the different forms of these extraction and nonextraction processes that define different industrial enterprises and their different class structures.

To ignore these differences is to vitiate Marxian analysis by conflating commodity production, supervision, private ownership of capital, and profits with capitalism. It is quite literally to see capitalist industrial enterprises wherever one sees the production of commodities for profit. Immanuel Wallerstein's work provides an excellent example of this approach. He defines capitalism as the "essential feature of a capitalist world economy, which is production for sale in a market in which the effect is to realize the maximum profit." [81] Using such a definition, he identifies the growth of capitalist enterprise with the growth of the world market or economy. Such a definition abstracts in particular from the fundamental class process developed and used by Marx to produce his different and new knowledge of capitalism. As a result, in Wallerstein's work feudal, slave, ancient, and capitalist commodity-producing enterprises often become indistinguishable from one another. [82] Their class differences are negated by the conceptual focus on the production and circulation of commodities for profitable sale as stressed by Marx:

> The production and circulation of commodities are, however, phenomena that occur to a greater or less extent in modes of production the most diverse. If we are acquainted with nothing but the abstract

categories of circulation, which are common to all these modes of production, we cannot possibly know anything of the specific points of difference of those modes, nor pronounce any judgment upon them.[83]

Profits are not unique to capitalist industrial or financial enterprises. Feudal, ancient, and slave merchants and moneylenders calculated profits on their respective merchant- and money-capital. Noncapitalist owners of means of production may have figured their profitable returns on land, tools, mills, and slaves rented to different fundamental extractors. Individuals occupying these different subsumed class positions established banks, trading houses, and merchant companies. Such enterprises could then service various segments of the noncapitalist social formation, including those who occupied the fundamental class position as surplus appropriators.

English merchants, for example, operating via the various chartered trading companies established after the turn of the seventeenth century, bought and sold commodities from and to feudal, primitive communist, slave, and ancient social formations all over the world. Such merchants provided to different fundamental extracting classes in these formations the nonclass process of circulation, selling their noncapitalist commodities at their values and receiving from them portions of the already extracted surplus labor. English merchants were subsumed to occupants of different noncapitalist fundamental class positions. These noncapitalist trading enterprises showed revenues, costs, merchant profits, and the return to the merchant capital invested. Similar examples exist for European feudal merchant enterprises selling the food grains produced by European feudal lords on the manor economy from at least the twelfth century onward; American and English slave merchants selling the cotton of American slave masters from the early 1800s until the Civil War; and English merchants selling the commodities produced by ancient American producers from the early seventeenth century onward.[84]

As pointed out in chapter 3, Marx specified repeatedly that merchants, money-capital, and profits earned on invested capital existed long before the development of capitalism (meaning the capitalist fundamental class process).[85] Noncapitalist commodity production also predates capitalism. Such commodities exist not as the effect of the capitalist fundamental class process (surplus value is not materialized in them) but rather as the overdetermined result of noncapitalist extraction and nonextraction processes. And again, individuals who hold noncapitalist fundamental class positions constituting the class structures of these commodity-producing enterprises can and did calculate costs of production, exchange values realized, and profits on the capital invested. What is unique to capitalism then is clearly not capital and profits, but rather the productive form of capital, the capitalist form of the fundamental class process and its quantitative measure, the value profit rate. This simple but powerful insight of Marx provides the theoretical basis to distinguish between capitalist and noncapitalist commodity-producing enterprises and their respective profit rates.

To underscore this key point let us specify the class structural equation for a feudal commodity-producing enterprise:

$$FSL = FSC_I + FSC_O, \qquad (4.27)$$

where FSL refers to feudal surplus labor, FSC_I to the surplus distribution to subsumed classes internal to the enterprise, and FSC_O to subsumed classes external to the enterprise. Now, from FSC_O subtract feudal ground rents, FR, paid to owners of land, and feudal interest, Fi, paid to moneylenders, and add the net total $(FSC_O - FR - Fi)$ to FSC_I. Call this new sum, $F\Pi$, the feudal profits of the enterprise.

Specifying equation (4.27), modified slightly by these changes, along with our previous class structural equation for the capitalist industrial enterprise (also changed slightly to facilitate comparison), we can readily compare the two different industrial enterprises:

$$CSL = C\Pi + CR + Ci; \qquad (4.28)$$
$$FSL = F\Pi + FR + Fi.$$

Both enterprises are exactly alike in that surplus labor is extracted and distributed under the headings of profits, rents, and interest. They are radically different in that the forms of surplus labor extraction and the meaning of the distributional headings are different. It is this subtle but key difference that informs the Marxian class theoretic approach, and it is its absence that marks the non-Marxian approach. The different forms of extraction and distribution in turn mean different impacts of these class processes upon all the other processes of the social formation.

Enterprises undergo a number of different kinds of transition, many of which we have already commented on. There is the transition within capitalism from the volume-1 industrial enterprise to the volume-3 enterprise that involves changes in ownership, management, credit, and accumulation. All these changes effect the fundamental class process. However, the industrial enterprise remains a capitalist site, despite its dramatic change from being a relatively small producing unit in which one or a very few individuals occupy the fundamental and most of the subsumed class positions to becoming a much larger unit in which the industrial capitalists no longer are the sole managers, owners, and creditors. Another kind of transition within capitalism involves the movement from a capitalist industrial to financial enterprise or vice versa. This form of transition may also occur in noncapitalist social formations between industrial and financial enterprises there. Finally, there are transitions between capitalist and non-capitalist enterprises. Here a transition involves revolutionary changes in both the left- and right-hand sides of our class structural equations. These changes involve revolutionary struggles over the fundamental and subsumed class processes. Other enterprise transitions do not.

Too often these different kinds of transition are collapsed into one—the movement from relatively small, national producing or financial units to the enormous multinational enterprises that operate across the contemporary world. This is far different from the Marxian class approach specified here. No matter how intriguing and complex is this alternative approach, its point of entry becomes the size and power of the producing or financial unit, be it capitalist in the Marxian class sense or not. Consequently, it at best produces a "class analysis" of the enterprise, focused on the latter's essentialized size and power, and at worst ignores class completely. Unlike this alternative, we use Marx's different forms of exploitation as the conceptual base from and with which we understand the changing class and nonclass nature of the enterprise.

5

Class Analysis: A Marxian Theory of the State

Introduction: The Capitalist State

The Marxian class analysis of the state consistent with the general Marxian theory advanced in this book begins by distinguishing the class and nonclass processes that comprise the social site called "the state." It proceeds to specify the interaction among and between class and nonclass processes in the state and such processes at other sites of the social formation. As with a Marxian analysis of any social site, one goal of this analysis is to comprehend the overdetermined and hence changing contradictions among the processes that comprise the state. The broader goal is to comprehend the interaction between the state's contradictions and the class structure generally. Achievement of such a comprehension is Marxian theory's contribution toward concrete social interventions aimed to transform class structure, state, and society.

We do not imagine that a chapter can pretend to present a Marxian analysis of the state. However, we can demonstrate many distinguishing aspects of this analysis—and of the concretization of Marxian theory generally—by narrowing the purview of this chapter to the class analysis of the revenue and expenditure flows of a capitalist state such as the current federal government of the United States. Accordingly, after a brief overview of the diverse processes occurring in the state, our discussion will concentrate upon the capitalist state budget.

The capitalist state is a site in society. By that we mean it is a location or grouping of specific relationships that each comprise a particular subset of social and natural processes. It is a place in society where various sorts of processes are performed and which define it qua social site. We will begin by illustrating some of them. States undertake natural processes such as seeding clouds to make rain, breeding animals threatened with extinction, altering the chemical compositions of air, water, and soil, converting water power into electricity, and so forth. Of course the state is not the only institutional site where these natural processes are performed. Some of them, for example, are performed in and by industrial enterprises. And indeed, the same can be said for the following economic, political, and cultural processes performed in and by the state in capitalist society.

The state performs certain political processes. It establishes rules of social behavior in the community, typically by the design and enactment of laws and public policies. It adjudicates disputes over the interpretation of such laws and policies, typically through judicial procedures. It administers the laws, typically through executive actions, and police and military proceedings. These political processes performed by the state share the common objective of securing particular authority relations (including concrete practices of sovereignty and nationality) among members of the society and with other societies.

The state performs a variety of economic processes. It controls, at least in part, the quantity of money in general circulation. It provides incomes via transfer payments to designated members of society. It taxes individuals and enterprises, lends to and borrows money from them, and both sells and buys commodities. It typically regulates different aspects of enterprise activities. It may itself produce capitalist commodities. If so, the state (i.e., state industrial enterprises) is the site of the two class processes. Except where otherwise indicated, our discussion of the state will focus upon its activities that do *not* involve capitalist commodity production, that is, that do not include the capitalist fundamental class process.

The state performs many cultural processes. It typically performs much of the formal education process. It maintains museums and usually a variety of offices charged with producing and disseminating officially endorsed interpretations of political and other social events (in some capitalist societies such offices include state-operated mass media). The state is thus the site and organizational form of a subset of the cultural processes within a social formation, that is, processes producing meanings therein.

Most of the social processes performed in and by the state are also performed at other sites in the society. The cultural process of education, for example, may also be produced in the household as a matter of interpersonal communications among family members. It may also occur in the enterprise in various forms, including the sale of educational services as a commodity by a private school. Similarly, the state's political process of policing often coexists with policing performed at other social sites: in troubled neighborhoods as residents rotate a patrol function among themselves or in enterprises whose employees include security personnel. Legislation and adjudication are processes occurring in enterprises, schools, and churches as well as in the state. Similarly, the economic processes performed by the state include many also performed at other social sites: borrowing and lending money are done by individuals and enterprises, controlling the money supply is done partly by institutions accepting demand deposits, and producing commodities is hardly an economic process limited to the state. On the other hand, the state is often the exclusive site of some social processes. Maintaining a full-time standing military force, manufacturing legal tender, allocating airspace for aircraft traffic, and rendering final legal judgments (supreme courts) are examples of social processes usually exclusively performed in and by capitalist states.

Keep in mind that social processes have been and still are continually shifted from one site to another in society. Each social site varies with the ever-changing composition and nature of the processes that comprise it. Indeed, in early feudal Europe, the industrial enterprise and state were often indistinguishable from one another. The feudal lords' manor-estates were places in society of production of use values perhaps in feudal commodity form; of feudal appropriation and distribution of surplus labor; of production, enforcement, and adjudication of laws; and of the production and dissemination of meanings concerning both secular and religious life. The lord was often at one and the same time an occupant of a fundamental class position as an extractor of surplus labor (in the feudal manor enterprise) and of a subsumed class position as a lawmaker (in the feudal manor state). This unity of social processes in the same institutional site was fragmented with the development of the feudal absolute state and feudal enterprise as separate sites in society. New political and philosophical theories of the state and its role in society developed as both conditions of and responses to this radical separation of state from industry.[1]

Currently in the United States, several processes produced within the state are under attack. It is argued (often by the Republican party) that certain nonstate sites in society, for example, the household and private enterprise, are the proper places for their production. A struggle may even occur within the state over this issue: some state officials push for reducing or ending particular social processes provided by the state while others resist such changes and may even call for expanding such state-run processes.

Marxian theory approaches the state as a site in society by specifying the particular social processes performed at and thereby defining that site at a particular time. This is how we approached the enterprise and how we would approach any other social site chosen for analysis. Household, school, two-person love relationship, sports team, church, union, working class, and individual are examples of other possible sites in society understood as particular subsets of social processes. Any relationship in society is such a site, whether formally institutionalized or not. Since we distinguish one site from another precisely in terms of which particular social processes comprise each one, states in different capitalist societies will differ according to which social processes are or are not performed by them. There are other differences between capitalist states and those occurring within noncapitalist societies, but these too are analyzed by Marxian theory in terms of the specific social processes performed by and thus defining such different states.

The capitalist state usually performs certain processes that are conditions of existence of the capitalist fundamental class process. For so doing, it often receives a share of surplus value, predominantly in the form of taxes on enterprises. On this point, Engels writes: "The state and municipal taxes, as far as they affect the capitalist class, the rent of the landlords, etc., are paid from (surplus value)."[2] Here is a relationship between state and industrial capital in which state-produced nonclass processes occur together with the subsumed class process. The state receives subsumed class revenues.

As we shall show in detail, subsumed class revenues are not the sole source of state income. Thus there can be no one-to-one correspondence between a particular state expenditure and the subsumed class revenue component of state income. Rather, each such expenditure will draw upon a heterogeneous—in class terms—state revenue flow. Indeed, the class impacts of both state expenditures and revenues are objects of intense struggles over state policies. However, at this point in our discussion we want to focus upon the *part* of the capitalist state that involves the subsumed class process between it and industrial capitalist enterprises.

The state performs *natural* processes that permit and shape, that is, participate in the overdetermination of, the capitalist fundamental class process. For example, state enterprises (nonindustrial, i.e., non–commodity producing) dig, dredge, and clean harbors, thereby facilitating trade, extending markets, and thus contributing toward the reproduction of the capitalist fundamental class process.[3] Other such state enterprises, often linked to military activity, produce new chemical compounds whose formulation is made known to capitalist industrial enterprises, enabling them to realize production economies, market altogether new commodities, and so generate greater surplus value. State enterprises operate various public health programs affecting population growth, length of productive life, and worker absenteeism—all factors directly related to the profitability and hence viability of capitalist industrial enterprises, of the capitalist fundamental class process. The managers and actual performers—all state employees— of these natural processes require personal incomes to reproduce such processes. In addition, the state enterprises in which they perform require funds to purchase the commodities, that is, buildings, equipment, and raw materials, necessary to perform these processes. The state's subsumed class (tax) revenue is used to pay at least partly for these state workers and these purchased commodities.

The state performs certain *economic* processes, which likewise are conditions of existence of the capitalist fundamental class process. The costs of these economic processes are similarly defrayed at least in part from subsumed class payments to the state. To prevent rapid price inflation, state enterprises may closely monitor private banking practices and monopolistic tendencies throughout the economy. The incomes of such monitors and the costs of the computers and other equipment they require are defrayed in part by subsumed class payments to the state. The masses of unemployed workers in capitalist societies often result in state policies of retraining, relocating, or, to reduce the risk of social disorder, minimally sustaining them for parts or all of the duration of their unemployment. The processes of retraining, relocating, and minimally sustaining what Marx calls this "reserve army of the unemployed" usually absorb subsumed class payments to the state to partly cover personnel and income maintenance costs. States typically build means of transportation, communication networks, and various other public works which condition the value profitability and development of industrial capitalist enterprises in innumerable ways: parts of the costs of such infrastructure are defrayed from subsumed class payments to the state.

The capitalist state passes laws in its legislatures and maintains administrative and judicial bureaucracies to enforce them. Consider, for example, the enactments establishing private property in the means of production. The existence of incorporated industrial enterprises requires the political processes of legislation, administration, and judicial decision which secure the rights of stockholders' private property in the means of production. To take another example, surplus value appropriation depends upon processes that secure the freedom of productive laborers and industrial capitalists to sell and buy the labor power commodity. Such processes are *political* conditions of existence of the capitalist fundamental class process, and their various costs are typically covered at least in part by subsumed class revenues to the state. Military and police forces perform the process of securing noninterference from potential (or actual) disrupters—foreign or domestic—of the fundamental capitalist class process. The typically enormous costs of the personnel and materials needed to perform these processes are likewise defrayed partly out of subsumed class payments to the state, which is charged with maintaining military and police forces.[4]

Public education is a major *cultural* process performed in large part by states in capitalist societies. Such education provides conditions of existence for the capitalist fundamental class process by systematically disseminating certain conceptions of the meaning of life, work, politics, justice, goodness, and so forth. The dissemination of such meanings is a condition of existence of the capitalist fundamental class process in the sense that workers, for example, have to understand the world in certain ways if they are to accept their conditions as workers. Such understandings also condition their productivity on the job. If workers thought that justice required that any surplus value they produced ought to be theirs, their ac ceptance of the capitalist fundamental class process in which such surplus passes rather to capitalists might be problematic. That would jeopardize the reproduction over time of that fundamental class process. If workers believed that the good life required and deserved, as a matter of basic human right, the distribution of produced goods and services according to individual human need rather than purchasing power, the existence of the capitalist fundamental class process would be similarly jeopardized. Public education is a state-run cultural process designed, among other things, to disseminate those particular concepts and meanings whose wide acceptance is a condition of existence of the capitalist fundamental class process. And this costs money, usually including subsumed class payments to the state.

The capitalist state also performs various social and natural processes whose costs are not defrayed by subsumed class revenues. This involves the state in relationships in which the subsumed class process does not occur. In such relationships, the state performs processes, for example, providing recreational facilities, certain property laws, communication networks, public education, road systems, and police protection, which are directed to nonindustrial capitalists—to productive and unproductive laborers and to various occupants of subsumed class positions. In such relationships, the costs of these processes are defrayed at least in part out of tax payments levied on the profits of nonindustrial enterprises and the personal incomes of productive and unproductive laborers. These particular tax payments do not involve the subsumed class process since the taxpayers are not appropriators of surplus value. These tax payments thus represent a portion of the nonclass revenues received by the state alongside its subsumed class revenues.

Beyond nonclass and subsumed class processes, the final sorts of processes in which the state may participate are fundamental class processes, including the capitalist fundamental class process. The production and sale of capitalist commodities in and by the state—that is, the existence of state capitalist industrial enterprises—mean that surplus value is appropriated in and realized by the state. This surplus value forms an additional possible source of the state's revenues, a fundamental class revenue. The state's surplus value, like that of any nonstate industrial capitalist, is distributed to occupants of subsumed class positions both within *and* without the state (as discussed further later). The extraction of surplus value within the state suggests the possibility of fundamental class struggle there. Indeed, this particular form of class struggle is possible in the state if and only if capitalist exploitation takes place there. Otherwise, fundamental class struggles take place in other social sites where the fundamental class process *does* occur.

In summary, the state performs an infinite variety of social and natural processes for occupants of both class and nonclass positions. Industrial capitalists, managers, bankers, merchants, landlords, property owners, productive and unproductive laborers are all, to varying degrees, beneficiaries of state processes and payers of state taxes. All the state-performed processes, and a fortiori that state itself as the site of them, are overdetermined by processes comprising all other social sites in society.

Two important and related points follow from our specifications so far. First, our definition of the state and the logic of overdetermination rule out the possibility that any one essential subset of processes governs its development. Often the political processes performed in and by the state have attracted the most analytic attention, which has not infrequently tended to reduce the state to a purely political site in society. By contrast, our Marxian approach cannot make such a reduction. Second, the state cannot be treated as the phenomenon, expression, tool, or creature of a subset of the above class groupings of individuals. A different Marxian approach with many adherents views the state as the creature and instrument of the industrial capitalists. We must reject such an essentialist approach. Before elaborating these two points further, we will specify systematically the class structure of the capitalist state.

Class Structure of the State

As noted, the subset of processes comprising the relations grouped together within the state may include the capitalist fundamental class process.[5] In this case, state industrial enterprises would be the sites of the fundamental class process (appropriating surplus value) and the capitalist subsumed class process (distributing such surplus value to various subsumed classes). A state's class structure includes then the state industrial capitalist fundamental and subsumed class positions associated with such enterprises. The conditions of existence of the state enterprise's fundamental class process include state processes of producing and selling commodities, and political processes establishing laws permitting such enterprises to operate and their commodities to be produced and state industrial capitalists to gain access to means of production. These conditions may be secured by distributions of surplus value to occupants of subsumed class positions within and without the state. State industrial enterprise managers and lawmakers are examples of two subsumed class groupings within the

state, while private moneylenders (e.g., holders of a state industrial enterprise's bonds) and merchants are examples of subsumed class groupings
external to it. Where such state industrial enterprises exist, the state is the
site of contradictions between occupants of the two fundamental class positions, productive laborers and surplus-value-appropriating capitalists. It is
also the site of contradictions among those who occupy subsumed class
positions within the state and between them and occupants of the two fundamental class positions. We can conclude then that the state itself can become a site in society of various class as well as nonclass struggles.

Parallel to the identification of the industrial capitalists in the previous
chapter, state industrial capitalists are the first receivers and distributors of
surplus value. To so receive and distribute the produced surplus value, such
individuals depend upon various social processes, some of which are listed
above and others variously mentioned in the two preceding chapters. However, in contrast to appropriators of surplus value in private industrial enterprises, state industrial capitalists may have to secure an appointment to
the enterprise's board from particular state officials rather than through
shareholders' elections. This political process of appointing could be in the
hands of Congress or the president, depending upon law and/or tradition.
It is likely this particular political difference between private and public
industrial capitalists extends to several other social processes as well. Such
differences also produce contradictions and developments unique to each
of these two social sites of surplus value appropriation and their respective
class structures.

Because of the essentialist approach to property ownership so prevalent
within the Marxian theoretical tradition, we must once again stress the
point that these state industrial capitalists need not own the means of production used by them. That they have access to such means is the issue—
access, not ownership, is a condition of their existence. A law may be enacted, for example, that gives the right of property ownership of such
means to all citizens of the nation. This establishes a subsumed class position for each citizen if a share of the state appropriated surplus value is
distributed to each of them (perhaps called a social dividend) for providing
state industrial capitalists with access to the publicly owned means of production. Of course, to be a citizen and thus occupy this particular subsumed class ownership position presupposes that the individual participates in numerous other social processes, for example, satisfying whatever
laws and/or customs have been established pertaining to an individual's acquisition of citizenship.

In contrast to our approach, if private ownership of the means of production is made the essential condition of (conflated with) the appropriation of surplus value, then the existence of both the capitalist state indus-

trial enterprises and their capitalists become equally problematic. Faced with a shift to public ownership of the means of production, practitioners of this alternative, essentialist approach might quite literally not see the existence of the capitalist fundamental class process within the state. Thus, the nature of these state enterprises and their social consequences would be very differently conceptualized within the alternative theory from that specified here.

For example, such an essentialist approach might define state capitalist enterprises as "socialist"—meaning not capitalist—by virtue of their public *property ownership* through the state (read public domain). Another conception, also different from ours, would refer to them simply as state-run enterprises—meaning neither properly capitalist nor socialist nor communist—whose essential feature is the bureaucratic *power and control* wielded by their directors and top managers. Typically at work within this latter conception is a definition of capitalism that makes its essential feature the particular power distribution among persons involved in enterprise relationships. Hence, despite being publicly owned, such enterprises are often thought in the last instance to be not socialist but a variant form of capitalist, for example, "state-capitalist," because centralized power (the essential feature of capitalism) is in the hands of these state bureaucrats who, in power terms, are essentially equivalent to industrial capitalists. Clearly this version recognizes the existence of something it calls capitalism within the state. This is a capitalism far different from the one presented in our approach: the former is defined by an essentialist focus upon political processes of power and authority while ours involves a nonessentialist focus on the economic process of surplus value production. Such alternative conceptions cannot produce the kind of Marxian class analysis of state industrial and nonindustrial enterprises undertaken here. They fail to identify the possibly significant location—the state within diverse societies—where the capitalist fundamental class process can exist and correspondingly exert complex determinations on the rest of society.

Like all capitalist commodities, those produced within such state enterprises are sold to individuals occupying different class and nonclass positions, including those within the state itself. In the United States, examples of state industrial enterprises and their commodities would be the Tennessee Valley Authority and the sale of electric power, and Amtrak and the sale of rail transport.[6] In other countries, state industrial enterprises are more common than in the United States: automobiles and recently much more in France, steel in India, electrical machinery in Italy, and so forth.

Besides the two class processes occurring within state capitalist industrial enterprises, a myriad of nonclass processes occur within the state generally. In performing many of these processes, the state provides certain conditions of existence for the capitalist fundamental class process located in enterprises, both private and state. To do so the state may require and obtain capitalist subsumed class distributions from both private and, where existing, state capitalist industrial enterprises. Individuals who receive such subsumed class distributions thereby occupy subsumed class positions in the state.

If a state nonindustrial enterprise makes land available to capitalist appropriators and receives rent distributions from the surplus value appropriated by those capitalists, then the board of directors of this state nonindustrial enterprise would occupy a subsumed class position as a state landlord. If a state nonindustrial enterprise provides industrial capitalists with access to money-capital and receives interest payments from their appropriated surplus value, its board occupies a subsumed class position as state financiers. These are but two of many such examples of specifically state-established nonindustrial enterprises whose board occupies subsumed class positions. Parallel to the existence of state industrial enterprises, these state nonindustrial enterprises and their class structures are the result of specific social processes, including particular laws enacted by legislators. Members of Congress may themselves receive such rents and interest by legislating themselves as the boards of state nonindustrial enterprises. Members of Congress would then occupy subsumed class positions in those enterprises. Alternatively, Congress could legislate the appointment of boards other than themselves and thereby place others in those subsumed class positions.

In the United States, Congress is the first receiver and distributor of all forms of tax revenues. By constitutional law, members of Congress originate (receive) and expend (distribute) all tax revenues.[7] Taxes are paid to Congress by industrial capitalists as a share of their appropriated surplus value to secure the state's provision of certain conditions of their existence. In this tax relationship, the nonclass process of tax collecting/paying occurs together with the subsumed class process. Consequently, members of Congress collectively occupy subsumed class positions within the state. As noted earlier, congressional members or their designees may also occupy additional subsumed class positions within nonindustrial state enterprises as state landlords and bankers. One condition, among many others, of their occupation of any of these different subsumed class positions in the state is their victory at the polls, that is, the securing of the political processes for acquiring congressional seats.

Congress also receives other kinds of revenues besides its share of surplus value in the form of taxes paid by industrial capitalists. Revenues are generated from taxes on performers of productive labor, on those who occupy subsumed class positions, and on those who occupy no class position whatsoever.[8] In these three tax relationships, the nonclass process of collecting taxes does *not* occur together with the subsumed class process: the tax paid is not an initial distribution of surplus value. As a result, members of Congress do not occupy a (subsumed) class position within those relationships and such tax revenues are therefore defined as part of the nonclass revenues collected by the state. Other nonclass (and nontax) revenues derive from those congressional relations with other individuals in society, which include neither of the two class processes nor the tax payments process. The interest received by the state on loans granted to nonextractors of surplus value, for example, homeowners for household repairs, is one such example. Another is rent received from making land available to such nonextractors.[9] Finally, a still different form of state revenues is generated from debt issued by Congress and sold to the public. Parallel to our discussion of debt in chapter 4, the state may borrow to establish fundamental, subsumed, and/or nonclass positions. No matter which is the case, the loans so received are part of the state's nonclass revenues.

In summary, members of Congress may occupy several different class and nonclass positions within the state. Such positions are associated with the different possible revenue flows: capitalist subsumed class positions as the receivers of taxes on surplus value and providers of certain conditions of its existence; possibly other subsumed class positions within nonindustrial state enterprises as the receivers of interest, rents, and such from industrial capitalists for making available to them money-capital, land, and so forth; and various nonclass positions as receivers of taxes, of borrowings, of interest and rental payments from productive and unproductive laborers. Congresspersons may also occupy a fundamental class position within the state if they serve as well on the respective boards of industrial state enterprises. Typically, however, such surplus-value-appropriating positions are delegated by law and custom to others.

Congress uses its class and nonclass revenues to secure its class and nonclass positions by purchasing unproductive labor power and other commodities (from public swimming pools to computers to tanks) to aid such unproductive labor in its tasks.[10] The unproductive labor power purchased by Congress includes its members' own as performers of labor—that is, the labor of legislation. Congress thus pays itself a salary and occupies in the state an additional nonclass position as seller of unproductive labor power to itself. As previously mentioned, a political condition of this purchase/sale of unproductive labor is accession to office by electoral means.

Congress also purchases the unproductive labor power of all other state employees. The latter include the president of the United States, all federal judges, military personnel, managers of various state enterprises, clerks, secretaries, health personnel, research scientists, and so forth. As developed in chapter 3, such individuals do not occupy class positions. Rather, they are simply sellers of labor power to other than industrial capitalists; they receive the wages (and salaries) denoted in chapter 3 by W^3. The relationship of state employees such as these to the Congress does not include either the fundamental or the subsumed class processes, although it does include the commodity exchange process (unproductive labor power for money). These employees' incomes are thus nonclass incomes.

The capitalist state's diverse class structure includes income-receiving occupants of both kinds of capitalist class positions—fundamental and subsumed—as well as of nonclass positions. In the United States, relatively few individuals in the state occupy either the fundamental or subsumed class positions. State industrial capitalist enterprises are traditionally frowned upon, and few have been established. Their existence is often seen as the first signs of an emerging socialism identified with the twin horrors of bureaucratic inefficiencies and antidemocratic centralized power. Members of Congress and boards of state nonindustrial enterprises that directly receive distributions of surplus value make up the subsumed class grouping. This too represents a relatively small number of individuals. By contrast, the vast majority of state employees are involved with performing unproductive labor. They sell their unproductive labor power in exchange for state wage and salary payments. They do not occupy class positions qua state workers. The numbers of these individuals have grown dramatically in the last decades. Thus a significant expansion of unproductive labor has taken place in American society. This expansion required a growth of state revenues, mainly from taxes on business profits (subsumed class revenues if a tax on surplus value and nonclass revenues if a tax on nonindustrial profits), on personal incomes (nonclass revenues), and from a steadily growing national debt (nonclass revenues).

Parallel to our enterprise discussion, within the class structure of the state there is no necessary connection between, on the one hand, an individual's class or nonclass position and, on the other, the political power he or she may wield. The president (and his or her office) holds considerable power in the state and the society at large. Yet, he or she occupies a nonclass position within the state. This may discomfit those who would deduce an individual's class position from his or her power to dominate others. In addition, the power held by centralized state bureaucracies often has been and still is a target of criticism articulated by those on both the Left and Right. Frequently such power, whether in the hands of a strong president or state bureaucracy, is understood to be the essential determinant of a society's development. A class analysis is either displaced completely or made derivative from a power analysis. So, for example, social analyses of the Soviet Union often focus on its state bureaucracies and the power held by a few individual members of the Soviet Communist party. This is understood to be what Russian socialism has achieved and why it is to be shunned or what state capitalism could develop into and why it is to be avoided. Paradoxically, the Marxian categories of class, contradiction, and overdetermination are rarely used in or outside of the Soviet Union to produce a class analytical study of the one society that first achieved a socialist revolution.[11]

We must emphasize once again that from our standpoint the nonclass process of ordering social behavior—a political process—cannot be confused with, conflated to, or be the essential cause of individuals' class or nonclass positions in society. In particular, the wielding of this political process by, say, the president, is different from and not related in an essential way to the capitalist class processes. The president in his or her nonclass position thus may enjoy power over members of Congress in their subsumed class positions. By logical extension, the president may also have power over any single capitalist or any particular group of capitalists, despite their alliance and opposition to this state leader. Notwithstanding this power, the president *exploits* neither Congress nor the capitalists: no surplus value is appropriated from them. And despite being subject to presidential command, Congress occupies its subsumed class position and capitalists their fundamental one. In like manner, a Soviet state bureaucracy may have the ability to order the social behavior of literally millions of Soviet citizens. Yet, this power is different from and not to be confused with the Marxian notion of exploitation. It is possible for a number of different fundamental class processes (capitalist, communist, feudal, slave) to exist with different forms of such centralized or, alternatively, decentralized power.[12] However, by itself a form of power does not signal which of these fundamental class processes is present. This type of reductionism is rejected in our approach: class and power are neither reducible to nor derivative from one another. Rather, each process participates in the overdetermination of the other.[13]

One consequence of this distinction between one's power and class position emerges in the analysis of struggles within the state. A conflict between two parts of government, president and Congress, over, say, the level and composition of revenues and expenditures can possibly threaten the social survival of both. The president (Congress) may believe its very existence as a governing institution in society is threatened by the Congress's (president's) actions or even nonactions. Here the effort by one part of the state to order and control the behavior of the other part may produce a struggle between them over power. A so-called constitutional crisis perhaps results: a struggle between occupants of various class and nonclass positions over this nonclass process of power. Each side produces its particular knowledge—a cultural process—of the Constitution to support and justify its position. Each side produces its truth and searches for allies both within and without the state to aid in its struggle.

This and similar type conflicts are not class struggles in the state. They refer to struggles over political and, as suggested, cultural processes. However, such contradictions and struggles within the state necessarily impact upon as indeed they are also shaped by struggles over the fundamental and subsumed class processes throughout the society. A political crisis in the state, for example, may well threaten particular conditions of surplus value's existence.

Suppose the crisis results in a stalemate between the president and Congress such that state processes to secure certain conditions of existence of industrial capitalists are not forthcoming. The latter's relationships to all sorts of individuals occupying different class and nonclass positions will be changed by this removal of state-secured processes. Productive laborers, unproductive laborers, managers, stock owners, landlords, bankers, and so forth will discover that their relationships to industrial capitalists and enterprises have changed, perhaps radically. These changes will in turn alter the complex relationships each one of these groups has with the others. In the specific relationship between productive laborers and industrial capitalists, the state perhaps no longer secures, say, laws of contract. Occupants of the two fundamental class positions may then attempt to alter the fundamental class process in some significant way. A struggle over the fundamental class process may result from these actions. So political and cultural struggles in the state may become conditions of existence of class struggles in society, as indeed the latter may become conditions of existence of the former.

Other social groupings within the state itself will be affected by a state political crisis. Of particular interest is the military. In reaction to threats to their particular conditions (e.g., the military budget delayed), they may move to correct the existing "disorder" within the state and society.[14] If successful, such a move would end the political crisis and resume what they understand to be the state's "traditional" role in society: securing the conditions of existence of private enterprise, which includes funding the military budget. In some instances, to accomplish this conserving of tradition, restoring what is considered to be normal state practice, segments of the military may seize, for a time, political power. They might then occupy one or more positions in the state besides that of the nonclass position of sellers of unproductive military labor power (e.g., providers of protection and security). Indeed, a dictator (or military junta) may be thought of as an individual who occupies several different class and nonclass positions within the state: chief of the armed forces (a nonclass position), president of the nation (a still different nonclass position), legislator of the nation (both a subsumed and nonclass position). Such an individual would then participate in the social processes associated with each position.

The concentration of power in the hands of one or more individuals does not in and of itself imply the ending of the capitalist fundamental class process. Indeed, such a radical political change in the state may end its political crisis, thereby allowing the extraction of surplus value to continue in society, albeit under a very different set of social processes. However, for those who understand the social totality within an essentialist conceptual framework focused on political processes of power, the capitalist nature of the changed society tends to fade into the background to be replaced by an analytic emphasis upon its new totalitarian structure. In fact, the logical extension of such approaches is for the class nature and analysis of such regimes to disappear completely. The dictatorship of power and its effectivity upon the lives of human beings become instead the logic and objects of the analysis. Within such frameworks, Hitler's Germany and Stalin's Russia become as one. Their essential common property is a monstrous dictatorship and consequent lack of freedom for so many.[15]

The horror and danger in and of such approaches is not so much in their essentialized treatment of power, but rather in what they tend not to see— how specifically class and nonclass processes interact to produce what they, we, and so many others abhor. Since we, like Marx, think this interaction is still of key importance in today's world, we fear that such theoretical blinders can produce, in part, the conditions for the emergence, yet once again, of such horrors. This then is one possible consequence of nonclass approaches to the state.

Revenues and Expenditures of the State

Our discussion so far of different forms of state revenue flows may be summarized in the following equation:

$$SV + \Sigma SCR + \Sigma NCR = R. \qquad (5.1)$$

The revenue category SV refers to the presence of the capitalist fundamental class process within the state (the existence of industrial capitalist state enterprises). Revenues are also generated from state subsumed class positions, denoted by ΣSCR. If a payer of taxes and/or interest, rent, and such to the state is also an appropriator of surplus value, then the capitalist subsumed class process occurs together with these different forms of nonclass processes—paying taxes, interest, rent, and such. So ΣSCR includes distributed shares of surplus value to the state in the form of taxes and of interest, rents, merchant fees, and such. Both tax and nontax payments are

made by industrial capitalists to state occupants of subsumed class positions. The third source of state revenues refers to its nonclass revenues,
ΣNCR. Taxes and interests, rents, and such are paid to the state by both
productive and unproductive laborers and by occupants of subsumed class
positions. In the case of these groups, the paying of taxes, interests, rents,
and such does not occur together with the subsumed class process: these
groups do not distribute surplus value since they do not appropriate it.
Thus, members of Congress, who receive such payments, do not thereby
occupy a class position. ΣNCR also includes state borrowings from individuals occupying different class and nonclass positions. The state's payments of interest on such national debt to these individuals does not occur
together with the subsumed class process unless the debt is issued by a
state capitalist industrial enterprise.

The state, we may initially presume, makes expenditures to secure the
conditions of existence of each of these different revenue flows. We write
such an expenditure flow equation for the state as follows:

$$\Sigma SC + \Sigma X + \Sigma Y = E. \qquad (5.2)$$

ΣSC refers to the payments securing the conditions of existence of state
capitalist industrial enterprises. Shares of surplus value appropriated within
state enterprises must be distributed to occupants of subsumed class positions both within and without the state. Such expenditures are analogous to
those analyzed previously in the enterprise chapter. ΣX refers to expenditures to secure the conditions of existence for the state's receipts of ΣSCR
from industrial capitalists. These state expenditures finance those state
nonclass processes that secure conditions of existence of surplus value.
These are precisely what we referred to in previous chapters as the state's
economic, political, and cultural processes which must be in place for surplus value to be appropriated in the society. State workers (including Congress itself) are paid by Congress to perform these social processes. They
sell and perform respectively unproductive labor power and labor. The
Congress also purchases commodities to aid state workers in their performance of this labor. In addition to these purchases of unproductive labor
power and other commodities, ΣX includes payments of interest, rents, and
such to bondholders, landlords, and others if such state (national) debt,
land, and so forth are used to establish state subsumed class positions. Finally, Congress makes a variety of different welfare payments to unemployed
individuals to retrain and relocate them and to secure social order. Industrial capitalists pay taxes to secure this sustaining of the reserve army, a
condition of their existence. ΣX is the sum of all these different forms of
state commodity and noncommodity expenditures aimed to secure the
state's subsumed class receipts.

ΣY refers to still other kinds of state expenditures—those to secure the conditions of existence of its nonclass revenues, ΣNCR.[16] The objective of such state expenditures, ΣY, is to provide direct benefits, use values, to those taxpayers who are not industrial capitalists distributing portions of their surplus value to the state. The relationship between such taxpayers and the state includes no class process, but it does include both the paying of taxes and the delivery of noncommodity "public" services. ΣY are the expenditures the state must make to accomplish such delivery and thereby secure those tax revenues (ΣNCR). Included in this category are commodity purchases of unproductive labor power and equipment, materials, and so forth needed to set in motion such unproductive labor. ΣY also includes the associated noncommodity expenditures in the form of rents to landlords and interest paid on the state (national) debt where the rented land and borrowed money make possible public service deliveries. Such processes of rent and interest payment establish nonclass positions within the state. Finally and parallel to its inclusion in ΣX above, ΣY includes welfare payments. In this case, productive and unproductive laborers pay taxes to the state to receive aid from it if they become unemployed, disabled, and so forth.

A particular identification problem concerns the classification of state expenditures. State expenditures are not classified easily or wholly into the categories ΣX or ΣY. Both the capitalist fundamental class process and the personal consumption processes of laborers may depend upon a particular state expenditure. For example, capitalists and these laborers pay, respectively, a tax share of surplus value and wages to secure police protection. The problem here is dividing state expenditures for police protection into one portion that secures class and another that secures nonclass processes. We may construct an expenditure classification as follows: allocate the police cost (patrol car plus officer) to the two categories, ΣX and ΣY, respectively, according to the hours spent providing security for each social grouping. If the car and different officer shifts were used on a twenty-four-hour basis, then one-third of the total expenditure would be allocated to ΣX if the car is used exclusively to patrol the business neighborhood from 9:00 A.M. to 5:00 P.M.; one-third to ΣY if it is used for the residential neighborhood from 5:00 P.M. to 1:00 A.M.; and one-sixth to each category if both neighborhoods are patrolled for the rest of the morning hours. There are a number of obvious problems with such a classification, including the assumption that only industrial enterprises operate within the so-called business neighborhood.

Such an analysis, notwithstanding the usual problems attending any set of allocation criteria, is required for each expenditure category. Thus, interest on the so-called public debt requires a disaggregation on the right-hand side of equation (5.2) into the three value categories, depending on whether such debt is used to secure conditions of existence of state surplus value appropriation, subsumed class revenues, or nonclass revenues. Expenditures on weapons and welfare, obviously not minor portions of state expenditures, require such a class analysis, despite and indeed in part precisely because of the thorny classificatory difficulties each category presents.

If we set equations (5.1) and (5.2) equal to one another, we may portray one economic feature of the state's multifaceted existence—a budgetary balance between its total class and nonclass revenue and expenditure flows:[17]

$$SV + \Sigma SCR + \Sigma NCR = \Sigma SC + \Sigma X + \Sigma Y. \qquad (5.3)$$

Parallel to our discussion of the industrial enterprise, there is no necessary one-to-one correspondence between the categories on the right- and left-hand sides of equation (5.3). So, for example, tax revenues from productive and unproductive laborers (components of ΣNCR) may change even if ΣY does not. However, if the conditions of existence of the changed ΣNCR are not secured in some way, such changed tax revenues would be jeopardized. Nonetheless, for a time a rise in the state's, say, nonclass revenues could be used to expand either or both ΣSC and ΣX. This possibility suggests that levels and changes in each of these revenue and expenditure categories are the result in part of diverse influences exerted from occupants of different class and nonclass positions both within and without the state. Further, such occupants will likely make complex alliances with one another to achieve particular tax and expenditure programs. Despite such alliances and compromises, struggles may break out within the state and outside of it over the distribution of taxes paid and expenditures received by these different social groupings.

For completeness, we should mention the possible complex struggles that may occur within the state when its class structural equation is extended to include revenues collected from and expenditures made to secure different forms of the fundamental class process: capitalist, feudal, ancient, slave, or communist. Equation (5.3) would have to be modified by adding to its left-hand side revenues collected from possibly different forms of the fundamental class positions occupied, from distributed shares of different forms of surplus labor appropriated in the society (including within the state), and from all the different nonclass positions that would then exist. On its right-hand side we would add expenditures to secure all these different revenue flows.

One of the interesting implications of such an extension is the state's securing simultaneously conditions of existence of radically different and perhaps directly contradictory forms of the fundamental class process. American society is replete with such examples. During its early history, the state secured political, economic, and cultural conditions for capitalist, ancient, slave, and likely feudal fundamental class processes. Congress became a site of contradictions and struggles emanating from the very different subsumed class positions occupied by its members. Other state officials were likewise pulled in different directions. We can illustrate this history with a simplification. Thomas Jefferson became the champion of the ancient form of the fundamental class process—each producer-citizen was to be an owner-operator, a farmer or craftsperson. Alexander Hamilton became the fighter for and defender of the early industrial capitalists— each producer was to be a consumer of labor power and thus a receiver of surplus value. Indeed, at this time it was difficult to distinguish between these two fundamental class processes because the early individual capitalist occupied so many different class positions. Wage labor became then a focus of attention and rhetoric. Struggles within the state, in Congress and elsewhere, erupted over a variety of different state policies fostering and discriminating against these different class processes in society.

Decades later congressional members divided literally into warring factions because of their inability to secure simultaneously certain conditions of existence of the contesting capitalist and slave forms of the fundamental class processes. They were required to preserve the rights of some individuals to sell their labor power while insuring that others could not do so. In capitalism, all are free before God, market, and law; in slavery, some are not. Yet the state was to reproduce both freedom and nonfreedom: a contradictory position whose complex effects still haunt the United States.

Equation (5.3) is a convenient vehicle to underscore our previous specification of the state as an overdetermined site in society and thus our rejection of different forms of both Marxian and non-Marxian essentialist treatments of it. The dominant non-Marxian approach considers the state to be a social institution existing as an effect of the will of its subjects. It is thus a site governed by an essence (a telos) reflecting the will of the subjects. This telos is the increase of social utility understood as wealth, which is defined as a mass of commodities. Thus the state exists at the will of its subjects, who establish and govern it so as to enjoy more utility (wealth) than they would without it.[18]

This state is to be socially neutral concerning conflicts among subjects, except insofar as these affect the utility—maximizing charge of the state— wealth enhancement. The state thus has assigned functions: to guarantee social contracts among individuals without which the utility maximization accomplished by private commodity markets might be jeopardized; to prevent all barriers to perfect competition for the same reasons; and likewise to prevent and/or offset externalities for which the private sector cannot account.

In this approach we note the *absence* of all references to class as process; the focus is rather on use values and individual utility maximizations. Thus when the state does intervene in society, it is judged and/or defended by whether and how it enhances the wealth of individuals. Budget growth, deficits, allocation of tax revenues and expenditures are all assessed in this way, that is, vis-à-vis the wealth-enhancing telos of the state. In terms of our class structural equation for the state, this approach abstracts from the class and nonclass positions of individuals. In this approach, all state revenues and expenditures are aggregated into class-neutral bundles of tax dollars received from these utility-maximizing individuals for the so-called public use values produced by the state and consumed by them. The only division that remains in this treatment of the state is between the level of private and public sector use values produced in the society. Ultimately, this allocation is to be decided by the will of the citizens of the society.[19]

This non-Marxian approach includes, of course, its debates over the state. In the United States, conservatives see the net effect of state actions as, on balance, typically negative, while liberals assess it differently. Both groups tend to use the same telos as the measuring standard. According to the conservative view, problems of the economy and perhaps even of the society are ultimately caused by state intervention in private (enterprise and household) decision making. The state's actions interfere with the market-mediated wealth enhancement of the individuals in society. They thus enjoy less utility with these state actions than without them. The policy effect of such an understanding is logically and clearly a decreased state: less state commodity production, less regulation, and crucially a radical cut in taxes collected and expenditures made.[20]

According to the liberal view, the problems of the economy and indeed of much of the society can be solved only by state intervention. There is nothing basically wrong with the structure of the economy or of the society of which it is a part. However, the market economy has certain "imperfections" and tends either to run out of gas, leading to recessions, or to run faster than it should, producing inflations. Thus the state's actions allow an otherwise healthy economic machine and society to operate smoothly and fairly. It follows that the state intervenes to avoid radical and perhaps dangerous economic and associated political swings. Such interventions permit individuals in society to enjoy more wealth than if the state took no action whatsoever.

In this debate, the conservatives see the state as the essential problem whereas for the liberals it is the essential solution. The key in both views is the role of the state in society: its active presence is the linchpin that makes the economy and society work smoothly in one view, and its absence (except for the previously listed functions) is essential to the economy's success in the other. Both views measure the state's actions in terms of their effects on the essential issue, which is the state's essential social role—increasing the wealth of the individuals in society.

There is a Marxian counteressentialism to this non-Marxian essentialism of the state: the state is not and cannot be a class-neutral social wealth enhancer. Rather, the state is the agent of one class against another: it is the "executive committee of the ruling class." Thus, Lenin writes: "The forms of bourgeois states are exceedingly variegated, but their essence is the same: in one way or another, all these states are in the last analysis inevitably a *dictatorship of the bourgeoisie.*" [21] In this Marxian approach, the state is defined by its essence which is also a telos, namely, to secure the political rule of one class over another. The state functions as an "executive committee" for managing the common interests of those who own and/or control the economic forces in society. Such owners/controllers of the economy, the "ruling class(es)," are understood to utilize their dominant power to shape state policies to meet their needs, above all their need to retain their ownership and control of the economy. Like any executive committee, the state has two basic functions: to arbitrate disputes within (among) the ruling class(es) whose interests it represents and serves and to secure those interests against challenges from the ruled class(es) or from the ruling class(es) of other societies. In this approach, then, the state has been reduced to a primary function of securing the essential conditions of capitalists' class position in society, chiefly the private ownership/control of private property. The state (politics) is thus derived from its essence; it is a reflection of class (economy). [22]

The state is understood as a class state in the sense that the economic class structure determines the goals and limits of state power and actions. From the standpoint of such a Marxian theory, for example, any state's claim to be democratic is tested and judged by asking whether economic ownership and control are democratically distributed across the population. If not, the claim is rejected.

Many Marxian economists and political scientists now vary this determinist approach by formulating a somewhat different essence/telos of the state—to increase productive capital accumulation and to legitimate (including by repression) the rule of capital. The state thus has assigned functions: the repression of one class by another via the monopoly of force (the class dictatorship); the fostering of capital accumulation, which aids one class at the expense of another; the legitimation of capital, that is, to mystify or hide the reality of capitalist exploitation via the ideology of bourgeois social theory.[23] Nonetheless, the state is still the phenomenon of an underlying essence: class (or perhaps class division and struggle). It follows that the capitalists' will to preserve their ruling positions governs the economic, political, and cultural functions of the state.

Some Marxian writers question the state's role as merely and simply a class agent, as in the well-known Poulantzas-Miliband debate.[24] Poulantzas provides a "structuralist" approach: it is the social nexus, the web of structural constraints in capitalist society, that forces the state apparatus to play the role of capitalist class agent regardless of particular "wills" of officials, communist and socialist parties, and others. In contrast, Miliband takes a position against "structuralism" by arguing for some residual "freedom of individual action" akin to the traditional humanist position we have already encountered in previous chapters. Miliband insists on inquiring about who becomes state operatives. Their values, social ties, ideologies will then explain why they act so as to make the state an agent of class rule. Miliband does not really deny Poulantzas' view, but he thinks it is insufficient and in need of the addition he provides.

Several Marxian writers, including some of those mentioned earlier (e.g., Poulantzas), concern themselves with the question of the "relative autonomy" of the state: can it ever move against a ruling class?[25] Some hold to a strictly economic determinant position and answer in a negative fashion. Others argue strongly for state autonomy. A widely held midposition posits a relative autonomy for the state, but in a very limited way. A relative autonomy of the state can exist just when oppositional classes or other social groupings in society are at a standoff, a kind of transitional conjuncture. A different position argues that a relative autonomy of the state is needed and put into effect by the ruling capitalist class precisely in order to perform its legitimation function. It is a ruse that nonetheless confers some real relative autonomy upon the state.[26]

It seems to us that within the Marxian tradition of notions of the state, essentialism (of economy, class, or politics) is ubiquitous.[27] Further, the different Marxian notions seem to be more reactions to the dominant bourgeois view of the state than carefully specified nonessentialist class analyses on their own theoretical terrain. Our definition of the state qua social site means that it only exists as the overdetermined result of the specific social and natural processes interacting and coexisting with it. Hence the state must possess its own unique pattern of change, in just that sense, its relative autonomy. The state does not merely derive from and reflect some subset of its constituent processes. Rather, the diverse social processes comprising the state overdetermine one another; they combine together to produce something different from each and all of them. It follows that the particular processes that comprise the state are neither dependent on nor independent of class. The state's "relative autonomy" refers precisely to the unique set of contradictions overdetermined in its component processes which give it its unique development. The conditions of existence of this set of contradictions and thus the state's relative autonomy have begun to be specified in this chapter. The state, for Marxian theory, is not reducible to an effect of the economy or any part of the economy (e.g., class). Rather than an entity determined by the economy or a particular economic class, the state is a specific subset of social processes, each of which is overdetermined by the other processes in that subset and by all the other political, natural, cultural, as well as economic processes in the society.

The State and Industrial Capital

State-produced nonclass processes that secure conditions of existence of the capitalist fundamental class process and are themselves secured by subsumed class payments impact industrial capitalist enterprises in contradictory ways. The state's provision of certain cultural processes, for example, mass public education, typically produces and disseminates particular meanings of capitalism that generally tend to equate it with the most efficient, the fairest, and the freest social system known so far to humankind. Such meaning production is a condition of existence of capitalist exploitation. The state's provision of mass education will also shape the productivity of the mass of productive and unproductive workers in society. If education enhanced the productivity of productive workers, then the exchange values of commodities would be reduced and thus the value costs to industrial capitalist enterprises. Their surplus value will be higher than what it would be otherwise. However, taxes on surplus value, destined in part to support expanded public education, result in less surplus available for productive capital accumulation, salaries of managers, dividends, land rents, acquisition of the stock of other enterprises, and so forth. This activity of the state thus expands surplus value while it may also require an increased tax claim on surplus value. In certain cases, as developed in the previous chapter, the industrial enterprises' expanded subsumed class payments to the state (components of λ in that chapter) could well be a condition for such a higher value profit rate (ρ) that the rate of distributions to secure these other social processes (productive accumulation, access to land and means of production, etc.) might expand as well. Nonetheless, industrial capitalists must distribute a share of their appropriated surplus value to secure the state's cultural (and other) processes, and this very distribution creates a tension between the payer and collector of taxes. No matter how much the state may secure the conditions for a higher value profit rate, industrial capitalists would still be better off receiving the same state-produced processes for less (tax) cost.

The cultural processes whereby the state produces and disseminates meanings are themselves overdetermined and hence contradictory: they may well have adverse effects on capitalist exploitation. The state establishes schools and hires teachers (unproductive laborers) to secure this cultural process. Once established, this part of the state has its own unique relative autonomy, its own contradictory effectivity upon industrial capital and the rest of the society.[28] The schools, for example, may introduce, knowingly or unknowingly, certain ideas that are in opposition to capitalist exploitation. Such knowledge production could severely strain the relationship between the state legislators (occupants of subsumed class positions) and the teachers (unproductive laborers). If continued, productive capital might resist paying a share of surplus value to the state for a cultural process it perceives as undermining its existence. Nonetheless, for a time such ideas may be taught. This suggests that education will be monitored to insure that industrial capital is receiving what it requires from the state.[29] In addition, mass education tends to bring together under one roof individuals from diverse backgrounds; it creates an opportunity for such individuals to play and communicate with one another, thus sharing experiences. Such sharing may well be a condition for groups to form, including groups possibly challenging capitalism itself. This example of education could easily be extended to all the other processes secured by the state. Private property laws, welfare payments to maintain the reserve army of the unemployed, road systems, and such both secure the conditions for surplus value's existence and undermine them.

Our example of public education as a particular cultural process over-determining the fundamental class process in different ways can be extended to encompass state economic processes necessary for the provision of public education. These include paying salaries to teachers, building schools, and buying materials such as books, paper, and so forth. These state economic processes of buying commodities and unproductive labor power shape capital, labor power, and consumer good markets directly and indirectly. The net effect of state demand for commodity materials and of state employees' demands for wage commodities may be to raise the prices of these commodities. A similar effect may be felt in the labor power market. If prices and money wages (price of labor power) do rise as a result, costs to industrial enterprises will rise and profits will be less than they might have been otherwise. However, the same spending by the state and its teachers can also be an important condition of existence of surplus value. The economic processes involved in providing public education may well provide an important market for the sale of capitalist commodities. Thus the state helps secure the realization of commodity values, itself a condition of existence of surplus value.

This example just begins to outline the different and contradictory ways any particular state activity, for example, public education, can overdetermine industrial enterprises. Typically, many state processes are combined together, depending upon the political environment within and outside of the state, to effect capitalist enterprises in particular ways. Thus, specific fiscal and monetary policies may be combined either to stimulate or constrain the economic activity of such enterprises. These policies include sets of particular economic processes involved with the purchasing of commodities, the taxing of individuals and enterprises, and the changing of the quantity of money in circulation. They also include certain political processes of the enactment and administration of laws establishing and funding such changed economic processes. Finally, they include certain cultural processes involved with producing explanations of the need for such policies and predictions as to their success in aiding enterprises. The state's fiscal and monetary policies cannot then be reduced to their economic component alone. Such policies are the combined result of the interaction of diverse social processes, economic and noneconomic, class and nonclass.

The location of state expenditures can be similarly shown to involve a combination of processes. It is influenced by the home districts of the legislators. As already noted, to occupy a state subsumed class position, individuals must secure political processes of election. One condition of such processes is the delivery of goods and services to one's home district. So the state's economic processes and their impact upon industrial enterprises are overdetermined by the political considerations of different occupants of state subsumed class positions. Indeed, it is possible that the very success of such a fiscal policy could be undermined by such political considerations of location. Each legislator in his or her subsumed class position lives a contradictory existence between serving industrial capital and securing the class position to do so among many other contradictory pressures.[30]

The aforementioned non-Marxian debate between conservative and liberal views of the state itself participates in overdetermining the economic processes developed within any fiscal and/or monetary policy. Since Keynes, liberal economists have often argued that the state can and should, more or less, keep the economy at close to full employment via the management of social demand. According to this view, state intervention can avoid the worst of the crises that periodically haunt capitalism and the unrecoverable losses associated with unemployed laborers and nonproduced use values (wealth). Keynesian policy thus secures certain important processes for industrial capital. It supports markets to prevent or minimize realization crises and thereby avoids radical income redistributions that might be required to clear markets in the absence of such policy. The risk here is that such changes in the distribution of income or still more radical changes might threaten the stability of capitalism. In this sense Keynesian policy saves capitalism from its own worse excesses and their possible consequences. In contrast to this view, conservatives see the intervention of the state, the very Keynesian policy advocated by the liberals, as the ultimate cause of economic crises. For them, the management of demand inevitably constrains the supply of commodities in society. Without this state management, we would have more jobs and output (wealth) and thereby greater capitalist stability. These very different views influence any fiscal policy adopted. In fact, the policy finally implemented often reflects a compromise between the camps. Industrial capitalists can be found on both sides.

Parallel to the state's fiscal and monetary policy, any actual state-run activity is not a political or economic or cultural or natural process. It is rather a specific combination, including some of each type of process. We have provisionally isolated the distinct processes so far only to explain them clearly. To analyze the state in capitalist society requires, for Marxian theory, understanding state policies and actions as specific combinations of these processes. For example, when a branch of the United States military builds a naval base in, say, Central America, the construction and maintenance of that base involves many different state-run social processes. Natural processes are involved—utilizing engineers and natural scientific personnel—to change land and water conditions appropriate to such a base. Other natural processes are involved as well, whether intended or not: possible air and water pollution, with secondary effects on fish and animal life, crop-growing conditions, and so on. The construction and maintenance of the naval base involves complex political processes as well. Not only is the security of the capitalist fundamental class process in the United States presumably enhanced thereby, but likely also that of the particular government that granted the United States permission for the naval base. Since the Central American government is itself subsumed to the fundamental class process(es) in its country, the United States naval base provides political conditions of existence to them as well as to the capitalist fundamental class process in the United States. State-run cultural processes enter the picture as naval personnel produce a flood of press releases, white papers, and research reports presenting the United States government's theory of what is occurring in Central America, why a United States naval base is appropriate, what its social consequences will be, and so forth. This theory will be systematically presented to the mass media here, there, and across the world. In different ways, these media will then reproduce this theory, which thereby becomes part of the educational process occurring in the United States and other societies. Teachers in schools will teach it. And in repressive periods the state might perform various police and judicial processes to enforce the dissemination and teaching of its theory and the banning of any alternative theory.

The naval base's construction and maintenance include economic processes as well. There will be purchases of U.S.-made commodities, both base equipment and consumer goods for United States personnel. Such purchases may stimulate a taste for United States goods in the local population and thus the export market for United States goods. Production technologies used at the base will have complex effects on local production methods; the same will likely apply to banking, communication, and transportation technologies. The local purchases by the base and its personnel will expand local markets, stimulate local production, and change local labor markets, wage rates, tax revenues, and credit conditions.

It would be misleading, therefore, to reduce the complexity of foreign naval base building and maintenance to only one of the many different sorts of processes involved. More than political processes are included; there are also natural, economic, and cultural processes inextricably woven together with the political to constitute the state action. In general, foreign policy by a state involves all of these processes. The economic and noneconomic policies of the state may include the distribution of aid, loans, military support to foreign countries, as well as the passing of laws regulating trade, immigration, and foreign investment. Treaties between states involve all these processes. Foreign policy may also include searching for and maintaining access to cheap raw materials for capitalist industrial enterprises, opening up markets for such enterprises and outlets for their capital exports, preventing foreign industrial enterprises and their capital from having easy access to such markets, resisting potential and actual threats from various states or movements, protecting the national honor, and so forth. Foreign action by a state can even generate an alliance among occupants of different domestic class and nonclass positions in the face of foreign threats.

The same complexity applies to all other state actions: setting an annual state budget, passing a law, operating a community college, changing a central bank rediscount rate, launching a space mission, and so forth. The state as a site in society is the locus of a specific subset of the full set of overdetermined processes that altogether comprise society. Each activity performed by the state is then a subset of the subset. Combine all its activities and we have what we understand Marxian theory to mean by the state. Combine the state with all the other sites and we have what is meant by the social totality, society as a whole. It follows that Marxian theory is inconsistent with and opposed to any other theory that reduces the state to merely a political institution or that explains the state as the effect merely of one or another kind of social process or subset of them.

Contradictions in the State

As a subset of social and natural processes, the state is the locus of all sorts of contradictions. It is pushed and pulled in contradictory ways by virtue of the overdetermination of each of its component processes. It is the site of contradictory movements emanating from all the other sites in society—industrial and nonindustrial enterprises, households, individuals, and so forth. Each other site (a particular subset of processes) exerts its particular determination upon the state. Individuals within the state who participate in its different processes, thereby occupying class and/or nonclass positions, are shaped by and are active participants in shaping the actions of each other as well as of those occupying different class and nonclass positions outside the state. So, for example, congressional members in their subsumed class and nonclass positions effect and are effected by the actions of various industrial capitalists, landlords, bankers, merchants, and productive and unproductive laborers outside the state. Congresspersons effect and are effected as well by the different unproductive laborers—the president, military, court, bureaucracy—and whatever industrial capitalists, subsumed classes, and productive laborers exist within the state. Their actions within the state are overdetermined by the very different determinations emanating from individuals both in and outside the state who participate in these different social processes.

The voting of congressional members on any particular piece of legislation is thus overdetermined by their participation in processes that secure conditions of existence of industrial capitalists, of occupants of various subsumed class positions, and of productive and unproductive laborers. It is also overdetermined by their participation in relationships among themselves and with various other state employees. Each of these and still other participations propel their voting behavior in conflicting directions. The political process of voting, then, is the site of all these contradictory movements. In parallel fashion, the whole range of behavior of each individual holding class and nonclass positions within the state is understood to be overdetermined and contradictory.

State legislators receive a share of surplus value, but theirs is only one share. Occupants of other subsumed class positions outside of the state claim their shares. The state's share will be larger or smaller in relation to the shares captured by other occupants. There is, in short, a competitive struggle among occupants of subsumed class positions for relative shares of surplus value. That struggle reflects some of the contradictions over-determined in the state.

Suppose that the state succeeds, for whatever reasons, in snaring a very large share of surplus value by a rapid increase in corporate tax rates. Industrial corporations forced to pay these higher taxes are left with less surplus value to meet their other subsumed classes' claims. Such an enterprise might inform its creditors that it must pay lower interest payments, or its landlords that it cannot afford the same rents, or its shareholders that it must cut dividends, or its managers that it must reduce their salaries and departmental budgets. Occupants of these subsumed class positions can fight back. Creditors threaten that if paid lower interest rates, they will never again provide credit. In other words, unless given their share of surplus value, they will cease to provide a condition of the industrial capitalist's existence, thereby jeopardizing it. Similarly, the landlords threaten eviction proceedings. Shareholders can sell off their holdings, which would depress the market prices of the corporation's shares. This would undermine its access to capital through the issue of more shares. Finally, managers can decrease their purchase of new machines and labor power, decrease their own labor, or move to other concerns, if paid less. Such managers thus threaten not to perform their functions, thereby undermining, for example, the accumulation of productive capital and the maintenance of work-force discipline which are conditions of existence for the production of surplus value.

Each occupant of these subsumed class positions might well resent the state's grabbing a larger share of surplus value at their expense. Industrial capitalists, under the pressures of this resentment and perhaps, as individuals, occupying some of these subsumed class positions themselves, might also be offended by higher taxes. Occupants of both fundamental and subsumed class positions may unite in a campaign for a cut in taxes, especially taxes on industrial corporations. A cry might rise up across the land that government is too big, taxes too high, state enterprises' productivity too low, freedom threatened, and so forth. Congressional members, sensing that their share of surplus value is under attack, would likely counter-threaten. They argue that lower taxes would compromise military security or the educational level of the work force or other state-performed conditions of existence. Each of these occupants of subsumed class positions threatens not to reproduce a condition of existence of the capitalist fundamental class process to maintain and, if possible, increase its share of surplus value. Of course, even if taxes on industrial enterprises are reduced, there is no guarantee that any particular subsumed class distribution will increase as a result. A reduction in corporate taxes does not necessarily imply that corporate productive capital accumulation and thus employment must rise. Instead, industrial corporations may redistribute the surplus value saved from taxes to higher dividends, salaries of managers, acquisition of other companies' stock, and so forth.

Contradictions in the state also arise as occupants of various subsumed class positions outside of the state seek simultaneously to reduce taxes on their revenues and increase state support of their respective social positions. Banks in difficulty seek state financial support at the same time as they seek to reduce their liability for the taxes from which such support might come. Stockholders seek reduced corporate taxes to free surplus value for more generous dividends at the same time as they seek greater government orders for the industrial enterprises whose stock they own, orders made possible by tax revenues. Landlords support reduced taxes at the same time as they pressure the state to pump mortgage financing into the construction industry to enhance the demand for and thus the value of their land holdings. The state is the site of contradictory pushes and pulls from these competing occupants of subsumed class positions in the society.

The state is the site of other contradictions that stem from industrial capitalists themselves. Confronted by the claims of their various subsumed classes, industrial capitalists may well seek to appease all of them at the expense of tax payments to the state. They will then join in the cry to reduce government, but simultaneously call for more government spending on the particular commodities they produce. Thus munitions producers couple their pressure for tax reduction with that for greater military spending. Construction companies demand tax reductions but without any reduction in government construction projects. Agribusiness wants lower taxes but no lowering in farm subsidies. Industrial capitalists compete with one another over access to particular state contracts, subsidies, depreciation allowances, and so forth. Different congressional members are pushed and pulled in different directions by these conflicting claims. These are all examples of contradictions and resulting struggles in the state over taxes and expenditures that stem from the nonclass struggles—competition—of industrial capitalists among themselves.

The state is the site of still other contradictions coming from a clash between industrial capitalists and the productive workers performing their surplus labor. The former want to save money by abolishing occupational health and safety regulations that hurt profitability. The latter want more health and safety inspectors to make the law genuinely effective in improving the job environment of workers. Capitalists want reduced taxes on industrial enterprises; workers prefer tax reductions on middle and lower personal incomes. Capitalists want legislation outlawing strikes; workers seek the extension of unemployment benefits to strikers.

There is one particular kind of contradiction in the state that may serve usefully to summarize much of the argument developed to this point. Industrial capitalists may, depending on the social circumstances, react in a special way to all the subsumed class demands on the surplus value they receive from their productive workers. Instead of playing them off against one another, paying one a larger share to the extent another can be satisfied with a smaller share, industrial capitalists move instead to alter the portion of total labor that is surplus. That is, they seek to reduce the value of labor power of productive workers and thereby enlarge the quantity of surplus value appropriated and available for distribution to the various subsumed classes. In this effort, industrial capitalists pressure Congress and/or the president for various policies designed to lower wage levels (the price of labor power): reducing or eliminating legal minimum wage levels, stimulating immigration to increase labor supply, reducing student loans to force students into the labor supply, reducing retiree's Social Security benefits to force them into the labor supply, and so forth. If successful, such policies reduce the price of labor power below its value and thus earn the industrial enterprise nonclass revenues (see n. 54 in the previous chapter). A subsequent fall in the value of labor power to its lower price would then enlarge the surplus value for the industrial capitalist. In this case, the state has become a vehicle for raising the rate of exploitation.[31]

Productive workers, through unions and otherwise, fight back by pressuring the state to reject such policies. They seek to have Congress lower taxes on industrial enterprises to ease pressure on their wage levels. Alternatively, they might demand state policies to nationalize banks, lower interest charges to industrial corporations, and thereby free surplus value for payments to occupants of other subsumed class positions without adding pressure on wages. Still other comparable strategies are available to productive workers.

There are innumerable ways besides those listed for industrial capital to influence the quantity of surplus value via its influence upon state activities. The state's various political, economic, and cultural processes have effects directly and indirectly on the value profit rate of corporations. For instance, state research and development, public road systems, mass public education, foreign policy, and so forth shape the cost of capital and labor power to corporations. Which measures are implemented at different times depends on class and nonclass pressures. It is even possible for higher taxes to the state to produce a particular pattern of state policies that so enhance surplus value that increased distributions can be made to occupants of all other subsumed class positions. In this case, higher taxes *and* higher dividends, interest payments, productive capital accumulation, rents, and such are possible because of the particular way state policies overdetermine the enterprises' value profit rate.[32]

Still other contradictions arise in the state from changes in the pattern of its revenues that do not match changes in its distribution of expenditures. For example, expenditures directed to secure the conditions of existence of industrial capitalists may rise without a corresponding increase in tax revenues from surplus value. This produced inequality between ΣSCR and ΣX may be financed in several ways that tend to create tensions and conflicts within the state. To see this clearly, let us rewrite the class structural equation (equation 5.3) for the state's revenues and expenditures: $(SV - \Sigma SC)$ + $(\Sigma NCR - \Sigma Y) = (\Sigma X - \Sigma SCR)$. Since in our example, $(\Sigma X - \Sigma SCR)$ > 0, $(SV - \Sigma SC)$ and/or $(\Sigma NCR - \Sigma Y)$ must be positive. If we assume that state industrial enterprises are not an important source of state revenues and outlet for state expenditures in the United States (i.e., that SV and ΣSC are not significant), then the focus falls upon ΣNCR and ΣY. ΣNCR comprises chiefly two sorts of revenues. The first is taxes on personal incomes of three groups: individuals who occupy subsumed class positions, those who occupy the fundamental class positions of productive laborers, and those who occupy nonclass positions as unproductive laborers. The second is government borrowing from individuals, and industrial and nonindustrial enterprises. Thus, in our example, the imbalance between ΣSCR and ΣX must be resolved by either raising taxes on personal incomes or raising government deficits. In the current circumstances of the United States, reducing a deficit caused by cuts in corporate taxes will mean increased income taxes on productive and unproductive laborers since they are the majority of personal income earners. Their taxes and other payments to the state must be raised and/or state expenditures directed to them reduced to finance the increased state processes directed to industrial capitalists.

Productive and unproductive laborers resist this change in state policy by pointing to its "unfairness." They may form complex alliances with one another to struggle over the direction of state revenues and expenditures. These are struggles—over both the class and nonclass processes involved in state revenues and expenditures—that produce contradictory pressures within the state. Congressional members and the office of the president are pressured by such groupings to alter in particular ways the source and direction of the state's taxes and expenditures, while industrial capitalists pressure Congress and the president to resist such changes.

There are, of course, complex compromises that can be struck. Suppose industrial capitalists and different occupants of subsumed class positions form an alliance with particular tax and expenditure objectives. As a result, taxes on individuals occupying these different subsumed class positions, as well as those occupying these fundamental class positions, are not raised, nor are expenditures directed to them cut. This relieves the pressure on the state by such individuals while also undermining whatever alliance might have or was formed between them and productive and unproductive laborers. Instead, the tax and expenditure burden falls on one or both of the latter two groupings.[33]

Contradictions over taxes and expenditures are hardly the only ones in the state. It is also the site for contradictory pushes and pulls concerning and shaping all the other economic, political, and cultural processes that it performs. State policies on religion, water fluoridation, voting procedures, abortion, tariff agreements, and so on are overdetermined in contradictory ways by citizens with different religious, ecological, political, and economic positions. Any citizen occupies not only one or more class positions in society, but also a great variety of other economic, political, and cultural positions. The citizen is a contradictory site in society. It follows that the pressures he or she exerts on the state are contradictory too. These pressures are themselves overdetermined by the class and nonclass positions he or she occupies.

A state decision to go to war against another state can hardly be reduced to some basic set of underlying economic conditions such as the securing of foreign markets and sources of raw materials for its national industrial capitalists. Nor can such a decision be reduced to noneconomic conditions such as different and conflicting religious, territorial, or political objectives among states. The contradictions necessarily overdetermined in industrial and nonindustrial enterprises, households, and individuals imply that the pressures of each of them on the state will be contradictory. Some but not all industrial capitalists may push Congress and the president to use force to secure commodity and raw material markets, to secure the national honor, to punish foreign infidels or transgressors, to protect national property and freedom. Other industrial capitalists may hold political, cultural, and even economic positions that influence them to hold one or more ór perhaps none of these objectives. Their pressure on Congress and the president may be different. The same complexity holds for each of our subsumed class and nonclass groupings.

A Concrete Example of Contradictions

A briefly elaborated example of certain contradictions in the relations among productive capital, productive labor, and the state in the United States during the last few years may illustrate the kinds of more concrete analyses implied by our notion of Marxian class analysis. High interest rates during the 1970s and early 1980s resulted, among other things, in drawing increasing subsumed class payments from productive capitalists who had to secure their credit requirements. These payments squeezed the amount of surplus value left to allocate to their other subsumed classes. This squeeze occurred when the United States faced increasingly effective price competition from technologically innovative capitalists in other countries. Just as rising interest rates reduced the surplus value left to be allocated to other subsumed classes, the competitive reproduction of the capitalist fundamental class process in the United States required additional allocations of surplus value to productive capital accumulation, that is, the purchase of new, additional means of production and the labor power needed to work with it. How was this dilemma to be resolved?

Two options presented themselves as general kinds of resolution: more industrial revenues might be received by a lowering of wages below the value of labor power and/or other subsumed class payments might be reduced to allow simultaneously for higher interest payments and higher allocations for productive capital accumulation. Economic struggles in the United States from 1975 to 1985 suggest that a mixture of both types of resolution had been accomplished. The mechanism of this accomplishment was a swelling attack upon the state. The attack had cultural as well as economic and political dimensions. The state was said to undermine, by its size and growth, the political powers that would better be vested in local, more "accountable" units of community control and in citizens themselves. It was likewise said to interfere in the intimate interpersonal affairs of home and the free contracts between employer and employee in the enterprise. It was accused of sapping citizens' incentives, self-reliance, and social responsibility and held responsible for maintaining a welfare population at immense and wasteful social cost. The state was pictured as a vastly excessive cost burden on the body politic.[34]

The attack on the state had many consequences, of which two reveal its particular usefulness as a strategy to resolve certain current contradictions of United States capitalism. First, corporate income taxes were sharply reduced.[35] The reduced subsumed class payments that industrial capitalists made to the state allowed for both higher interest payments and more productive capital accumulation to take place. Second, reduced state revenues increased public sector unemployment sharply. This drove former state employees to compete in the productive labor market. The resulting weakening of labor unions and the glut of labor power generally pushed wages (price of labor power) down below the value of labor power, thereby increasing industrial enterprises' nonclass revenues available for distribution to subsumed classes.

The attack on the state also produced a cut in its nonclass revenues: personal income taxes were reduced.[36] The reduction in the state's nonclass revenues along with its reduced subsumed class revenues produced sizable deficits unless there were substantial cuts in its expenditures. Cutting back state policies and personnel was in line with the conservative Reagan administration's view of the state, namely, that social sites other than the state (private enterprises and households) should become the location of formerly state-run social processes.[37] Pressures mounted in Congress to cut expenditures along with revenues. Congressional occupants of subsumed class positions were pushed in this direction by the president as well as by a growing consensus that emerged from occupants holding many different class and nonclass positions. In their view, the president should be given the opportunity to implement his ideas and his traditional faith in capitalism. The consensus held that state intervention in a private enterprise society was the ultimate cause of the society's social difficulties and the key barrier to its economic development.

Significant cuts in one segment of state expenditures, namely, those directed to industrial capitalists and certain occupants of subsumed class positions, for example, nonindustrial capitalists, were not favored generally by the private-enterprise-oriented administration. Indeed, in part the administration's expansive military expenditure program may be considered as the rather traditional imperialistic emphasis on policies and personnel to secure foreign protection and hegemony for United States enterprises' portfolio and direct investments abroad and for their various import and export interests. Consequently, the focus of expenditure cuts became largely ΣY, and especially those programs and policies directed to productive and unproductive laborers. Struggles emerged in the state between the president and Congress and within Congress itself over what elements of ΣY to cut and over the expansion of military budgets considered here to be chiefly part of ΣX. The battle between the conservative and the liberal views of the state emerged once more. Notwithstanding a gradual redistribution of state expenditures from ΣY to ΣX, the level of the total redistributed expenditures still exceeded the lowered revenues and, at least in the short run, large state deficits emerged and were financed by state debt.[38]

State debt, Marx's "fictitious capital," has, as he says, "its own laws of motion."[39] A generalized rise in market rates of interest initially set off by the Fed's policy of restricting the growth of the money supply and then enhanced by growing state debt increased creditors' claims on productive capital's surplus value. Less was thus left to distribute to other subsumed class groupings. In addition, higher interest rates also necessarily expanded state expenditures (interest payments on its debt). The annual deficits thus grew.[40]

To struggles over state taxes and expenditures were added struggles over deficits per se. In general, the struggles over the processes involved in state activities included both class and nonclass struggles. The sides struggling against each other varied according to which class or nonclass process was the issue of the struggle. For example, industrial capitalists found allies in many persons occupying either surplus labor performing fundamental or various subsumed and nonclass positions. The former's efforts to cut subsumed class payments to the state became allied with the latter's efforts to cut their personal income taxes. The alliance was built around the demand to cut "taxes" per se. Yet this very alliance was strained and sometimes broken when the issue was not the payment of taxes per se but the mix of government policies and programs to be cut or retained. To take another example, the alliance of persons occupying various class and nonclass positions who shared the demand that government prohibit abortion disintegrated when those persons confronted issues that affected their varying class positions very differently, for example, when the issue was lowering minimum wages or reducing governmental Social Security support to the aged.

In any case, from the standpoint of productive capital, the Reagan attack on the state had achieved desirable consequences in the early 1980s in terms of lower wages and reduced subsumed class payments to the state.[41] The alliances of persons from various class and nonclass positions struggling to diminish the state by reducing taxes achieved these consequences, among others. From the standpoint of Marxian theory, the class analysis of the struggles producing these consequences implies new objects of further analysis. Were these consequences sufficient to offset the squeeze on surplus value distributions that was the big problem? Will the more recent fall in interest rates produce new alliances and struggles? Will the reduction of the state prevent it from providing certain conditions of existence of surplus value appropriation and if so, which ones? How will industrial capital respond to such a dilemma? How will productive and unproductive laborers understand the relation between lowered real wages, reduced public services, and reduced taxes on their incomes? How can Marxian theory maximize its chances of informing that understanding? What lessons can be drawn from the alliances formed in struggles over various nonclass processes (abortion, school curricula, environmental protection, etc.) regarding the problems and possibilities of forging alliances over class processes generally and in particular over the capitalist fundamental class process?

From the standpoint of Marxian theory, all these objects of analysis require elaborate treatment by means of the kind of class analysis presented in this book. Such treatment is one condition of existence of the formation of effective alliances for *class* struggles in the United States today. The justification of Marxian theory, as we understand it, lies precisely in the circumstance that its formulations themselves are conditions of existence for class struggles aimed at qualitatively altering the fundamental class process from a capitalist to a communist form.

The State and Revolution

A basic change in the nature of the state and its relations with the rest of society requires—has as one condition of its existence—a basic change in its class structure. There is a tradition in Marxism that distinguishes between basic changes that are reforms and those that are revolutions. We might interpret that tradition as follows: a reform of the capitalist state is a change in its position as a provider of conditions of existence of the capitalist fundamental class process. A revolution of the capitalist state involves two interdependent parts: its goes beyond reformist change to considerably or entirely eliminate its capitalist subsumed class position and at the same time to impede or block other sites in society from securing those capitalist conditions no longer provided by the state. Some changes in the state will be judged as neither reformist nor revolutionary.

This last sort of change in the state may be illustrated by several examples. An election in the United States that replaces Democrats with Republicans in the White House and Congress is highly unlikely to involve either reform or revolution in the state. Congress will retain its capitalist subsumed class position. The changes that do occur will be more or less limited to alterations in tax rates, to relatively minor alterations in spending for the different social processes performed by the state, and to changes in regulations aimed at modifying the actions of other sites in society. No challenge will be mounted to the capitalist subsumed class position occupied by congressional members, their task of securing certain conditions of existence of the capitalist fundamental class process. Nonclass changes in the state—that is, changes in its cultural, political, and other policies— will be limited by the commitment to maintain its capitalist subsumed class position. The changes of faces and policies usually produced by United State elections will not basically alter the class nature of the state, however much particular groups may benefit or lose economically, politically, or culturally from such limited changes.

It is not necessarily different if the new faces and policies are labeled socialist or communist or anything else. The analytic question for Marxian theory remains the same: do the changed faces, labels, and policies basically change the class nature of the state? Do they alter fundamentally its role as provider of certain conditions for the existence of surplus value? If they do not, their accession to state power may involve reform, but not revolution. If the state's position as a receiver of subsumed class revenues and performer of certain conditions of existence of the capitalist fundamental class process is basically altered, it remains to ascertain whether it is a reformist or a revolutionary alteration.

An example currently receiving wide attention around the world may illustrate our argument. The states of certain countries during the twentieth century have experienced changes widely considered reformist and/or revolutionary. Socialist and communist governments in the Soviet Union, Eastern Europe, Scandinavia, China, Africa, Latin America, and elsewhere have been so considered. We propose to examine the question of the reformist or revolutionary changes in their states from the vantage point of the Marxian theory developed here.

Typically, such changed states have taken a series of steps to nationalize private property in the means of production and circulation of commodities.[42] They did this to varying degrees, but in all cases a sizable portion of previously owned means were nationalized, with or without compensation to the former owners, depending on each country's particular history and conditions. Typically, such states have also established or taken over considerable private capitalist commodity production. State industrial enterprises generally have flourished. The state's position in society was certainly changed by these steps.

It had changed its position as a receiver of capitalist subsumed class revenues. It was no longer dependent chiefly on the tax portion of surplus value for its existence as a performer of certain conditions of existence of the capitalist fundamental class process. If it had nationalized banks, the state was henceforth the agency extending credit, for which it received the subsumed class payment of interest in addition to the taxes it levied. If it had nationalized all or much of the land, it added rent payments from industrial capitalists to its other subsumed class receipts. If it had nationalized portions of the privately owned shares of capitalist industrial enterprises, then it added dividend payments to its subsumed class receipts. The state had also changed its position by newly establishing and/or extending the fundamental class position within state enterprises. Appropriated surplus labor within these state enterprises was then added to its other (changed) revenue.

The point is that the legislative bodies that undertook these sorts of changes altered their subsumed and fundamental class positions. Their alteration took the historically important form of a greater or lesser *extension* of their subsumed and fundamental class positions into areas previously restricted largely to private ownership (of money, land, stock, etc.) and private production of capitalist commodities. This strikes us as clearly a reform in and of the state. We do not deny that such a reform will have far-reaching social effects. Capitalist industrial enterprises will function differently when they borrow, rent from, and pay dividends as well as taxes to a single state. Productive laborers will act differently when they work for and pay taxes to a single state. Such a state will display a different pattern of class and other contradictions from the sort of pattern we discussed earlier as appropriate to the United States–type capitalist state. The society in which such a state exists will display a different dynamic than one in which the state is limited to subsumed class payments in tax form.

But the important question remains: however altered by the extension of its class positions, has the state in any sense eliminated its capitalist subsumed class position and restricted other sites in society from securing those conditions it no longer provides? Only an affirmative answer would qualify the changes involved as revolutionary alterations of the state. However, despite the enormous volume of both Marxian and non-Marxian literature on the subject of state changes in these countries across this century, the question still lacks an answer.

Socialists and communists who insist on the most profound theoretical and practical differences between them nonetheless widely share the identification of the nationalization of means of production with the demise of capitalism. Social democratic politicians worldwide and official pronouncements from Moscow echo the view that capitalism weakens and vanishes in proportion to the state's takeover of both formerly privately owned means of production and industrial enterprises. We argue that such viewpoints evade rather than answer the basic question. By equating the end of the capitalist fundamental class process to the nationalization of the means of production and of industrial enterprises, they need not analyze what kind of fundamental class process(es) is (are) in place after the state extends its fundamental and subsumed class positions. Hence they collapse reform and revolution into one undifferentiated theory of state change in which both are virtually identical or at most differentiated by degree.[43]

Neither the logic of Marxian theory nor research into the concrete histories of the countries whose states have so extended their subsumed and fundamental class positions supports the collapsing of reform and revolution into one another when state changes are analyzed. Suppose that a state in capitalist society is so changed that not only does it extend its subsumed class position to become the owner of all formerly privately owned means of production, but it also takes over the capitalist fundamental class process of producing surplus labor. The state would then be both the direct receiver of produced surplus labor (in state industrial enterprises) and the subsumed class receiver of distributed shares of that surplus labor (in state nonindustrial enterprises). Individuals located in such different enterprises of the state would then play the different roles of industrial capitalists and occupants of various subsumed class positions. Payments would flow among them in ways perfectly analogous with those among capitalist directors and managers within and between private enterprises in a United States–type capitalist society. Of course, a state directly involved and perhaps even predominant in the society's fundamental and subsumed class processes would develop differently from one occupying a far more socially restricted position. But the question remains: are individuals within the state still subsumed to the capitalist fundamental class process?

We answer yes. This book has, after all, been repeatedly concerned to argue and elaborate the proposition that Marx's concept of capitalism refers centrally to a particular process of producing surplus labor and not to a particular process of allocating ownership of objects among individuals. The state may own all the means of production; it may employ productive workers and receive the surplus value they produce; it may then distribute that surplus value to its various branches which provide the conditions of existence of its appropriation of surplus value.

The fundamental class process in this state and society is still capitalist. In the United States, the government owns, as nationalized property, large tracts of land. It leases some of these to capitalist industrial firms (in oil and gas production, in agriculture, etc.), who must pay rent to the state, which thus receives subsumed class revenues. It gets both taxes and rents from such firms. The United States government also lends money to industrial capitalists; hence it gets interest payments from them. United States government pension funds own large blocks of shares in United States firms. United States government industrial enterprises (for example, the Tennessee Valley Authority) also produce capitalist commodities for sale and thus appropriate surplus value from their productive employees.

Capitalism in the United States is not weakened by these aspects of the state, these extensions of its subsumed class position, and even this occupation of a fundamental class position (in the TVA case). The question is whether the state in a society like that of the Soviet Union presents us with a revolutionary as opposed to a reformist change. The answer hinges on a Marxian analysis of the fundamental class processes currently existing in the Soviet Union and on the Soviet state's relation to them. If these fundamental class processes do not include the capitalist form or do so only to a socially minimal degree, we would conclude that the Soviet change of state was indeed revolutionary as various of its defenders and critics alike claim. However, neither the Marxian theoretical tradition (nor any other) has yet to produce developed analyses, concrete or abstract, of what the communist fundamental class process involves, how it influences the position of the state within a society that is predominantly communist, or the extent of the existence of such communist class processes within actually existing socialist societies. This absence within Marxian theory must be addressed to formulate a properly Marxian analysis of such societies.[44]

What distinguishes this theory of Marxism from other Marxian and non-Marxian theories, however, is that we identify this absence in a particular way, give priority to producing the absent theory, and consistently refuse to reduce change in state and class to mere patterns of ownership of means of production and of social location of industrial enterprises. We also believe it to be proper to Marxian theory to emphasize the fundamental class processes in the determination of whether any given state change is revolutionary.

One implication of this theory is that even if a law is passed vesting collective ownership of the means of production in the performers of surplus value, we would still raise the question of the revolutionary nature of such state action. Suppose that under such a law workers now own collectively the means of production and receive a so-called social dividend for distributing these means for use in the fundamental class process. These workers now occupy two class positions: the fundamental class one as performers of surplus labor and the subsumed class one as receivers of dividends for providing a condition of existence (access to collectively owned means) of this surplus labor. Suppose in addition that the means are distributed to state industrial enterprises that exhibit the following class structure: the same workers who own the means produce the surplus labor, they are supervised by state managers, and the surplus labor is received by the state directors of such enterprises. This surplus labor could still be appropriated in capitalist form despite the fact that workers, the proletariat, own the means of production.

However, the general collectivization in a capitalist society of hitherto private property in the means of production is no doubt a massive, historically epoch-making change. The state that administers such collectivized property is a changed state: its officials will initially occupy the capitalist fundamental class position as receivers of surplus value and the subsumed class position of managers of state-run industrial enterprises as well as possibly other class positions. These profound changes, interacting with all the other class and non-class processes in such a society, *may* overdetermine the conditions of existence and growth of the communist fundamental class process. They *may* produce the conditions for the demise of the capitalist fundamental class process (within the state and/or nonstate enterprises). They also *may* produce neither of these developments. The epoch-making social change of the general collectivization of ownership in means of production is no essential, inevitable determinant of a necessary chain of subsequent epoch-making changes in class and nonclass processes, eventualizing in a communist social formation. To suppose so is to deny the need for the Marxian class analysis and practical social intervention to which this book and, we believe, the Marxian tradition are committed. And such a denial can only harm the development of Marxism everywhere.

Another implication of this Marxian theory of the state is a particular view of citizens' efforts to change state policies and structures within a capitalist social formation. Any change produced in the state will have effects, including effects on the various fundamental and subsumed class processes in the society. Persons using this Marxian theory to produce social analyses must then continually assess and reassess the likely effects of the various changes being pressed on the state by all sorts of groups in society. For example, women's groups who produce changes in state support for women seeking abortions will thereby produce changes throughout the society, including class changes. Different changes will flow from altered state policies on the environment, race relations, minimum wage rates, and public education. One major goal for Marxian theory is to specify the social effects of these different changes with particular reference to their effects on the various fundamental and subsumed class processes in the society.

Another goal is to specify the conditions that overdetermine how successful any particular effort to change the capitalist state is likely to be. The desire to change the state can hardly suffice to determine such a change; the desire requires organized actions under certain social conditions if it is to succeed. Marxian theory seeks to specify, for example, whether any particular proposed change in the state would, intentionally or otherwise, undermine its provision of a condition of existence of the capitalist fundamental class process. If so, the expectation would be that industrial capitalists and others with whom they might ally would fight strenuously against such a change. By contrast, proposed state changes that leave intact the state's effectivity as the performer of social processes providing the conditions of existence of the capitalist fundamental class process would be opposed less or perhaps endorsed by industrial capitalists.

From assessments such as these, whereby Marxian theory produces its particular class knowledge of the social conditions for and effects of different state changes, the Marxian practitioners of the theory draw practical conclusions. Doing such Marxian theory is one determinant, among many others, that participates in the overdetermination of the strategies and tactical decisions taken by Marxian organizations concerned with the transformation of society with special reference to its class structure. This Marxian theory precludes certain views sometimes found in other Marxian theories. For example, adherents of this theory could not reject practical efforts to alter state policies—on the grounds of some general or principled irrelevance of the state or its different branches to class change, including revolutionary change. Nor could adherents of this Marxian theory take the opposite tack and propose a practical attitude toward the state that imagines that changes in it would necessarily or inevitably produce a social transformation, including revolutionary alteration of the class structure. This theory's commitment to overdetermination as against the determinism of this or that aspect of society, such as the state, precludes precisely either of these two views found in alternative Marxisms.

One final implication of this Marxian theory of the state may be briefly mentioned to illustrate its explanatory powers. The state as the social site where certain conditions of existence of the capitalist fundamental class process are produced need not *always* be the site where they are produced. That is, what the state does may at other times be done at other sites. For example, mass education is only sometimes a state activity. While mass education is clearly a condition of existence of the capitalist fundamental class process, it need not always or ever be done in and by the state. Currently in the United States, a significant part of mass education of children is being shifted to nonstate sites, for example, capitalist industrial enterprises that sell education as a commodity in the market. Similarly, local police functions formerly performed by state employees (unproductive laborers) are increasingly being performed instead by private security enterprises selling protection as a capitalist commodity.

The logic of this Marxian theory insists that the conditions of existence of the capitalist fundamental class process be reproduced, not that the state need be the only site for their reproduction. Thus the size and sorts of processes performed in and by the state will vary across the history of capitalist societies—and noncapitalist societies as well. No necessary trend to bigness or smallness of the state apparatus is inscribed in this theory. Indeed, what Marxian theory would suggest is that one determinant of expanding versus shrinking states would be capitalist perceptions of whether their conditions of existence would be more securely reproduced by the state versus alternative social sites. In the 1930s the United States state appeared to be, in this regard, the social site of last resort; so it grew. In the 1940s the state was needed to provide military security in a world war; it grew further. In the 1960s the maintenance of social peace in the face of demands by black Americans, women, poor people, and others, and another war, in Vietnam, combined to make for another growth spurt in the state. By contrast, the 1950s and again in the later 1970s and early 1980s were periods when capitalists opposed growth in subsumed class payments to the state, preferring to see their conditions of existence reproduced at other social sites. In these latter periods, the state shrank; its relative position as a site in society was curtailed. Presumably, Marxian strategies for social change must adjust to the kind of social changes involved in differing relative positions of the state in capitalist society.[45]

This Marxian theory of the state suggsts a complex knowledge of the position and history of the state in capitalist society. It is a knowledge that recognizes and elaborates the state as an overdetermined, contradictory site in society. It is a knowledge that focuses upon and emphasizes the relationships of this state to the fundamental and subsumed class processes in the society. It carries far-reaching implications for the practical activities of Marxian adherents to the theory.

Alternative theories produce their alternative knowledges of the state; they make sense of the state differently. Their theories help shape different practical attitudes of their adherents toward the state. Indeed, our struggle in theory against those theories—our critiques of them—is a part of our practical struggles. That is, we seek changes in the state which we theorize about. We oppose the changes sought by adherents of the theories we oppose. To paraphrase Marx, life is a struggle, with the struggles in theory complexly interwoven and interdependent with the struggles in practical activity to change society and ourselves.

Epilogue:
Purposes of This Book

What Is a Book?

We understand this book or any book to be a moment in the human interaction called communication. As its authors, we see ourselves as partial agents of this interaction. Our goals and writings techniques are only some among the divers determinants of whatever communication with our readers may occur. The social totality in which we write and our readers read shapes us, them, and the different relations we and they establish with the text of this book.

At the same time, our goals and writings are constituent parts of the social totality; the same holds for our readers and their readings. We play a part in shaping the social totality that shapes our readers, as they do vis-à-vis us. We are acutely aware of the tensions and contradictions in our thinking determined by the divers influences working on us. This book is one result of and response to them. Its production adds another influence to the many at work determining our readers. Their readings of our text will add new influences determining us.

There is not and cannot be anything finished about a book. What readers grasp in a text is always changing. A book is thus a moment within an ever-changing relation of communication among people caught up and shaped within an ever-changing social totality. Both the writing and the reading of any text are processes comprising the relations of communication that such a text may help establish.

This book came into existence as the result of a myriad of determinations too numerous and complex to list. They overdetermined all the aspects of writing this book, including the existence of the process itself. While we will not use this epilogue to list the determinants of our writing or our general theory of the overdetermination of social process, we do want to draw our readers' attention to certain qualities of our text. Underscoring these qualities for our readers enhances the likelihood of the particular kind of communication we intend.

This Book and the Marxian Tradition

This book participates in the Marxian tradition. This means that we share many of the basic assumptions and goals that typify that tradition: interest in a social transition to socialism, concern with a historical conceptualization of society as a totality, opposition to the injustices and oppressions that distort the present and future of social life, focus on class structure and struggle, and so forth. Our contribution is to that tradition. As such, it comes into existence as the complex result of many, divers theoretical influences. Some of these lie within the Marxian tradition itself. We understand that tradition to encompass several distinct theories. Certain of them have influenced us quite positively in the sense that we accept and build upon some of their major arguments. Others have influenced us negatively; we reject their major arguments and build such a rejection into the core of our theory. To a lesser degree, but in the same way, we have been both positively and negatively influenced by much non-Marxian theory.

The theoretical influences upon this book are but one kind among the economic, political, and cultural determinations that have made it what it is. We emphasize the book's theoretical conditions of existence because it is a theoretical construct, not because those conditions played any greater role in its production than its nontheoretical conditions. Any assertion claiming to rank the relative importance of the book's various determinants (i.e., its various conditions of existence) would violate the logic (overdetermination) of the Marxian theory that the book constructs.

We are ambitious regarding the contribution this book can make to the Marxian theoretical tradition. We intended to formulate a distinct theory within that tradition, one that stands in sharp contrast and contradiction to those theories that have long predominated within the tradition. Our theory is hardly new or original since Marx and influential Marxists after him made many of the points we assemble and develop in our work. Indeed, our theory is one way of reading that tradition, that is, the classic Marxian texts treated in chapters 2 and 3.

What is distinctively ours in the contribution made by this book is first, the particular manner of extending certain lines of argumentation within the Marxian tradition. Second, we sought critically to juxtapose them to the predominant theories of that tradition in a particular way. The Marxian tradition badly needs and will, we believe, greatly benefit from the theoretical debates we want this book to join and encourage.

This Book's Methodological Self-Consciousness

The method of this book is the method of the theory that the book elaborates. We began by posing some initial concepts. We entered into our discourse with these entry-point concepts. These entry-point concepts were themselves results; their existence and qualities were complexly determined by all manner of economic, political, and cultural (including theoretical) influences. However, the analysis of their complex determination is another book, although we would use the method elaborated in this book to construct that book.

Our entry-point concepts are defined and deployed in a distinctive way to construct our theoretical system. Our particular definitions and deployments are what qualify our book as a Marxian work, a participant in the Marxian theoretical tradition. By the deployment of our entry-point concepts we mean two different but interrelated theoretical procedures. First, we link these concepts together to produce additional concepts. Second, we use these concepts to work upon, to interpret, to reconceptualize, and so to integrate into our system the different concepts of other theoretical systems as we encounter them in the activities of daily life (conversations, readings of texts, etc.). The deployment of our entry-point concepts is the means for the construction and elaboration of the particular Marxian theory the book intends to propound.

The process of deploying our entry-point concepts changes them as well as changing, as noted, the other concepts we encounter. It changes as well the additional concepts we construct as our theorization proceeds. In the course of our book, then, our concepts change. This change is unavoidable because the definition of any concept is nothing other than the varied relations in which it stands to other concepts. Since our entry-point concepts are deployed so as to produce and interact with other concepts, it follows that we continuously bring these entry-point concepts into new relations with these other concepts. Hence the entry-point concepts change, and the same holds for all the other concepts by virtue of the ceaseless deployment that is theory.

Each step in the deployment of the concepts of our theory adds determinations to those concepts, enriching and thereby changing their meanings. Our entry-point concepts such as class, surplus, and contradictions as well as our produced concepts such as capital, enterprise, and state, to take some examples, were all initially posed and defined so as to permit their further deployment. Their further deployment then develops, enriches, and changes the determinations (relations to other concepts) that give them their definitions, that is, meanings. Our book comprises a phase, a moment, in the changing determinations of our concepts. Our concepts have changed from what they were before our book came into existence; they change across the text of our book itself; and they will no doubt change as our readers and we deploy them after the writings and readings of the book are done.

This Book's Political Position

A book is one way of expressing a theoretical position, one way of making sense of the world. It is a particular way of constructing a knowledge of the social totality that it defines as the object of its knowledge. This book represents our theoretical position within the Marxian tradition. It is written from the standpoint that the predominant theories within the Marxian tradition understand differently the object of Marxian theory and hence the questions it must resolve, and that they understand differently what theory is and hence proceed to theorize in a manner we reject. Their different notions of the object and method of Marxian theory leave definite traces in their Marxian analyses of and participations in concrete economic, political, and cultural processes. We occasionally distanced ourselves from such concrete consequences, but we did so to underscore our focus on the theoretical differences.

Where the predominant social theories within the Marxian tradition display various economic and/or humanist determinisms, our concern was to reject them and offer an alternative to *any* determinism. Where the predominant Marxian theories assert and "prove" their correspondence to the "real world," we argued for the need to criticize such conventional, essentialist epistemologies and for one way to formulate an antiessentialist alternative (our understanding of dialectical materialism). Where the predominant theories treat class in terms of property ownership and/or interpersonal relations of domination, we offered instead a concept of classes (more than two) that defines class as a social process precisely different from either the processes of ownership or domination. Moreover, we constructed a social theory—which we read in Marx—by means of our concepts of social overdetermination, nonessentialist epistemology, and the class processes.

This book seeks to change the terrain of Marxian theoretical discourse, discussion, and debate. Our theory is a political response—in theory—to the current terrain. We do this in the conviction that Marx's goals in formulating his theoretical breakthroughs remain the goals we recognize in formulating ours. A brief statement of these goals may serve to summarize the political position we occupy.

A wide variety of movements for social change existed in Marx's time, much as another set of such movements exist now. Persons sensitive to different injustices and oppressions gather together, forge alliances, and struggle actively for all manner of economic, political, and cultural changes in capitalist social formations. With many of them, Marx then and we now feel a sense of close agreement and sympathy; with many of them we join forces struggling for the various desired social changes. Together with them we seek a society freed of self-perpetuating inequalities of power, wealth, and social standing which constrict and distort the potentialities of human life. However, as allies in struggles for a new and better society, we like Marx have something distinctive to contribute to the alliance.

We are often asked the question Why choose class as an entry point rather than, say, racial or sexual oppression? Our answer may serve to clarify our relations both to Marx and to those people today (including friends) whose entry points and hence theories differ more or less from ours. What Marx sought and we continue to seek to contribute to struggles for social change are not only our practical energies but also certain distinctive theoretical insights. The most important of these for us concerns class. Marx discovered, we think, a specific social process that his allies in social struggle had missed. The process in question is the production and distribution of surplus labor in society. Marx's contribution lay in defining, locating, and connecting the class process to all the other processes comprising the social totality they all sought to change. Marx's presumption was that programs for social change had less chance of success to the degree that their grasp of social structure was deficient. The deficiency that absorbed Marx's attention and powered his theoretical and practical strivings was the understanding of class and its role in social structure and social change.

Marx's consequent focus on class in his writings did not stem from some spurious claim that the particular process he discovered was "more important" in shaping the social totality than the myriad other processes comprising that totality. This sort of absolutist claim represented a kind of reasoning he often ridiculed. Rather, Marx's focus on class and hence on economics represented the much more modest self-awareness of someone who knew he had something particular to *add* to certain forces for social change. To borrow language from elsewhere, Marx's insistence on the existence and interdependence of class with every other aspect of social life stemmed from his implicit sense that class was a "repressed" element in the consciousness of his time, including the consciousness of social revolutionaries. The repressed element represented to him a critical lapse in the knowledge of society which he felt was needed to make possible the desired social changes. So he undertook to make conscious sense of and to popularize what had been repressed: to show the interconnections of class with every other aspect of society. This, we believe, is the unifying thread of all his mature work.

We believe that Marx's goal ought properly to be ours because we find that Marx's writings were only very partially successful in defining and popularizing class analysis. Simply, many readings of Marx by friends and foes alike understandably missed much of what he sought to add. Rather they assimilated Marx's work to that already circulating broadly within movements for social change. Such readings often lost Marx's contribution of something radically new, different, and consequential to movements for social change. On the other hand, other readings formulated their enthusiasm for Marx's work by raising his theory of class to a claim to have found *the* essential, last-instance determinant of social life and history. This essentialization of Marx's theory lost the point that he had something to *add,* something to interweave with other social processes in a particular conception of society. The rush to essentialize Marx's insights produced as troublesome a distortion of Marx's theory as did the rush to assimilate his work to what preexisted him. Indeed, not a few readings rushed in both directions at once.

It remained to us in this book to reconstruct and emphasize the cutting edge and specific differences of Marx's theory of class. They continue to be repressed in various ways by both friends and foes of the sorts of social changes Marx and Marxists typically endorse. As we showed, both friends and foes continue to assimilate class to property and/or domination; many continue to essentialize it into the final determinant of social life and hence of political efforts to change such life. Marx's work is not accomplished. In new and altered—if not altogether different after all—circumstances, the goals remain of integrating the insights of specifically Marxian class analysis into the social analyses and programs of complex, multifaceted movements for social change. That is what we want this book to help accomplish.

Marx's distinctive contribution lies not only in the discovery of class and its complex interconnections with all the other aspects of society. He also deployed a specific method of social analysis intricately connected to what he understood theory to be. His distinctive epistemology—built from his intellectual debt to as well as criticism of Hegel—conditioned his method, which in turn conditioned his distinctive class analysis. Indeed, in our view, the lack of attention to and understanding of Marx's distinct epistemology helps explain why his class analytics have not been more widely accepted and critically developed. Therefore, we felt it necessary to make a detailed and explicit presentation of that epistemology in chapters 1 and 2. This was all the more necessary since Marx himself did not produce an explicit statement of his epistemology in the way he did for his class theory.

Nowhere does Marx's complex debt to Hegel emerge more clearly than in Marx's concern to specify what he means by class by reference to what is not class in society. The definition of his object implies and requires defining its opposite, what it is not. What is more, it requires constant attention to the complex linkages between class and nonclass, linkages that comprise precisely the specific difference and hence social effectivity of class. The Marxian theory constructed from our readings of Marx is self-consciously concerned throughout with the complex interdependencies of class and nonclass aspects of social life, interdependencies that neither Marx nor we reduce to cause-effect or determining-determined essentialisms.

The basic entry-point concepts of our Marxian theory, overdetermination and class processes, then represent positions we have taken up in theoretical struggles within Marxism as well as between Marxian and non-Marxian theories. These positions have specific political, economic, and cultural aspects, that is, specific conditions as well as consequences of their existence. This book is a beginning effort to make these positions, conditions, and consequences clear and persuasive.

Notes

Chapter 1

1. The term *overdetermination,* in the broad sense that interests us, was first articulated by Sigmund Freud in *The Interpretation of Dreams* (1900), although the term itself appeared earlier in *Studies on Hysteria* (1895), coauthored with Joseph Breuer. Freud deploys the term to explain what he means by dream interpretation, the process of constructing the sense of a dream content. The means for this construction are the dream thoughts elicited from the dreamer by the analyst after the dream: "a complex of thoughts and memories of the most intricate possible construction." The interpreter's task, for Freud, is to show the relations among them that combine to produce the dream content; i.e., how the dream thoughts overdetermine the dream content. Freud's formulation of overdetermination already goes well beyond a simple notion of multiple causation among independently existing entities that merely influence each other complexly. Freud's formulation implies constitutivity—the idea that the dream content is constituted by the thoughts that happen to be elicited after the dream. Our development of the term is a goal and preoccupation throughout this book. On Freud's usage, see particularly the chapter "The Dream Work," in *The Interpretation of Dreams,* trans. A. A. Brill, New York: Modern Library, 1950, pp. 174–205; and also *Studies on Hysteria,* ed. and trans. James and Alix Strachey, Harmondsworth: Pelican, 1974, pp. 289 and 346. Lukács's and Althusser's usages are discussed at length in chap. 2.

2. By the term *idealism* we understand an essentialism that reduces natural and/or social processes to an ideal or theoretic origin or cause. Marxian theory's commitment to overdetermination, and hence antiessentialism, implies its rejection of idealism. The charge that our view of theory's constitutive role vis-à-vis all the other processes in society amounts to idealism is a red herring. It takes our assertion that ideas or theories participate in the overdetermination of everything else for the reductionist assertion that they are final determinants, essences. Richard Rorty has recognized a similar red herring in the charges of idealism thrown against the work of Thomas Kuhn and others: *Philosophy and the Mirror of Nature,* Princeton: Princeton University Press, 1979, pp. 276–79. Marx's *Theses on Feuerbach* summarize his rejection of materialism in the sense we mean here.

3. Our concept of contradiction builds upon Althusser's specification of "complex" as differentiated from "simple" contradiction: Althusser attributes the latter to Hegel. The point for Althusser is to emphasize the multifaceted differences or

contradictions embedded within a social process as the consequence of its over-determination and to break from a traditional notion of contradiction as a simple juxtaposition or clash of two opposing forces. See Louis Althusser, "Contradiction and Overdetermination," in *For Marx,* trans. Ben Brewster, New York: Vintage, 1970, pp. 100–101.

4. This formulation of indexes of difference among theories is indebted particu-larly to Michel Foucault's comparable formulation of such indexes distinguishing what he terms "discursive formations"; see *The Archaeology of Knowledge,* trans. A. M. Sheridan Smith, New York: Harper and Row, 1976, especially pp. 21–79.

5. Change, like other basic concepts in Marxian theory, is presented initially, and then progressively elaborated throughout this book. At this level it is under-stood as the consequence of contradictions. Later in this chapter the concept of change is further elaborated to produce the concept of uneven development in the relationships that comprise any society.

6. Our criticism of rationalism is not any endorsement of irrationalism. Ours is strictly a critique of a particular epistemological position appropriately designated "rationalist" as explained in the text. While we depart in fundamental ways from their deployment of the two terms, we are indebted to Barry Hindess and Paul Hirst for their early formulations of empiricist and rationalist epistemological positions; Hindess, *Philosophy and Methodology in the Social Sciences,* London: Routledge and Kegan Paul, 1977, pp. 1–22 and 196–228; and Hindess and Hirst, *Mode of Production and Social Formation,* London: Macmillan, 1977, pp. 15–16 and 23–28. Terms other than *empiricist* and *rationalist* have been used to characterize the predominant epistemological positions of recent Western philosophy, e.g., positivism, modernism, and realism. There are also conceptualizations of *empiri-cism* and *rationalism* different from those we use. Our usages facilitate the specifi-cation of Marxian theory's specific differences from other theories in terms of epistemologies.

7. Rorty, *Philosophy,* pp. 8–9 and *passim.* This project of analytical philosophy must presume linguistic or logical standards independent of all theories against which to measure and judge the relative adequacy of different theories' efforts at "adequate mirroring of reality." This is analogous to the empiricist presumption of given facts—independent of all theories—against which to judge their relative adequacy.

8. While this is evident from the body of literature comprising the Marxian tra-dition, two recent discussions, alike stimulated by Marx's *Grundrisse,* focus upon the problems of interpreting Marx's method of analysis, including his episte-mological position: Roman Rosdolsky, *The Making of Marx's Capital,* trans. Pete Burgess, London: Pluto, 1977, pp. 561–70 and 25–32; and Martin Nicolaus, "Foreword," in *Grundrisse,* by Karl Marx, trans. Martin Nicolaus, New York: Vintage, 1973, pp. 29–44. As if to illustrate the point, our reading of Marx's method and his epistemological position, as developed in chap. 2, differs from both Rosdolsky's and Nicolaus's.

9. V. I. Lenin, *Collected Works,* vol. 38, Moscow: Progress Publishers, 1972, especially the section "Conspectus of Hegel's Book, *The Science of Logic,*" pp. 85–238.

10. *Cf.* György Lukács, *History and Class Consciousness,* trans. Rodney Livingstone, London: Merlin Press, 1971; and idem, *The Ontology of Social Being,* vol. 2: *Marx,* trans. David Fernbach, London: Merlin Press, 1978.

11. Cf. Antonio Gramsci, *Selections from the Prison Notebooks,* trans. and ed. Quintin Hoare and Geoffrey Nowell Smith, New York: International Publishers, 1971, pp. 321–472.

12. David Pears, *Ludwig Wittgenstein,* Harmondsworth: Penguin, 1977, p. 145. See Ludwig Wittgenstein, *Philosophical Investigations,* 3d ed., trans. G. E. H. Anscombe, New York: Macmillan, 1968, pp. 48ff. and *passim.* Our emphasis on the specific, unique epistemology accomplished in Marx's break from traditional epistemologies is not intended to minimize similar formulations constructed by non-Marxists. The social formation that overdetermines a particular epistemology in those who identify themselves as Marxists will likely do so occasionally in those making no such identification.

13. Thomas S. Kuhn, *The Structure of Scientific Revolutions,* Chicago: Chicago University Press, 1962, p. 168.

14. Thomas Kuhn, "Reflections on My Critics," in *Criticism and the Growth of Knowledge,* ed. Imre Lakatos and Allan Musgrave, Cambridge: University Press, 1979, pp. 265–66.

15. Paul Feyerabend, *Against Method,* London: New Left Books, 1975, p. 168. In all quotations containing italics, emphasis is in the original unless otherwise noted.

16. Willard Van Orman Quine, "Two Dogmas of Empiricism" (1951), reprinted in *From a Logical Point of View,* 2d rev. ed., New York: Harper, 1961, pp. 20–46; the quotation appears on p. 45.

17. Quine speaks of one epistemological position as being "more efficacious" for coping with "experience" than others or having a greater degree of "simplicity," ibid., pp. 44–46; see also his "On What There Is," in *Logical Point of View,* esp. pp. 17–19. This begs the question since definitions of *efficacious* and *simple* vary across theories much as epistemological positions do. If theorists, following Quine, are conservative and pragmatic in choice of epistemological position, then the questions they immediately pose themselves concern the determinants of what is "conservative" and "pragmatic" at any time and for whom the different meanings of these terms hold true and with what social consequences. Quine ignores these matters, while they are central to the epistemological position of Marxian theory.

18. Hilary Putnam, "Realism and Reason," in *Meaning and the Moral Sciences,* Boston and London: Routledge and Kegan Paul, 1978, pp. 123–38. Putnam designates his own position as "internal" rather than "metaphysical" realism.

19. Hilary Putnam, "Meaning and Knowledge," ibid., pp. 18–19.

20. The relevant portions of Carnap's essay appear in Ernest Hegel and Richard B. Brandt, eds., *Meaning and Knowledge,* New York: Harcourt, Brace and World, 1965, pp. 298–305.

21. We may note the arresting parallel between Carnap et al. and Hindess and Hirst. Both equate epistemology per se with the traditions of empiricist and rationalist proofs of absolute validity. Both therefore "reject epistemology" in favor

of different notions of "practicality." Both ignore the claim that Marx contributed to an "epistemological break," a nontraditional epistemological standpoint. Both therefore miss the problems, insights, and issues posed and treated from such a standpoint. For a further discussion of Hindess and Hirst on this point see chap. 2.

22. J. M. Bochenski, *The Methods of Contemporary Thought*, trans. Peter Caws, New York and Evanston: Harper Torchbooks, 1968, pp. 78–129; Bochenski is himself a specialist in the logical, or, in his preferred usage, axiomatic method of thought. For a detailed critique of epistemological positions in mathematics, see Philip J. Davis and Reuben Hersh, *The Mathematical Experience*, Boston: Birkhauser, 1981; and Morris Kline, *Mathematics: The Loss of Certainty*, New York: Oxford University Press, 1980.

23. Bochenski, *Methods of Contemporary Thought*, p. 79. The appeal to "simplicity" is a criterion for choice among theories widely proposed by those who dissent from traditional epistemology.

24. The quotation is a paraphrase of Saussure by Jonathan Culler in *Ferdinand de Saussure*, Harmondsworth: Penguin, 1977, pp. 52 and 122.

25. Ferdinand de Saussure, *Cours de linguistique generale*, Paris: Presses Universitaires, 1965, p. 168, quoted in Frederic Jameson, *The Prison House of Language*, Princeton: Princeton University Press, 1972, p. 17.

26. This point is made clear in John Sturrock, *Structuralism and Since: From Lévi-Strauss to Derrida*, Oxford: Oxford University Press, 1979. Sturrock undercuts the notion that structuralism is a school. It is rather a variegated group of elaborations from some provocative initial theoretical breaks and shifts linked to Saussure. "These 'structuralists' may lack a common programme but they do not lack a common ancestry" (p. 5).

27. In this connection it is important to note that both Foucault and Althusser—certain of whose formulations have been particularly influential on our approach—have taken pains to argue how *structuralist* is an inappropriate label for their work: Michel Foucault, *The Order of Things*, New York: Vintage, 1973, p. xiv; and Louis Althusser, *Essays in Self-Criticism*, trans. Grahame Lock, London: New Left Books, 1976, p. 131.

28. Rorty, *Philosophy*, pp. 7, 12, 315, 318, and 377. See also idem, *Consequences of Pragmatism*, Minneapolis: University of Minnesota Press, 1982, pp. 160–75. Rorty attacks epistemology per se, pointedly refuses to endorse any epistemological position, and seems to reject the notion that his is one particular epistemological position. Much the same approach is taken by Barry Hindess and Paul Hirst. Our criticism of Rorty on this point parallels our criticism of Hindess and Hirst in chap. 2.

29. Rorty, *Philosophy;* see especially pp. 264–72 and 324.

30. Ibid., p. 294.

31. Ibid., p. 335; see also pp. 10–11. A recent case study shows precisely how the search for agreement among a group of theorists (scientists) takes the particular form of their assertion that the finally-agreed upon statement is more than merely a statement they agree upon. From their agreement to endorse (for different personal and social, as well as scientific, reasons) one of several alternative explanations, these theorists move to transform agreement into the "discovery" of *the* truth of *the*

nature of an external objective reality. The study shows how this leap is just one step in the process of securing the widest possible agreement for the endorsed explanation. Bruno Latour and Steve Woolgar, *Laboratory Life: The Social Construction of Scientific Facts,* Beverly Hills and London: Sage Publications, 1979, especially pp. 174–83 and 235–62. This book reports on a two-year study of scientists working at the Salk Institute for Biological Studies in La Jolla, California.

32. Rorty, *Philosophy,* pp. 333–35 and 389–94. Rorty's approach has found expression in economics through the work of Donald N. McCloskey, *The Rhetoric of Economics,* Madison: University of Wisconsin Press, 1985.

33. One completes Rorty's impressive volume with the sense that he supports a new philosophic tradition in which different theories converse without empty claims that one or the other more or less adequately mirrors "reality." How the birth, development, and demise of such theories are explained and how the constitution of theory is understood are questions of little or no interest for Rorty. He assigns all that to an untheorized "history," thereby removing the social constitution and effects of theories from the discussion of epistemology. Life in its complexity produces theoretical diversity. By contrast, Marxian theory builds its conceptualization of the social constitution and social effectivity of theories into its epistemological position. Hence its critique of traditional epistemology is not Rorty's, couched merely in terms of openness versus closure, but rather proceeds in terms of traditional epistemology's overdetermined social position. For Marxian theory the specification of epistemological positions and their differences necessarily includes and involves the specification of their historical location within societies understood as distinct overdetermined totalities. Our criticism of Rorty on this point has certain similarities to the critique of Michel Foucault's concept of "discursive formations" (see n. 4, this chapter) by Dominique Lecourt, *Marxism and Epistemology: Bachelard, Canguilhem and Foucault,* trans. Ben Brewster, London: New Left Books, 1975, pp. 187–213.

34. Of course, different theories will produce different knowledges of what is understood by these terms. Rorty writes as if the definitions of these terms were universally agreed upon, which, in out view, they are not.

35. Our emphasis on the uniqueness of each social process and its unique participation in the overdetermination of all other social processes bears a particular relationship to the literature on overdetermination. Our concept of uniqueness is an effort to change, develop, and make more precise what we think Althusser began to articulate with his notion of "relative autonomy," in "Overdetermination and Contradiction," p. 111. The problems we see in the usual connotations of the term *autonomy*—however "relative" it is thought to be—prompt us to discard Althusser's initial formulation.

36. It is in the sense of this paragraph that we read Marx's methodological proposals in "The Method of Political Economy" in *Grundrisse:* "The concrete is concrete because it is the concentration of many determinations" (p. 101); "Capital . . . must form the starting-point as well as the finishing point" (p. 107); and "the . . . conception of a whole . . . as a rich totality of many determinations and relations" (p. 100). Marx's notion of capital as the starting point—our entry point—is a notion, as Marx often repeats, of a relationship, not a thing. In our terminology,

what Marx calls the capital relation amounts to the capitalist form of the class process, as we shall show in chap. 3.

37. Ibid., p. 100.

38. Ferdinand de Saussure, *Course in General Linguistics*, New York: McGraw-Hill, 1959, p. 120.

39. Ibid., p. 114.

40. Ibid., p. 122.

41. A comment on the term *overdetermination* is in order here. We have come to appreciate Althusser's qualms about using it: "I am not particularly taken by this term *overdetermination* (borrowed from other disciplines), but I shall use it in the absence of anything better" ("Overdetermination and Contradiction," p. 101). Nothing better has yet occurred to us. In particular, we shy away from using the term *dialectics*. The troublesomeness of *overdetermination* is as nothing compared to the vagueness, definitional chaos, and polemical intentions that clutter and embitter the history and variegated usages of the term *dialectics*. Our strategy here is to specify our meaning in using *overdetermination* precisely enough to lessen the likelihood of it going the way of *dialectics*.

42. An essay that typifies empiricist formulations within the Marxian tradition and also cites works by other Marxian writers that endorse such formulations is Oskar Lange's *Political Economy*, vol. 1, New York: Macmillan, 1963, pp. 278–342.

43. E. P. Thompson, "The Poverty of Theory or an Orrery of Errors," in *The Poverty of Theory and Other Essays*, New York: Monthly Review, 1978, pp. 1–210. We discount the possibility that Thompson means by empiricism something radically different from what we do. In this we follow Thompson, who admits no such radical difference when he refers to Althusser's concept of empiricism which is similar to ours.

44. Ibid.; see especially pp. 18–32, as well as *passim*.

45. See, for some examples, Rudolf Hilferding's critique of Eugen von Bohm-Bawerk in the latter's *Karl Marx and the Close of His System*, ed. Paul M. Sweezy, London: Merlin, 1975, pp. 132–33; Samir Amin, *Accumulation on a World Scale*, vol. 1, trans. Brian Pearce, New York and London: Monthly Review, 1974, pp. 5–7; and David Mermelstein, ed., *The Economic Crisis Reader*, New York: Vintage, 1975, where the editor, in typically rationalist fashion, faults orthodox economic theory because its concept of the economy ("the competitive model") is "ill-suited" for, i.e., cannot grasp, "the real world of monopoly, multi-national corporations and political manipulation of national and world economies" (p. x).

46. Two clear formulations of this position among Marxian theorists are Russell Keat and John Urry, *Social Theory as Science*, London: Routledge and Kegan Paul, 1977, p. 196. The most ambitious work in recent years seeking to specify the particular Marxian epistemological position is chiefly an effort to establish Marxian theory as "realist": John Mepham and David-Hillel Ruben, eds., *Issues in Marxist Philosophy*, vol. 3: *Epistemology, Science and Ideology*, Brighton: Harvester Press, 1979; see especially the essays by Roy Edgley, Derek Sayer, Andrew Collier, and Roy Bhaskar, where the last-named seems to exercise the widest influence among the realists. Across the Atlantic, in the United States, much the same sort of

position is taken, although with far less theoretical self-consciousness, by Erik Olin Wright, *Class, Crisis and the State,* London: New Left Books, 1978, pp. 11–12; Wright calls his approach "structuralist" and cites Althusser. This is the sort of association that might explain why Althusser took pains to dissociate himself from structuralism in his *Essays in Self-Criticism;* see n. 27.

47. Keat and Urry, *Social Theory,* p. 5.

48. Ibid., p. 5. The most careful of recent empiricists, mindful of the criticisms of empiricism produced by Quine, Kuhn, and Feyerabend, works his way to an epistemological position that he terms "internal realism"; see Putnam, *Meaning and the Moral Sciences,* pp. 123–40.

49. See Frederick Engels, *Ludwig Feuerbach and the End of Classical German Philosophy,* Moscow: Progress Publishers, 1969, p. 14; V. I. Lenin, *Materialism and Empirio-Criticism,* in *Collected Works,* vol. 13, New York: International, 1927, pp. 105–6; and idem, "On the Question of Dialectics," in *Collected Works* (1972 ed.), vol. 38, p. 360.

50. Rorty, *Philosophy,* p. 4.

51. Ibid., p. 10.

52. Ibid., p. 11.

53. See Raymond Aron, *Introduction à la philosophie de l'histoire,* Paris: 1938; Hans Meyerhoff, ed., *The Philosophy of History in Our Time,* New York: Doubleday, 1959, pp. 18–25; Peter Winch, *The Idea of a Social Science and Its Relation to Philosophy,* London: Routledge and Kegan Paul, 1958, pp. 100–101; Harold Bloom, *A Map of Misreading,* New York: Oxford University Press, 1975, p. 33. For references to Foucault, Kuhn, and Feyerabend, see earlier notes; references to Bachelard and Canguilhem are presented and discussed in Lecourt, *Marxism and Epistemology.*

54. See Lecourt, *Marxism and Epistemology,* pp. 17–19. The quotation from Kuhn appears in *Structure of Scientific Revolutions,* p. 64.

55. Rorty, *Philosophy,* p. 377. Rorty dissolves relativism into a pragmatism; the former becomes a nonissue and the latter becomes *the* issue: see idem, *Consequences of Pragmatism,* pp. 166ff.

56. Feyerabend, *Against Method,* p. 306.

57. Cf. the related critiques of Rorty in John Rajchman and Cornel West, *Post-Analytic Philosophy,* New York: Columbia University Press, 1985, especially the essays by the two editors; see also the critique of Kuhn in Lecourt, *Marxism and Epistemology,* pp. 7–19.

58. Rorty, *Philosophy,* pp. 378–79.

Chapter 2

1. On Adorno's attacks, see Martin Jay, *The Dialectical Imagination,* Boston: Little, Brown, 1973, pp. 68–69; and Andrew Arato and Eike Gebhardt, *The Essential Frankfurt School Reader,* New York: Urizen Books, 1978, pp. 497–511. For examples of the monotheism to which we refer, see Herbert Gintis, "On the Theory of Transitional Conjunctures," *Review of Radical Political Economics* 11:3 (Fall

1979), pp. 23–31; and William Lazonick, "Discussion," *Journal of Economic History* 42:1 (March 1982), pp. 83–85. Many other examples are discussed in this chapter.

2. One recent compendium of attitudes of this minority tendency (or rather tendencies) is Dick Howard and Karl E. Klare, eds., *The Unknown Dimension: European Marxism since Lenin*, New York and London: Basic Books, 1972. This volume is doubly useful in that it offers readings of the major figures that are as indicative of the minority tendencies as are the figures themselves.

3. The humanist Marxian tendency, while developed earlier, became particularly popular and widely elaborated after World War II, especially in France (by both French thinkers and other Europeans living in France). A sympathetic study of the various articulations of humanist Marxism and their vicissitudes is contained in Mark Poster, *Existential Marxism in Postwar France: From Sartre to Althusser*, Princeton: Princeton University Press, 1975. A critical review of humanist Marxism, not only in its Western European but also in its Eastern European and particularly Soviet forms, is contained in Louis Althusser, *For Marx*, trans. Ben Brewster, New York: Vintage, 1974, especially essays 2, 5, and 7.

4. Engels to H. Starkenburg, January 25, 1894, in Karl Marx and Frederick Engels, *Selected Correspondence*, Moscow: Foreign Languages Publishing House, n.d., p. 549.

5. Engels to J. Bloch, September 21–22, 1890, ibid., p. 500.

6. See Max Horkheimer, *Critical Theory: Selected Essays*, trans. Matthew J. O'Connell and others, New York: Seabury Press, 1972, particularly the essays "Materialism and Metaphysics" and "Traditional and Critical Theory" (especially pp. 226 and 251). In these two essays Horkheimer not only illustrates the tension in his thinking between the pro- and anti-economic-determinist readings of Marx; he also produces important critical commentaries on Marxian epistemology which fully deserve to be included among the passages paving the way for the resolution of the debate, a resolution he never did produce. See also Jay, *Dialectical Imagination*, pp. 82–84.

7. A recent example of the old debate flaring up again was the publication of G. A. Cohen, *Karl Marx's Theory of History: A Defense*, Oxford: Oxford University Press, 1978, which advanced a technological variant (the forces of production are the primary essence of social change) of the economic determinist position. In response, variations on the usual replies to this position were produced: Andrew Levine and Erik Olin Wright, "Rationality and Class Struggle," *New Left Review* 123 (September–October 1980), pp. 47–68, among others.

8. Howard and Klare's *Unknown Dimension* and Stanley Aronowitz's introduction to Horkheimer's *Critical Theory* offer many examples of such rediscovery.

9. Herbert Gintis reproduces E. P. Thompson's arguments in "On the Theory of Transitional Conjunctures," pp. 23–31. Gintis there worries about statements of other Marxists that "result not from the nature of the world, but the commitments of the theory" (p. 29). Like Thompson, he rejects empiricism but then relapses back into it when confronted with the notion that different theories contest as totalities in the social arena (p. 26). Like Thompson, he recoils from the notion of Marxism as "only" a distinctive set of concepts: "how utterly, utterly distressing"

(p. 28). For Gintis there must be something more, something beyond theory that guarantees Marxism as truer than other conceptual frameworks in terms of some universal standard of truth (pp. 24–25).

10. See Erik Olin Wright, "Alternative Perspectives in Marxist Theory of Accumulation and Crisis," in *The Subtle Anatomy of Capitalism*, ed. Jesse Schwartz, Santa Monica: Goodyear Publishing, 1977, pp. 195–231. Wright resolves his worry over which crisis tendency developed in *Capital* actually explains economic crises in a remarkable fashion: he offers a periodization of capitalism according to which of *Capital's* formulations of tendency to crisis were the essence of capitalist accumulation in each period.

11. An instructive text exemplifying the epistemological coexistence of both empiricism and rationalism is the work of the Soviet economist (at one time vice-president of the USSR Academy of Sciences) Alexei M. Rumyantsev, *Categories and Laws of the Political Economy of Communism*, Moscow: Progress Publishers, 1969, pp. 13–75.

12. See, for example, Lenin, *What Is to Be Done?*, International, 1929, pp. 46ff., 76ff., and *passim*, where Lenin attacks economism for tending toward Marxian political subservience to trade unionism, etc., which in his view produced disaster for Marxian political practice.

13. See Lenin's *Materialism and Empirio-Criticism* and also a recent essay on just the link between the ideas of Mach and Bogdanov and the political practices Lenin was concerned to defeat: Dominique Lecourt, "Bogdanov: Mirror of the Soviet Intelligentsia," in *Proletarian Science: The Case of Lysenko*, trans. Ben Brewster, London: New Left Books, 1977, pp. 137–62.

14. As noted in chap. 1, we accept that for specific reasons different conceptual frameworks may agree *for a time* on the validity of certain propositions of the sort: "That is a brown tree" or "Napoleon was a ruler of France" or "A dropped coffee cup will break." We do not, of course, accept that such agreement warrants any belief that those propositions (or "facts") are independent of the agreeing frameworks: a clear non sequitur. More important, it is *always* necessary to interrogate any proposed "given" in order to ascertain its status—its place within the structure of meaning—within our own as opposed to different theoretical frameworks. Omitting such an interrogation—the hallmark of empiricism—is what we criticize here. Perhaps it is still necessary to add that, in our view, any theory can and must contend with each and every "fact" confronting its proponents, whether that "fact" arises within their own framework or is thrown up to them from alternative frameworks.

15. Lukács, *History and Class Consciousness*, pp. 150ff. We stress that we understand Lukács in the manner indicated, despite occasional ambiguities in his usage of *immediacy*.

16. Karl Marx, *Theories of Surplus Value, Part II*, Moscow: Progress Publishers, 1968, p. 106. Emphasis added.

17. Our specification of overdetermination goes well beyond Althusser's original formulations in 1963: "On the Materialist Dialectic" and "Overdetermination and Contradiction," in *For Marx*, pp. 161–218 and 87–128. It is closer to his later emphasis on the notion of a process without a subject: see Althusser, "Marx's Rela-

tion to Hegel" (1968), in *Politics and History*, trans. Ben Brewster, London: New Left Books, 1972, pp. 161–86; and idem, "Reply to John Lewis" (1973), in *Essays in Self-Criticism*, especially pp. 94–99. Our readily acknowledged debt to Althusser should not obscure the particular way we have further developed and changed the notion of overdetermination.

18. Marx, *Grundrisse*, pp. 101–2.

19. See Barry Hindess and Paul Q. Hirst, *Pre-Capitalist Modes of Production*, London and Boston: Routledge and Kegan Paul, 1975, pp. 21–22. The authors later criticized this view in *Mode of Production and Social Formation*.

20. The comment in the *Grundrisse* (p. 101) about concentrating many determinations may serve to correct the impression of those who read Marx's fragmentary chap. 52, entitled "Classes," in *Capital*, vol. 3, New York: International, 1967, pp. 885–86, as if it were Marx's first definitional effort. (Lukács, for example, writes in this vein in his essay "Class Consciousness" [1920], in *History and Class Consciousness*, p. 46.) Marx's earlier writings were involved in working up an understanding of class. What Marx proposed at the end of *Capital*, vol. 3, was not an initial definition but rather a "concentration of many determinations," most of which were already theoretically produced in the earlier works. Indeed, it was those earlier determinations, each building upon those that preceded them, that alone made possible the projected *concentration* of determinations and that provide the indispensable context and basis for our work here and in the paper cited in n. 26. On this point see the complementary comments of Roman Rosdolsky, *The Making of Marx's Capital*, trans. Pete Burgess, London: Pluto Press, 1977, pp. 39 and 54; Rosdolsky is here attempting to demonstrate the logic of Marx's decisions on how to present his theoretical findings.

21. Marx to Engels, January 14, 1858, in *Selected Correspondence*, p. 121. In *Capital*, vol. 1, pp. 19–20, Marx refers to himself as "the pupil of that mighty thinker."

22. See the examples noted in Terrell Carver, ed. and trans., *Karl Marx: Texts on Method*, Oxford: Basil Blackwell, 1975, pp. 126–42.

23. Richard Norman, *Hegel's Phenomenology: A Philosophical Introduction*, Sussex: Sussex University Press, 1976, p. 12. The first chapter of this work, entitled "The Dilemma of Epistemology," is a very useful text in terms of this chapter's objectives. Along similar lines, see David Lamb, *Hegel*, Hague: Martinus Nijhoff, 1980. See also G. W. F. Hegel, *Science of Logic*, trans. A. V. Miller, London: George Allen and Unwin, 1969, pp. 75–76.

24. The quotation is from G. W. F. Hegel, *The Phenomenology of Mind*, trans. J. B. Baillie, 2d ed., London: George Allen and Unwin, 1931, p. 135. Marx could not, we believe, countenance any discussion of the different forms of knowledge, the different claims to truths, that pretended to operate outside one or another of those forms and claims. What Marx rejected in Hegel is discussed in Joseph O'Malley, ed., *Marx's Critique of Hegel's "Philosophy of Right,"* Cambridge: Cambridge University Press, 1972.

25. Hegel, *Philosophy of Religion*, in *Werke*, vol. 11, pp. 158–59, as cited and quoted by Lukács in the latter's "Reification and the Consciousness of the Proletariat," in *History and Class Consciousness*, pp. 163 and 218.

26. Hegel, *Science of Logic*, p. 43.

27. Marx to L. Kugelmann, June 27, 1870, *Selected Correspondence*, pp. 290–91. The other admirer in question was F. A. Lange. In this light, note Marx's comment on the worker-philosopher Joseph Dietzgen, whom he admired, although critically: "It is his hard luck that precisely Hegel he did *not* study," Marx to Engels, November 7, 1868, ibid., p. 262.

28. Karl Marx, *Economic and Philosophic Manuscripts of 1844,* trans. Martin Milligan, Moscow: Foreign Languages Publishing House, 1961, p. 107.

In this connection note the parallel conclusion reached by Edwin H. Land in his Phi Beta Kappa lecture at Harvard University in 1977. His point was that what humans see in the world is not "what is out there," but rather is a complex mediation/interaction between external stimuli and complex eye-brain responses; see "Our 'Polar Partnership' with the World Around Us," *Harvard Magazine*, January/February 1978, pp. 23–26.

29. Marx, *Grundrisse*, p. 101.

30. Marx to Kugelmann, July 11, 1868, *Selected Correspondence*, p. 252.

31. Marx to Engels, March 25, 1868, ibid., p. 243.

32. Karl Marx, *Critique of Political Economy*, trans. N. I. Stone, Chicago: Charles H. Kerr, 1904, pp. 11–12.

33. Marx, *Grundrisse*, p. 101.

34. This play on Hegelian notions of negation, contradiction, and synthesis is appropriate because of Marx's closeness to them; see Hegel, *Science of Logic*, pp. 54ff.

35. Hegel insists that "the whole of the science be within itself a circle in which the first is also the last and the last is also first" (*Science of Logic*, p. 71). Another commentator on Marx's relation to Hegel has noted the same quality:

> The cyclical form of [Hegel's] *Logic* is expressed in the phrase: 'Being is Meaning and Meaning is Being.' The starting point is immediacy, or Being-in-Itself which pretends to be an absolute origin, and which, in so far as it develops, assumes its proper expression as meaning. (Jean Hyppolite, *Studies on Marx and Hegel*, trans. John O'Neill, New York: Basic Books, 1969, p. 179)

As shown below, later Marxists returned frequently to this cyclical notion in their search to specify and emphasize the meaning of dialectical materialism. The concept of the relation between concrete-real and thought-concrete as circular is also in Galvano della Volpe, *Rousseau and Marx,* trans. John Fraser, London: Lawrence and Wishart, 1978, pp. 191, 200.

36. The terms *concrete-real* and *thought-concrete* are taken from *Grundrisse,* pp. 101–2. However, we build upon and also depart from Althusser's usage of them: see *Reading Capital*, trans. Ben Brewster, London: New Left Books, 1970, pp. 54ff. Marx's connection to Hegel is suggested also in the parallel terminology deployed by a major Hegel scholar in elucidating Hegel's work:

> The concrete Real (of which we *speak*) is both Real revealed by a discourse, and Discourse revealing a real. . . . And since it [Hegel's work] is itself a

revealing Discourse, it is itself an aspect of the concrete Real which it describes. (Alexandre Kojève, *Introduction to the Reading of Hegel,* trans. James H. Nichols, Jr., New York: Basic Books, 1969, p. 178)

See also nn. 82, 83.

37. Hegel, *Science of Logic,* p. 75.

38. As Marx puts it: "[Thinking] can vary only gradually, according to maturity of development, including the development of the organ by which the thinking is done" (Marx to Kugelmann, July 11, 1868, *Selected Correspondence,* p. 252).

39. Engels, *Feuerbach and the End of Classical German Philosophy,* p. 39.

40. This is the formulation toward which the following early comment of Marx was an initial gesture: "Thinking and being are thus no doubt *distinct,* but at the same time are in *unity* with each other" (*Economic and Philosophic Manuscripts,* p. 105).

41. In his *Theses on Feuerbach* (especially numbers 1, 3, 5, 9, and 11), Marx strives to emphasize the active, constituent role of thought vis-à-vis social life as against the passivity of previous materialism, its "chief defect." In the preface to his *Critique of Political Economy* (n. 40), Marx stresses that "social existence" determines "consciousness." By putting these, or any of many comparable pairs of remarks together, we see how Marx's goal was to unify the activity/passivity, the determining/determined relations of thought and being, to make materialism dialectical, to break from, among other things, the epistemological tradition of empiricism and rationalism.

42. This point is developed considerably from a simpler formulation made by Althusser: "It was a question of recalling with Marx that knowledge of reality changes something in reality, because it *adds* to it precisely the fact that *it* is known, though everything makes it appear as if this *addition* cancelled itself out in its result" (*Essays in Self-Criticism,* p. 194).

43. Engels to C. Schmidt, March 12, 1895, *Selected Correspondence,* p. 563.

44. Marx, *Theories of Surplus Value, Part II,* p. 437.

45. Marx distinguishes between his critique of sciences different from his own (as "false" or "erroneous") and his critique of what he terms "base" or "vulgar" elements associated with such sciences. Thus he arrives at a double criticism of Malthus's science as "erroneous" (as was Ricardo's) and also "base" (unlike Ricardo): "When a man seeks to *accommodate* science to a viewpoint which is derived not from science itself (however erroneous it may be) but from outside, *from alien, external interests,* then I call him 'base'" (*Theories of Surplus Value, Part II,* p. 119).

Marx here gestures toward some notion of at least partial autonomy for science. Althusser's transformation of this notion, his "relative autonomy," is discussed later and further developed by us as an important part of our conclusion.

46. This argument is developed in detail in Richard D. Wolff, Bruce Roberts, and Antonino Callari, "A Marxian Alternative to the Traditional 'Transformation Problem,'" *Review of Radical Political Economics* 16:2–3 (Summer and Fall 1984), pp. 115–36.

47. Of course, for polemical purposes, that is, to prepare the way for the crucial

juxtaposition of sciences (Marxian versus others), Marx or any theorist may expose and attack internal inconsistencies within the opposed theories. As noted earlier, every theory continually produces, resolves, and thereby produces new inconsistencies. Indeed, the resolution of such inconsistencies is the goal of much work done within each science by its scientists. Critics may often find and expose such inconsistencies. However, doing so is merely the prelude for the main point of criticism as here understood.

Thomas Kuhn elegantly recognizes this point in a critique of Karl Popper, using the work *puzzle* for what we term *internal inconsistency:* "I use the term 'puzzle' in order to emphasize that the difficulties which *ordinarily* confront even the very best scientists are . . . challenges only to his ingenuity. *He* is in difficulty, not current theory" (in Lakatos and Musgrave, *Criticism and Growth of Knowledge*, p. 5).

48. Marx to Kugelmann, July 11, 1868, *Selected Correspondence*, p. 251.

49. Consider this paraphrase of the later Wittgenstein:

When we judge deviant systems of nonratification [sciences] by our standards of correctness, and reach the inevitable verdict that they are mistaken, we must realize that this judgement can be reciprocated, and that it does nothing to show that our system has any independent backing. (Pears, *Ludwig Wittgenstein*, p. 147)

50. In the preface to his *Critique of Political Economy*, pp. 12–13, Marx writes: "No social order ever disappears before all the productive forces . . . in it have been developed. . . . Mankind always takes up only such problems as it can solve . . . the problem itself arises only when the material conditions necessary for its solution already exist."

In our reading, this passage views "problems" and "solutions" as conceptualizations within theories. The conditions of existence of a theory are nothing other than the conditions of existence for the concepts it deploys to pose and resolve its problems in the ceaseless theoretical process. Here is yet another affirmation by Marx of the internality of "problems" and "their solutions" within the lifetime of each socially conditioned theory.

Marx also makes this point in *Economic and Philosophic Manuscripts*, p. 109.

51. Engels, *Feuerbach and the End of Classical German Philosophy*, p. 14.

52. Karl Marx, *Theories of Surplus Value, Part III*, Moscow: Progress Publishers, 1971, p. 502.

53. Engels to J. Bloch, September 21–22, 1890, *Selected Correspondence*, p. 498.

54. Engels to H. Starkenburg, January 25, 1894, ibid., p. 549.

55. Marx, *Grundrisse*, p. 99.

56. Lenin, *Materialism and Empirio-Criticism*, pp. 1, 270, 284–85, 290, and 298. See also Lecourt, *Proletarian Science*, pp. 137–62.

57. See Lenin, *Collected Works*, vol. 38, pp. 85–326. Lenin's many appreciations of Hegel occur throughout this text. During 1914–16 Lenin also wrote *Imperialism, the Highest Stage of Capitalism, Socialism and War, The Junius Pamphlet,* and other pamphlets. The philosophical notebooks published in this volume provide

ample evidence to contradict the epistemological simplemindedness and disregard of Hegel's achievements occasionally attributed to Lenin, as in Charles Taylor, *Hegel,* Cambridge: Cambridge University Press, 1975, pp. 552–55. What eludes Taylor is how Lenin reads Hegel differently.

58. Lenin, "Conspectus of Hegel's Book, *The Science of Logic,*" p. 180; hereafter referred to as "Conspectus."

59. In his 1873 "Afterword to the Second German Edition" of *Capital,* vol. 1, Marx expressed his outrage at the then fashionable treatment of Hegel in academic circles as a "dead dog," pp. 19–20. See also Engels, *Feuerbach and the End of Classical German Philosophy,* pp. 14–18. A useful commentary upon the demise of Hegel's influence and its relation to Marxian theory's own development is in Karl Korsch, *Marxism and Philosophy,* trans. Fred Halliday, New York: Monthly Review, 1970, pp. 37–38 and *passim.*

60. See, for example, Lenin, *Materialism and Empirio-Criticism,* pp. 100 and 293; the theme that Russian Marxists had, to a significant extent, lost touch with Hegel's and Marx's epistemological standpoints and fallen back to the basic positions of Hume and Kant is repeated throughout this work.

61. Lenin, "On the Question of Dialectics," p. 362. Our treatment of Lenin's response to (reading of) Hegel, while in substantial agreement with Althusser's treatment, has a different emphasis and so proceeds differently. Where Althusser focuses mainly upon the antihumanism clearly embedded in Lenin's reading (the notion of history as a "process without a subject"), we are interested in the important epistemological relevance of the parallel notion of knowledge as a process without a subject in the precise sense elaborated in our text; see "Lenin before Hegel" (1969) in Althusser, *Lenin and Philosophy and Other Essays,* trans. Ben Brewster, London: New Left Books, 1971, pp. 116–20.

62. Hegel, *Science of Logic,* pp. 755–60.

63. Lenin, "Conspectus," p. 192. The words here underlined were both underlined and capitalized in Lenin's notebooks. Lenin refers here also to Hegel's parallel formulations in his *Encyclopedia of Philosophy,* trans. Gustav Emil Mueller, New York: Philosophical Library, 1959, pp. 67ff.

64. Lenin, "Conspectus," pp. 207–8.

65. Lenin, *Materialism and Empirio-Criticism,* pp. 73ff. and especially p. 77.

66. Kojève, *Reading of Hegel,* p. 174. Kojève's work is useful because he reads Hegel with concerns that are significantly similar to Lenin's; see particularly the section of this work entitled "The Dialectic of the Real and the Phenomenological Method in Hegel," pp. 169–260.

67. Ibid., p. 177.

68. "The *totality of all* sides of the phenomenon, of reality and their (reciprocal) *relations*—that is what truth is composed of" (Lenin, "Conspectus," p. 196).

69. Ibid., pp. 196–97.

70. Cf. "Man's consciousness not only reflects the objective world, but creates it" (ibid., p. 212); "The activity of Man . . . *changes* external actuality" (ibid., p. 218).

71. Ibid., p. 195. As Marx did, so Lenin also shares Hegel's notion of knowl-

edge as a cyclical process, beginning and ending with concretes: the Hegelian ana-
logue for the passage from concrete-real to thought-concrete is the passage (via
"dialectic" or "logic") from immediate to mediated being. Lenin specifically endorses Hegel's view that each of the particular sciences is a "circle of circles"
("Conspectus," p. 233). See also n. 33.

72. However, Hegel and Lenin make their approaches to such a conception of
the concrete-real in very different ways. Hegel does so through his definitions of
logic as having three constituent elements: the abstract, the negating, and the speculative. For Hegel, the elements of logic are those of the reality revealed through that
logic. He sees reality as composed of elements, each as abstractions from totality,
which are in the perpetual process of self-negation and which are enmeshed within
a network of relations linking each to all. Truth, then, is the comprehension of the
totality of these elements in the movement of their negation and in the relationships
among them through which they forever transform one another. See Hegel's explanation of the theoretical need to go beyond concepts of causality or even reciprocity
in order to get to the adequate conception of totality and its constituent aspects or
elements: pp. 153–56 in the *Encyclopedia of Philosophy*. Korsch notes these paragraphs in the same kind of argument in *Marxism and Philosophy*, p. 79; and Kojève
summarizes Hegel's approach to what we term overdetermination in *Reading of
Hegel*, pp. 195–203.

73. Lenin, "Conspectus," p. 159. A similar approach is in evidence in Lenin's
notion that social analysis must "present the sum-total of social and economic relationships as the result of the mutual relations between these groups [all, divers
groupings of persons in society], which have different interests and different historical roles" (*The Development of Capitalism in Russia*, Moscow: Foreign Languages Publishing House, 1956, p. 660).

It seems to us that Lenin was not able to go beyond Hegel's approaches to a
concept of an overdetermined totality; indeed, Hegel's formulations are generally
far richer and more comprehensive. On the other hand, as discussed later, Lenin
never went so far as Hegel toward absolutizing his theory, toward making it the end
or final summation of all prior thought. Lenin confronted the relativity of theories
and their truths in ways Hegel did not. Hegel's valuable critiques of essentialism left
him nonetheless something of an essentialist since he could not relativize his own
thought.

74. Lenin, *Materialism and Empirio-Criticism*, pp. 105–6. See also n. 75.

75. Lenin, "On the Question of Dialectics," p. 360.

76. Lenin makes an explicit attack against eclecticism in theory—as in "the
mixture of Marxism and bourgeois science in [P. B.] Struve's views"—in his essay "Uncritical Criticism" (1900), in *Development Of Capitalism in Russia*,
pp. 695–96.

77. "You will say that this distinction between relative and absolute truth is indefinite. And I will reply that it is sufficiently indefinite to prevent science from
becoming dogmatic, in the bad sense of the word, from becoming dead, frozen,
ossified: but it is at the same time sufficiently 'definite' to preclude us from espousing any brand of fideism or agnosticism, from embracing the sophistry and philo-

sophical idealism of the followers of Hume and Kant. Here is a boundary which you have not noticed, and not having noticed it, you have fallen into the mire of reactionary philosophy. It is the boundary between dialectical materialism and relativism" (Lenin, *Materialism and Empirio-Criticism,* pp. 107–8).

78. On the other hand, consider this comment: "Of course, we must not forget that the criterion of practice, in the nature of things, neither confirms nor refutes completely any human presentation" (ibid., pp. 113–14).

79. "The materialist dialectics of Marx and Engels certainly does contain relativism, but it is not reduced to it, that is, it recognizes the relativity of all our knowledge, not in the sense of the denial of objective truth, but in the sense of the historical conditions which determine the degrees of our knowledge as it approaches this truth" (ibid., p. 108).

80. Lenin, "Karl Marx: Brief Biographical Sketch with an Exposition of Marxism" (1914), in *Marx, Engels, Marxism,* Moscow: Foreign Languages Publishing House, n.d., p. 26.

81. See Lukács, *History and Class Consciousness,* pp. xliii–xlvii and 34–35; idem, "Art and Objective Truth," in *Writer and Critic,* trans. Arthur Kahn, London: Merlin Press, 1970, pp. 29–60, especially the section entitled "The Objectivity of Truth in Marxist-Leninist Epistemology," pp. 25–29; and idem, *Lenin: A Study on the Unity of His Thought,* trans. Nicholas Jacobs, Cambridge: MIT Press, 1971.

82. Lukács, "Art and Objective Truth," pp. 44–45.

83. These terms appear in Taylor, *Hegel,* p. 557.

84. See, for example, Andrew Arato, "The Concept of Critique," in Arato and Gebhardt, *Essential Frankfurt School Reader,* pp. 197–204; and Jurgen Habermas, *Theory and Practice,* trans. John Viertel, Boston: Beacon Press, 1973, pp. 34–36. Habermas here presents a caricature of Lukács as a crude and vulgar apologist of and for Party expediency. Compare also Henri Lefebvre's attack on Gramsci as well as Lukács along similar lines in *The Sociology of Marx,* trans. Norbert Guterman, New York: Vintage Books, 1969, pp. 36–37. There are also those who reject Lukács precisely because they see him going too far toward championing, within Marxism, the concepts of subjective freedom and "praxis"; John Hoffman, *Marxism and the Theory of Praxis,* New York: International, 1976, pp. 18–19.

85. See, for example, Rosalind Coward and John Ellis, *Language and Materialism,* London: Routledge and Kegan Paul, 1977, pp. 34–36. Barry Hindess finds in Lukács a rationalist notion of discourse, i.e., the idea that particular theories can be reduced to the direct product or expression of some extradiscursive "reality," in this case class: see *Philosophy and Methodology in the Social Sciences,* pp. 214 and 232. Then, again, there are those Marxists who congratulate Lukács for what Coward, Ellis, and Hindess denounce, namely, his "realism," understood as his affirmation that historical materialism is both "correct" and "the" theoretical articulation of the class consciousness of the proletariat: Keat and Urry, *Social Theory as Science,* pp. 206–7.

86. Istvan Meszaros, *Lukács' Concept of Dialectic,* London: Merlin Press, 1972, especially pp. 41–45.

87. Frederic Jameson, *Marxism and Form*, Princeton: Princeton University Press, 1971, pp. 160–205, and especially pp. 189–90.

88. Lukács, *Schriften zur Ideologie und Politik* (1967), quoted in Meszaros, *Lukács' Concept of Dialectic*, p. 73.

89. Lukács, *History and Class Consciousness*, pp. 203–4.

90. Lucien Goldmann, *Lukács and Heidegger*, trans. William Q. Boelhower, London and Boston: Routledge and Kegan Paul, 1979, p. 6. Goldmann's work on Lukács has been particularly useful for the arguments offered in our text because of his special interest in Lukács's contributions to a Marxian epistemological standpoint. Moreover, Goldmann offers a suggestive interpretation that non-Marxists such as Husserl and particularly Heidegger shared Lukács's rejection of the post-Hegelian European epistemological tradition, although they took it to very different destinations.

91. Lukács, *History and Class Consciousness*, p. 178. Lukács's endorsement of Lenin is in *The Ontology of Social Being*, vol. 1: *Hegel*, trans. David Fernbach, London: Merlin Press, 1978, p. 78.

92. "Historical materialism both can and must be applied to itself. . . . The substantive truths of historical materialism are of the same type as were the truths of classical economics in Marx's view: they are truths within a particular social order and system of production" (Lukács, *History and Class Consciousness*, p. 288).

93. Ibid., p. 9.

94. Ibid., p. 179.

95. Ibid., p. 19. Lukács's style of addressing such imperatives led his readers often to conclude—as Lukács himself seems to do—that the proletariat had been only an object and not yet also a subject in history. Given the broad context of Lukács's epistemological standpoint and the many formulations of his concept of totality, we read even his imperatives as calls to a proletariat—which had always been both object and subject—to become subjective in a particular way, namely in a Marxian-defined class revolutionary direction.

96. Ibid., p. 13.

97. "The Tasks of Marxist Philosophy in the New Democracy," delivered in the Congress of Marxist Philosophers, Milan, Italy, December 20, 1947, quoted in Meszaros, *Lukács' Concept of Dialectic*, pp. 63–64. See also the formulations of an overdeterminist viewpoint in Lukács's last major work, which was left unfinished at his death in 1971: *Toward the Ontology of Social Being*. One of this work's eight chapters has been published as *The Ontology of Social Being*, vol. 2: *Marx:* see in the present context particularly pp. 30, 76, and 146.

98. Lukács, *History and Class Consciousness*, p. 187. As shown in n. 108, Lukács applied this viewpoint to his own theory as well.

99. Ibid., pp. xlvi–xlvii.

100. Goldmann, *Lukács and Heidegger*, p. 35.

101. Lukács, *Ontology of Social Being*, vol. 2: *Marx*, p. 34.

102. Ibid., pp. 30–38.

103. Ibid., p. 130.

104. Ibid., p. 63.

105. Ibid., p. 49.

106. Ibid., pp. 54–55.

107. It is in this sense that we read Lukács's endorsements of economic determinism: "If historical materialism is deployed to discover the *sociological meaning* of these struggles, economic interests will doubtless be revealed as the decisive *factors in any explanation*" (*History and Class Consciousness*, p. 58). In his essay on Rosa Luxemburg's accumulation theory, he endorses in his own dramatic style her statements of the inevitability of capitalism's demise: "[capitalism's] ghastly dance of death . . . the inexorable march of Oedipus to his doom" (ibid., p. 33). It is also in this sense that we view his occasional lapses into traditional epistemological standpoints, which he himself rejects in his formulation of dialectical materialism: for example, his comment on Rickert's concept of machine, "We see further that to view the machine thus is to distort its true objective nature" (ibid., p. 153).

108. Gramsci, *Selections from the Prison Notebooks* (hereafter referred to as *Selections*). The section "The Philosophy of Praxis" comprises pp. 321–472. Because of his subjection to the prison censor, Gramsci often used the phrase "Philosophy of Praxis" to denote Marxian philosophy.

109. Ibid., p. 406. Emphasis added.

110. Gramsci read Lenin's notebooks on Hegel, his elaboration of the dialectic, in a manner directly opposed to what were becoming the dominant philosophical and epistemological tendencies of the Third International after Lenin's death. See Leonardo Paggi, "Gramsci's General Theory of Marxism," in *Gramsci and Marxist Theory*, ed. Chantal Mouffe, London: Routledge and Kegan Paul, 1979, especially pp. 133–34.

111. Gramsci, *Selections*, pp. 435 and 464. See also Gramsci's affirmation of the specifically "epistemological value" of Marx's famous preface to *Introduction to the Critique of Political Economy*, ibid., p. 465.

112. Ibid., pp. 434ff. Paggi also concludes that for Gramsci "this conception of the dialectic was the most complete and mature weapon for attacking philosophical materialism *and* every economistic practice of historical materialism" ("Gramsci's General Theory of Marxism," p. 137).

113. Gramsci, *Selections*, pp. 440–45.

114. Ibid., p. 446.

115. Ibid., p. 437. Emphasis added.

116. Ibid., p. 435.

117. Some read Gramsci as a subjective humanist for whom "man" becomes the origin/cause of social changes, as in Romano Giachetti, "Antonio Gramsci: The Subjective Revolution," in Howard and Klare, *Unknown Dimension*, pp. 147–68. Others read his work as clearly antisubjectivist and antihumanist in a sense linked to Althusser's formulations, as in Chantal Mouffe, "Hegemony and Ideology in Gramsci," in *Gramsci and Marxist Theory*, pp. 168–204.

118. Gramsci, *Selections*, pp. 163ff.

119. Ibid., pp. 427–28.

120. Ibid., p. 437.

121. Ibid., p. 437.

122. Ibid., p. 352.

123. Ibid., p. 366. We understand Gramsci's choice of the word *reciprocity* to lie within the tradition of Hegel's and Lenin's use of that same word. Thus, Gramsci's particular theoretical development of reciprocity constitutes another step toward the formulation of the concept of overdetermination.

124. Antonio Gramsci, *La Construzione del Partito Comunista, 1921–1926*, Turin, 1971, quoted in Paggi, "Gramsci's General Theory of Marxism," p. 124.

125. Gramsci, *Selections*, p. 353.

126. Mao Tse-tung, "On Practice," in *Four Essays on Philosophy*, Peking: Foreign Languages Press, 1968, p. 13; see also "On Contradiction," ibid., pp. 23–78.

127. It is in this context that Mao insists that contradictions, while profoundly different after the revolution, remain the dialectical law of Chinese development just as class struggles, although radically changed, remain a basic feature of that development: see "On the Correct Handling of Contradictions among the People," ibid., pp. 91–92.

128. Mao, "On Correct Handling of Contradictions," pp. 95 and 91.

129. Mao, "Where Do Correct Ideas Come From?" in *Four Essays on Philosophy*, p. 116.

130. Ibid., p. 136; and also Mao, "On Correct Handling of Contradictions," pp. 91 and 118–19.

131. Mao, "On Contradiction," pp. 60–61 and see also p. 30.

132. Ibid., p. 61.

133. Ibid., pp. 58–59. Note in this connection Mao's attack on the Soviet philosopher Deborin and through Deborin also on Bukharin. Mao criticizes them for their formulation of Marxian theory, a formulation that does not seek to specify the contradictory aspects constituting every possible object for Marxian theory. Mao finds that such a version of Marxian theory "reverts to the metaphysical theories of eternal causality and of mechanism" (ibid., p. 33).

134. Ibid., p. 62.

135. While no work, to our knowledge, adequately investigates Althusser's relation to the structuralist movements, one specifies his links to and differences from the tradition of Bachelard and Canguilhem, focusing upon the important concept of the "epistemological break": Lecourt's *Marxism and Epistemology*.

136. For Althusser's statement of his purposes in writing his major philosophical essays, see the foreword, "To My English Readers," in *For Marx*, pp. 9–15; our quotations in this paragraph are all taken from these pages.

137. Althusser, "Philosophy as a Revolutionary Weapon" (1963), in *Lenin and Philosophy and Other Essays*, p. 20. See also idem, *Reading Capital*, pp. 73–78.

138. Korsch's call appears in his essay "Marxism and Philosophy" (1923), and its sequel "The Present State of the Problem of 'Marxism and Philosophy'—an Anti-Critique" (1930), both in his *Marxism and Philosophy*, pp. 29–144. The remarks referred to in the text, which Korsch himself admits were undeveloped philosophic positions (p. 122), appear on pp. 86–97.

139. Various versions of this argument occur in Althusser's work; one concise formulation is in *Reading Capital*, pp. 189–93. The complex struggle of Althusser with the conceptualization of the science-ideology couple offers a particular focus around which he elaborates his epistemological standpoint: see in particular *Read-*

ing Capital, pp. 62ff; "Ideology and Ideological State Apparatuses" (1969), in *Lenin and Philosophy*, especially pp. 154–65, and *Essays in Self-Criticism*, especially pp. 189–95. We return to the science-ideology issue later in this chapter.

140. Althusser's work strikes us as quite clear on the point that Marxian theory's concepts of knowledge and science are different from those of non-Marxian theories and on the related point that no transtheoretical canon of scientificity is possible for Marxian theory. Hence we must disagree with Alex Callinicos's contention that Althusser claims to establish such a transtheoretical canon of scientificity. When Callinicos embellishes his contention into the "deep contradiction within Althusser's epistemology," our reaction is to suppose at the very least that Callinicos reads Althusser differently from the way we do. For us, the power and thrust of Althusser's epistemological arguments are exactly to deny and reject the transtheoretical truths, measures, or canons that Callinicos charges him with. See Alex Callinicos, *Althusser's Marxism*, London: Pluto Press, 1976, pp. 60, 72, and 102.

141. A strict construction of structuralism that builds upon its linguistic foundations in Saussure readily concludes that Althusser is no structuralist: see, for example, Philip Pettit, *The Concept of Structuralism: A Critical Analysis*, Berkeley and Los Angeles: University of California Press, 1977, p. 69. Althusser himself explicitly rejected any characterization of his approach as structuralist: *Essays in Self-Criticism*, pp. 126–31. The linking of a structuralism in Althusser to a rationalist epistemology attributed to him is found in the work of Barry Hindess and Paul Q. Hirst: see the critical discussion of their argument in the last section of this chapter.

142. The many-centuries-old philosophical tradition of seeing epistemological standpoints as necessarily variants of either rationalism or empiricism (or some combination) is carried forward in these critical readings of Althusser. Their outright, although hardly direct or explicit, rejection of Althusser's point on the specific difference of Marxian epistemology is accomplished by assimilating him to rationalism and thus precisely to the old philosophical tradition he rejects. Some relevant texts by Hindess and Hirst are the following: *Pre-Capitalist Modes of Production*, pp. 308–23, and *Mode of Production and Social Formation*, pp. 15–16. See also Hindess, *Philosophy and Methodology in the Social Sciences*, introduction and chap. 7.

143. Althusser, "Montesquieu: Politics and History" (1959), in *Politics and History*, p. 34.

144. Althusser, "Marx's Relations to Hegel," ibid., p. 175. This essay, recognizing Marx's major indebtedness to Hegel, corrected much of Althusser's earlier attacks on Hegel; see pp. 181–83.

145. Althusser, "Contradiction and Overdetermination," pp. 87–128. As noted above, Lukács finds Freud's analysis of dreams—the locus of the notion of overdetermination—as useful as Althusser does. Althusser tends to omit mention of natural processes; our formulation remedies this omission as noted in the previous chapter.

146. Ibid. Althusser's emphasis on "complexity" in his concept of contradictions is partly his further development of Mao's contribution toward the specification of the complexity of contradictions noted earlier. Althusser's emphasis is also

yet another critical attack upon tendencies within Marxism that reduced the complexity of contradictions to simple oppositions of two entities (e.g., forces and relations of production, base and superstructure, mental and manual labor, etc.).

147. We may summarize a major insight of Althusser's *Reading Capital*. The meaning of each of *Capital*'s concepts must change as its discourse develops, for that is precisely how discursive development is understood. To posit the existence, i.e., the meaning, of any concept (object of analysis) in *Capital* is to specify its conceptual conditions of existence. Their interaction is the overdetermination of and hence the development process of that concept and, by extension, of all concepts constituting *Capital*. Althusser's elaboration of the epistemological break of Marx becomes a key theoretical condition of existence for this particular overdetermined reading of *Capital*. For a related point see pp. 28–29 in chap. 1.

148. Althusser's recognition of and plan to overcome the problem of a "relativist" reading of dialetical materialism appears in "Marx's Relation to Hegel," pp. 175ff.

149. Althusser, *Essays in Self-Criticism,* p. 130.

150. This notion of hegemony refers, of course, to argument, theoretical struggle, and conviction; no implication of extratheoretical coercion is intended.

151. See Althusser, *Reading Capital,* pp. 71–198. In another sentence Althusser argues for the key link between any theory and *its* object, as follows: "Every abstract concept therefore provides knowledge of a reality whose existence it reveals" ("Preface to *Capital,* Volume One," in *Lenin and Philosophy,* p. 75).

152. Althusser, "Marx's Relation to Hegel," p. 185.

153. See, for example, Norman Geras, "Marx and the Critique of Political Economy," in *Ideology in Social Science,* ed. Robin Blackburn, New York: Vintage, 1973, pp. 284–305. Most sharply to the point were John Lewis's 1972 articles, "The Althusser Case," in the January and February issues of *Marxism Today* and Althusser's 1973 reply; see *Essays in Self-Criticism,* pp. 35–39.

154. See Althusser, "Marxism and Humanism," in *For Marx,* pp. 219–48, and idem, "Marx's Relation to Hegel," pp. 176–86. Cf. Max Adler's early (1914) anticipation of Althusser's focus on Marx's break from Feuerbach in Tom Bottomore and Patrick Goode, eds., *Austro-Marxism,* Oxford: Clarendon Press, 1978, pp. 59–60.

155. Althusser, *For Marx,* p. 205. Althusser's critique and problematization of economic determinism and the predominant Soviet endorsement of such a position runs continuously from implicit to explicit expression *throughout his published work.* From his 1959 concern over "determination in the last instance" in "Montesquieu" (pp. 47–52), to his sharp problematization of such determination in 1969 in "Ideology and Ideological State Apparatuses" (pp. 129–30), to his remarks in 1974 in "Is It Simple to Be a Marxist in Philosophy?" (*Essays in Self-Criticism,* pp. 175–87), Althusser's work is a constant challenge to the predominant economic determinist position within the Marxian tradition. The challenge continues in his later journalistic critiques directed to the French Communist party: see his "On the Twenty-Second Congress of the French Communist Party," *New Left Review* 104 (July–August 1977), pp. 3–24. The ambivalences and incompletenesses that beset Althusser's critical challenge are addressed later.

156. Althusser, *For Marx,* p. 113.

157. Althusser, *Essays in Self-Criticism*, pp. 115–87.

158. See Althusser's essay, "From *Capital* to Marx's Philosophy," in *Reading Capital*, especially pp. 54–63.

159. Althusser, "Ideology and Ideological State Apparatuses," p. 152.

160. Althusser, *Reading Capital*, p. 56.

161. Althusser, *Lenin and Philosophy and Other Essays*, p. 160. This classifying notion of the ideological/scientific differentiation between sciences is developed and usefully applied to a Marxian critique of modern sociobiology and ethology in Dominique Lecourt, "Biology and the Crisis of the Human Sciences," *New Left Review* 125 (January–February 1981), pp. 90–96.

162. Althusser, *Essays in Self-Criticism*, pp. 119–25.

163. Althusser comes close to this position in the following appreciation of Spinoza (ibid., p. 188): "Thus Spinoza *in advance* makes every theory of knowledge, which reasons about the *justification* of knowledge, dependent on the *fact* of the knowledge which we already possess."

164. Ibid., pp. 201–2. This retrospective reflection by Althusser on his anti-humanism is the best brief summary of his position: pp. 195–207.

165. Two of these, *Pre-Capitalist Modes of Production* and *Mode of Production and Social Formation*, were coauthored by Barry Hindess and Paul Hirst; *Philosophy and Methodology in the Social Sciences* was authored by Barry Hindess; in the most recent books, *Marx's Capital and Capitalism Today*, vols. 1 and 2, London: Routledge and Kegan Paul, 1977 and 1978, Antony Cutler and Athar Hussain joined Hindess and Hirst as authors. Since the basic critique of Althusser begins initially with the separate and joint work of Hindess and Hirst, we will refer to them only when discussing this critique: no downgrading of Cutler's and Hussain's contributions is intended.

166. We are not surprised that Hindess and Hirst must reckon first with Althusser before proceeding to a critique of Marx. After Althusser, it is difficult to read Marx without being acutely aware of the epistemological reading accomplished by Althusser. In this sense Althusser represents to Hindess and Hirst what Hegel did to the "young Hegelians." They must "settle accounts" with Althusser, this "mighty thinker," since—as they acknowledge—he has rigorously and aggressively dealt with the most basic philosophical and epistemological questions and problems that have plagued Marxism for over one hundred years. For Hindess and Hirst, the critique of Althusser becomes their rejection of epistemology, the final rejection of what they conceive to be the dogmatism embedded in the epistemological enterprise as such. Once liberated from epistemology (from Althusser's fundamental reformulation of the Marxian philosophical position), they can finally begin their own reformulation of Marxism at its most basic conceptual level. However, this rejection also involves their nonrecognition of the centrality of contradiction embedded in the notion of overdetermination. Althusser's formulation of Marx's "epistemological break" implies Marxism's theoretical commitment to the concepts of overdetermination and contradiction. This, in turn, precludes ascribing any notion of rationalism or economism to Marxism, *as elaborated by Althusser*. Therefore, the final reckoning and eventual break with Althusser by Hindess and Hirst effectively prevent them from reading Marx as immune to the charges of rationalism and economism they throw at him.

167. Hindess reads Althusser's attack on empiricism as including rationalism and thus as an attack on epistemology per se. See Hindess's *Philosophy and Methodology in the Social Sciences,* pp. 5, 196–97. However, in that same work Hindess faults Althusser for "rationalist slippage" around the notion that he collapses (conflates) the logic (problematic) of a discourse with the logic of its formulation (production). Hindess reads Althusser as having legitimately constructed the systematic problematic of a discourse and illegitimately made the problematic into an essence or cause of that discourse, i.e., an "extradiscursive" rationalist "cause" of discourse. For us, the theoretical commitment to overdetermination (in the matter of production of a discourse as of everything else) effectively precludes assigning any essence or cause to a discursive formation. Hindess's definition and refutation of epistemology per se prevents him from understanding this key point.

168. Cutler, Hindess, Hirst, and Hussain, *Marx's Capital and Capitalism Today,* vol. 1, p. 214.

169. Ibid., pp. 211, 215. Such absolutist formulations are scattered throughout their work, e.g., Paul Hirst, *Durkheim, Bernard and Epistemology,* London and Boston: Routledge and Kegan Paul, 1975, pp. 2–7; and Hindess, *Philosophy and Methodology in the Social Sciences,* p. 20.

170. For elaboration of this position, see Cutler, Hindess, Hirst, and Hussain, *Marx's Capital,* vol. 1, pp. 107–34, and Hindess and Hirst, *Mode of Production and Social Formation,* pp. 9–33.

171. Paul Hirst, *On Law and Ideology,* London: Macmillan Press, 1979, p. 18. Hindess and Hirst, who elsewhere attack deduction, come very close to deducing the essentialism they read *in* Marx's and Althusser's social theory from the essentialism *of* their theory, i.e., the rationalism they read in it.

172. The first chapter of Cutler, Hindess, Hirst, and Hussain, *Marx's Capital and Capitalism Today,* vol. 1, contains a critique of Marx's value theory. Consistent with their view of Marxism as characterized by a classical form of rationalism, they understand Marx's value theory to include the epistemological claim that it is the essence governing phenomenal historical forms: exchange values and prices of production. In effect, the logic they use to criticize Marx's value theory in *Capital* is similar to that used elsewhere in their work. They charge Marx with an essentialist formulation of the relationships among the concepts of his theory that parallels his essentialist epistemological (rationalist) standpoint. Marx is read as follows: his initial abstract concepts (value, exchange value, money, etc.) are understood to form a basic unrevised set (essence) from which all other concepts (prices of production, profit rates, credit, etc.) are derived as necessary effects (phenomenal forms). Value theory is rejected as essentialist both for the reductionist deployment of its concepts and for its rationalist claims to give the essence of the real and an economistic essence at that. Hindess and Hirst read *Capital,* then, as providing evidence for their view of value theory, while Marx's rationalism is confirmed for them by those few famous pages on method in the *Grundrisse.* The logic of the argument is tight. We, of course, understand that the concept of value is used in Marx's discourse as one among the means to produce—not deduce—the further concepts of exchange value and prices of production. This further theoretical elaboration/production not only produces both the concepts of exchange value and prices of production; it also *necessarily works changes* in the initial concept of value itself,

thereby producing a new revised concept reflecting and consistent with the further elaborated level of the discourse. (For further discussion of this reading of value theory, see the article cited in n. 46.)

Hindess and Hirst and we articulate two different positions offering two different truths and having different political consequences. We understand a critical debate to be both necessary and possible between the two positions, but we also understand that the two are in conflict with one another.

Chapter 3

1. See the perceptive discussion of "ambiguity" and "confusion" in both Marxian and non-Marxian formulations of "class" in Raymond Williams, *Keywords*, New York: Oxford, 1976, pp. 51–59. We are indebted to Williams's useful specifications of certain of these confusions.

2. Cf. Ralph Miliband, *Marxism and Politics*, Oxford: Oxford University Press, 1977, pp. 21–22. Miliband conceptualizes class in ways very different from ours.

3. Hegel, *Phenomenology of Mind*, p. 134. Hegel is here referring to basic epistemological terms such as *knowledge*, *subjective*, and *objective*. As argued in previous chapters, we agree with Hegel on this point if not with the particular conceptions he goes on to propound. We want here to extend his point to cover the terms of class as well.

4. The classic formulation in such Hegelian terms is in Lukács's *History and Class Consciousness;* see also Nicos Poulantzas's intense dismissal of these terms in *Classes in Contemporary Capitalism*, trans. Timothy O'Hagan, London: Verso, 1978, p. 16.

5. In his notebook struggles to specify capital and the capitalist class, Marx writes: "Capital is not a simple relation, but a process, in whose various moments it is always capital" (*Grundrisse*, p. 258).

6. Marx's preface to the first German edition of *Capital*, vol. 1, p. 10. See also ibid., p. 85; *Capital*, vol. 3, pp. 289–90 and 819; idem, *Theories of Surplus Value, Part I*, p. 389, and *Part III*, p. 296; and idem, *Grundrisse*, p. 452.

7. Was a Russian citizen who sided with Lenin in 1917 a member of the working class because of that decision or because of property that he or she did or did not own, or again because of his or her position as a performer or receiver of surplus labor? Clearly, class position by one definition is not generally consistent with the other two unless one makes any two of these definitions derivative from the third. This would amount to deriving our Russian's property position and participation in the surplus labor process from the side taken in social struggles in 1917. Alternatively, such an approach might reduce the side taken to a necessary consequence of such position and/or participation. While such reductionisms (essentialisms) still flourish within the Marxian tradition, we are among the considerable group disaffected from them.

8. Marx, *Capital*, vol. 2, chaps. 12–14; vol. 3, pts. 3–7; idem, *Theories of Surplus Value, Part I*, chaps. 3, 4, 6, and addenda; and *Part III*, chap. 20 and addenda.

9. See, for example, Ralf Dahrendorf, *Class and Class Conflict in Industrial*

Society, Stanford: Stanford University Press, 1959, pp. 19–20. Like many Marxists, the non-Marxian Dahrendorf attributes to Marx the view that in capitalism all other classes are eventually drawn into two great oppositional classes. Dahrendorf is also concerned to improve upon Marx's dichotomous theory by affirming that capitalism does contain more than two classes, which are not dissolving into the two great oppositional classes (pp. 32–33). See also Anthony Giddens, *The Class Structure of Advanced Societies,* New York: Harper and Row, 1975, pp. 28–29.

10. Cf. Miliband, *Marxism and Politics,* pp. 20–21; Poulantzas, *Classes in Contemporary Capitalism,* p. 23; and Paul M. Sweezy, "The American Ruling Class," in *The Present as History,* New York: Monthly Review, 1953, pp. 128–29.

11. Poulantzas, *Classes in Contemporary Capitalism,* pp. 14ff. Here Poulantzas criticizes the traditional Marxian focus on two classes for its underlying economic determinism. He has class places determined at the political and ideological as well as the economic levels (see his discussion of foremen, managers, and supervisors on pp. 227–28). In an earlier work, Poulantzas develops a more subtle and less mechanical concept of social class as the "effect of an ensemble of" levels and structures, rather than a concept of classes determined more or less separately at each level: *Political Power and Social Classes,* trans. Timothy O'Hagen, London: New Left Books, 1978, pp. 67–70. This book was originally published in France in 1968, while *Classes in Contemporary Capitalism* was first published in 1974. Poulantzas's earlier concept, which shows a close affinity to an Althusserian notion of class as overdetermined by *all* the levels of social totality, seems to have given way to the quite different and non-Althusserian formulations of the later book.

12. Wright, *Class, Crisis and the State,* pp. 61–96; see also idem, *Class Structure and Income Determination,* New York: Academic Press, 1979, especially chap. 2.

13. Wright, *Class, Crisis and the State,* pp. 88ff. Wright reasons in a rather circular manner here. He uses concepts of class position to derive the "fundamental interests" of their occupants. Then he uses shared fundamental interests to derive class positions for the housewives, students, pensioners, and others who do not fit immediately into his initial six class positions (locations). While Wright's work invites criticism on many other points, that is not our purpose here. We wish only to prepare the basis for our argument that Marx's complex conceptualization of multiple class positions in capitalism is very different from Poulantzas's or Wright's.

14. Barbara Ehrenreich and John Ehrenreich, "The Professional-Managerial Class," *Radical America* 11:2 (March–April 1977), pp. 7–31. C. Wright Mills's formulations are in *White Collar: The American Middle Classes,* New York: Oxford, 1951, pp. 65ff. See also the similar approach of Michel Aglietta, *A Theory of Capitalist Regulation,* trans. David Fernbach, London: New Left Books, 1979, pp. 174ff.

15. Beyond the works of Poulantzas and Wright cited, Miliband's work also belongs in this group: see *Marxism and Politics,* p. 18.

16. See Samuel Bowles and Herbert Gintis, *Democracy and Capitalism,* New York: Basic Books, 1986, especially pp. 92ff.

17. Implicit in class fraction theories is the presumption that Marx misses divisions within classes. Thus Poulantzas distinguishes "fractions, strata and catego-

ries" within classes by incorporating non-Marxian concepts of social differentiation into his theory: *Classes in Contemporary Capitalism,* pp. 23–24. Francesca
Freedman, in "The Internal Structure of the American Proletariat," *Socialist Revolution* 26 (October–December 1975), pp. 41–84, worries about how to determine
whether a fraction is within this or that class; she concludes that a fraction's property relation to "productive assets" is the test. Guglielmo Carchedi insists on last-
instance economic determination of classes while also deploying class fraction
analysis: *On the Economic Identification of Social Classes,* London and Boston:
Routledge and Kegan Paul, 1977, pp. 1–13. Miliband, like Poulantzas, seeks to
incorporate standard concepts of bourgeois sociology to supplement Marx's class
designations; he suggests "income" and "status" along with "subordination" and
refers to these as essential to accomplish the "differentiations which the class structure of capitalist societies obviously requires" (*Marxism and Politics,* p. 24). By
contrast, we shall argue that Marx has a concept of divisions within classes but
conceives of them very differently from all of the formulations propounded by class
fraction theorists. In simple terms, the Marxian commitment to overdetermination
implies that occupants of the same class position will still be divided by the literally
infinite different positions they variously occupy in the nonclass processes of social
life. How such different, that is, divided, individuals who occupy the same class
position will group themselves vis-à-vis social conflicts and change is itself overdetermined and hence not reducible to any one or another different process such as
income distribution, sex, race, etc.

18. Marx, *Theories of Surplus Value, Part III,* p. 360. Marx scorns this simplification as a "bourgeois ideal."

19. Marx criticizes Ricardo and post-Ricardians such as John Stuart Mill on
their tendencies to collapse complex theoretical constructs into simple one-to-one
derivations. They fail, in his view, to properly develop the basic insights of the theory of value because they do not theorize the complex linkages, the added determinations, that connect (and thereby transform) abstract concepts into more concrete ones in social analysis. Instead, they leap over these complexities toward a
simple and usually essentialist bridge between highly abstract and very concrete
(conjuncturally specific) concepts: "Here the contradiction between the general law
and further developments in the concrete circumstances is to be resolved not by the
discovery of the connecting links but by directly subordinating and immediately
adapting the concrete to the abstract" (ibid., p. 87).

20. See Marx's many references to the "pumping out" of surplus labor in *Capital,* vol. 3, pp. 791 and 819–22; see also vol. 1, p. 564.

21. Note Marx's explicit precision in making this distinction in *Capital,* vol. 1,
pp. 216–20; see also vol. 3, pp. 632–33.

22. Nothing is quantitatively fixed in the Marxian concepts of necessary and
surplus labor. What is necessary labor depends upon the overdetermined, historically variable social standards for the reproduction of the direct producers and on
their overdetermined productive efficiency in meeting those standards. See Marx's
brief chap. 22, "National Differences of Wages," in *Capital,* vol. 1, pp. 559–63,
and also vol. 3, pp. 877ff. Similarly, the amount of surplus labor depends on the
overdetermined, historically variable standards for reproducing the lives and activi-

ties of those who live off the products of that surplus labor—as later elaborated further.

23. Marx, *Theories of Surplus Value, Part I*, pp. 55, 81, and 316; see also idem, *Capital*, vol. 1, p. 534.

24. The reference to wages appears in Marx, *Grundrisse*, p. 570, and the reference to profit appears in idem, *Theories of Surplus Value, Part III*, p. 495. The italics appear in Marx's original text.

25. Marx, *Capital*, vol. 1, p. 217. See also Marx's historical formulation in *Theories of Surplus Value, Part III*, p. 400: "In all previous forms, it is the landed proprietor, not the capitalist, who directly appropriates the *surplus labor* of other people."

26. The concept of "conditions of existence" is deployed clearly and creatively in Hindess and Hirst, *Pre-Capitalist Modes of Production*, and *Mode of Production and Social Formation*. As noted in chap. 2, these authors do not share our conceptualization of overdetermination.

27. Consider, for example, Marx's reflection on the class positions—plural—a direct producer may hold if he owns, say, certain of the means of production he deploys in his productive activity: "He himself is divided up into different categories. As his own workman, he gets his wages, and as capitalist, he gets his profits" (*Theories of Surplus Value, Part III*, p. 423).

28. The term *fundamental classes* is Marx's own: *Grundrisse*, p. 108. In that book he also discusses several of these two-class groupings: pp. 471–513. Further attempts to specify these different kinds of fundamental class dichotomies may be found in Hindess and Hirst, *Pre-Capitalist Modes of Production*; John G. Taylor, *From Modernisation to Modes of Production*, London: Macmillan 1979; and Aidan Foster-Carter, "The Modes of Production Controversy," *New Left Review* 107 (January–February 1978), pp. 47–77. However, these writers read and develop Marx's concepts of class very differently from what we undertake in this book.

The primitive communist form of the fundamental class process is here understood to involve a particular manner of the performance and appropriation of surplus labor. What distinguishes this form is the manner in which the surplus labor is appropriated, in particular the identity of the persons who occupy both fundamental class positions. The direct producers *collectively* perform and appropriate their *own* surplus labor. Strictly speaking, then, it is inaccurate to propose a notion of a "classless" society, notwithstanding the evident intent of the term to highlight the absence of fundamental class divisions between persons in such a society.

29. Marx, *Theories of Surplus Value, Part I*, pp. 85–86.

30. Marx, *Capital*, vol. 1, p. 564.

31. Marx, *Theories of Surplus Value, Part III*, p. 471.

32. Marx, *Capital*, vol. 2, p. 421.

33. Marx, *Theories of Surplus Value, Part III*, p. 455.

34. Marx, *Capital*, vol. 1, p. 175. In this passage Marx adds that the production of surplus value occurs "outside the limits of the market or of the sphere of circulation."

35. Marx, *Grundrisse*, p. 413. We are mindful that Marx is often quoted to the effect that the final cause of crisis is the insufficient purchasing power of wage ear-

ners. Such quotation is usually intended to reduce crisis to fundamental class issues. In our view this involves a double error. First, it reduces wages to a matter merely of the fundamental class process which we do not find acceptable or compatible with Marx's notion of wages (see *Grundrisse*, p. 557). Second, such quotation ignores Marx's alternative formulations such as we have here cited. Instead of seeking theoretically to connect and integrate both types of formulations or, failing that, to justify the preference for one over the other, most treatments reduce crisis—like most other issues Marx raises—to phenomena of the "essential" or "primary" contradiction between the fundamental classes. Our effort is to break from this reductionist tendency within the Marxian tradition.

36. See Marx, "Appendix: Results of the Immediate Process of Production," in *Capital*, vol. 1, trans. Ben Fowkes, New York: Vintage, 1977, p. 1022. What we call prevalence will be constructed differently depending on the analyst's theoretical framework. For us, it is possible for the majority of people in a social formation to be engaged, say, in a noncapitalist fundamental class process and yet for a capitalist fundamental class process to be prevalent by virtue of its effectivity upon the nonclass processes of that formation.

37. See R. Wolff and S. Resnick, "The Theory of Transitional Conjunctures and the Transition from Feudalism to Capitalism in Western Europe," *Review of Radical Political Economics* 11:3 (Fall 1979), pp. 3–22.

38. Marx specifically criticizes the German Workers' party for its 1875 Gotha Programme in which it disregards the continuing need for a communist society to produce and distribute surplus labor (communist fundamental and subsumed class processes). What matters, he argues, are the differences between capitalist and communist fundamental and subsumed class processes. Communism is not to be understood as the absence of the class processes, but rather as the all-important transformation of them. Marx also discusses the changes in communist subsumed class processes to be expected in later versus earlier phases of a communist social formation. Karl Marx, *Critique of the Gotha Programme*, Moscow: Foreign Languages Publishing House, n.d., sec. 3, pp. 18–23. Engels makes the point again in his 1884 preface to the first German edition of Marx's *The Poverty of Philosophy*, New York: International, 1963, p. 21.

39. For example, Marx's detailed discussion of the subsumed class of merchants—subsumed to the capitalist fundamental class process—pinpoints how they were individuals who often also occupied the fundamental capitalist class position as appropriators of surplus value. See *Capital*, vol. 2, pp. 129–52, and idem, *Theories of Surplus Value, Part III*, pp. 423, 473–74, and 479. This point is developed further in our text.

40. Cf. Marx, *Capital*, vol. 3, pp. 290 and 298–301.

41. Cf. ibid., pp. 268–73, and vols. 1 and 2, *passim*.

42. See ibid., vol. 3, pp. 287 and 325ff. In vol. 2, pp. 136–52, Marx discusses how merchants may also be involved in what he terms productive functions: the storage and transportation of commodities. He argues that if and when they do so, they occupy both a fundamental class position as capitalists as well as the subsumed class position as buyers/sellers of commodities produced in capitalist enterprises.

43. Ibid., vol. 3, pp. 324–25. Marx read classical political economists as

having confused the fundamental class of industrial capitalists not only with merchant capitalists but with such other capitalist subsumed classes as moneylenders, owners, landlords, etc. See also Marx's letter to Engels of August 24, 1867, in *Selected Correspondence*.

44. Marx, *Capital*, vol. 3, p. 280, as well as entire section, pp. 267–314. Cf. also Marx's remark in *Capital*, vol. 2, p. 111: "Trading in commodities as the function of merchant's capital is a premise of capitalist production and develops more and more in the course of development of such production."

45. Ibid., vol. 3, p. 279.

46. The logic of this analysis is not affected if the argument is expressed in terms of "prices of production" rather than values of commodities.

47. The mechanism in the case of the moneylender is the interest payment made out of surplus value by the fundamental class of capitalists, what Marx refers to as industrial capitalists. For Marx, the determination of the rate of interest is then a particularly complex affair involving not only the relation between this fundamental and this subsumed class but also the many other sources of both supply and demand of loanable funds. These include persons occupying all the other fundamental and subsumed class positions in the social formation as well as those who borrow/lend without occupying a class position. See *Capital*, vol. 3, pp. 358–69. On money-dealing capital see pp. 315–22.

48. See ibid., pt. 6, and idem, *Theories of Surplus Value, Part II*, pp. 44 and 152–53. There is a useful summary discussion in Roman Rosdolsky, *Making of Marx's Capital*, pp. 33–34.

49. Marx, *Capital*, vol. 3, p. 821.

50. Marx, *Theories of Surplus Value, Part III*, p. 472.

51. The market price of any comparable limited-access situation (i.e., any effective monopoly over a condition of existence of the capitalist fundamental class process) would be calculated in the same way.

52. Marx, *Capital*, vol. 3, p. 625.

53. Ibid., pp. 436–37 and 382–88.

54. Ibid., pp. 436–37.

55. Ibid., pp. 338–57 and 370–90.

56. Ibid., p. 339. Cf. Marx's remark that "the capitalist exists here in dual form, as the owner of capital and as the industrial capitalist who really converts money into capital" (*Theories of Surplus Value, Part III*, p. 458).

57. See Marx, *Capital*, vol. 3, pp. 382–88, and vol. 1, pp. 448–50. Marx distinguishes the technical coordination of production necessitated by advanced degrees of division of labor within enterprises from the supervision of workers stemming from class relations and antagonisms. Coordination is a process linked to the fundamental class process within the relationship of production; Marx considers coordination as productive labor. By contrast, supervision is a process he links to a subsumed class process; Marx signals this linkage by applying his phrase "faux frais" to the costs of such supervision. We argue that it is entirely possible for the supervision process to occur alternatively in a relationship with a capitalist fundamental class process: for example, when supervisory services are produced and sold as a commodity by a capitalist enterprise. Marx's linkage of supervision with

the subsumed class process was meant to illustrate the latter process, but not to exhaust the possible social forms of the former process.

58. The state apparatus is not the only possible site of subsumed classes providing cultural conditions of existence of the capitalist fundamental class process. Alternative sites include, for example, religious institutions, private philanthropic foundations, and in-house corporate counseling programs. The analysis of the state's provision of cultural conditions of existence could be readily applied as well to such alternative sites where contributions out of surplus value would replace taxes on surplus value as the social mechanism for distributing shares of surplus value.

59. In other terms, let C = constant capital; V = variable capital; $C + V$ = productive capital; S = surplus value; U = unproductive capital; X = portion of surplus value distributed to subsumed classes deploying U; $C + V + U$ = total social capital; and $S - X$ = conventional definition of profit on productive capital. A hypothetical equilibrium state would then require that

$$\frac{S - X}{C + V} = \frac{X}{U}.$$

It follows that

$$U(S - X) = X(C + V).$$

Adding UX to both sides of the equation yields

$$US = X(C + V + U).$$

This equality implies that the average rate of profit in value terms is

$$\frac{S}{C + V + U} = \frac{S - X}{C + V} = \frac{X}{U}.$$

60. This is unproductive labor power since it is not productive of surplus value; the distinction between productive and unproductive labor power and laborers will be developed further.

61. It is, however, possible that surplus value will be allocated to the direct purchase of commodities other than labor power. For example, if supervisory personnel employed in a capitalist enterprise use commodities to carry out their functions, then these are purchased by the capitalist. Their purchase, alongside the purchase of the unproductive labor power of the supervisory personnel, are payments that combine the subsumed class process and commodity exchange process as we have noted.

62. This point usually occasions no theoretical difficulty in the case of, say, supervisory personnel using their wages to buy commodity means of consumption for themselves. However, more difficulty usually attaches to the parallel case of a nonemployee subsumed class—for instance, a banker—who uses subsumed class receipts (interest) to buy not only his or her means of consumption but also the labor power needed to manage a bank. Indeed, the difficulty is explained in part by the likelihood that such a banker will purchase his or her own labor power alongside

that of others. The next section of this chapter specifies how and why such labor power purchased by subsumed classes is also unproductive.

63. Cf. Marx's reference to the unproductive labor power of a person engaged in the exchange of commodities: "He performs a necessary function, because the process of reproduction itself includes the unproductive functions. . . . But this furnishes no ground for confusing the agents of circulation with those of production. . . . The agents of circulation must be paid by the agents of production" (*Capital*, vol. 2, pp. 131 and 127).

64. Engels's review appeared in the *Demokratisches Wochenblatt*, Leipzig, March 21 and 28, 1868; it is reprinted in *Engels on Capital*, 2d ed., New York: International, 1974, p. 16.

65. In volume 1 of *Capital* there is the famous summary statement containing the promise of a fuller and historical treatment of these concepts in vol. 4 (trans. by Ben Fowkes, Harmondsworth: Penguin Books, 1976, p. 644). The historical treatment appears in chap. 4 (pp. 152–304) and Marx's own views in the addenda (pp. 393–413) of *Theories of Surplus Value, Part 1*, Moscow: Progress Publishers, 1963. In volumes 2 and 3 of *Capital* there are many references to unproductive laborers as employees of the unproductive capital, which Marx wants to distinguish from productive capital: see especially vol. 2, pp. 124–33, and vol. 3, pp. 267–301 and 383–84, New York: International Publishers, 1967. There are also useful discussions in Marx's *Grundrisse*, pp. 272–73, and in the appendix to vol. 1 of *Capital*, pp. 1038–49.

66. Marx, *Theories of Surplus Value, Part 1*, p. 396.

67. Ibid., p. 399. The same point is made in Marx, *Capital*, vol. 1, p. 644.

68. Cf. "The designation of labour as *productive labour* has absolutely nothing to do with the *determinate content* of the labour, its special utility" (Marx, *Theories of Surplus Value, Part 1*, p. 401).

69. Ibid. On page 157 of the same volume, Marx makes the argument in slightly different terms: "A jobbing tailor who comes to the capitalist's house and patches his trousers for him, produces a mere use-value for him, is an unproductive labourer." We might point out, to clarify Marx's statement, that the singer's song and the tailor's patching are commodities—both use values and exchange values; what they are not are *capitalist* commodities and hence the labor in them is unproductive. Marx also recognizes that there is some unproductive labor that "does not enter into, and whose aim and purpose is not, the production of commodities" (*Theories of Surplus Value, Part III*, p. 432). Our reading of Marx's work on productive and unproductive labor supplements that of I. I. Rubin, *Essays on Marx's Theory of Value*, trans. M. Samardzidja and F. Perlman, Detroit: Black and Red, 1972, p. 264. We have here also corrected our earlier formulation of the productive/unproductive distinction in "Classes in Marxian Theory," *Review of Radical Political Economics* 13:4 (Winter 1982), pp. 1–18, and especially pp. 6–10.

70. Marx, *Capital*, vol. 2, p. 131.

71. Marx, *Theories of Surplus Value, Part III*, p. 432.

72. Marx, *Capital*, vol. 2, pp. 126–27.

73. Marx's own usage certainly sanctions this sort of approach. See, for example, Marx's references to productive and unproductive laborers as different

classes in *Theories of Surplus Value, Part I,* pp. 200 and 228; in *Grundrisse,* p. 468; and in *Capital,* vol. 3, p. 491.

74. Marx, *Theories of Surplus Value, Part I,* p. 159.

75. Consider these two seemingly contradictory passages from Marx:

The determinate material form of labor, and therefore of its product, in itself has nothing to do with this distinction between productive and unproductive labor.

The fact is that these workers, indeed, are productive as far as they increase the capital of their master; unproductive as to the material result of their labor.

This first quotation is taken from *Theories of Surplus Value, Part I,* p. 159; the second from *Grundrisse,* p. 273. These statements clash unless they are interpreted to mean that "unproductive" in the second statement is intended to apply to the consumption of the material result rather than the labor embodied in it. We interpret them in this way because we can thereby clearly distinguish between unproductive consumption—an important concept in its own right—and the different concept of unproductive labor.

76. Wright, *Class, Crisis and the State,* p. 48. Wright credits James O'Connor and the San Francisco *Kapitalistaat* group for his ideas.

77. Ibid., pp. 48–50 and 90. Wright repeatedly writes here of the "struggle for socialism" as synonymous with an interest in a noncapitalist mode of production. This is, to say the least, a problematic and controversial usage which is left basically untheorized despite its central importance to his notion of "interests".

78. Braverman, *Labor and Monopoly Capital,* New York: Monthly Review, 1974, p. 423.

79. Poulantzas, *Classes in Contemporary Capitalism,* pp. 20 and 94–95. Poulantzas argues that the productive/unproductive labor distinction demarcates the "boundary between the working class and the new petty bourgeoisie in a rigorous manner" (p. 256). He attacks those who include in the working class all wage earners, even if they are unproductive; he mentions specifically Christian Palloix, Pierre-Philippe Rey, Arghiri Emmanuel, and Andre Gunder Frank (pp. 94–95). While Poulantzas claims that Marx's texts support his view, he does so without citations; we too can find none.

80. Carchedi, *Economic Identification of Social Classes,* pp. 55–57, 64, and 88–91.

81. Paul Sweezy, *The Theory of Capitalist Development,* New York: Monthly Review, 1956, pp. 280–84.

82. John Harrison, "The Political Economy of Housework," *Bulletin of the Conference of Socialist Economists* (hereafter *BCSE*), Winter 1973, pp. 35–52; Bob Rowthorn, "Skilled Labor in the Marxist System," *BCSE,* Spring 1974, pp. 25–45; Ian Gough, "Marx's Theory of Productive and Unproductive Labor," *New Left Review* 76 (November–December 1972), pp. 47–72; Ian Gough and John Harrison, "Unproductive Labor and Housework Again," *BCSE* 4:1 (February 1975); and Alan Hunt, "The Differentiation of the Working Class," in *Class and*

Class Structure, ed. Alan Hunt, London: Lawrence and Wishart, 1977, pp. 81–112. The quotation is from Hunt, p. 94.

83. "It is time we rejected Marx's simple dichotomy and used terms that are more precisely definable," say Gough and Harrison in "Unproductive Labor and Housework Again." While these authors' rejection of Marx's terms is clear, as is their alternative, it is far from clear that the difference has much to do with "precise definition." Both Marx's and their notions of the productive/unproductive labor distinction encounter certain difficulties or "gray areas" in categorizing certain workers, as indeed all categorizations do (Marxian and non-Marxian alike). The point is that the imprecisions of theories differ and have different consequences.

84. In a recent debate (chiefly among British theorists) that covers many issues, including the productive/unproductive labor distinction, the debaters are divided between "neo-Ricardians" and "fundamentalists." Among the former are Gough, Harrison, and others discussed earlier; the latter include Bullock and David Yaffee. A third tendency is exemplified by Ben Fine and Laurence Harris, who offer critiques of both groups of debaters: *Rereading Capital,* New York: Columbia University Press, 1979, pp. 5–6 and 49–57. We share Fine and Harris's rejection of the neo-Ricardian view—that nearly all workers are productive—as losing most of the analytical distinctions central to Marxian theory. We also share Fine and Harris's critique of the fundamentalists' making the laborer's contribution to capital accumulation into the criterion for the productiveness of labor rather than, as Marx did, making surplus value production the criterion. However, we do not share Fine and Harris's own definition, which makes all labor "performed under the control of capital . . . and in the sphere of production, productive" (p. 56). That definition conflates and thus loses all the distinctions between fundamental and subsumed (productive and unproductive) laborers *within* the group they define as productive. The basic problem for Fine and Harris, as with so many Marxists, lies in their adherence to essentialist reasoning, in their case a "production is ultimately determinant" formulation. They follow the early Althusser (or *For Marx* and *Reading Capital* rather than *Essays in Self-Criticism*) and the early Hindess and Hirst (of *Pre-Capitalist Modes of Production* rather than *Mode of Production and Social Formation*) in affirming that production is determinant in the last instance upon a structure of social levels that is understood hierarchically, some levels "dominating" others. As we argued earlier concerning Althusser and his predecessors as well as Hindess and Hirst, "last-instance determinism" is best understood as a way station on the road to rejecting essentialist reasoning within Marxian epistemology and social theory generally, a road projected by many of the greatest contributors to the Marxian tradition. Fine and Harris, by contrast, are determined not to go down that road, to stay within a sophisticated economic determinist framework: production determines "ultimately" (p. 53). Thus their focus becomes the articulation of the subtle hierarchical structures through which such last-instance determination is effected. Notwithstanding the structuralist determination/domination formulation, a determinist view of economy and society will reach different analyses of society and social change from the antideterminist or rather overdeterminist approach developed in this book. Hence their concept of productive/unproductive labor is very different from ours.

85. In many writers, the expression of this theme overlaps with an expression of the first theme mentioned earlier: the two are separated here for analytical purposes only.

86. Ernest Mandel, *Marxist Economic Theory*, vol. 1, trans. Brian Pearce, New York and London: Monthly Review, 1968, p. 191.

87. Paul Baran, *The Political Economy of Growth*, New York and London: Monthly Review, 1957, p. 26.

88. Michael Kidron, *Capitalism and Theory*, London: Pluto Press, 1974, p. 38; and Oskar Lange, *Political Economy*, vol. 1, trans. A. H. Walker, New York: Macmillan, 1963, pp. 6–7.

89. See items cited in n. 82 and also Paul Bullock "Defining Productive Labor for Capital," *BCSE* 9 (Autumn 1974), p. B6.

90. Paul Baran and Paul Sweezy, *Monopoly Capital*, New York: Monthly Review, 1966, especially pp. 281–368.

91. Marx makes just these points regarding the positive contributions of such unproductive laborers: "For the capitalist this is a positive gain, because the negative limit for the self-expansion of his capital-value is thereby reduced" (*Capital*, vol. 2, p. 132).

92. For example, "moneyed" and "operating" capitalists. For a nearly complete catalog of Marx's usages, see *Theories of Surplus Value, Part III*, pp. 471–90.

93. When Marxian analyses differentiate capitalists at all, little attention is usually paid to the logic of Marx's particular class differentiations. For example, the focus by Marxists on finance as opposed to industrial capital is thought to originate with Lenin and Rudolf Hilferding (*Das Finanzkapital*), and Marx's analysis of the so-called managerial revolution is overlooked. Indeed, having missed Marx's class differentiation among capitalists, many Marxian writers "supplement" or "correct" Marx by their own differentiations: Yankee versus cowboy, hi tech versus low tech, center versus peripheral, and other "fractions" among capitalists. Cf. n. 17.

94. Marx, *Capital*, vol. 1, p. 564.

95. Marx, *Grundrisse*, pp. 513 and 331.

96. Ibid., p. 253; see also idem, *Capital*, vol. 1 (Fowkes edition), p. 975. As Marx notes, "the production and circulation of commodities do not at all imply the existence of the capitalist mode of production" (ibid., p. 949).

97. See Marx, *Theories of Surplus Value, Part III*, pp. 527, 458, and 468; idem, *Capital*, vol. 1, p. 146; and vol. 3, pp. 327 and 376.

98. Marx, *Grundrisse*, pp. 536 and 270; and idem, *Theories of Surplus Value, Part I*, p. 392. Cf. "Capital manifests itself as capital through self-expansion" (idem, *Capital*, vol. 3, p. 354).

99. Marx, *Capital*, vol. 2, p. 105.

100. Ibid., vol. 3, p. 375; and idem, *Theories of Surplus Value, Part III*, p. 473.

101. Cf. Marx's remark that lending at interest can "also take the form of transactions which have nothing to do with the capitalist process of reproduction" (*Capital*, vol. 3, p. 350).

102. Marx, *Theories of Surplus Value, Part III*, p. 457. See also p. 486, where Marx makes this point again for emphasis.

103. Ibid., p. 471.

104. Ibid., *Part I*, p. 78; see also idem, *Capital*, vol. 2, p. 29; and idem, *Grundrisse*, pp. 266 and 462–63.

105. Marx, *Grundrisse*, p. 452.

106. Ibid., p. 492; and idem, *Theories of Surplus Value, Part III*, p. 272.

107. Marx, *Grundrisse*, p. 317.

108. Marx, *Theories of Surplus Value, Part I*, p. 81; see also Marx's parallel attack on the "vulgarians" who speak of capitalists' labor, in *Part III*, p. 497.

109. Ibid., *Part III*, p. 74.

110. Marx, *Grundrisse*, p. 265.

111. Marx, *Theories of Surplus Value, Part III*, p. 423. For Marx's explicit references to the other fundamental and subsumed class positions that a capitalist may occupy, see *Theories of Surplus Value, Part I*, p. 408, and *Part III*, pp. 423, 473–74; and idem, *Capital*, vol. 1, p. 330, and vol. 3, pp. 291 and 375.

112. Marx, *Capital*, vol. 1, p. 332.

113. Marx, *Theories of Surplus Value, Part III*, p. 497. Marx explicitly notes how much supervision of labor is also a condition of existence of other fundamental class processes, not only the capitalist form. This shows that such supervision does not define the capitalist and is not a function specific to the capitalist per se: see *Capital*, vol. 3, pp. 384–86.

114. Marx, *Capital*, vol. 3, p. 387; and earlier n. 108.

115. Ibid., vol. 1, p. 332; Marx elaborates this in *Theories of Surplus Value, Part III*, p. 495.

116. Marx, *Capital*, vol. 3, p. 312.

117. Ibid., p. 267.

118. Ibid., pp. 370–83.

119. Ibid., p. 387.

120. Ibid., pp. 388–89.

121. Ibid., p. 830; the general argument is made in pp. 814–31.

122. Marx, "Preface to the First German Edition," in *Capital*, vol. 1, p. 10.

123. See the famous section entitled "The Valorisation Process," in Marx, *Capital*, vol. 1, chap. 7.

124. Ibid., vol. 3, p. 48.

125. In the celebrated volume-3 discussion of the transformation of values into prices of production, Marx begins to specify profits by showing how the profits of a capitalist commodity-producing enterprise are its share of total surplus value produced economywide. He shows this share to be different from the surplus labor usually appropriated from the enterprise's own productive laborers. The point is that all his other comments on merchant and money-lending capital, landlords, managers, state, monopoly—in a word, capitalist subsumed classes—remain to be integrated into a specification of profits to make the latter complete.

126. See Marx's explanation of his choice not to explore the many "wage forms," in *Capital*, vol. 1, p. 543.

127. Ibid., vol. 3, p. 235.

128. Marx, *Grundrisse*, p. 557.

129. Cf. Marx, *Capital,* vol. 2, p. 509, where Marx speaks of himself "assuming, for instance, in Book 1 of *Capital,* that the capitalist pays labor power at its real value, a thing which it mostly does not do."

130. Cf. Marx, *Grundrisse,* p. 593, where Marx repeats his insistence that "the *act of exchange* itself, as we have seen, is not a moment of the direct production process, but rather one of its conditions." See also Marx's discussion in *Capital,* vol. 2, pp. 29–30 and 387.

131. Marx, *Capital,* vol. 2, p. 508, and vol. 3, p. 627.

132. Ibid., vol. 1, p. 553.

133. Ibid., vol. 3, p. 439. See also chap. 4.

134. Marx, *Theories of Surplus Value, Part III,* pp. 480 and 508–9. See also chap. 4.

135. Ibid., p. 356; see also idem, *Capital,* vol. 3, pp. 358 and 382ff.

136. One problem here concerns what is to be counted in the denominator of the profit-rate fraction. Shall it be only the constant and variable capital $(C + V)$ of Marx's usual notation, or shall certain subsumed class payments (e.g., managers' salaries, rents, etc.) also be accounted as "costs"? Here too conventions have varied and been objects of controversy.

137. Another example would be a capitalist enterprise's receipts of its wage laborers' implicit payments (as earlier when $W^3 < 0$) to obtain access to the market for the sale of their labor power.

138. Such firms may operate feudal or slave plantations, merchant houses marketing the corresponding feudal or slave commodities, etc.

139. "We intentionally present this law before going on to the division of profit into different independent categories. . . . The profit to which we are here referring is but another name for surplus-value itself . . . and is for this reason independent of any division whatsoever of this surplus-value among the various categories" (Marx, *Capital,* vol. 3, p. 214). Nothing is more illogical for Marxists than to incorporate into their theories the statistics on "profits" produced and collated by non-Marxian statisticians who have no knowledge of or interest in what Marx means by profits. Marx explicitly criticizes bourgeois efforts to understand the economy by means of what they misunderstand—in Marx's view—as profits. Ibid., p. 213.

140. Ibid., p. 198.

141. Ibid., vol. 1, p. 235.

142. Marx, *Theories of Surplus Value, Part III,* p. 509.

143. Marx to Engels, April 30, 1868, in *Selected Correspondence.*

144. Individuals obtaining income via gifts from relatives, for example, need not participate in either fundamental or subsumed class processes, assuming that their gift income suffices to permit them to exist. Class payments, fundamental and subsumed, are different from incomes. The latter can and often do comprise both class and nonclass income flows or either one of them. For an extended discussion of income and its distribution in class-analytical terms, see Stephen Resnick and Richard Wolff, "A Marxian Reconceptualization of Income and Its Distribution," in *Rethinking Marxism: Essays for Harry Magdoff and Paul Sweezy,* ed. Stephen Resnick and Richard Wolff, Brooklyn, N.Y.: Autonomedia, 1985, pp. 319–44.

Chapter 4

1. It seems to us that much of the Marxian literature has often reduced the behavior of the industrial enterprise to a small number of economic processes within it. These processes are understood to be the ultimate determinants of an industrial enterprise's development. Typically, they include such (nonclass) economic processes as the purchase of additional constant and variable capital (accumulation of capital), the determination of market prices, and the physical/technical labor process of producing commodities.

Perhaps the best example of one such approach within the Marxian literature is provided in the famous work by Paul Baran and Paul Sweezy, *Monopoly Capital.* This book has also spawned numerous articles by the same and other authors as well as several other books. Bruce Norton's recent study of a portion of this literature, "Market Structure and the Accumulation of Capital: A Critique of the Theory of Monopoly Capitalism," shows that it advances an essentialist argument: industrial capitalist enterprises are shaped and driven by their need to expand. This drive is theoretically located in the notion of capital as the self-expansion of value. Since the enterprise is taken to be a unit of capital, it follows that it must expand. The accumulation of capital and the determination of prices are then merely mediums to accomplish this self-expansion of capital. In a broad sense, Norton shows that, for this literature, production (which is understood as inherently expansionary in capitalist producing units) governs in the last instance all other social processes both within and without the enterprise.

The differences between such alternative theories and ours revolve around two main issues. First, parallel to these approaches, we too begin our analysis with a focus on economic concepts, but for us the conceptual entry point is the fundamental class process and not the other processes associated with expansion. Second, unlike these approaches we do not make our entry point into an economic essence that determines, no matter how complexly, the behavior of the industrial enterprise. Ours is a dialectically constructed class theory of the enterprise rather than some essentialized expansion, production, or circulation theory. We thus do not discover or pose any fundamental economic contradiction within an industrial enterprise that governs in the last instance its corporate behavior. In contrast to much of the Marxian literature, we discover no inexorable drive of the capitalist industrial enterprise to accumulate productive capital, to alter its gross profit margin so as to maintain or increase its surplus, or to produce and sell commodities for maximum profit.

Instead, we show, for example, how an enterprise's productive capital accumulation and its value profit rate are each contradictorily effected by class and nonclass processes. Thus each of them exists only in contradiction; each is the site of different effects propelling each of them in contradictory directions. Because of this method, we, again in contrast to this literature, do not understand distributions of shares of surplus value in the form of salaries of advertising managers, rents to landlords, taxes to the state, dividends to stockholders, and interest to bankers to be necessarily a "drag" on or a "barrier" to an industrial enterprise's growth and development. Instead, we understand such distributions in general to be conditions for its continued existence and development.

For an insightful analysis of the theory of the industrial enterprise specified in some of the most well-known texts within the Marxian literature, we refer the reader to the previously mentioned dissertation by Bruce Norton, "Market Structure and the Accumulation of Capital: A Critique of the Theory of Monopoly Capitalism," Ph.D. dissertation, Department of Economics, University of Massachusetts, Amherst, 1983. In this work Norton presents a comprehensive critique of the economic essentialism referred to above and discovered in the approaches by Baran and Sweezy, *Monopoly Capital;* Josef Steindl, *Maturity and Stagnation in American Capitalism,* Oxford: Basil Blackwell, 1952; and David Levine, "The Theory of the Growth of the Capitalist Economy," *Economic Development and Cultural Change* 12:3 (October 1975). Norton also demonstrates several consequences that follow from an essentialized entry point that is not the fundamental class process. His thesis begins to explore concretely one of the key questions of this book: What difference does a nonclass theory (of an enterprise) make?

The non-Marxian approach is typified by the "theory of the firm" chapters found in most standard textbooks on neoclassical theory. Here the behavior of the enterprise, like the behavior of any site in society, is reduced ultimately to the given preferences of individuals, whether located within or without the enterprise, and to the inherent marginal productivities of the factors of production. These essences determine firm behavior. In contrast to our approach, the class processes do not exist within this theory. For the neoclassical theorist the appropriation and distribution of surplus labor are absent from society and thus it would make no sense in that theory to discuss the theoretical location of class.

2. As developed in chap. 3, these managers perform unproductive labor within the enterprise. Their salary represents the share of surplus value received for occupying a subsumed class position, which is the payment received for selling a commodity, their labor power. For further discussion, see chap. 3.

3. Advertising, financial planning, public relations, and forecasting may alternatively be produced and sold as service commodities. If an enterprise purchases them, then a subsumed class distribution is the payment for a commodity purchase by that enterprise. In this case, appropriated surplus value is distributed to purchase these commodities (see chap. 3 for a similar example in which an enterprise may purchase water as a condition of existence of its fundamental class process). In the producing and selling enterprise, these services may be produced either as capitalist commodities containing value and surplus value or as noncapitalist commodities containing value but not surplus value.

4. In the two key chapters, 23 and 27, of *Capital,* vol. 3, Marx begins to discuss the transformation of what we have called the "early capitalist" into his industrial capitalist, a mere recipient of surplus value dependent upon others to supply him with capital, management of labor, and credit. He explicitly discusses this transformation along with that of industrial enterprises from owner-operated to joint stock companies. For further discussion of this transformation, see the section "Once Again: What Is a Capitalist?" in this chapter.

5. Marx, *Capital,* vol. 3, p. 375.

6. As specified in chap. 3, individuals who occupy the surplus value extracting position must also be the initial distributors of that surplus value. They therefore occupy both fundamental and subsumed class positions.

7. When such a fee is paid, board members participate in the subsumed class process as both distributors and recipients of a share of appropriated surplus value. They buy labor power from themselves. As analyzed in chap. 3, the subsumed class process occurs together with the commodity exchange process.

8. Chapter 5 specifies the class position of individuals who pass such laws in the state as members of a subsumed class. State legislators are the receivers of shares of surplus value in the form of taxes on industrial enterprises and are thus subsumed to the industrial capitalists. Individuals who enforce and adjudicate such laws are understood to be unproductive laborers who sell their labor power to this state subsumed class. They do not therefore occupy a subsumed class position within the state, nor, of course, a fundamental class position either: they occupy a nonclass position.

9. Marx, *Capital,* vol. 1, p. 332.

10. Alfred D. Chandler, Jr.'s recent book, *The Visible Hand: The Managerial Revolution in American Business,* Cambridge: Harvard University Press, 1981, presents a superb study of the historical development of a new "business class," the managers, whose rise in American life is inexorably linked to the emergence of what he calls "modern business enterprises." In our terms, it is a study of the rise and growing importance and influence of one particular subsumed class, the managers, who are understood by Chandler to "play a far more central role in the operations of the American economy than did the robber barons, industrial statesmen, or financiers" (p. 491).

11. As our example suggests, most managers within a corporate hierarchy both give and receive orders within a complex chain of authority. Of course, this particular political process—the wielding of power—should not be confused with the economic process of surplus appropriation.

12. The distinction between order-giving and order-taking positions refers to only *one* among many differences among individuals who occupy the same class position. Other differences among those who occupy the *same* class position can include those associated with sex, race, age, education, weight, and so forth. All of them, including the political process of command, overdetermine the appropriation of surplus value. However, they are different from and are not to be conflated with the capitalist fundamental class process. To underscore our point, occupants of the *same* class position can have *different* positions of domination/subordination. We could easily add other such differences among them, including sexual, racial, and religious ones.

13. For further discussion of this point, see chap. 3.

14. The particular subsumed class payment to productive laborers in the form of wages exceeding the value of labor power is developed and discussed in the previous chapter.

15. Marx, *Capital,* vol. 3, p. 439.

16. Ibid., pp. 814–51.

17. Ibid., p. 821.

18. For further discussion, see chap. 3.

19. Marx, *Capital,* vol. 3, p. 814.

20. Ibid., p. 834.

21. Marx also abstracts from all noncapitalist class incomes. To include, for

example, noncapitalist commodity production would be to specify the total income in a social formation of which the capitalist class structure is only one component. Thus, the total income might be written as $Y_T = \Sigma_i Y_i$, where Y_i refers to the ith class structure's income. All categories are measured in abstract labor hours to derive the total income, Y_T. The total thus abstracts from the different values (e.g., capitalist values, feudal values, slave values, and so forth) produced in and by each class structure.

22. Dividing the categories specified in equations (4.10) and (4.11) by $C + V$, the total productive capital of the industrial enterprise, produces two different calculated profit rates, one for each equation. Each of them differs differently from the value profit rate. Each of them can fall while the value profit rate rises. In addition, as noted in chap. 3, the value categories included in the denominator of such calculated ratios may also vary and they may even vary with different definitions of the numerator (profits of the enterprise).

23. Marx, *Capital*, vol. 2, p. 79.

24. Ibid., pp. 126–27.

25. For a discussion of three such texts and the essentialized treatment of capital accumulation found therein, see Norton, "Market Structure and Accumulation of Capital."

26. According to equation (4.9) in the text, for a given level of Y, a rise in the rate of exploitation is a shift in the income distribution ratio, $(\hat{\Pi} + GR)/V$, against productive laborers and in favor of occupants of subsumed class positions.

27. Using the notation of equation (4.12), retained earnings—sometimes understood as corporate profits—can be defined as $\Pi' = SC_I + SC_O = SV - SC_C - SC_R$. The difference between the previously defined net profits of the enterprise, Π, and this new profit category, Π', is $\Pi - \Pi' = SC_R - (SC_O + GR)$. Board members decide how to allocate the enterprise's retained earnings between a share to owners in the form of dividends (SC_O) and a share to managers in the form of salaries and budgets (SC_I).

28. To see this, partially differentiate equation (4.15) with respect to λ: $\partial K^*/\partial \lambda = \partial \rho/\partial \lambda - 1$, where $\partial \rho/\partial \lambda$ is assumed > 0. Now, $\partial K^*/\partial \lambda \gtreqless 0$ if $\partial \rho/\partial \lambda \gtreqless 1$. So the inverse relationship between K^* and λ depends upon either $\partial \rho/\partial \lambda \leq 0$ or if positive, then $\partial \rho/\partial \lambda < 1$. A positive relationship between K^* and λ requires that the quantitative relationship between ρ and λ be positive and greater than one.

The significance and validity of these mathematical expressions are meant only to illustrate and explain a particular feature of the text. We do not intend to attach any general validity to our formulae. We do not want readers to think that these expressions capture some truth of the world. They are merely points in an argument.

29. In this case, the relationship between ρ and λ is positive and greater than one; see n. 28.

30. Like all social processes provided by occupants of subsumed class positions, those secured by state officials are conditions for both an expanded and diminished rate of surplus value appropriation: they have contradictory effects. Courts and public laws protect capitalist private property; they may also safeguard the rights of labor unions to organize, bargain for higher wages, and strike. Public education improves labor skills, teaches work discipline, and justifies capitalist

profits; it also improves the ability of workers to organize themselves into groups antagonistic to the interests of industrial capitalists and classes subsumed to them. Welfare payments and unemployment compensation help maintain a reserve army for capital and dampen revolutionary fires that may arise against capitalism; they may also keep wages higher than they would otherwise be and jeopardize the work ethic by supporting individuals who do not work. State regulation of capitalist business improves the safety, health, and longevity of workers—important conditions of the reproduction of labor power; it also can interfere with the ability of managers to run machines and labor as efficiently as desired.

31. The definition of an enterprise's profits would have to be changed once again to include these revenues. The effects of receiving such subsumed class revenues will be discussed later; see the section "Overdetermination of Productive Capital Accumulation."

32. An enterprise that changes in the manner described in the text may be considered to become a holding company to the degree it holds shares of stock of other industrial enterprises.

33. We hasten to add that this example only illustrates a point; there is no necessity for K^* to fall when these subsumed class revenues rise. For an examination of some of the conditions under which K^* may fall, rise, or remain unchanged, see the section in this chapter, "A Concrete Example."

34. The purchase of such common stocks/shares establishes a subsumed class position for board members as recipients of other industrial capitalists' surplus value distributions. Board members may invest in other enterprises for different reasons—e.g., to secure conditions of existence of their own surplus value appropriation, or to establish a new (subsumed) class position for themselves. The first type of distribution may be done for competitive reasons while the second may involve a transition of an enterprise's class structure from one that includes the fundamental class process to one that does not.

35. The policy of the Reagan administration in the United States (1980–84) suggests such an example. Elected state officials representing the Republican party advocated, as part of their party's platform, the reduction of state-secured processes to be matched by an expansion of those provided by particular nonstate sites—households and private enterprises. The decreased role of the state in society was to be coupled with tax cuts, especially on corporate profits (a reduction of the share of surplus value directed to the state).

36. We may assume a constant proportionality between the value of raw materials used and the use values produced.

37. For simplicity, we assume here an unchanged demand by other enterprises for this C-commodity and the market price always equal to the exchange value per unit use value. In market terms the supply of use values has shifted to the right, and with an assumed unchanged demand for the commodity, its market price falls to its lower per unit exchange value.

38. Marx, *Capital*, vol. 1, pp. 316–19, and vol. 3, pp. 178–99 and 641–45. Also, see idem, *Theories of Surplus Value, Part II*, pp. 204–6, and Isaak Illich Rubin, *Essays on Marx's Theory of Value*, pp. 173–221. The term *super profits* sometimes replaces *surplus profits*.

39. Changes in labor productivity may be a result of an enterprise's changed λ, as suggested in the text's previous examples, or changed k, or changed K^*. Marx, *Capital*, vol. 3, p. 644, provides a similar summary of possible causes of an enterprise's reduction in its production costs:

> This reduction arises either from the fact that capital is used in greater than average quantities, so that the faux frais of production are reduced, while the general causes increasing the productiveness of labour (co-operation, division of labour, etc.) can become more effective to a higher degree, with more intensity, because their field of activity has become larger; or it may arise from the fact, aside from the amount of functioning capital, better methods of labour, new inventions, improved machinery, chemical manufacturing secrets, etc., in short, new and improved, better than average means of production and methods of production are used.

40. Once again (see n. 37) we assume that demand does not shift to the right and that market price does not deviate from exchange value per unit. The labor times in question here, as per Marx's repeated insistence, are in terms of "abstract" labor.

41. Such tensions and conflicts can alter a number of different social processes constituting the enterprise. The adversely affected industrial capitalists may shift surplus value to accumulation of productive capital in response to the innovative capitalist's increased productivity. They may also attempt to change the fundamental class process, perhaps by lowering the wages of productive laborers, thereby raising the realized rate of exploitation.

42. If a director's fee is paid, then board members also purchase their own directing labor power. See n. 7.

43. Stock purchase is only one of several ways to improve the competitive position of an industrial enterprise. Others include the purchase and renting of land, acquisition of a monopoly position, purchase of bonds, and so forth. In these cases, the board, personifying the industrial enterprise, receives collectively rents, monopoly revenues, and interest, which are subsumed class revenues when they originate from surplus values of other enterprises. Then the total revenues of the enterprise exceed its surplus value by these subsumed class receipts. Particular subsumed class positions occupied by one industrial enterprise also affect other industrial enterprises' competitive positions by restricting their access to land and to required means of production commodities by virtue of having to pay ground rent and monopoly prices to the industrial enterprise holding the land and the monopoly position. In addition, higher enterprise revenue resulting from these subsumed class positions allows a changed distribution to take place that also can improve a competitive position even more.

44. The increased stock purchase must come at the expense of other surplus value distributions. The resulting impact of these changes upon total revenues and then upon total distributions is explored further later.

45. Marx, *Capital*, vol. 3, p. 388, and see discussion to follow.

46. Ibid., p. 436.

47. We can divide these approaches into three according to the subsumed class group essentialized in each of them. One approach essentializes the managers. The

processes in which they participate, the most important being the political one of control, determine the development and growth of the enterprise and by extension of the economy as well. There is a two-step essentialist logic at work here: the development of the enterprise is reduced to the processes participated in by its managers and the economy is reduced to the development of the enterprise. It follows that the corporate managers become the most important group in society, determining its economic development. We may call this a Chandler-Galbraith-Berle-Means school: Chandler, *Visible Hand: The Managerial Revolution in American Business;* John Kenneth Galbraith, *The New Industrial State,* Boston: Houghton Mifflin, 1967; and Adolf A. Berle and Gardiner C. Means, *The Modern Corporation and Private Property,* New York: Harcourt, Brace and World, 1967. A different approach, one within the Marxian tradition, essentializes the top managers of large corporations who are also the most important property owners in society. These corporate capitalists (i.e., the most important manager-owners) control the enterprise, and their chief objective becomes the maximization of surplus value (the urge to expand) achieved via the medium of productive capital accumulation. We may call this a Baran-Sweezy school: Baran and Sweezy, *Monopoly Capital.* A third approach, formulated both within and without the Marxian tradition, is a finance capitalist one. Here the lenders to (and/or owners of) the enterprise are essentialized. This subsumed class group of financiers are thought to control the enterprise, its managers, and industrial capitalists, in the current age of "Finance Capitalism"; Robert Fitch and Mary Oppenheimer, "Who Rules the Corporations?" *Socialist Revolution* 1: 4, 5, 6 (1970–71).

All three approaches share an essentialism within theory but embrace very different conceptual points of entry: managers in the management school, corporate capitalists in the monopoly capitalist school, and financiers in the finance capitalist school. Each approach attempts to separate itself from the others, often appealing to the facts of History to prove the validity of its particular theory of the enterprise and to disprove the others. They thus share an empiricist epistemology.

The Baran-Sweezy school's notion of a corporate capitalist differs in particular with our concept of an industrial capitalist. In *Monopoly Capital* (pp. 34–35) they seem to identify the corporate capitalist with two key processes:

> managers are among the biggest owners; and because of the strategic positions they occupy, they function as the protectors and spokesmen for all large-scale property. Far from being a separate class, they constitute in reality the leading echelon of the property-owning class.

For Baran and Sweezy, an individual is an appropriator of surplus value if two key processes are secured: supervision (read corporate management) and ownership (read capitalist). Together, these two, supervision and ownership, produce the corporate capitalist.

48. Adolf A. Berle, Jr., *Power without Property,* New York: Harcourt, Brace, 1959.

49. Marx, *Capital,* vol. 3, p. 389.

50. Ibid., p. 388.

51. Since individuals who are industrial capitalists need no longer own their

capital privately, it is possible that those who perform productive labor do so. The latter may save in the form of purchasing stock of industrial enterprises, as in the example of employee pension plans. These individuals then occupy two different class positions: the fundamental one as performers of surplus value and the subsumed one as owners of means of production. They receive as their personal income wages from the former position and dividends from the latter one.

Suppose some of these individuals through some form of concerted action are able to displace the existing board and hire themselves as the new managers as well. The productive laborers who sit on the board now extract surplus value, manage, and, along with the other workers, own the industrial enterprise. They might turn next to the development of new organizational and bureaucratic forms in and through which all productive laborers will supervise the efforts of one another, hold self-critical discussion meetings, decide on the kind of capital equipment to purchase, and so forth. The Marxian problematic still requires the question: Is this still a capitalist industrial enterprise? Such a question pertains to similar type examples of state- and worker-owned and -run enterprises.

The answer depends on the kind of qualitative transformation of the mode of appropriating surplus labor that occurs with such altered social conditions. If the conditions of existence for the capitalist fundamental class process remain, no matter what their changed form, then it still exists. Even if the proletariat owns the means of production and manages the factory, and even if both are accomplished in a democratic and egalitarian fashion, capitalist exploitation still may occur. A radical change in the form in which conditions of existence are secured does not *necessarily* imply a revolution over the fundamental class process. However, such changes as these in the pattern of occupation of class positions by individuals may produce the conditions for a qualitative change in the form of exploitation. Indeed, socialist revolution may be viewed as precisely that time when such occupation patterns are changing to produce such conditions. But we emphasize that to establish such conditions (e.g., communal ownership of means of production, worker-controlled enterprises, and so forth) is different from and does not necessarily imply a change from the capitalist to a communist fundamental class process.

52. Frederick Engels, *Anti-Duhring,* New York: International Publishers, 1976, p. 304.

53. According to equation (4.17), the presence of some form of monopoly power by the industrial enterprise in and of itself does not necessarily imply a class position and class revenues for the industrial capitalist. The board receives SCR if a monopolized means of production commodity is sold to other industrial capitalists, and NCR if a monopolized wage commodity is sold. In the relationship between buyer and seller of the wage commodity, no subsumed class process occurs because there is no distribution of surplus value. This is a nonclass revenue by the monopolist-seller because the buyer of the wage commodity receives no equivalent value for the monopoly payment made (the excess of its price over the commodity's value). The difference between the two forms of monopoly has a number of consequences. Any analysis of a rise in SCR for some enterprises due to their ability to raise prices above values of means of production depends, in part, on the different reactions of the differently affected enterprises. In contrast, an analysis of a rise in

NCR due to higher prices for monopolized wage goods depends upon the reactions, not of enterprises, but rather of the sellers of productive and unproductive labor power.

54. For our discussion of the wages of productive labor, see chap. 3. Population growth and immigration, for example, can act to shift the supply of labor power to the right, which, along with an unchanged demand for labor power, will depress the price below the value of labor power. Capitalist commodity production itself can produce a deviation of price from value of labor power by competitively driving noncapitalist and capitalist commodity producers out of business (see Stephen Resnick, "The Decline of Rural Industry under Export Expansion: A Comparison among Burma, Philippines, and Thailand, 1870 to 1938," *Journal of Economic History,* March 1970). Labor tied to those failed enterprises is released on the market, adding its numbers to those already looking for work. If not employed by the successful commodity producers, the price of labor power will tend to fall below its value. There are a number of such examples illustrating how industrial enterprises may earn such nonclass revenues (*NCR*) without distributing revenues explicitly to ΣY. Indeed, as Marx suggests, capitalism produces its own law of population— supplies of labor power are altered by changes in the distribution of surplus value to occupants of different subsumed class positions. Here a change in the distribution to particular occupants changes *NCR*. See, for example, his discussion of productive capital accumulation's effect on the supply of labor power in *Capital,* vol. 1, pp. 612–712.

55. The equation would read

$$SV + SCR + (NCR+l_1+l_2+l_3) = (\Sigma SC + RP_1)$$
$$+ (\Sigma X + RP_2) + (\Sigma Y + RP_3),$$

where l_i refers to the new borrowings or stock issues to establish the three different nonclass revenue positions mentioned in the text and RP_i the repayments and retirements of such debts and stock equities placed in the appropriate expenditure categories.

56. This distribution of surplus value to establish new subsumed class positions means, of course, less surplus allocated to secure the board's fundamental class position. This may involve the enterprise in a transition from an industrial to, say, a financial enterprise. If accomplished, board members would no longer occupy a fundamental class position. They would become occupants of new subsumed class positions as in a banking enterprise that makes loans to industrial capitalists. So the same individuals may remain on the same board, but a radical change would have occurred in their class position. There also would have been other changes in the nature of the enterprise's class structure. See section "Industrial versus Financial Enterprises" for further discussion of the differences between the two types of enterprises.

57. This will be explored in more detail later. In particular, we will show how the purchase of stock could become a condition for expanding and not contracting other processes.

58. A "complex profit rate" different from $\bar{\rho}$ could be calculated on the basis of

the total wealth of the enterprise rather than only on its productive capital. To see this, divide the total revenues received by an enterprise by $(C + V + X_T + Y_T) = W$, its total wealth: $\rho' = (SV + SCR + NCR)/W$. Comparing the two differently calculated "complex profit rates," we have: $\hat{\rho} = \rho' [W/(C + V)]$. Since $W/(C + V) > 1$, $\hat{\rho} > \rho'$. So a change in an enterprise's accounting practices leading to a calculated ρ' instead of $\hat{\rho}$ produces a lowered "complex profit rate," despite there being no change in its organic composition of capital or rate of exploitation.

59. We focus only on so-called foreign portfolio investment. If the board directs surplus value to its managers to establish or expand a foreign commodity-producing branch, we then have so-called direct foreign investment or the foreign accumulation of productive capital. Managers of such a plant, be they foreign nationals or not, would be subsumed to industrial capitalists in the "home" enterprise. So, in contrast to portfolio investment, expanding a foreign industrial plant involves the further appropriation of surplus value and thus involves exploiting foreign labor. Whether portfolio or direct foreign investment has the bigger impact upon the enterprise's complex profit rate $(\hat{\rho})$ is a separate and different question. For an extended discussion of these and related issues in class-analytical terms, see Stephen Resnick, John Sinisi, and Richard Wolff, "Class Analysis of International Relations," in *An International Political Economy*, ed. W. Ladd Hollist and F. LaMond Tullis, Boulder, Colo.: Westview Press, 1985, pp. 87–126.

60. As noted in the text, the assumption of $\Sigma X = 0$ does not necessarily imply that $r_1 = 0$. Foreign portfolio investment is considered to secure a condition of the fundamental class position and not to establish a new subsumed class one. That the latter has in fact been established is interesting and important to our example, but it does not require as a prior condition that ΣX must have been positive. However, for analytical purposes only, we ignore all other possible subsumed class revenues even if, like the example of foreign investment, they are generated without ΣX. In effect, SCR in equation (4.18) equals only $r_1 A$ where A represents the value of foreign portfolio assets. Changing any of these assumptions (including $\Sigma Y = NCR = 0$) would add complexity to, but would not qualitatively change, the results.

61. Note that $\Sigma \overline{SC} + \Delta A = (1 - \beta)SC_I + SC_C + SC_O + SC_R$ in equation (4.18).

62. See n. 68.

63. To see this, differentiate equation (4.26) partially with respect to α_1: $\partial \hat{K}^*/\partial \alpha_1 = (r_1 - \rho + \bar{\lambda})/(1 + \alpha_1)^2$. $\partial \hat{K}^*/\partial \alpha_1 \gtreqless 0$ iff $r_1 \gtreqless \rho - \bar{\lambda}$.

64. We can rewrite n. 63 by letting $\rho_1 = \rho - \bar{\lambda}$. It then reads simply: $\partial \hat{K}^*/\partial \alpha_1 \gtreqless 0$ iff $r_1 \gtreqless \rho_1$.

65. Employment will expand if there are no direct or indirect changes in ε, k, or the other components of λ.

66. Assume that $\partial \rho/\partial \alpha_1 > 0$. Differentiating equation (4.26) with respect to α_1, and assuming a positive relationship between α_1 and ρ, yields:

$$\frac{\partial \hat{K}^*}{\partial \alpha_1} = \frac{(1 + \alpha_1)\partial \rho/\partial \alpha_1 - \rho + r_1 + \bar{\lambda}}{(1 + \alpha_1)^2}$$

$$= \frac{(1 + \alpha_1)\partial \rho/\partial \alpha_1}{(1 + \alpha_1)^2} + \frac{r_1 - \rho + \bar{\lambda}}{(1 + \alpha_1)^2}.$$

Let us call the first term in this expression the value-cheapening effect and the second the portfolio effect. Then $\partial \hat{K}^*/\partial \alpha_1 \gtreqless 0$, depending on the sign and magnitude of the two effects. By assumption the value-cheapening effect is positive. If, as before, $r_1 > \rho - \bar{\lambda} = \rho_1$, then the two effects work together to raise capital accumulation. If, however, $r_1 < \rho_1$, then capital accumulation can still be positive if the positive value-cheapening effect outweighs the portfolio effect. There will be no effect on capital accumulation if a negative portfolio effect is equal to a positive value-cheapening effect.

If domestic competition results in a particular tendency for the internal profit rate in several industries to decline, we might then expect the portfolio return to be higher than the falling internal rate (ρ_1). In this case, industrial enterprises seek to make foreign investments for both the portfolio and value-cheapening effects. This suggests a transition to a subsumed class position as a result of domestic industrial competition.

67. If α_1 is not constant, then the equation in n. 66 must be changed as follows:

$$\frac{\partial \hat{K}^*}{\partial \alpha_1} = \frac{(1 + \alpha_1)\partial \rho/\partial \alpha_1}{(1 + \alpha_1)^2} + \frac{r_1 - \rho + \lambda}{(1 + \alpha_1)^2} - \frac{(1 + \alpha_1)\partial \lambda/\partial \alpha_1}{(1 + \alpha_1)^2}$$

$$= \quad \text{cheapening} \quad + \quad \text{portfolio} \quad - \quad \text{nonaccumulation}$$
$$\text{effect} \qquad\quad \text{effect} \qquad\qquad \text{effect.}$$

If $r_1 > \rho_1$, then $\partial \hat{K}^*/\partial \alpha_1 + \partial \lambda/\partial \alpha_1[1/(1 + \alpha_1)] > 0$, and if $\partial \hat{K}^*/\partial \alpha_1 = 0$, then $\partial \lambda/\partial \alpha_1[1/(1 + \alpha_1)] > 0$, as in the text.

68. Assuming α_1 to be affected by changes in ρ and r_1 produces a complex expression which we will not present here. We can summarize the result by stating that the three effects specified so far (see n. 67) would have added to them the effects upon ρ and λ of changes in α_1. So, for example, an increased α_1 would raise the domestic ρ because less capital would be seeking a return there and domestic competition is thereby reduced. However, an increased α_1 would tend to drive down the foreign return (r_1). These effects would be weighed against the other three to examine the final effect upon productive capital accumulation.

69. When the *same* enterprise becomes the site of both fundamental and subsumed class revenues, its board members *and* its managers and clerks occupy very different positions. For example, managers of an enterprise that receives both fundamental and subsumed class revenues may occupy for a portion of the day subsumed class positions. They would be subsumed to the board in the latter's industrial capitalist position. These managers sell unproductive labor power to the industrial capitalists. For a different portion of the day, such managers may secure processes that are conditions of existence of the board in its subsumed class position, say, as lender of credit to other industrial capitalists. In this capacity, managers do not occupy any class position, but they do perform additional unproductive labor. This labor power is sold to the board in its subsumed class position. The salaries of these managers would combine together income from these two very different class and nonclass positions.

70. If they were elected to the board of a financial institution serving only pro-

ductive laborers and occupants of subsumed class positions, they would occupy nonclass positions.

71. V. I. Lenin, *Imperialism, The Highest Stage of Capitalism*, New York: International Publishers, 1969, pp. 41–42.

72. Marx, *Capital*, vol. 3, p. 436.

73. Ibid., pts. 2, 3, and 4, *passim*.

74. In the case of industrial enterprises, a process of declining exchange value per unit use value due to capitalist competition may make it increasingly difficult for the relatively inefficient enterprises within the industry to cover their costs of production. Such enterprises cannot reproduce their conditions of existence. For them this is a survival crisis solved by their going out of business or being bought up by their competitors. A similar development can occur in the case of financial enterprises. Competition among them may produce a tendency for interest rates to fall. Those enterprises not as efficient as others will have difficulty covering costs of materials and wages and salaries of unproductive labor. They may suffer the same fate as the industrial enterprises. In both cases the number of enterprises declines, leaving fewer industrial capitalists and financial capitalists to satisfy the respective demands for commodities and credit.

75. We hasten to add here that the emergence of such a monopoly position in any industry does not imply that competition has forevermore disappeared there. Indeed, a monopoly position in one industry may serve as the basis for entry into different industries, whether the latter are monopolized or not. A recent example would be the changed industrial activity of American Telephone and Telegraph. Its monopoly position in telephone service was, in part, a condition of its entry into new industries, creating in the process competition there. In general, the emergence of our two forms of monopoly can create the conditions of competition in both means of production and wage-good industries, while at the same time competition over these same commodities creates the conditions for monopoly to emerge. Marx captured this process of continual change:

> Monopoly produces competition, competition produces monopoly. Monopolists are made from competition; competitors become monopolists. . . . The synthesis is of such a character that monopoly can only maintain itself by continually entering into the struggle of competition. (*Poverty of Philosophy*, New York: International, 1963, p. 152)

76. Productive laborers may be able to achieve some monopoly over their labor power and thus to raise the price of labor power pari passu with higher monopoly prices on wage goods. As developed in chap. 3, they then would occupy a subsumed class position to those industrial capitalists forced to pay higher wages (W^2). For those industrial capitalists selling such monopolized commodities, their higher nonclass revenues earned will be offset by the higher cost of labor power. However, other industrial capitalists are forced to pay the higher wages without enjoying a similar monopoly position.

77. Lenin, *Imperialism*, p. 42.

78. Perhaps the often-used phrase *state-monopoly-capitalism* can be understood in terms of the class structural features just outlined. It refers, in part, to a moment

of capitalist development in which the emergence of monopoly conditions from competition is coupled with the appearance of a relatively small number of individuals sitting on the boards of the monopolized industrial and financial enterprises. Such individuals occupy multiple capitalist class positions; they are the industrial capitalists and monopoly capitalists within the industrial enterprise *and* the owning capitalists and financial capitalists within the financial enterprise. This is Lenin's "personal union" between banks and industry. It specifies a class meaning of the *monopoly-capitalism* part of the term. Some of these same financial and industrial board members may occupy class and nonclass positions within the state as well. Thus this state feature is added to Lenin's "personal union" to complete the term, state-monopoly-capitalism.

79. Lenin elaborates much more than we have here on the importance and effectivity of capital export on different industrial enterprises in different nations. However, the story told in the text for the interactions among the class structures of different industrial enterprises could be extended to those among different nations. Consider different competing industrial enterprises within a given national industry as different national enterprises competing within a given "world industry." Then as each national industrial unit reproduces its conditions of existence, it affects the conditions of all the other national units. Each utilizes its surplus value in a variety of ways to protect and reproduce its survival. War, as Lenin well understood, is only one form of the possible struggles among these different national units over different social processes.

80. Galbraith, *New Industrial State,* pp. 46–59.

81. Immanuel Wallerstein, *The Capitalist World-Economy,* Cambridge: Cambridge University Press, 1979, p. 15.

82. See Immanuel Wallerstein, *The Modern World System,* New York: Academic Press, 1974, pp. 67–129.

83. Marx, *Capital,* vol. 1, p. 114.

84. The particular example of American and English slave merchants as occupying subsumed class positions has been examined in Susan Feiner, "The Financial Structures and Banking Institutions of the Antebellum South, 1811–1832," Ph.D. dissertation, Department of Economics, University of Massachusetts, Amherst, 1981; and the English merchant as subsumed to the American ancient in Rona Weiss, "The Development of the Market Economy in Colonial Massachusetts," Ph.D. dissertation, Department of Economics, University of Massachusetts, Amherst, 1981.

85. See chap. 3, and Marx, *Capital,* vol. 3, p. 593. For example, in the *Grundrisse,* p. 327, Marx discusses the calculation of profits in an economy based on slavery.

Chapter 5

1. Marx often refers to a changing configuration of processes occurring in particular sites and the continual emergence of new sites in society. We have already mentioned his changing notions of enterprise and capital in the previous chapters. One recurring theme in his early and later writings on the transition from feudalism to capitalism concerns the separation of towns and manufacturing from the country-

side and its agricultural production. In early feudalism, the countryside's manor-estates and households were sites of both food and nonfood production (Marx's "rural domestic industry") and whatever small towns existed were feudal append-ages of these estates. The primary accumulation of capital produced a double frag-mentation within the countryside; the town emerged out of it as a new and distinct site in society in which manufactures were produced (to paraphrase Marx, now "ur-ban industry") and traded for food items produced in the now specialized agricul-tural countryside. Marx discusses such a transformation first in *The German Ide-ology,* New York: International Publishers, 1968, pp. 43–58, and then in *Capital,* vol. 1, pp. 713–49.

2. Friedrich Engels, *Engels on Capital,* 2d ed., New York: International Pub-lishers, 1974, p. 16.

3. Throughout this chapter when referring to the institutional form in which state natural and social processes take place, we use the term *state enterprise* (as distinguished from a state *industrial* enterprise that produces commodities) rather than *state agency, department, office,* or *bureau.* We are not concerned here to specify the differences among all these different institutional forms—e.g., the rela-tive degree of decision-making autonomy enjoyed by the members of one state in-stitution as opposed to another. Our focus is only on whether the state institution is the site of the fundamental (state industrial enterprise) or subsumed (state enter-prise) class process.

4. In the United States, military weapons production is accomplished typically in capitalist private industrial enterprises whose produced commodities (military goods) are sold to the United States state or to foreign states. As argued in chap. 3, there is no question but that productive capital and labor take place in these enter-prises. However, an interesting, controversial, and different question arises if and when such enterprises are able to achieve a monopoly position. In our approach, they would then receive nonclass (monopoly) revenues in their commodity ex-change process with the state. These revenues would rise to the degree that the price of military commodities sold to the state exceeded their exchange value (or "price of production"). This unequal exchange between state and industrial capital might, in turn, force the state to alter its tax and/or expenditure policies. If the securing of the particular political process of national protection is sacrosanct no matter the costs involved, then the state must either raise additional class and non-class revenues, cut other expenditures, or use combinations of increased taxes and decreased expenditures to finance the monopoly payments to these industrial enterprises.

5. It is, of course, possible that noncapitalist fundamental class processes may occur within the state besides the capitalist one. We will not treat this here. For further discussion, see later text and n. 44.

6. In the United States, a conservative argument often advanced is that state production of commodities is inherently inefficient. The claim is that resources would be more efficiently used by private as compared to state industrial enter-prises. A related argument is that state commodity production would threaten pri-vate enterprise and open the door to socialism. Since socialism often is identified in the United States with the end of democracy, any attempt to extend the state's

economic powers in such a direction is viewed with antipathy. In other words, various cultural processes in the United States, some of which are provided by the state itself in the form of public education, produces a particular knowledge of *state* commodity production and its consequences, whose effect is to restrict that production.

7. The president participates in the development of such tax and expenditure bills in the sense that he or she must sign all bills passed by Congress. In that somewhat limited sense the president could be thought to occupy a subsumed class position also. However, because the president cannot expend a dollar unless first authorized (and received) by Congress and cannot pass any tax law, he or she is not the first receiver and distributor of a tax share of surplus value. Nonetheless, if his or her signature on all such bills is not secured, the subsumed class position of Congress is thereby jeopardized.

The Internal Revenue Service is understood to be a collector of taxes for Congress; its personnel are paid in and through the budgets passed by Congress. IRS personnel thus occupy, as noted throughout this book, nonclass positions as unproductive laborers. That such laborers are part of the administrative rather than the legislative branches of the state does not alter, but does overdetermine in a particular way, their nonclass position within the state.

8. Included in this state nonclass revenue category are: (1) taxes on the wage and salary incomes of both productive and unproductive laborers; (2) taxes on the revenues of occupants of subsumed class positions, including bankers, merchants, landlords, and owners, whether doing their respective business in incorporated enterprises or not; and (3) taxes on the realized capital gains from the selling of assets or on incomes gained through the redistributions of wealth such as inheritances and gifts.

The imposition of a tax on productive laborers reduces their real wage, i.e., the bundle of wage goods consumed by them. It has no necessary impact upon the market wage (the price of their labor power) or the value of their labor power. Of course, a lowering of productive laborers' means of consumption below their value of labor power may jeopardize the reproduction of their fundamental class position and lead to a number of different actions whose outcomes depend on the totality of social conditions. That, however, would be a different point to explore. In parallel fashion, taxes on unproductive laborers may threaten the reproduction of their nonclass position qua sellers of (unproductive) labor power. Here too a lowering of their real wage below the value of their unproductive labor power may lead them (and others) to take different actions. Finally, taxes on occupants of subsumed class positions reduce the portion of the share of surplus value received by them, which they in turn can spend. Such taxes upon subsumed class revenues may also produce a variety of overdetermined results, including possibly demands for higher revenues from industrial capitalists to offset such taxes. However, parallel to the impact of taxes on productive and unproductive laborers, that is another and different story.

9. We are assuming here that such loans and land are made available by members of Congress in their nonclass position. If, alternatively, nonindustrial enterprises are set up by Congress with noncongressional boards of directors who receive and distribute such nonclass revenues, then congressional members would

no longer occupy this particular nonclass position. In either arrangement, it is non-class revenues that would still flow to the state, and that is what is of importance here.

10. We are ignoring here the fundamental class position possibly occupied by congressional members. It may be assumed that state industrial enterprises have been established in which boards of directors, composed of other than congressional members, receive and distribute surplus value.

11. An exception to this is Grahame Lock's short but provocative "introduction" to Althusser, *Essays in Self-Criticism*, pp. 1–32. Although our approach differs basically from Bettelheim's, we must also mention his ambitious effort to construct a class analysis of the Soviet Union: Charles Bettelheim, *Class Struggles in the USSR*, vols. 1 and 2, New York: Monthly Review Press, 1976 and 1979.

12. Cf. the parallel conclusions reached apropos the concept of the "dictatorship" of the proletariat by Etienne Balibar, *On the Dictatorship of the Proletariat*, trans. Grahame Lock, London: New Left Books, 1977, pp. 1–156.

13. It follows that we must then distance ourselves from those formulations within Marxism that react to economism by counterposing power as the alternative essence of social structure and development and that, therefore, define revolution or communism in basically antistatist terms. For the same reasons we must reject those anti-Marxian formulations that equate Marxism with economism and consequently reject it in favor of a focus on power and on the state as the source of the oppression of people. In this two-sided rejection of contesting essentialisms in favor of a reading and development of Marxism that seeks rather to theorize the ever-changing intereffectivity of economy and power, we share a perspective of Suzanne de Brunhoff, *The State, Capital and Economic Policy*, trans. Mike Sonenscher, London: Pluto Press, 1978, pp. 2–4. However, our book aims in large part to specify—by means of our elaborated concepts of overdetermination and class—the precise nature of that intereffectivity which de Brunhoff affirms but does not work out. A critical and provocative discussion of tendencies within Marxism to essentialize power in place of economics is presented in Alex Callinicos, *Is There a Future for Marxism?* Atlantic Highlands, N.J.: Humanities Press, 1982, pp. 149–54.

14. We do not wish to suggest that the military (or any other social grouping in or outside of the state) would only attempt to intervene and/or seize power in reaction to such a budgetary crisis. Certainly there may be innumerable reasons for such attempts, even when no political crisis exists.

15. An extreme example of how far the theoretical slide into an essentialism of power can carry former Marxists is presented by the *nouveaux philosophes* in France: see André Glucksmann, *Les maitres penseurs*, Paris: Grasset, 1977, pp. 239–50.

There is a related if not complementary approach in which, again, power analysis overwhelms and absorbs class analysis. Here, the *absence* of such centralized power and its decentralization into freely constituted individual units corresponds to the absence of class exploitation. The development of democracy for all citizens is understood necessarily to coincide with the disappearance of exploitation of one group by another. In both approaches, class analysis is displaced by the essentialist focus on centralized power: its presence or its absence. For us there may be a broad range of different forms of political processes, from centralized to decentralized, which are conditions of existence of different forms of the capitalist fundamental class process. Political democracy may be and often is a particular political condition of today's capitalism. However, to avoid misunderstanding on this point, we must reiterate that such a political condition, like all conditions, has contradictory effects. It creates particular contradictions that, at any moment, may threaten the continued existence of the fundamental class process. One such contradiction comes quickly to mind: productive laborers help elect occupants of state subsumed class positions despite the latter's role in securing processes that are conditions of the exploitation of these same laborers.

16. Included in ΣY are those state expenditures that produce particular noncommodity use values for productive laborers. Such items are "free" (services received from public education, police protection, and the like) and must be included in any calculation of the laborers' standard of living. An interesting question concerns how such noncommodity use values effect the value of labor power. Our answer is that there is *no* a priori necessary effect on V from a change in ΣY directed to productive laborers: any particular effect depends on the context in which such state expenditures occur. For example, suppose the state produces certain free use values for productive laborers that are good substitutes for some of their purchased wage commodities. Assume that the workers' standard of living does not change with these added state use values, and there are no other changes, i.e., no change in any other class or nonclass position occupied and no change in commodity exchange values. Under these conditions, by definition V must fall, and industrial capitalists will thus benefit from a higher rate of exploitation. So the state's provision of social processes for productive laborers may become a condition for a higher rate of exploitation for industrial capitalist enterprises. We must underscore, however, the *may* for these workers need not accept a constant standard of living nor are these private and public use values necessarily good substitutes for one another. In addition, recall that workers pay taxes, in part, to secure such use values. These taxes tend to reduce the real bundle of use values consumed by them (see n. 8). We have then two offsetting effects on productive laborers: state use values, which are substitutes and free, tend to raise such workers' standard of living while taxes lower it. Without further specification, it is not possible to analyze the resulting impact of state taxes and public goods on the value of labor power (the value of the *commodities* needed to reproduce labor power).

17. Two qualifications of this equation are in order. First, the left- and right-hand sides of equation (5.3) need not be in balance because the state may seek to establish new class and nonclass positions. In this case, the state redirects its expenditures from reproducing the conditions of existence of one or more of its existing revenue flows to secure those new conditions of existence of its anticipated new revenue flows. Formally, this may be written as $SV + \Sigma SCR + \Sigma NCR = \Sigma SC + \Sigma X + \Sigma Y + Z$. The term Z represents the redirected state expenditures to establish new revenue flows. When realized, such revenue flows would be added to the left-hand side of the state's budgetary equation. Such a changed expenditure pattern by the capitalist state would jeopardize continued receipt of its prior revenue pattern. Certain of the conditions of existence of the latter are not being reproduced, as indi-

cated by the Z term in the previous equation. Second, a word is necessary concerning state deficits and changes in the money supply. The capitalist state may establish a monetary institution such as the Federal Reserve System to monitor and control changes in the money supply and credit. One effect of such a system, besides the obvious one of its replacement of commodity with noncommodity money, concerns the Fed's purchase of debt issued by the state's treasury department. If the state runs a deficit (i.e., it raises nonclass revenues [ΣNCR] via the sale of bonds), the Fed can become an indirect lender of money to the treasury via its purchase of state bonds. In so doing, it changes the money supply. However, we are not concerned here with the important effects of such purchases on interest rates, bank loans, etc. Nor can we here explore the implications of a different form of money for Marx's value theory.

18. Within this non-Marxian approach there exists a definite calculus of the costs and benefits of the state: citizens give up some of their liberty and recognize state authority (the cost) for the greater liberty of added wealth that results from state authority (the benefit). Such calculations are related to John Locke's political philosophy of social contracts: each individual consents to give up some of his or her individual liberty, assets, etc. to the state for the presumed greater benefits thereby obtained from or via state actions. According to this view, the state authority exists as the ultimately voluntary expression of such individuals. The writings of Locke, Hobbes, and Rousseau are all important influences upon this dominant non-Marxian approach to the state. Recent exemplary formulations are found in Richard A. Musgrave and Peggy B. Musgrave, *Public Finance in Theory and Practice,* 2d ed., New York: McGraw-Hill, 1976, esp. pp. 3–21; and Charles E. Lindblom, *Politics and Markets,* New York: Basic Books, 1977, pp. 21ff and *passim.*

19. The logical extension of such an approach in modern neoclassical economic theory is found in Paul Samuelson, "The Pure Theory of Public Expenditure," *Review of Economics and Statistics* 36: 4 (1954), pp. 387–89.

20. Since inflation, low or negative growth in productivity, breakup of the family, and creeping socialism are often traced ultimately to the ubiquitous interference of the state in the free market system, it follows that the solution is to reduce, if not eliminate, state interference by economic, political, and cultural reforms. Thus, private enterprise, family, and individual become the proper sites in society to carry on several former state activities, including welfare, pensions, environmental control, education, and health maintenance. The reasoning in this approach is essentialist: it identifies the state as the ultimate cause (essence) of societal problems. The essentialist political policy implemented follows logically from the essentialist theory advanced.

Milton Friedman, perhaps the leading American conservative in economic theory, sees two ultimate evils threatening American society: Russian communism and the centralized power of the American state. And, according to him, they "unfortunately reinforce one another." His hope is to maintain the strong military program while radically reducing the power and interference of the state in the domestic economy; a simple but powerful two-pronged strategy and one that certainly informed the Reagan administration and its supply-side economics. Milton Friedman, *Capitalism and Freedom*, Chicago: University of Chicago Press, 1963, pp. 201–2.

21. V. I. Lenin, *State and Revolution*, New York: International Publishers, 1969, p. 31. Lenin counterposes as his goal the dictatorship of the proletariat (the opposite essence). According to him, this latter dictatorship will make possible communism, whose consequence will be the withering away of the state as a significant social institution/site. See especially chaps. 2 and 5 of *State and Revolution*.

22. For a short but cogent argument supporting such an approach to the state, see Sweezy, *Theory of Capitalist Development*, pp. 240–50. More recent but very similar formulations may be found in Cohen, *Marx's Theory of History*, pp. 216–48; Goran Therborn, *What Does the Ruling Class Do When It Rules*, London: New Left Books, 1978, p. 34; Nicos Poulantzas, *State, Power, Socialism*, London: New Left Books, 1978, pp. 129–32; and John Holloway and Sol Picciotto, eds., *State and Capital*, London: Edward Arnold, 1978, p. 14.

23. See the useful survey of the Marxian literature in Bob Jessop, *The Capitalist State: Marxist Theories and Methods*, London: Basil Blackwell, 1978, and the many exemplars in the journal *Kapitalistate* since 1973, especially the work of Claus Offe and James O'Connor.

24. Ralph Miliband, *The State in Capitalist Society*, London: Weidenfeld and Nicholson, 1969. Nicos Poulantzas, "The Problem of the Capitalist State," and Ralph Miliband, "Reply to Nicos Poulantzas," both in *Ideology in Social Science*, ed. Robin Blackburn, New York: Vintage, 1973, pp. 238–62. Poulantzas, *Political Power and Social Classes*; idem, *Classes in Contemporary Capitalism*, esp. pp. 177–79. See also Michael H. Best and William E. Connolly, *The Politicized Economy*, Lexington, Mass.: D. C. Heath, 1976, pp. 173–76; and Ernesto Laclau, "The Specificity of the Political," in *Politics and Ideology in Marxist Theory*, London: New Left Books, 1977, pp. 51–79.

25. A sophisticated midposition is found in Ralph Miliband, "State Power and Class Interests," *New Left Review* 138 (March–April, 1983), pp. 57–68 and especially p. 61. Miliband credits Poulantzas with "the most thorough exploration" of the concept of such relative autonomy (p. 58). See also the survey of Marx's views on state "autonomy" in Hal Draper, *Karl Marx's Theory of Revolution*, vol. 1: *State and Bureaucracy*, New York: Monthly Review, 1978, chaps. 14–23. James O'Connor, *The Fiscal Crisis of the State*, New York: St. Martin's, 1973, argues that the state functions differently in the phase of monopoly capitalism from the way it did under competitive capitalism. The capitalist state can be torn apart in trying to perform its two key functions: accumulation enhancement and repression/legitimation. It is being torn apart under monopoly capitalist conditions, he argues, as gains from enhanced accumulation are kept privatized by monopolies while "interest groups" make mushrooming demands for state support. Strong arguments for state autonomy appear in Fred Block, "Beyond Relative Autonomy," in *The Socialist Register 1980*, London: Merlin, 1980, esp. p. 229; and Theda Skocpol, *States and Social Revolution*, Cambridge: Cambridge University Press, 1979, esp. p. 27.

26. See, for example, Wright, *Class, Crisis and the State*, pp. 157–58.

27. An exception is Barry Hindess, "The Concept of Class in Marxist Theory

and Marxist Politics," in *Class, Hegemony and Party*, ed. John Bloomfield, London: Lawrence and Wishart, 1977, pp. 95–108. In this essay, the state has a general relative autonomy. It can move against industrial capitalists.

28. All unproductive laborers within the state, no matter their place in its bureaucracy, have this relative autonomy, this unique and contradictory effectivity upon industrial capital. The performance of social processes directed to industrial capitalists requires state workers. The actions of these workers are overdetermined not only by the complex relationships they have with one another within the state, but also by all the relationships entered into as part of their daily lives outside of the state. The processes directed to industrial capitalists can be postponed, eroded, eliminated, or even reversed by a variety of different pressures operating upon these state workers. The frustrations and tensions often experienced by industrial enterprises in trying to get state workers to perform in the ways they prefer attest to the contradictory relationship between them and the state.

29. This presumes that social conditions exist that permit the conscious (or unconscious) identification of such ideas as dangerous.

30. His or her subsumed class existence is also overdetermined by the need to serve occupants of subsumed class positions and productive and unproductive laborers in these home districts. Every legislator is pulled in conflicting directions by these different pressures emanating from individuals occupying such diverse class and nonclass positions. Of course, the grand idea of state leadership is to be able to rise above such pressures so as to serve all individuals equally, unencumbered by the selfish interests of class (read business) and of nonclass (read politics) processes. But in this world we deal with human beings and not spirits.

31. There is no necessity for the value of labor power to fall to its lower price. Wages (price of labor power) may rise back to the unchanged value of labor power or there may be a combination of rising wages and falling value of labor power. If social conditions do produce a fall in the value of labor power, it would have to be the result of a lowered real bundle of use values consumed by productive laborers since the exchange values of these wage commodities have been assumed here to remain unchanged. This would be an instance of what Marx refers to as the "historical and moral element" determining the average amount of this means of subsistence bundle (*Capital*, vol. 1, p. 171). In our terms, society's political, cultural, and economic processes have interacted in such a particular way as to (over)determine a lower real wage, i.e., a lower real bundle of use values needed to reproduce the productive laborer's labor power.

32. The logic at work in this particular situation is as follows. Increased state expenditures (ΣX) directed to industrial enterprises raise ρ within these enterprises. If the value profit rate is increased sufficiently, it permits them to pay these higher taxes to the state as well as distribute increased shares to other subsumed class requirements. Higher tax payments increase state revenues and permit, yet once again, increased state expenditures directed to industrial enterprises. We can conclude then that the initial increase in state expenditures directed to these enterprises may produce a sequence of changes that permits increased state expenditures to be made in subsequent periods. Under these conditions, a current reduction in state spending will produce even lower future spending by the state because of the

adverse effect this will have on private enterprise. It depends upon the totality of natural and social processes whether the direction or composition of state spending at one moment can become a condition of existence for higher or lower state spending at a different moment.

33. One or both of these two groups must now finance the entire inequality ($\Sigma X > \Sigma SCR$) specified in the text's revenue/expenditure equation. To see this clearly, let us rewrite the tax portion of ΣNCR in terms of its three different sources: $\Sigma NCR_{TX} = NCR_{SC} + NCR_{PL} + NCR_{UPL}$, where the subscripts on NCR indicate, respectively, total taxes and taxes on subsumed classes, productive laborers, and unproductive laborers. Similarly, rewrite the expenditures directed to these three groups into the following equation: $\Sigma Y = Y_{SC} + Y_{PL} + Y_{UPL}$. Since we have assumed that, for conjunctural reasons, taxes on subsumed classes (NCR_{SC}) cannot be raised or expenditures (Y_{SC}) directed to them lowered, then ($NCR_{PL} + NCR_{UPL}$) − ($Y_{PL} + Y_{UPL}$) > 0. So this equation illustrates the conclusion of the text, namely, that productive and unproductive laborers would bear the entire tax/expenditure burden resulting from the assumed alliance between industrial capitalists and occupants of subsumed class positions.

34. The hegemony during the last few years of conservative over liberal views of the state does not guarantee its long-run dominance. For many years these views have existed in a contradictory relationship within American society—at times liberalism is hegemonic as in the Roosevelt-Kennedy-Johnson years, and at other times the conservative view is dominant as in the Nixon-Ford-Reagan years. On the one hand, it is likely that the conservative understanding is more in tune with an American capitalist ideology that many would like to be predominant. On the other, reform of capitalism's excesses is widely understood to be a necessary cost, and thus the cultural and political space is created for the liberal view. The implied compromises with ideology have a long history in capitalist development. The German industrialists and Junker landowners may have preferred Bismark's repressive attack on the German working class, but they too likely understood the necessity for state intervention and Bismark's welfare reforms which were aimed at quieting unrest among productive and unproductive laborers.

35. We have so far ignored the difference between a change in tax rates and in revenues collected. The state's subsumed class revenues are equal to a tax rate times surplus value: $SCR = t_1 SV$. Revenues may thus rise even if there is no change in this corporate tax rate, t_1. In like manner, the state's total nonclass revenues are composed of assumed proportional taxes on subsumed class revenues, $t_2 SCR$, on the value of labor power, $t_3 V$, and on wages of unproductive labor power, $t_4 W$. Each of these rates may be different and each is often the site of intense lobbying to alter it in particular ways. We did not introduce these different proportional (or even progressive) tax rates into our argument to avoid complicating an already complex argument.

36. For data on declining United States corporate tax rates, etc. see Howard J. Sherman, *Stagflation,* 2d ed., New York: Harper and Row, 1983, pp. 158–63; on personal income tax cuts, see "Effects of Tax and Benefit Reductions Enacted in 1981," Special Study of the United States Congressional Budget Office, Washington, D.C., February 1982.

37. We should mention that some conservatives expected state deficits to be small, if they appeared at all. Consistent with their essentialist view of the state—it is a barrier to a growing economy—a cut in state expenditures and taxes would lead to a rapidly growing national income, and since tax revenues are roughly proportional to income, growing revenues as well. So there is in this "supply side" view a necessary inverse relationship between changes in tax rates and revenues collected.

38. As outlined in n. 33, such a redistribution of state expenditures, combined with radically reduced corporate taxes, implied that the revenues from personal taxes, although lowered slightly, became relatively more important as a source of state revenues, and thus productive and unproductive laborers tended to "finance" state expenditures directed to industrial capitalists. Labor paid for the state's military buildup.

39. Marx, *Capital*, vol. 3, p. 465.

40. Growing state deficits produced counterpressures on and in Congress to raise taxes. Once again, the question became the class and nonclass division of such increased taxes.

41. As discussed previously, and assuming no other changes, the imposition of a tax on productive laborers reduces their real wages, a lowering of the real bundle of means of subsistence consumed by them. There is no necessary corresponding effect on the value or price of labor power. Now, assume the text's example of job-hungry former state workers pushing the private sector wage (the price of labor power) below the value of labor power. The real wage thus falls once again, but this time to a lowered price of labor power as an effect of unemployment. There is still no necessary effect on the value of labor power from these assumed changes. Let us now assume that personal taxes on productive laborers are cut, as in the text's example. Their real wage will now rise even if we assume no other changes. It is under these particular conditions that a change in the value of labor power may occur. Suppose industrial capitalists and the state point to decreased personal taxes on labor as an argument for unions to accept a somewhat lower permanent real wage. After all, the initial lowering of the real wage due to the imposition of a tax has been diminished to a degree by the new policy of reducing taxes. In the face of such a "historical and moral" argument, unions may indeed accept a long-run reduced average quantity of means of subsistence—the value of labor power falls toward the still lower price of labor power. Of course, a substantial pool of unemployed workers and relatively weak unions strengthen such tendencies.

42. For completeness we add here the notion of means of circulation. When we use the phrase *means of production*, it should be understood to include means of circulation of capitalist commodities.

43. A good example of this conflation can be found in Rumyantsev, *Categories and Laws of the Political Economy of Communism*, p. 19:

> However, this outward formal semblance conceals a different essence, which the outward appearance does not show, and which needs to be disclosed. Only by penetrating into the depth of these relationships can we see that in the one case—at capitalist enterprises—labour power is bought and sold as a commodity and that the worker is exploited by the capitalist; while in the

other—at socialist enterprises—one of the co-owners of the public means of production enters into comradely cooperation with another similar co-owner, and that he works both for himself and for his society and that, hence, there is not and cannot be any exploitation.

In this short but remarkable paragraph, Rumyantsev succeeds in specifying a dichotomy between appearance and reality, a definition of capitalist enterprise as buying-selling of labor power and hence exploitative, a definition of socialist enterprise as collective property ownership and hence not exploitative, and a displacement of the issue of surplus labor appropriation in favor of notions such as "comradely cooperation." A class analysis as we understand it has vanished from the analysis of reform, revolution, and alternative social systems.

44. We should mention the research of Rolf Jensen and Jack Amariglio, who have attempted to construct the primitive communist fundamental class process in different concrete social formations. Rolf Jensen, "The Transition from Primitive Communism: The Wolof Social Formation of West Africa," *Journal of Economic History* 42: 1 (March 1982), pp. 69–76. Jack Amariglio, "Economic History and the Theory of Primitive Socio-Economic Development," Ph.D. dissertation, Department of Economics, University of Massachusetts, Amherst, 1984.

We might for a moment leap heroically over the profound difficulties and problems that remain to be overcome in the specification of a communist fundamental class process. We could then conjecture how the sort of analysis we need might proceed. Let us assume a particular transitional conjuncture in which only the capitalist and communist fundamental class processes are present. The majority of individuals within the social formation may be assumed to be still involved with the capitalist fundamental class process. However, a socialist transition policy has been adopted by a newly established "communist" state. In this policy, the revolutionary goal set for each site in society—enterprise, state, household—is to create the social conditions of existence for the prevalence of the communist fundamental class process.

Under these assumed conditions, the state must secure particular processes for each of these fundamental class processes and receive from each a share of its appropriated surplus labor. Suppose the policy of the state—consistent with its communist objectives—is to foster the development of the communist fundamental class process while it erodes the conditions of the capitalist one. The following development strategy or plan might emerge. First, establish communist enterprises within the state while minimizing the state's tax share of their produced surplus labor. More communal surplus labor is thus left to the enterprise to secure its other processes, including the communist accumulation of means of production. Second, tax private capitalist enterprises heavily while redistributing state expenditures away from them and toward the communist ones within the state. Such a plan is consistent with the revolutionary objectives of the state—the deliberate removal of its capitalist subsumed class position in the social formation.

A contradiction appears. If the capitalist fundamental class process is an important source of state subsumed class revenues, then this revenue source may be undermined by the state's biased policy against it. To the degree that the state does not secure their diverse conditions of existence, it jeopardizes the existence of the capitalist enterprises and thus the state's source of revenues from them. However, if the state does secure these conditions, then it maintains its capitalist subsumed class position, which is not in accord with its objectives. In addition, if the state does secure some of their conditions of existence, such capitalist enterprises may prosper and thus pose a still additional threat to the revolutionary aims of the state. Such is one of the contradictions that emerge between the socialist state and different fundamental class processes. (One example of such contradictions can be found in the Soviet state's "transitional policies" of the 1920s; they remain the focus of debate and controversy.)

45. There is a question here of whether the state may wither away under capitalism. If what is meant by this is that all the economic, political, and cultural processes performed by the state as conditions of existence of the capitalist fundamental class process will *also* disappear, then clearly our answer must be no. However, we see no necessity for the capitalist state as a particular social site/institution to remain as some essential part of capitalist society if the conditions of existence it provides for the capitalist fundamental class process are performed in and by other sites in society. The boundaries of what processes a state performs, and, indeed, what the term means in a society, shift continually along with all the other changing class and nonclass processes in society. Such shifting is an important object of Marxian theory.

Name Index

Adler, Max, 303 n.154
Adorno, Theodor W., 38
Aglietta, Michel, 307 n.14
Althusser, Louis, 2, 14, 81–108, 283 n.3, 288 nn.43, 46, 291 n.17, 293 n.36, 294 nn.42, 45, 296 n.61
Amariglio, Jack, 341 n.44
Amin, Samir, 288 n.45
Aron, Raymond, 34
Aronowitz, Stanley, 290 n.8

Bachelard, Gaston, 34, 81, 82, 301 n.135
Balibar, Etienne, 334 n.12
Baran, Paul, 139–40, 319 n.1, 324 n.47
Barthes, Roland, 17
Berle, Adolf A., 205, 324 n.47, 325 n.48
Bernstein, Eduard, 46
Bettelheim, Charles, 334 n.11
Bhaskar, Roy, 288 n.46
Block, Fred, 337 n.25
Bloom, Harold, 34
Bochenski, J. M., 16
Bohm-Bawerk, Eugen von, 288 n.45
Braverman, Harry, 137
Breuer, Joseph, 283 n.1
Bukharin, Nikolai, 76–77
Bullock, Paul, 139

Callinicos, Alex, 302 n.140, 334 n.13
Canguilhem, Georges, 34, 81, 301 n.135
Carchedi, Guglielmo, 307 n.17
Carnap, Rudolf, 15, 16, 285 n.21
Chandler, Alfred D., 324 n.47
Cohen, G. A., 290 n.7
Collier, Andrew, 288 n.46
Coward, Rosalind, 298 n.85
Croce, Benedetto, 46

Davis, Philip J., 286 n.22
Deborin, Abram, 301 n.133
de Brunhoff, Suzanne, 334 n.13
della Volpe, Galvano, 293 n.35
Derrida, Jacques, 17
Descartes, Rene, 17, 32–34
Dewey, John, 33, 36
Dietzgen, Joseph, 293 n.27
Draper, Hal, 337 n.25

Edgley, Roy, 288 n.46
Ehrenreich, Barbara, 113
Ehrenreich, John, 113
Ellis, John, 298 n.85
Engels, Friedrich, 33, 40–41, 48, 56, 58–60, 87, 132, 207, 234, 310 n.38

Feiner, Susan, 331 n.84
Feuerbach, Ludwig, 37, 303 n.154
Feyerabend, Paul, 15, 34–35, 289 n.48
Fine, Ben, 315 n.84
Fitch, Robert, 324 n.47
Foster-Carter, Aidan, 309 n.28
Foucault, Michel, 17, 34, 284 n.4, 287 n.33
Freedman, Francesca, 307 n.17
Freud, Sigmund, 2, 283 n.1
Friedman, Milton, 336 n.20

Galbraith, John K., 225, 324 n.47
Giachetti, Romano, 300 n.117
Gintis, Herbert, 290 n.9
Glucksmann, Andre, 334 n.15
Goldmann, Lucien, 299 n.90
Gough, Ian, 137, 139, 315 nn.83, 84
Gramsci, Antonio, 40, 43, 46, 74–78, 90–91, 298 n.84, 303 n.150

Habermas, Jurgen, 298n.84
Harris, Laurence, 315n.84
Harrison, John, 137, 139, 315nn.83, 84
Hegel, Georg W. F., 13, 28, 45, 53, 55–56,
　59, 63–65, 67–70, 82–83, 87, 280,
　283n.3, 292nn.21, 23, 24, 293nn.27,
　34, 35, 36, 295n.57, 296nn.59, 60, 61,
　63, 66, 71, 297nn.72, 73, 300n.110,
　302n.144, 304n.166, 306n.3
Heidegger, Martin, 33, 299n.90
Hersh, Reuben, 286n.22
Hilferding, Rudolf, 46, 288n.45
Hindess, Barry, 86, 101–8, 284n.6,
　285n.21, 286n.28, 298n.85, 302nn.141,
　142, 304nn.165, 166, 305nn.167–72,
　309n.28, 337n.27
Hirst, Paul Q., 86, 101–8, 284n.6,
　285n.21, 286n.28, 302nn.141, 142,
　304nn.165, 166, 305nn.167–72,
　309n.28
Hobbes, Thomas, 336n.18
Hoffman, John, 298n.84
Horkheimer, Max, 41, 290n.6
Howard, Dick, 290n.2
Hume, David, 296n.60
Husserl, Edmund, 299n.90
Hyppolite, Jean, 293n.35

Jameson, Fredric, 68
Jensen, Rolf, 341n.44
Jessop, Bob, 337n.23

Kant, Immanuel, 17, 32–34, 296n.60
Keat, Russell, 288n.46, 298n.85
Kidron, Michael, 139
Klare, Karl E., 290n.2
Kline, Morris, 286n.22
Kojeve, Alexandre, 293n.36, 297n.72
Korsch, Karl, 40, 43, 83, 296n.59,
　297n.72, 301n.138
Kuhn, Thomas, 14, 15, 33–37, 289nn.48,
　57, 294n.47

Lacan, Jacques, 17, 81
Land, Edwin H., 293n.28
Lange, Oskar, 139, 288n.42
Latour, Bruno, 286n.31
Lecourt, Dominique, 287n.33, 304n.161
Lefebvre, Henri, 298n.84

Lenin, V. I., 33, 46, 62–67, 223–26, 251,
　291nn.12, 13, 330n.78, 337n.21
Lévi-Strauss, Claude, 17, 81
Levine, Andrew, 290n.7
Lewis, John, 303n.153
Lindblom, Charles, 336n.18
Lock, Grahame, 334n.11
Locke, John, 17, 32–34, 336n.18
Loria, Achille, 77
Lukács, György, 2, 40, 43, 47, 53, 67–74,
　291n.15, 306n.4
Luxemburg, Rosa, 300n.107

McCloskey, Donald M., 287n.32
Mandel, Ernest, 138–39
Mao Tse-tung, 78–81
Marcuse, Herbert, 40, 43
Mepham, John, 288n.46
Mermelstein, David, 288n.45
Meszaros, Istvan, 68
Meyerhoff, Hans, 34
Miliband, Ralph, 252, 306n.2, 307n.17,
　337n.25
Mills, C. Wright, 113
Montesquieu, Charles de Secondat, 83,
　86
Mouffe, Chantal, 300n.117
Musgrave, Peggy B., 336n.18
Musgrave, Richard A., 336n.18

Norman, Richard, 292n.23
Norton, Bruce, 319n.1, 322n.25

O'Connor, James, 314n.76, 337nn.23, 25
Offe, Claus, 337n.23
O'Malley, Joseph, 292n.24
Oppenheimer, Mary, 324n.47

Paggi, Leonardo, 300nn.110, 112
Pettit, Philip, 302n.141
Popper, Karl, 294n.47
Poster, Mark, 290n.3
Poulantzas, Nicos, 112–13, 137, 139, 252,
　306n.4, 307nn.11, 13, 17, 314n.79,
　337n.25
Putnam, Hilary, 15, 289n.48

Quine, Willard Var Orman, 15, 285n.17,
　289n.48

Rajchman, John, 289n.57
Reich, Wilhelm, 40, 43
Resnick, Stephen, 310n.37, 313n.69,
    318n.144, 327n.54, 328n.59
Ricardo, David, 47, 58, 294n.45
Rorty, Richard, 17–19, 33–37, 283n.2,
    284n.7, 286n.28, 287nn.33, 34,
    289nn.55, 57
Rosdolsky, Roman, 284n.8, 292n.20,
    311n.48
Rousseau, Jean-Jacques, 336n.18
Rubin, David-Hillel, 288n.46
Rubin, I. I., 313n.69
Rumyantsev, Alexi M., 291n.11, 340n.43

Samuelson, Paul, 336n.19
Sartre, Jean-Paul, 40
Saussure, Ferdinand de, 17, 28–29, 81,
    286n.26
Sayer, Derek, 288n.46
Sherman, Howard, 339n.36
Sinisi, John, 328n.59
Skocpol, Theda, 337n.25

Spinoza, Baruch, 83, 304n.163
Sweezy, Paul M., 137, 140, 288n.45,
    319n.1, 324n.47, 337n.22

Taylor, John, 309n.28
Thompson, E. P., 30–31, 86, 106,
    288n.43, 290n.9

Urry, John, 288n.46, 298n.85

Wallerstein, Immanuel, 227
Weiss, Rona, 331n.84
West, Cornel, 289n.57
Williams, Raymond, 109, 306n.1
Winch, Peter, 34
Wittgenstein, Ludwig, 14, 33, 295n.49
Wolff, Richard, 310n.37, 313n.69,
    318n.144, 327n.54, 328n.59
Woolgar, Steve, 286n.31
Wright, Erik Olin, 113, 136–37, 139,
    288n.46, 290n.7, 291n.10, 307n.13,
    314n.77

Subject Index

Abstraction, 182–83
Accumulation of capital: critique of when used as essence, 319 n.1; within enterprise, 184–91, 207–18; equation for, 187–89, 211–15; and foreign portfolio investment, 213–18, 328 nn.59, 60, 66, 329 nn.67, 68; overdetermination of, 185–91, 199, 207–18; related to subsumed class distributions, 184–91, 194, 196, 198, 211. *See also* Competition, among industrial enterprises
Activity. *See* Relationship
Ancient class process. *See* Fundamental class process
Antifoundationalism, 18. *See also* Overdetermination, in epistemology
Appropriation of surplus labor. *See* Fundamental class process; Surplus labor
Aspect. *See* Process
Austrian School, 59

Base versus superstructure, 39, 164
Board of directors: class positions of, 172–74, 200–204, 207–18, 321 n.7; income of, 173, 200–204, 207–18; nonclass positions of, 172–74, 207–18. *See also* Class analysis of, board of directors
Bourgeois economics. *See* Neoclassical economics

Capital: centralization of, 199; productive, 141–49, 311 n.59; productive versus unproductive, 130–31, 141–49, 316 nn.92, 93, 96, 101. *See also* Accumulation of capital
Capitalist, 114: functioning, 149, 207; industrial, 118, 119, 124–26, 131, 141–

49, 155; Marxian definition of different kinds of, 141–49; Marxian notions of, 204–7; Marx on, 309 n.25; merchant, 141–49; moneylending, 141–49; productive versus unproductive, 141–49, 316 nn.92, 93, 96, 101; as receiver of surplus value, 309 n.25; volume-1, 141, 143, 147, 148, 205–6, 223, 229; volume-3, 141, 148, 204–7, 223, 229. *See also* Class analysis of, capitalists; Fundamental class process, capitalist
Causality, and overdetermination, 4, 25, 65
Class: alliances, 225–26; consciousness, 110; as an entry point, 26, 50, 52, 109, 116, 319 n.1; as an essence (economic determinism), 114; fractions, 114, 307 n.17; in itself versus for itself, 110, 306 n.4; Marxian definitions of, 109–17; two-class model, 112–15. *See also* Capitalist; Class analysis of; Class positions; Class process; Class structure; Class struggles; Working class
Class analysis of: board of directors, 172–74, 200–204, 207–18; capitalists, 141–49, 204–18, 316 nn.92, 93, 96, 101; displayers, 179–80; financial enterprise, 219–26; income distribution, 180–83, 318 n.144; industrial enterprise, 166–218; landlords, 127–28; managers, 128–29, 174–76; merchants, 124–27, 310 nn.39, 42, 43, 311 n.44; moneylenders, 177, 219–26; monopolists, 128, 157, 326 n.53; owners, 128–29, 176–77; profits, 149–58, 181–83, 212–13, 317 n.125, 318 nn.136, 139, 322 n.27; social formation, 122–24, 310 nn.36–38; state officials, 129–30, 237–45, 333 n.7;

Class analysis of (*continued*)
taxes, 245–53, 259–66; wages, 149–58,
317n.126, 318nn.129, 137; working
class, 132–41, 161
Class analytical approaches, 111–12
Class interests, 163
Class positions, multiple, 128, 146–48,
172–74, 192–200, 309n.27, 310nn.39,
42, 311n.56, 325n.51, 329nn.69, 70,
330n.78
Class process: definition of, 20, 110–11,
115–17, 306n.5, 308nn.20, 21; overdetermination of, 23, 111, 116, 118; relationship to nonclass processes, 116,
125, 184–92, 278, 281. *See also* Fundamental class process; Subsumed class,
process
Class structure: of enterprise, 129, 170–77,
180, 219–26; of state, 231–45
Class struggles: definition of, 122, 158–63;
in enterprise, 192–95, 198–99, 204;
fundamental, 158–63; and person, 158–
63; in state, 258–63; subsumed, 158–63;
in theory, 60
Commodity exchange, differentiated from
class process, 22, 121, 126, 132, 227,
309n.34
Communism, 267–70, 325n.51, 341n.44
Communist class process. *See* Fundamental
class process, communist
Competition: effect on exchange value,
330n.74; effect on interest rate, 330n.74;
among industrial capitalists, 126;
among industrial enterprises, 192–200,
323n.34, 324nn.41, 43; relation to monopoly, 223–25, 330n.75; relation to
super profit, 197–98, 323n.38
Concrete-real, 84, 87–89; definition of, 55,
61, 65; relation to thought-concrete,
55–62, 84, 86, 89, 293nn.35, 36,
296n.71, 297n.72; overdetermination of,
55–56, 62. *See also* Reality, as concrete-
real
Conditions of existence, 34, 37, 51, 59,
121, 128–31, 253–58, 281, 295n.50,
303n.147; definition of, 116, 309n.26
Consumption, productive versus unproductive, 136, 138, 140
Contradiction, 89, 322n.30; Althusser's
notion of, 283n.3, 302n.146; creates

change, 7, 24, 284n.5; definition of,
5–6, 283n.3; in enterprise, 169–70,
192–200; Lenin on, 65; Mao's notion of,
78–80, 301n.133; relationship to overdetermination, 5–7, 24; in social formation, 122; in state, 258–66, 341n.44
Crisis, 122, 309n.35
Criticism, 5, 57–58, 294n.47
Cultural process. *See* Process, cultural

Determinism: economic versus political,
113–15; in last instance, 39–41, 45, 67,
77, 96–99, 115, 315n.84; debate over
economic, 104–5, 113–15, 290n.7. *See
also* Essentialism; Humanism
Dialectical materialism, 29–30, 57, 66, 97,
278; definition of, 86–91. *See also* Overdetermination, in epistemology
Dialectics, 63–64, 69–73, 75–77,
288n.41, 296nn.61, 66, 300n.112
Displayers: class and nonclass positions of,
179–80; income of, 179–80. *See also*
Class analysis of, displayers; Subsumed
class, of displayers
Dividends, 128–29. *See also* Class analysis
of, owners
Domination, relationship to class, 112–15,
204–7. *See also* Power

Economic determinism: Althusser's relation
to, 93, 303n.155; debates over, 38–108;
and empiricism, 44–45; Gramsci's attack
on, 40, 43, 76–78; within Marxism, 38,
73, 80, 300n.107; versus noneconomic
determinism, 42–43; related to rationalism, 44–55; within the URPE, 42–45
Economic process. *See* Process, economic
Empiricism, 7–10, 28, 30–32, 284n.6;
Althusser's rejection of, 81–108; Bukharin's 76–77; critique of, 15, 47–49,
54–55, 57, 101–8, 291n.14; and economic determinism, 44–45; within
Marxism, 46–49, 63, 66, 288n.42; E. P.
Thompson's, 30–31, 44. *See also*
Epistemology
Enterprise: accumulation in capitalist,
184–91, 207–18; board of directors of,
172–74, 200–204, 207–18, 321n.7;
capitalist, 124–26, 164–230; class and
nonclass expenditures and revenues of,

180–91, 209–18; class structure of, 129, 170–77, 180, 219–26; class struggles within, 192–95, 198–99, 204; contradictions in, 169–70, 192–200; definition of, 166; feudal, 226–29; financial, 219–26 (*see also* Moneylenders); industrial, 166–218; merchant, 125, 127 (*see also* Merchants); noncapitalist, 226–30; nonclass positions within, 128, 146–48, 172–74, 192–200, 309 n.27, 310 nn.39, 42, 311 n.56, 325 n.51, 329 nn.69, 70, 330 n.78; transition of, 229–30, 327 n.56. *See also* Board of directors; Managers; Subsumed class, shareholders; Working class

Entry point, 287 n.36; overdetermination of, 27, 52, 99, 279–81; role in Marxian theory, 25–29, 62, 72–73, 99, 122, 277–78. *See also* Class, as an entry point

Epistemology: in Althusser's theory, 81–108; Cartesian, 53; consequences of, 47–48, 58, 62, 67, 79–81, 89; as empiricism, 7, 284 n.7, 291 n.11; and essentialism, 8, 9, 30–32, 37, 43; Hindess and Hirst's views on, 101–8; Kantian, 53; in Marxian theory, 6, 7, 9, 10, 13, 19, 39, 67, 287 n.33, 296 n.61, 302 nn.140, 141, 142; as rationalism, 9–10, 291 n.11; Rorty's view of, 17–19; science ideology issue, 32, 94, 304 n.161; and standards, 6, 29; thinking versus being approach to, 39, 40, 64, 68–70, 84–85. *See also* Dialectical materialism; Ideology; Truth

Essentialism: definition of, 2–4; as power determinism, 113–15; in theories of enterprise, 324 n.47; in theory, 3, 12, 23, 49–52, 305 n.172; of theory, 8–10, 12, 49–52; versus antiessentialism, 3–4, 12–13, 23–25, 91–93, 96–99, 101, 114–15, 272–73, 278–81, 309 n.35. *See also* Epistemology

Exploitation, Marxian definition of, 20–22, 213–14. *See also* Fundamental class process

Finance capital, Lenin's theory of, 223–26, 330 n.78

Financial enterprise. *See* Enterprise, financial

Financiers. *See* Moneylenders

Foreign portfolio investment. *See* Accumulation of capital, and foreign portfolio investment

Frankfurt school, 40, 41

Fundamental class process, 109–63, 309 nn.25, 28; ancient, 118; capitalist, 118, 122–24, 145–49, 205–7, 309 n.25; communist, 117, 122–24, 309 n.28, 310 n.38; definition of, 115–19, 309 n.28; feudal, 117, 122–23; slave, 116–17, 122–23

Historical materialism, 29–30

History as the real, 31

Humanism, 25, 45; Althusser's rejection of, 81–82, 91–92, 100, 290 n.3, 296 n.61; definition of, 100; within Marxism, 40, 77, 278, 290 n.3, 300 n.117

Idealism, 5, 81–82, 283 n.2. *See also* Rationalism

Ideology, relation to truth, 18. *See also* Epistemology, science ideology issue

Income. *See* Class analysis of, income distribution

Individual. *See* Person

Interest, 120

Labor. *See* Necessary labor; Productive labor; Surplus labor; Unproductive labor

Labor power, consumption of, 121, 151

Laborers, 114

Landlords, 119; class and nonclass positions of, 124, 127–28, 310 n.43; income of, 119, 127–28, 132. *See also* Subsumed classes, landlords; Class analysis of, landlords

Managers: as essentialized, 204–5, 321 n.10, 324 n.47; class positions of, 124, 128–29, 174–76, 311 n.57; income of, 128–29, 174–76; nonclass positions of, 321 nn.11, 12. *See also* Subsumed class, managers; Class analysis of, managers

Materialism, 5, 283 n.2; Marxian critique of, 56, 294 n.41. *See also* Dialectical materialism

Means of production. *See* Property

Merchants: class positions of, 124–27,

Merchants (*continued*)
310nn.39, 42, 43, 311n.44; income of,
127. *See also* Subsumed class, merchants; Class analysis of, merchants
Mode of production, 45, 51, 112, 309n.28,
316n.96
Moneylenders, 120, 127, 311n.47; class
positions of, 124, 177, 219–26,
310n.43; income of, 120, 177; nonclass
positions of, 219–26, 311n.47. *See also*
Subsumed class, moneylenders; Class
analysis of, moneylenders
Monopolists, 332n.4; class positions of,
128, 157, 326n.53, 330n.76; competition as cause and effect of, 223–
25, 330n.75; definition of, 311n.51,
330n.78; income of, 128, 157, 224,
330n.76; effect on interest rate, 224;
nonclass positions of, 326n.53. *See also*
Subsumed class, of monopolists; Class
analysis of, monopolists
Natural process. *See* Process, natural
Necessary labor, 20, 115–16, 308n.22. *See
also* Fundamental class process
Neoclassical economics, 59; notion of income distribution, 183; theory of the
firm, 319n
New Left, 41–43
Nonclass: positions, 173; processes, 116,
123, 149–58; revenue, 149–58, 245–53.
See also Class process, relationship to
nonclass processes

Ontology, 49–50, 72–73
Overdetermination: Althusser's notion of,
87, 287n.35, 288n.41, 291n.17,
302n.145; definition of, 2, 49–52,
87–89, 116; in epistemology (dialectical
materialism), 4, 8–10, 14, 29, 32,
70–71, 288n.41, 303n.147; as used by
Freud, 87, 302n.145; implies change,
98–99; as used by Lukács, 299n.97,
302n.145; of process, 5, 20, 24, 30,
287n.35; in social theory, 12, 52, 70–71,
303n.147; versus determinisms, 2, 5,
50–51, 105–6, 114–15. *See also* Class
process, overdetermination of; Contradiction, relationship to overdetermination
Owners: class positions of, 176–77,
310n.43; income of, 176–77. *See also*

Subsumed class, of shareholders; Class
analysis of, owners

Person: class position of, 158–63; nonclass
positions of, 158–63; overdetermination
of, 163. *See also* Class analysis of
Political process. *See* Process, political
Positivism, 31, 83. *See also* Epistemology,
as empiricism
Power: as essence, 245, 324n.47, 334nn.13,
15; relation to class, 113–15, 242–45,
334nn.13, 15
Practice. *See* Relationship
Pragmatism, 15, 81, 108, 285n.17,
289n.55
Price of labor power, 116, 209, 261,
309n.24, 327n.54, 330n.76, 340n.41
Primitive communism, 309n.28, 341n.44
Process (aspect): cultural, 20–21, 130, 169,
232, 235–36, 311n.58; definition of, 7;
economic, 20, 22, 168, 232, 234–35;
natural, 20–23, 168, 231, 234; political,
20–22, 129, 169, 232, 235; relation to
activity and relationship, 19–25, 116–
17, 164. *See also* Overdetermination, of
process
Productive labor, 118, 125–26, 132–41,
313nn.63, 65, 68, 69, 73, 314n.75
Profit: complex rate of, 212–13, 311n.59,
327n.58, 328n.59; corporate, 172–
73, 322n.27; of enterprise, 181–83,
323n.31; meaning of, 149–58, 183,
212–13, 228–29; relation to surplus
value, 180–83. *See also* Class analysis
of, profits; Value rate of profit
Proletariat. *See* Working class
Property: ownership of and separation from,
144–45, 172–73, 176, 204–18; private,
22, 144, 235; relation to class, 144–45,
238–39, 268–71

Rationalism, 7, 10, 28, 30–32, 284n.6;
Althusser's rejection of, 81–108; critique
of, 46–49, 54–55, 57, 101–8; and
Lukács, 68; within Marxism, 31–32,
46–49, 63, 288n.45. *See also* Epistemology; Economic determinism, related to rationalism
Realism, 31–32, 58–59, 68, 288n.46,
289n.48, 298n.85

Reality, 6–12, 30–32, 297 n.72; as concrete-real, 58; as essence, 29, 38, 44, 83–85; Marxian theory of, 32, 64–65, 76
Reductionism, 2, 40, 80, 110. *See also* Essentialism
Relations of production. *See* Fundamental class process
Relationship (activity, practice): definition of, 19–20, 24, 116–17, 138; working as a, 20–21, 138. *See also* Sites in society
Relativism's relation to Marxism, 31, 33–36, 59–60, 63, 65–66, 71, 74–75, 89, 289 n.55, 297 n.77, 298 n.79, 299 n.92
Rent, 119, 128, 132. *See also* Class analysis of, income; Landlords

Science, 33, 55, 57, 59–61, 81, 86, 294 n.45. *See also* Epistemology, science ideology issue; Truth
Shareholders. *See* Subsumed class, of shareholders; Owners
Sites in society, 164–65, 231–33, 237–38, 249, 260, 263, 273, 331 n.1, 342 n.45
Slave class process. *See* Fundamental class process, slave
Social formation, 118. *See also* Class analysis of, social formation; Transition in social formation
Socialism, 123–24, 126, 239, 267–70, 332 n.6
Society, 4–5, 19, 24, 132. *See also* Social formation
Soviet Union, class analysis of, 124, 242–43, 270, 334 nn.11, 12
State, 127, 132, 311 n.58; capitalist enterprise within, 237–40; class and nonclass expenditures and revenues of, 245–53, 335 nn.16, 17, 338 n.32, 339 nn.33, 35, 36, 340 nn.37, 38, 40, 41; contradictions in, 253–66, 338 n.30, 341 n.44; Marxian versus non-Marxian approaches to, 249–53, 256, 270–74, 336 nn.18, 19, 20, 337 nn.21, 22, 25, 27; and monopoly capitalism, 330 n.78; nonclass struggles in, 243–45, 249, 258–63; overdetermination of, 252–53; reform and revolution over, 267–74, 340 n.43; relative autonomy of, 252–53, 337 n.25. *See also* Class structure of, state; Class struggles,

in state; Surplus value, relation to state; State officials
State officials: class positions of, 129–30, 237–45; income of, 130, 237–45; non-class position of, 237–45. *See also* Subsumed class, of state officials; Class analysis of, state officials
Structuralism, 17, 83, 100, 252, 288 n.46, 302 n.141
Structuralists, 17, 286 n.27
Subsumed class, 109–63; definition of, 118–19, 130–31; of displayers, 179–80; of landlords, 119, 124, 127–28, 178, 310 n.43; of managers, 124, 128–29, 174–76, 184–91; of merchants, 124–27, 178, 310 nn.39, 42, 43, 311 n.44; of moneylenders, 120, 124, 177, 219–26, 310 n.43, 311 n.47; of monopolists, 128, 179, 326 n.53; positions, 118; process, 118; of shareholders (owners), 128–29, 176–77, 310 n.43; of state officials, 120, 129–30, 178, 237–45. *See also* Class analysis of
Surplus labor: definition of, 20, 115–17; distribution of, 119; overdetermination of, 308 n.22. *See also* Fundamental class process
Surplus value: distribution of, 118–21, 124–32, 175–91, 202–4, 208–18; and foreign portfolio investment, 213–18; fundamental and subsumed classes, relation to, 132; interest as part of, 180–83; profit as part of, 180–83; relation of state to, 180, 190, 234–36, 240–41, 246–47, 253–63; rent as part of, 180–83. *See also* Fundamental class process, capitalist; Labor power, consumption of; Subsumed class

Taxes, 120, 121, 132. *See also* Class analysis of, taxes; State, revenue of
Theory: concept of, 6; consequences of, 59; contradictions within, 5–7; Marxian definition of, 2, 10, 12, 28, 55–59; overdetermination of, 2, 5, 7; as a process, 2, 5, 7, 295 n.50. *See also* Concrete-real, relation to thought-concrete; Entry point; Essentialism, in theory, of theory; Epistemology; Overdetermination, in epistemology

Thought-concrete, 55, 98. *See also* Concrete-real, relation to thought-concrete; Theory
Totality, 24–25, 29; essentialism of, 50; Hegel on, 297 nn.72, 73; Lenin on, 297 nn.72, 73; Lukács on, 71, 74; Mao on, 79–80. *See also* Concrete-real
Transition in social formation, 122–24. *See also* Communism; Enterprise, transition of
Trinity Formula, 149, 181–82
Truth, 6, 29, 40, 90, 108; empiricist, 8, 44, 57, 87; Hegel's notion of, 297 nn.72, 73; Lenin's conception of, 65–66; overdetermination of, 50; rationalist, 45, 87; versus truths, 6, 32, 34, 60, 74–75, 85, 94–95, 100–101, 103

Uneven development, 24, 199, 284 n.5
Unproductive capital, 311 n.59; definition of, 130, 141–49, 316 nn.92, 93, 96, 101; forms of, 141–49. *See also* Landlords; Merchants; Moneylenders; Monopolists

Unproductive labor, 125–26, 132–41, 311 nn.60, 61, 62, 313 nn.63, 65, 68, 69, 73, 314 n.75
URPE (Union for Radical Political Economics), 42–45

Value rate of profit: and accumulation of capital, 188–91, 197, 199, 215; overdetermination of, 191, 197, 199; and subsumed class distributions, 188–91, 197, 199, 215. *See also* Profit

Wage equation, 152–54
Wages, meaning of, 149–58, 308 n.22. *See also* Class analysis of, wages, income distribution; Price of labor power
Workers. *See* Laborers
Working class: different definitions of, 109, 313 nn.63, 65, 68, 69, 73, 314 n.75; productive and unproductive labor as parts of, 132–41, 313 nn.63, 65, 68, 69, 73, 314 n.75. *See also* Class analysis of, working class